BARRY FLANAGAN

EARLY WORKS 1965–1982

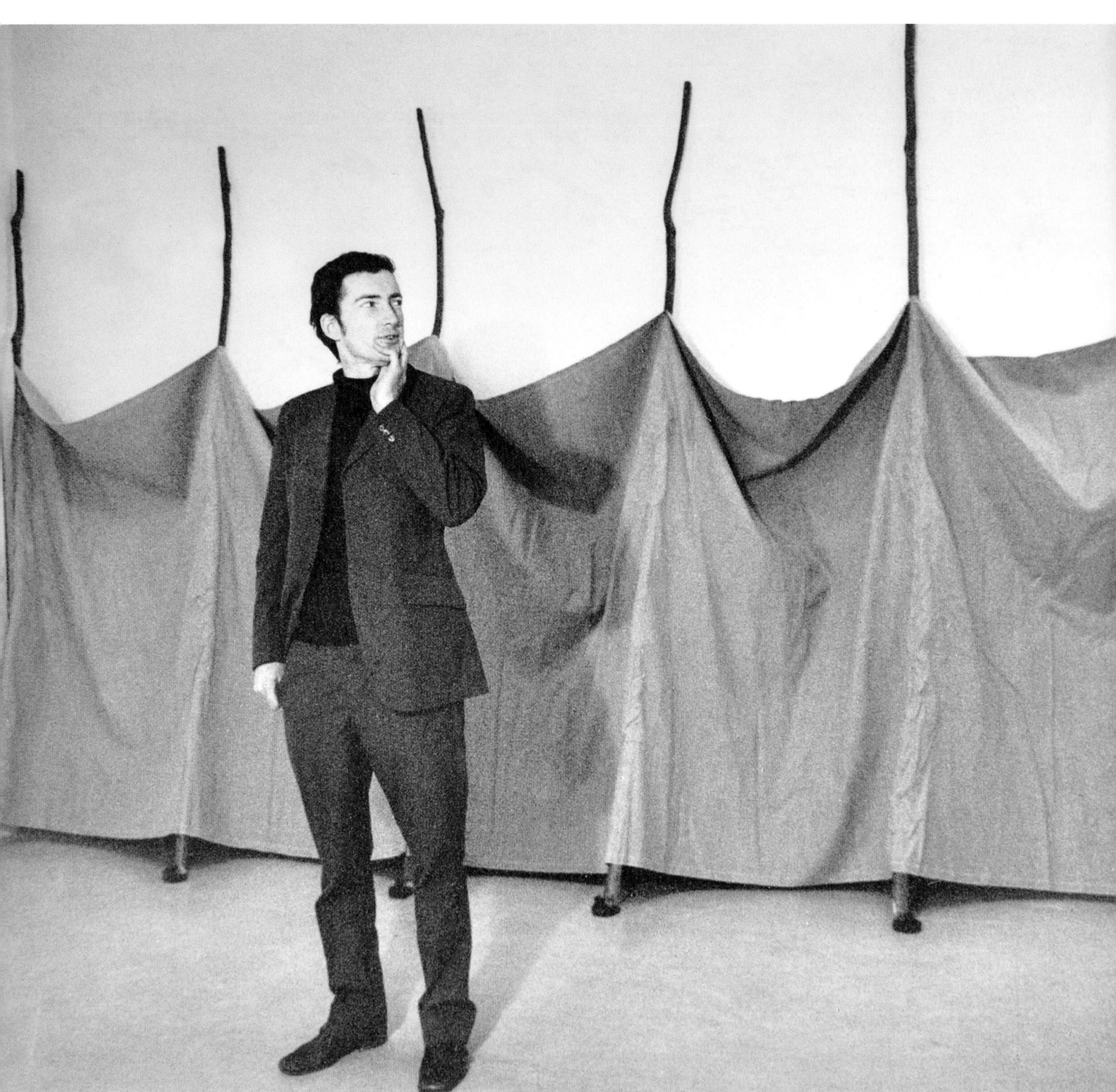

EDITED BY

Clarrie Wallis and Andrew Wilson

WITH CONTRIBUTIONS BY

Jo Melvin Jennifer Powell
Clarrie Wallis Andrew Wilson

BARRY FLANAGAN

EARLY WORKS 1965–1982

Tate Publishing

First published 2011 by order of the Tate Trustees
by Tate Publishing, a division of Tate Enterprises Ltd,
Millbank, London SW1P 4RG
www.tate.org.uk/publishing

on the occasion of the exhibition

BARRY FLANAGAN
EARLY WORKS 1965–1982

Tate Britain
27 September 2011 – 2 January 2012

A catalogue record for this book is available from the British Library

ISBN 978 1 85437 997 9

Distributed in the United States and Canada by ABRAMS, New York

Library of Congress Control Number: 2011924275

Designed by Philip Lewis
Colour reproduction by DL Imaging, London
Printed in Italy by Mondadori

FRONT COVER Barry Flanagan, *4 casb 2 '67* 1967, studio installation 1967
BACK COVER Barry Flanagan at Rowan Gallery, London, 1968
FRONTISPIECE Barry Flanagan beside *aug 8 '69* 1969
THIS PAGE Barry Flanagan in his studio 1972

Measurements of artworks are given in centimetres, height before width and depth

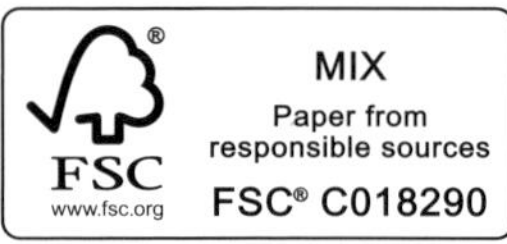

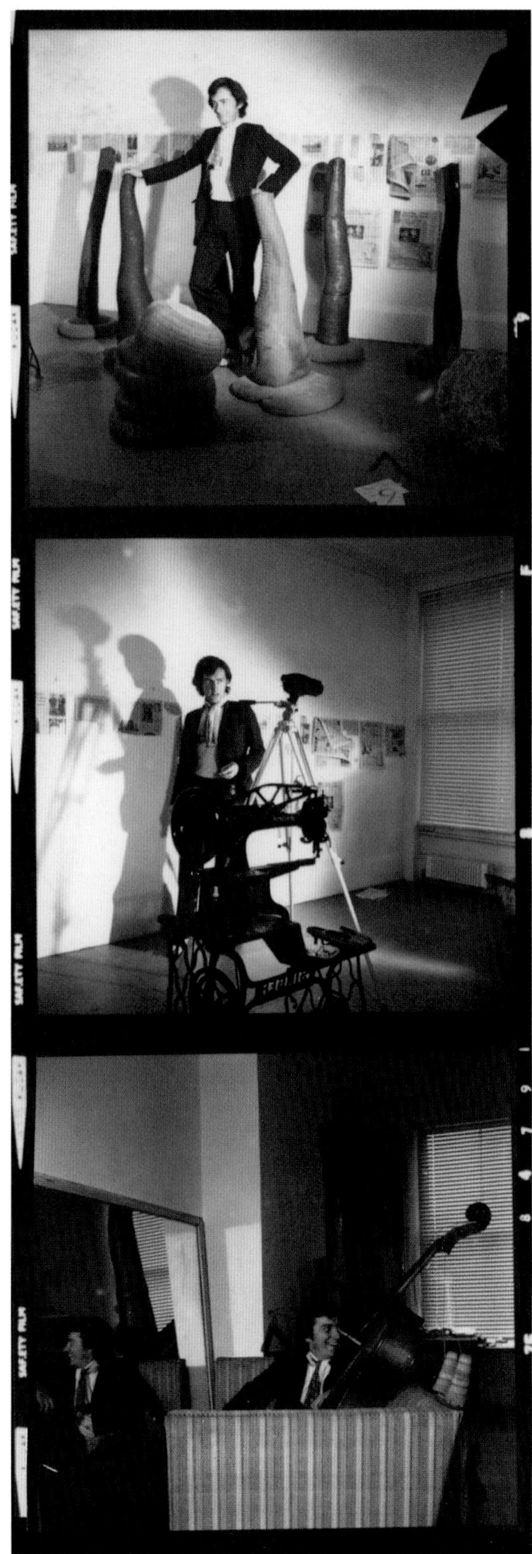

Contents

Foreword

One of the pleasures of arriving as a new Director at Tate Britain was having the opportunity to programme an exhibition devoted to Barry Flanagan. Another was to be able to do so knowing that in Clarrie Wallis and Andrew Wilson the show already had its curators.

From the outset we agreed to focus on Flanagan's early work as being not only inventive but also foundational. If Flanagan came to be most frequently represented by his later bronzes, this early work is more intimately connected to those monumental figures than has perhaps been generally understood. Rather than dealing with two distinct artistic phases, this exhibition suggests an underlying continuity to a career which is usually polarised. At the same time, in concentrating on the early work itself, the fullness of the selection reveals its internal logic, and exposes its materials and methods for what they are. Flanagan's work – and his career – is characterised by this dual fascination with, and knowledge of, the thinking head and the making hand; concept and method, the thought and its expression.

Barry Flanagan was born in 1941 and died in 2009. He was a maverick figure but a maverick who was absolutely central to the artistic conversation of the 1960s and 70s. This was a conversation which was based not just in London but in mainland Europe and North America, where Flanagan contributed to a number of the exhibitions which came to define a new art. The range of lenders to this exhibition, to whom we are most grateful, is an immediate indication of how well connected Flanagan was to an emerging European network of collectors and galleries who supported this new way of understanding the possibilities of visual thinking. In its very singularity Flanagan's art helps us to think more generally about these expanded horizons.

By bringing together here, from across Europe, a fully representative selection of work from this period, we show a much more rounded picture of an artist who has become known by a relatively small number of early works, notably from the Tate's own collection. Now we see how the line – incised, torn, engraved – acts as a key device. We see how the plane – the wall, the painting, the sheet of paper or cloth – plays a stronger role than was previously obvious. We see how the support – the floor, the prop, the plinth – is always in question. Gravity is marshalled to take its effect, whether on piles of sand on the ground, or on pieces of suspended cloth. We see how sculptural Flanagan is, and how classic a sculptor. Modelling and carving, addition and subtraction, plinth and ground: these are his concerns.

Clarrie Wallis's essay concentrates on Flanagan's relationship with materials and Andrew Wilson looks at materials of another kind, in the form of words. Flanagan's fascination with the French writer Alfred Jarry (1873–1907) whose creations *Ubu Roi* (first published and presented in 1896) and *Gestes et Opinions du Docteur Faustroll*, published posthumously, helped to establish a theatre of the absurd. Flanagan's intimate knowledge of Jarry's fertile literary geography echoed the interest of other artists including Picasso and Hockney, but pushed further into language and its material means. Perhaps it was also the Ubu characters who encouraged Flanagan in his theatrical bent, setting up sculptural scenes which might have encouraged their actors to animate them, complete with stage and lights. And it was perhaps the companionship of poets which allowed Flanagan to be so fleet of foot and light of touch, escaping from some of the weight and permanence of sculpture and allowing it to become more like a play of words which has no particular permanent residence. By combining words – or letters – in mysterious liaison with three-dimensional forms, Flanagan adds to the enduring character of his sculptures while refuting any obvious signification. These titles are like the forms themselves, both less and more than is conventional. The gaps – in material and in meaning – are exactly what we remember.

The fact that Flanagan died so very recently makes this a good and a bad moment for an exhibition. It is perhaps easier now to think of making the type of more heavily curated selection which defines the retrospective exhibition, but the very suddenness of the artist's departure has left any number of loose ends. Helping us throughout have been the artist's family, especially Flan Flanagan, and Jo Melvin of the artist's Estate. We thank them very sincerely for enabling this exhibition to happen. Flanagan's almost magical appeal to his colleagues, artists and curators, left a reservoir of people who were happy to talk to the curators; we thank them for giving so generously of their time. It was clear to us that many people wished this project well and wanted to add to the record.

We are enormously grateful to The Henry Moore Foundation for their generosity, and to Romulus Construction for their invaluable support. This exhibition has been made possible by the provision of insurance through the Government Indemnity Scheme. Tate Britain would like to thank HM Government for providing Government Indemnity and the Department for Culture, Media and Sport and the Museums, Libraries and Archives Council for arranging the indemnity.

The Collège de 'Pataphysique, founded in Paris, in part to collect, annotate and publish the writings of Alfred Jarry, underlined the importance of opposites. Dr Faustroll himself proposes that 'pataphysics be understood as the science of imaginary solutions. Even if it is no more than a pseudo-science, it still has lessons for us, and perhaps especially in relation to this show. 'Pataphysics 'will study the laws which govern the exceptions'; it explains 'a universe which one can see in place of the usual universe, and which, indeed, perhaps one ought to see.'

PENELOPE CURTIS
DIRECTOR, TATE BRITAIN

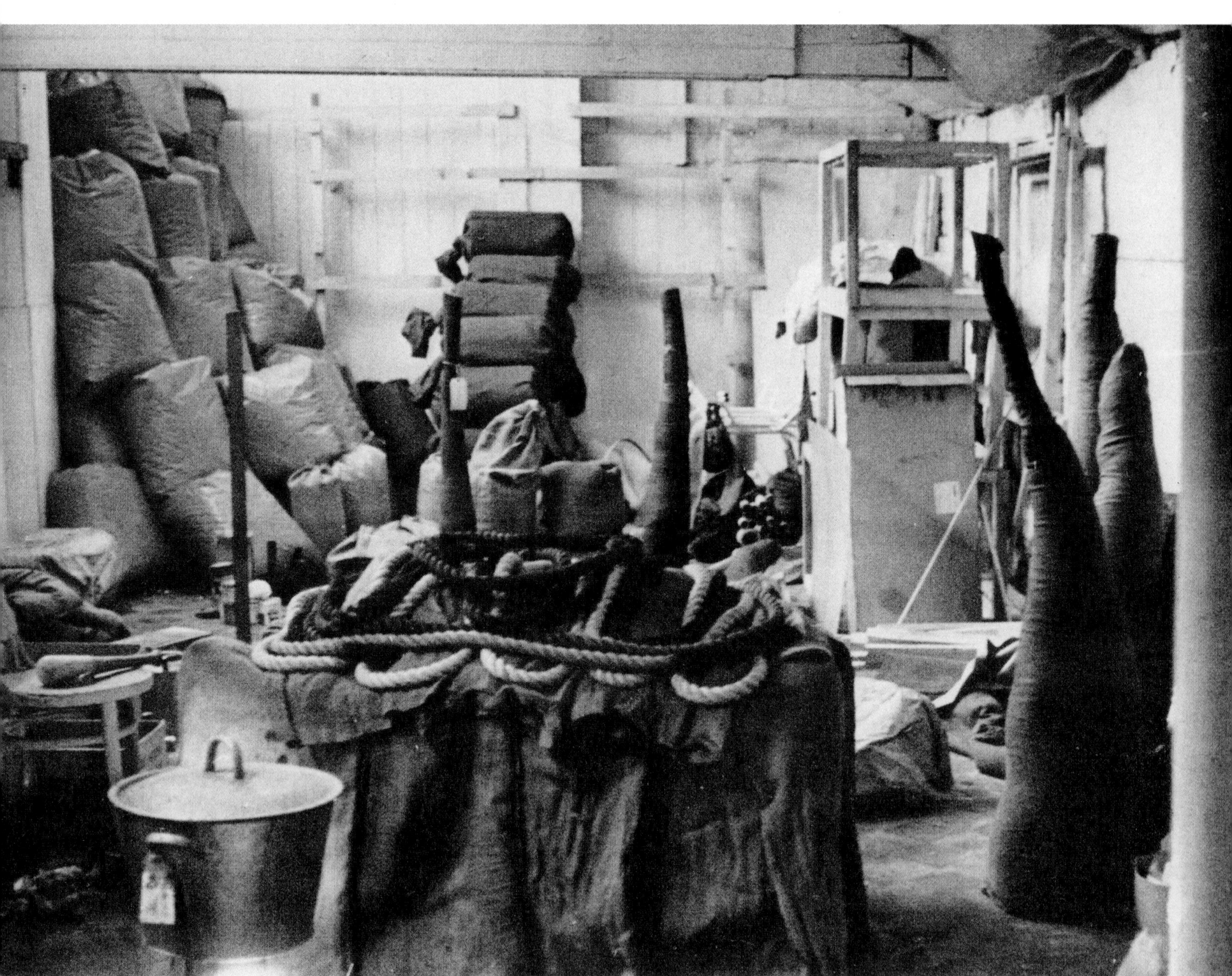

Barry Flanagan's studio/store. Invitation card,
Fischbach Gallery, New York 1969

Acknowledgements

Barry Flanagan was one of Britain's most original and inventive artists and challenged the nature of sculpture as it was understood in the mid-1960s. We are extremely proud to be given the opportunity to mount this major exhibition of his work, the first in London since his show at the Whitechapel Art Gallery almost thirty years ago. Flanagan is well known for the bronze work he produced in his later career. However, this exhibition concentrates on his early work and positions him as one of the key figures in the development of British and international sculpture, which was signalled by the first international presentation of his stone and bronze work at the Venice Biennale and the *Documenta* and *Zeitgeist* exhibitions in 1982.

In developing and preparing the exhibition we are especially indebted to the artist's family, in particular Flan Flanagan, and the Estate for providing such generous assistance on so many aspects of the project, and also for the support of Leslie Waddington and Felix Mottram of Waddington Custot Galleries, London and Patrice Cotensin at Galerie Lelong, Paris; thanks also go to the staff at Plubronze Limited, Meirian Jump, Ashley Mottram, Thomas Walker and Alfred Widmann. Jo Melvin's expert opinion has been crucial to the success of this project. We have been very fortunate to have had the active encouragement of Nicholas Serota and Penelope Curtis, in addition to the invaluable advice of Teresa Gleadowe and Catherine Lampert who have shared their deep knowledge and understanding of Flanagan's work.

We are deeply grateful to all the individuals and institutions who have lent so generously to the exhibition. It is rare for an exhibition of this sort to be met with such positive enthusiasm and willingness to lend unreservedly – testament to the high regard in which Flanagan's sculpture is held. We would also like to convey our thanks to those who have assisted us in the course of our research including Henry Abercrombie, Barry Barker, Ian Barker, Lewis Biggs, Marja Bloem, Peter Briggs, Sue Brown, Anthony Caro, Michael Compton, Michael Craig-Martin, Jan Dibbets, Andrew Dipper, Colin Dyer, Ger van Elk, Andy Elton, William Feaver, Barry E. Flanagan, Flan Flanagan, Glyn Foulkes, Alan Gouk, Hilary Gresty, Jackie Harding, Rupert Harris, Jim Haynes, Jerry Hughes, John James, Elisa Kay, Phillip King, Victoria Lane, Paul Levy, Richard Long, Bruce McLean, Jill McManners, Penelope Marcus, Barry Miles, Jonathan Park, Judith Patrick, David Plante, Cheryll Potter, Peter Randall-Page, Jasia Reichardt, John Retford, Patrick Reyntiens, John Sharkey, Seth Siegelaub, Barbara Steveni, Ann Stokes, Anthony Stokes, Jake Tilson, Charles Verey, Nicholas Wadley, Brian Wall, Alister Warman, Nick Wayte, Lawrence Weiner and Hester R. Westley.

Thanks also go to the following individuals for practical help on many fronts: Sebastiano Barassi, Alastair Brotchie, Gina Buenfeld, Rachel Chatalbash, Julie Defrenne, Arnaud Desjardin, Sarah den Dikken, Diana Eccles, Ton Geerts, Harry Gilonis, Pamela Griffin, Alan Halsey, Stella Halkyard, Michelle Harvey, Susanna Heron, Maxine Hodsdon, David Huntington, Geurt Imanse, Martin Jenkins, David Juda, Alexia Kirk, Paul Luckraft, Laura MacCulloch, Sally McKay, Biddy Peppin, Amy Pettifer, Peter Philpott, Justin Reay, Richard Riley, Charlie Rossow, Martijn Sanders, Sheena Stoddard, Reka Szili, Nancy Thompson, Jennifer Tobia, Connie Wan, Fiona Waterhouse, Diana Wood, and Margaret Zoller.

At Tate Britain we would particularly like to thank Jennifer Powell, Assistant Curator, who has helped steer preparations for the exhibition through to completion. Thanks are also due to Carolyn Kerr, Melanie Greenwood, Shoair Mavlian, Lorna Robinson, Sarah Walsh and Amy Thompson for their contribution to different stages of the organisation. The complexities of delivering and installation the exhibition have been ably handled by Kiko Noda and Alyson Rolington, in addition to Andy Shiel, Art Installation Manager, assisted by Juleigh Gordon-Orr, the Art Handling team and Tate conservators. We are also grateful to all those who have contributed to the wide range of activities that support the exhibition including Jennifer Batchelor, Helen Beeckmans, Claire Eva, Bronwyn Gardner, Clare Gill, Simon Grant, Selina Jones, Madeleine Keep, Billie Lindsay, Celeste Menich, Lucie Sherwood, Nikki Young and staff in the Tate Library and Archive.

We are grateful to the Tate Publishing team – Nicola Bion, Roanne Marner, and Miriam Perez – for their work on the catalogue, and to Philip Lewis for his sensitive design. We would also like to thank Sally O'Reilly for her skilful editing and Tate Photography, in particular Lucy Dawkins, Samuel Drake, Mark Heathcote, David Lambert, Marcella Leith and Rod Tidnam.

CLARRIE WALLIS AND ANDREW WILSON

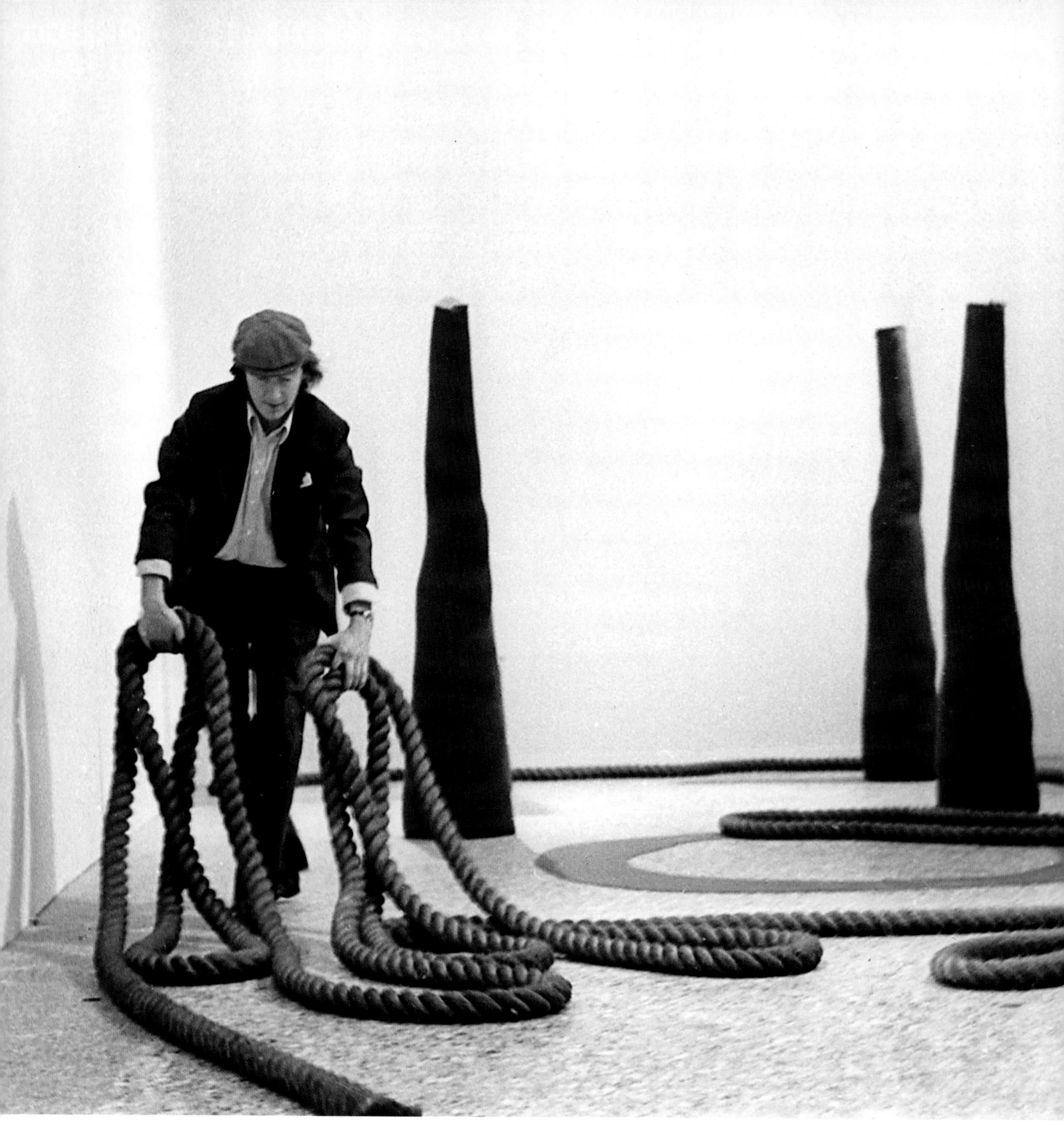

Flanagan installing *4 casb 2 '67* 1967 at
Arte Inglese Oggi, Milan 1976

'The business is in the making'[1]

Clarrie Wallis

In 1982 the British Pavilion at the Venice Biennale celebrated Barry Flanagan's work, presenting a selection of stone and bronze sculptures made during the previous decade. In the same year his first *Large Leaping Hare* 1982 caught the world's attention at *Documenta 7*, while a group of bronze hares and other animals appeared at *Zeitgeist*. These exhibitions had been preceded by eighteen years of sculptural innovation, fuelled by an idiosyncratic approach with an unusually wide frame of reference. These shows may have cemented Flanagan's reputation, but did they reflect a fundamental change in his practice or a coherent trajectory within the work?

At first glance Flanagan's work seems to fall easily into a number of discrete periods, with a distinct shift from the use of soft materials to stone and then to bronze casting. It is often assumed that his adoption of the traditional process of bronze casting signalled an abandonment of avant-garde practice. However, what it actually reveals is a deeper continuity running beneath a changing surface; a continuity based on his engagement with certain contradictions that have remained constant throughout a career marked by an intense search for a practice that answers the aporias and contradictions involved in making sculpture.

Flanagan's often conflicting interests in materials, sculptural processes, the acceptance of a given structure and yet openness to chance was reconciled by his working relationship with the foundry and based on a sophisticated understanding of the workings of trade within and beyond the art community he embraced. Teresa Gleadowe captures this well when she writes of Flanagan's 'consistent attitudes, representing not the adoption of an artistic stance, but simply opening a new area of research, a material to be tested and a tradition to be investigated.'[2] These issues are both internal to art world debates relating to the nature of sculpture and to other, wider discussions: tradition versus anti-tradition, work versus play, chance versus deliberation, spirit versus matter, craft versus art, to name but a few. From the outset Flanagan constantly sought solutions to these contradictions, not at a level of high theory, but in a spirit of playful openness, with varied approaches to material and the making of sculpture. And so 1982 marks a point when Flanagan showed how his characteristic lightness of touch could be projected through the solidity of bronze, the apparent contradiction typically suggestive of new solutions to sculptural problems.

Flanagan was born in 1941 in Prestatyn, North Wales. After studying architecture and art for a brief period at Birmingham College of Arts and Crafts he moved to London, later enrolling at St Martin's School of Art, to study sculpture from 1964 until 1966. The Head of Department at

1 Untitled statement, invitation card for *barry flanagan: sculpture*, Rowan Gallery, London 1966.
2 Teresa Gleadowe, 'Stone and Bronze Sculptures,' pamphlet to accompany *Barry Flanagan Sculpture*, British Council, 1982.

St Martin's during this period was Frank Martin, who transformed a place of amateur study into an international centre for professional sculptors; and in the late 1950s Anthony Caro's experimental evening classes pioneered fresh approaches to medium and form, attracting a group of students who became known as the New Generation: David Annesley, Michael Bolus, Phillip King, Tim Scott and William Tucker. They moved away from figurative and pastoral sculpture to urban, formal abstraction fashioned in colourful new materials and based on a modernist conception of sculpture that owed much to the writings of Clement Greenberg, the influential American critic, who called it 'the strongest new sculpture done anywhere in the world at this moment'.[3] Following international acclaim in the early 1960s, these sculptors went on to become tutors at St Martin's, seeking new teaching methods to complement their sculptural practice.

Flanagan had attended Caro's sculpture class for three months in 1960, where he was encouraged to take an experimental approach to making art. In 1963, prior to applying to the Sculpture Department, he wrote to him:

> '... The Friday evening classes at St Martin's were good meat for my imagination. These classes prompted the writing of poetry, a play, film scripts, songs, the purchase of cine equipment, and work on a means to translate movement and atmosphere into music. I might claim to be a sculptor and do everything else but sculpture. This is my dilemma.'[4]

When he enrolled at St Martin's in the autumn of the following year, Flanagan joined the unaccredited 'vocational' or 'advanced' sculpture course, which resembled a post-graduate programme. The students pursued an independent practice and received critical feedback in the form of a studio crit, where several visiting tutors would get together with the students to discuss a work. The course aimed to stimulate debate around the nature of sculpture and, as Flanagan recalled, 'Frank Martin and Tony Caro took Black Mountain College, North Carolina as a model. There was almost constant debate, profusely illustrated by the goods.'[5] It was an approach that prompted experimentation with non-conventional materials, reflecting a tendency among young artists of Flanagan's generation to employ a wide variety of strategies for rethinking the role of the artist and the form of the art object. Flanagan's use of impermanent or 'self forming' materials allowed results beyond his immediate control, while Bruce McLean pushed the territorial limits of sculpture by removing it from the studio and re-contextualising it in the street. Gilbert and George's performances challenged the viewer to consider questions

3 Letter from Clement Greenberg to Frank Martin championing the Sculpture department, 3 Feb. 1964. Frank Martin Papers, accepted by HM Government in lieu of Inheritance Tax and allocated to Tate 2010 (TGA 201014).

4 Letter of June 7 1963, printed in *Silâns*, no.6, Jan. 1965, unpag. *Silâns* was a magazine edited in the St Martin's Sculpture Department by Barry Flanagan, Alastair Jackson and Rudy Leenders and circulated within the college and through Better Books. Sixteen issues were published between September 1964 and June 1965.

5 *Barry Flanagan: Sculpture*, exh. cat., Venice Biennale, British Council, London 1982, p.79.

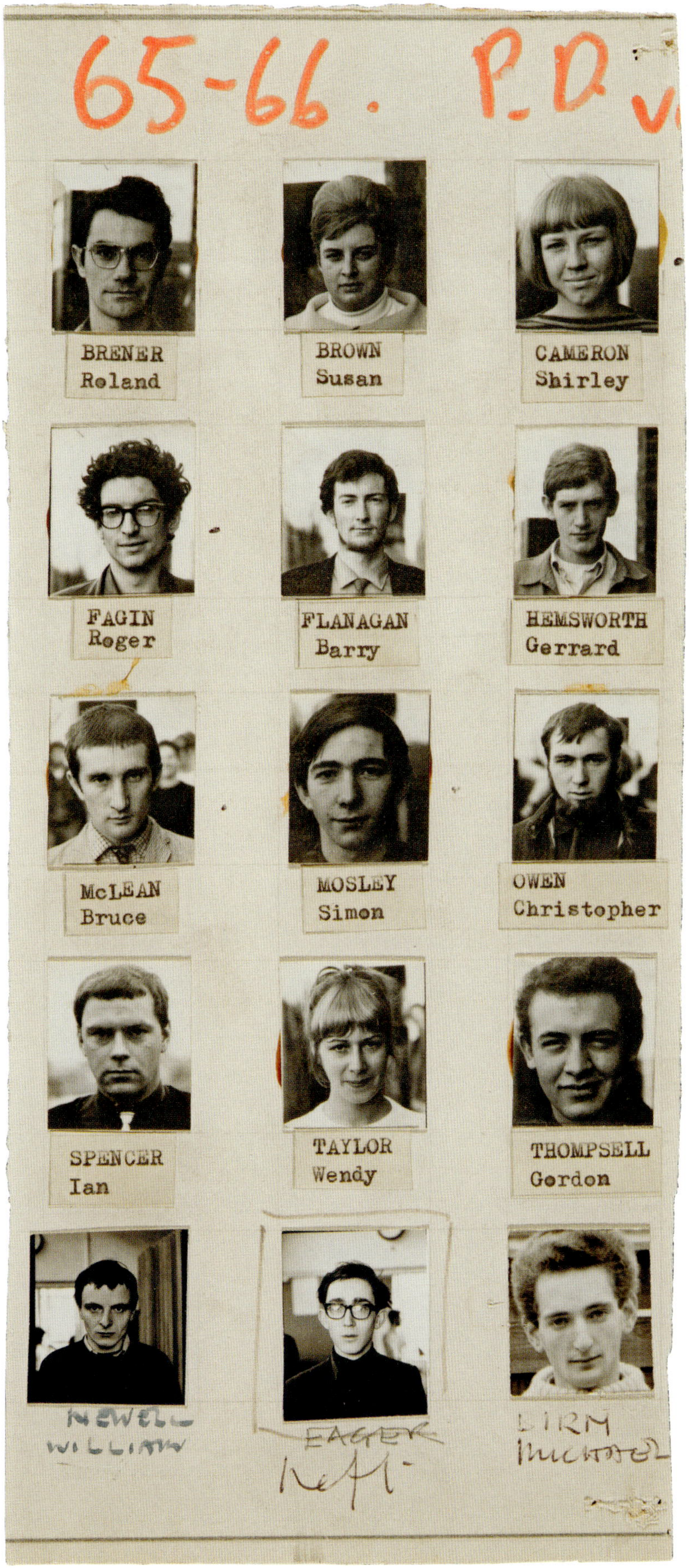

Student card for the vocational sculpture course at St Martin's School of Art 1965–6

regarding ephemerality, time, decay and, above all, the relationship of art and life.

In a special edition of the magazine *Studio International* the cartoon *St Martin's-in-the Fields* by Glyn Foulkes, featured 'some aspects of contemporary British Sculpture'.[6] A sheep bearing the date 1968 on its body stands in front of a gate, a large question mark above its head. On the other side of the fence are clearly identifiable sculptures by artists associated with the St Martin's Sculpture Department – including *Declaration* 1961 by Phillip King, *Swing Low* 1964 by David Annesley, *Four Part Sculpture 1* c.1966 by William Tucker, *4 casb 2 '67* 1967 and *rope (gr 2sp 60) 6 '67* 1967 by Flanagan – and the image is captioned with a quote by David Annesley: 'Sculpture then seemed a vast empty field, and we had just climbed over the gate'. The cartoon satirised the idea of a new tendency, of progressive artists increasingly rejecting traditional boundaries in favour of new forms of expression. The issue coincided with a large retrospective of Caro's work at the Hayward Gallery, London, and included coverage of the sculpture course at St Martin's, as well as Tucker's *Essay on Sculpture*; a discussion on Caro's work by Annesley, Roelof Louw, Tim Scott and Tucker; articles on colour in sculpture and on the Stockwell Depot, and a piece by Charles

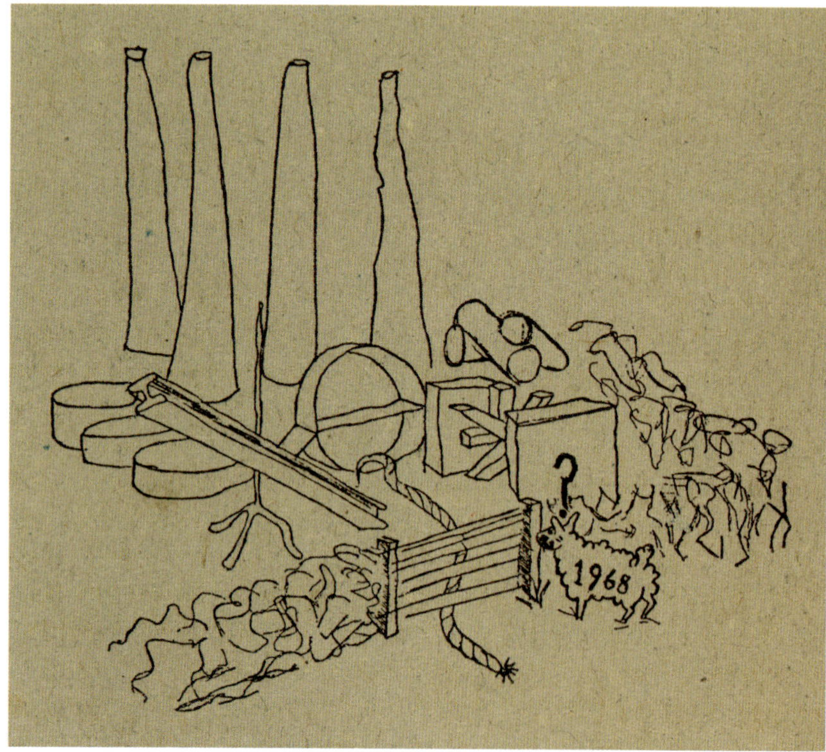

St Martin's-in-the-Fields by Glyn Foulkes, reproduced in *Studio International*, January 1969

6 Email exchange with Glyn Foulkes, 15 Feb. 2011. The cartoon first appeared in the second edition of *Potlatch*, Oct. 1968, a magazine produced at St Martin's School of Art and edited by Glyn Foulkes and Roger Bates. It was reproduced in *Studio International*, vol.177, no.907, Jan. 1969, p.8.

Harrison called 'Some recent sculpture in Britain', featuring the work of Roland Brener, Flanagan, Richard Long, Louw and McLean.

The shift in the way these artists were thinking can be put in the context of London's countercultural scene, not to mention the wider social and political context of the 1960s. It was a period of fundamental and far-reaching change in Britain, when the values and structures of society were shifting almost as fast as the technology that was reshaping daily life, and equally radical changes were taking place in the form and content of art. At the heart of this counterculture was an attack on the conformity of mainstream society and the breaking down of social boundaries to claim personal freedoms. On the one hand this formed the basis for a British version of the American West Coast flower power and hippie lifestyle; on the other, it consolidated more directed ethics of personal liberation.

Better Books, a bookshop near St Martin's, became a centre for countercultural events and happenings, initially organised by Barry Miles, until he left in late 1965 to co-found the Indica Gallery and Bookshop, when the concrete poet Bob Cobbing took over as manager. The many events at the bookshop included the *sTigma* exhibition in March 1965, inspired by Alex Trocchi's *Project Sigma*, and readings by the American poet Allen Ginsberg. Flanagan was attracted to the concrete poets that gathered there and co-produced, with Rudy Leenders and Alastair Jackson, a college magazine, *Silâns* (an approximate phonetic version of the word 'silence'), distributed free at St Martin's and at Better Books. *aaing j gni aa* 1965, Flanagan's six-part biomorphic sculpture, was first exhibited in the basement of Better Books alongside a 'magic poem' by John Sharkey, which used 'alchemical symbols printed out on a metre wide strip of paper nearly twenty feet in length [. . .] The poem surrounded Barry's sculpture which was set out on the floor so that people could walk in and around and through the combined work.'[7] The sculpture's mysterious, totemic forms bear some resemblance to the work of Joan Miró, and were enclosed within what could also be interpreted as a fairy ring or magic circle.

Better Books, together with the Institute of Contemporary Arts and the Indica Bookshop and Gallery, gave prominence to developments in experimental art, film and theatre. Much of this revolved around the Happenings movement, as it was registered in the Destruction in Art Symposium (specifically the work of Gustav Metzger, John Latham, Mark Boyle and Yoko Ono), the Arts Labs movement founded by Jim Haynes, the London Filmmakers Co-op, UFO, the Anti-University and Peter Brook's theatre company. At Better Books, and later at Miles's own Indica, we can see a fertile meeting of influences: trends from Europe and the United States were aired and 'high art' rubbed shoulders with popular culture.

7 John Sharkey in a letter to Andrew Wilson, 24 Feb. 2011.

There was also an explosion of interest in alchemy, the occult, psychic research, ley lines and Eastern religions. Louis Pauwels and Jacques Bergier's *The Dawn of Magic* was a key text and a major bestseller at the time, staying in print for decades.[8] This heady mix of alchemy, magic, witchcraft, secret societies and lost civilizations introduced many themes taken up by the counterculture, including the tension between science and a hidden 'irrationalist' mode of knowledge.

Flanagan certainly read *The Dawn of Magic* and it may have helped establish a set of reference points that were to have particular relevance in the future when combined with the Swiss psychiatrist Carl Jung's take on alchemy.[9] Particularly important was the '*coniunction oppositorum*', or conjunction of opposites, that is, the unity of seemingly opposed ideas, such as base matter and spiritual principles – in laboratory alchemy *coniunctio* meaning the mixing of two chemicals to produce a third – and we might view this as Flanagan's way of mediating the contradictions within which he created his work.

To confine the discussion of new tendencies in sculpture to its British protagonists is misleading, however, for it was part of a much wider phenomenon that included artists associated with Arte Povera, in addition to the work of Joseph Beuys. It was also evident in the United States in certain types of post-minimalist work, most notably that of Eva Hesse, and in the sculpture and writing of Robert Morris, in particular his essay 'Anti-Form', which was published in *Artforum* in 1968 and provided a philosophy of process, chance, random order, indeterminacy and impermanence. He describes the new approach as follows:

> 'Random piling, loose stacking, hanging, give passing form to the material. Chance is accepted and indeterminacy is implied since replacing will result in another configuration. Disengagement with preconceived enduring forms and orders for things is a positive assertion. It is part of the work's refusal to continue estheticizing form by dealing with it as a prescribed end.'[10]

An interest in chance and the idea that meaning appears beyond the control of the author was also explored by the highly influential experimental American composer John Cage. Cage experimented with unconventional material and, instead of a self-expressive art, he advocated techniques of composition through chance and indeterminacy. The composer's borrowings from South Asian aesthetics and philosophy included the *I Ching*, or the ancient *Chinese Book of Changes*, as a mechanism by which to generate compositions.[11] This opening up to the aleatory appealed to Flanagan's way of making sculpture.

8 The book *Le Matin des Magiciens* appeared in Paris in 1960. A translation by Rollo May was published in Britain in 1963 under the title *The Dawn of Magic* and made its way to the US a year later as *Morning of the Magicians*.

9 The possible impact of *The Dawn of Magic* on Flanagan was verified in an email from Barry Miles, 2 Mar. 2011.

10 Robert Morris, 'Anti-Form', *Artforum*, vol.6, no.8, Apr. 1968, pp.33–5.

11 The *I Ching* was a book that Flanagan highly valued and often gave as a gift.

While Minimal art had relatively little direct effect in Britain, the first half of the 1970s was dominated by Conceptual and Performance art and by sculpture in an expanded sense of the term, with installation, Land art and site-specific works receiving wide public attention through the exhibition *Live in Your Head: When Attitudes Become Form (Works – Concepts – Processes – Situations – Information)*, at the Kunsthalle Bern and the ICA, London, in 1969.[12] Significantly, Flanagan was the only British artist to be included in *When Attitudes Become Form* and the concurrent exhibition *Op Losse Schroeven (Situations and Cryptostructures)* at the Stedelijk Museum, Amsterdam.[13] Both landmark exhibitions brought together the 'new art' of the late 1960s: Arte Povera, anti-form, Conceptual and Land art. Although the complex nature of Flanagan's activities has prompted critics to brand his practice at one time or another with all these labels, his work defies such easy categorisation, and he was quick to assert that these debates were not principally about definitions. A statement prepared by Peter Fuller and Flanagan in 1970 declared that his work 'has been wrongly associated with Surrealism, Dada, Funk, Environment, Conceptualism, Happenings, the protest art of an Avant Garde, and even 'The English Tradition' of sculpture'.[14]

Flanagan was never greatly interested in theory, but instead created by way of an openness to sculptural processes and materials themselves. He considered the fundamental role of the sculptor to be to express himself in a three-dimensional way while holding on to the notion of doubt and enquiry; and his early investigations of form, as revealed through the inherent qualities of materials, highlight how his enquiries into the nature of sculpture combined with an ambition to explore the physical world. If the work seemed removed from 'traditional' sculptural activity, it nevertheless remained firmly engaged with a critique of sculpture, asking viewers to rethink their assumptions about space, form and materials. For example, constructed metal pieces realised while at St Martin's, such as *metal 2 '64* 1964 and *metal 3 '66* 1966 can be understood as formal investigations into abstract form and as a practical critique or response to modernist sculpture as identified within the very tradition of modernism. As Hilary Gresty describes:

> 'They clearly display the mode of their physical production – simple methods of jointing are left clearly visible, and a strange deployment of balance – of cause and effect – become apparent. *metal 2 '64* shows the intuitive application of unpredictable laws – a precarious balance is attained, the pipe being gently bent to display the possibilities of the material, the final form being off-set by the clean cut of the metal strip which is so positioned as to allow the plate to balance on an apex.'[15]

12 *Live in Your Head: When Attitudes Become Form (Work – Concepts – Processes – Situations – Information)*, exh. cat., Kunsthalle Bern 1969.

13 *Op Losse Schroeven (Situations and Crypostructures)*, exh. cat., Stedelijk Museum, Amsterdam 1969.

14 'Barry Flanagan; sculptor', *Connoisseur*, vol.174, no.701, July 1970, p.210.

15 *1965 to 1972 – When attitudes became form*, exh. cat., Kettle's Yard, Cambridge; Fruitmarket Gallery, Edinburgh 1984, p.43.

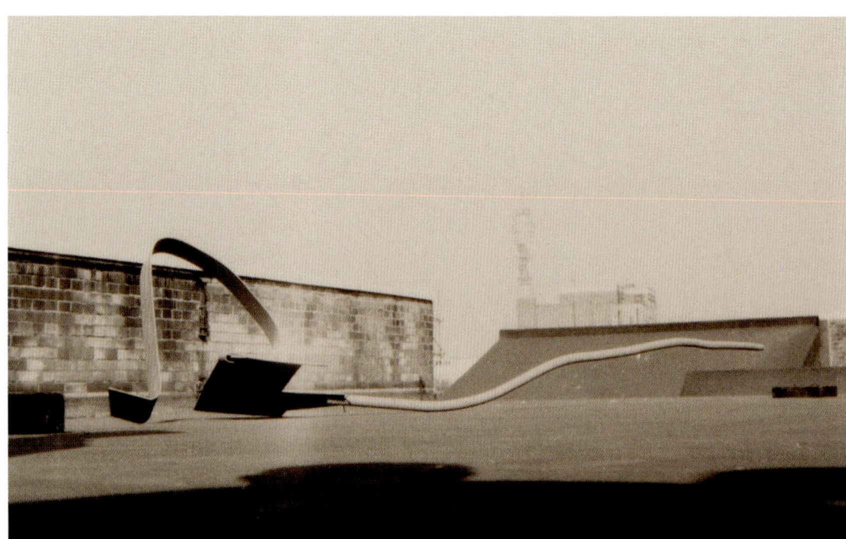

metal 2 '64 1964
on the roof of St Martin's

She goes on to add that 'the predictability of metal was unsatisfying – whereas the "New Generation" exploited their materials to make statements, for Flanagan it was a question of contemplation'.[16]

While Flanagan's early works, especially his metal sculptures, have been interpreted as a playful response to sculpture being made by Caro and his followers, his relationship with his tutors, in particular King and Latham, is more complex. Certainly his decision to include both *metal 2 '64* and *metal 3 '66* alongside *ho* 1966 and *four rahsb 1 '67* 1967 in *Ventures*,[17] an Arts Council touring exhibition in 1967, suggests that he did not think of these works as student experiments, but rather as significant in the development of his own concept of sculpture.

Flanagan may have ultimately found the predictability of metal unsatisfying, but what is noteworthy here is how, with a number of works, each element was allowed to take its own form. Flanagan cut, heated and then formed the steel while it was hung from a beam.[18] The metal's reaction depended in part on the amount of heat applied as well as the laws of gravity. So, even at this early stage, there is the sense of a sculptor not so much using materials to achieve a form in the way Caro had, but standing back and seeing how materials conducted themselves.

The complexity of Flanagan's interactions with the teachers at St Martin's is highlighted by his relationship with his first year tutor and subsequent friend Phillip King, who studied modern languages at Cambridge University before turning to sculpture. They shared an interest in concrete poetry, which had its roots in Mallarmé, Apollinaire and Dada, and also the French playwright and author Alfred Jarry, inventor of a logic

16 Ibid.
17 *Ventures*, exh. cat., Arts Council Gallery, Cambridge 1967.
18 Conversation with Henry Abercrombie, 9 Feb. 2011.

of the absurd, which he called 'pataphysics. This 'science of imaginary solutions' was a principle that underpinned much countercultural activity of the 1960s, and which Flanagan was introduced to shortly before his arrival at St Martin's. It remained an essential reference point throughout his career, signalling an (a)rationality that encompassed the absurd and the contradictions of making art, which Flanagan embraced and followed as 'solutions'. As he explained:

> 'I was drawn to Jarry not so much as a writer but as a poetic character. I first read him in 1963. I was lent a book, and I immediately adopted him as my historical hero, a symbolic figure emblematic of the individual imagination in revolt. What I liked best about Jarry was his invention of the science of 'pataphysics, or the science of imaginary solutions. It's a kind of anti-philosophy that challenges traditional ideas.'[19]

From 1965 Flanagan began to explore more malleable materials and, having access to a sewing machine, he used pre-sewn canvas shapes that were filled with plaster or sand and allowed to find their own form. It was, he noted, 'an elegant solution to the difficulty of making three-dimensional form.'[20] In other works simple found materials such as sisal rope were investigated for their shape-making qualities, their ambiguities and aporias playfully explored. The inherent malleability of the materials was important and the chance settling or falling of sculptural elements was allowed to happen in a spirit of ludic openness.

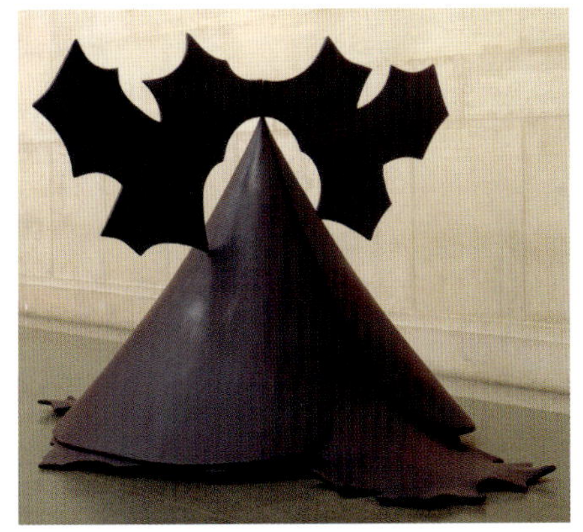

Phillip King *Genghis Khan* 1963
Tate. Presented by the Friends of the Tate Gallery 1970

Flanagan's first 'soft' sculpture was a cone. This was partly influenced by King who, since the early 1960s, had used the form as a central motif in sculptures such as *Rosebud* 1962, a baby pink cone divided down the middle to reveal a grey-green interior, or *Genghis Khan* 1963, the same shape rendered in dark purple with a crown of holly-like antlers. King considered the confidence of Flanagan's re-working of ideas, images and forms to be striking. In particular he admired the way Flanagan used the cone 'structurally as opposed to symbolically'.[21] He also marvelled at how he circumvented the problem of moving heavy plaster sculptures, as sand could be obtained almost anywhere and used to fill the bags.

Although there is a sense of a sculptor not using materials to achieve an effect in the way that King had, but rather seeing how materials conducted themselves – for example how piled hessian cloth folds or how poured sand heaps – the works Flanagan was producing at this time reflect a preoccupation with arrangements of different components. King recalls seeing Flanagan working on plaster and cloth elements of the sculpture *aaing j gni aa* 1965 in his studio at St Martin's, and suggesting

19 *Barry Flanagan Sculpture 1965 – 2005*, exh. cat., Irish Museum of Modern Art, Dublin 2006, p.59.
20 Ibid., p.68.
21 Conversation with Phillip King, 14 Dec. 2010.

that he pull the disparate components of the work together to form a single piece contained within a circle. He also proposed the addition of a plastic flower purchased from Seven Dials, near Charing Cross Road, and went on to recommend Flanagan to the Rowan Gallery, with which King also showed. They offered Flanagan his first solo exhibition, which took place in August 1966, only a couple of months after he had graduated from St Martin's.

Flanagan exhibited twelve sculptures, including *aaing j gni aa* and *ringn '66* 1966. Having seen the exhibition, Gene Baro devoted an entire article to Flanagan in the September edition of *Art and Artists*.[22] Opposite a full-page illustration of *pdreeoo* 1965 – suggestive of a large, shrivelled fruit and made by filling a pre-sewn shape with plaster which hardened within the restricting skin – he described how the work had 'no over-riding formality [. . .] principally, they come out of intuition and process'.

While Flanagan arrived at his concept of sculpture through an idiosyncratic route, he was also influenced by John Latham, who also taught part-time at St Martin's. His friendship with Latham was to prove to be of great consequence, not only because of Latham's recognition of art as a form of knowledge in itself, but also because of his questioning of the art object as a finite and discrete entity. Rather than focusing on the production of objects, Latham declared the importance of process, which he came to define as 'event structure', emphasising the importance of 'becoming' over 'being' and 'time' over 'space'. Although the scientific and philosophical underpinnings of Latham's time-based practice were complex, as Gresty notes, comparisons can be made between Flanagan's interest in process and Latham's idea of 'event as a sculptural component'.[23]

Latham's thinking remained closely informed by a scientific model, while Flanagan drew on a more eclectic range of influences. Both, however, saw their practice as generating a mode of knowing that was reducible neither to an autotelic artwork nor to the discourses that prompted the work, such as science or alchemy. This mode of knowing would have its own laws and rationality. In this light Flanagan's 'pataphysical explorations can be seen as comparable to Latham's work; but where Latham could be likened to the theoretical physicist with a great faith in an *a priori* conceptualism, Flanagan is better characterised as a laboratory tinkerer or *bricoleur* – empirical and experimental.

In August 1966 Flanagan took part in Latham's *Still and Chew* event, for which he also designed the invitation. Guests were invited to Latham's home to participate in an event-based work with the aim of extracting and capturing the 'essence' of Greenberg's influential collection of essays *Art and*

22 Gene Baro, 'Animal Vegetable and Mineral', *Art and Artists*, vol.1, no.6, Sept. 1966, p.63.

23 Hilary Gresty, 'Sculpture in Britain in the early '70s', M.Phil, Courtauld Institute, University of London, 1983, p.46.

Still and Chew invitation 1966

Culture 1961 – which Latham regarded as a 'fixed mode of knowledge' – and highlighting Latham's ideas about art, event and time, in opposition to Greenberg's emphasis on form and space. Everyone was asked to select and chew pages from the book, on temporary loan from the college library. The masticated pages were then immersed in acid and fermented to form a sugar, and later 'an alien culture' was added.[24] Following an overdue notice from St Martin's School of Art Library in May 1967, the liquid was distilled and returned, labelled *The Essence of Greenberg*. Latham's contract at the college was subsequently not renewed.

Flanagan's own tussles with the history of sculpture form a rough-and-ready dialectic, which attempted to mediate the contradictions of his practice, both internal and external to the art world. He wanted to find 'elegant solutions', to present sculpture free from preconceptions, without 'its myth'.[25] By this he meant that he was interested in making non-literary sculpture with no prior explanation for it.

In his statement for British Artists at the Biennale des Jeunes in Paris in 1967 he described how 'one merely causes things to reveal themselves to sculptural awareness'.[26] This approach was noted by Gene Baro: 'the work expresses on one level a dialogue of materials, the vital reaction of one substance to another; but there is also what we might call a sophisticated judgment here, a standard of preference deeply personal and not to be explained readily'[27]; and also by Charles Harrison:

> 'the life of Flanagan's sculptures is dictated by internal considerations; that is, by the behaviour of the inorganic substances used in their construction. In the case of two related sculptures, *Heap* is differentiated from *Rack* largely by the degree to which the behaviour of hessian bags filled with sand is different from the behaviour of hessian bags filled with

24 *John Latham: Least Event, One Second Drawings, Blind Work, 24 Second Painting*, Lisson Publications, London 1970, p.8.
25 See statement published by Flanagan on the occasion of his first exhibition at the Rowan Gallery in August 1966.
26 'British Artists at the Biennale des Jeunes in Paris', with text by Barry Flanagan, *Studio International*, vol.174, no.893, Sept. 1967, pp.98–9.
27 Gene Baro, 'Animal Vegetable and Mineral', *Art and Artists*, vol.1, no.6, Sept. 1966, p.63.

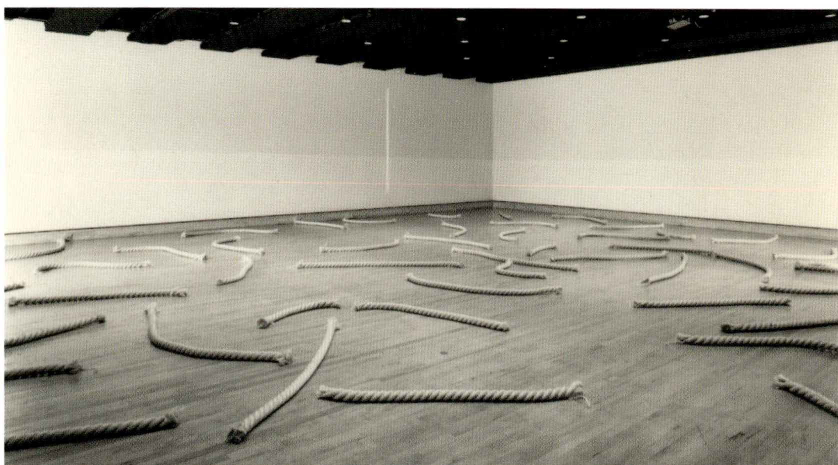

light on light on white on white (Hayward I) 1969

polystyrene chips: they have a different weight, lie differently, create different surfaces and are enlivened by different tensions. Yet we don't perceive the sand, or the polystyrene: we perceive the results of their behaviour as manifested in the form taken by the hessian bags.'[28]

Flanagan's desire to rid the work of all but the physical facts so that they have their own 'material reality' is further highlighted by the use of codes to title his early sculptures. A rope piece installed in two spaces, for example, was titled *2 sp rope '67/69* 1967–9, whereas works such as *heap 1 '68* 1968, *bundle 2 '67* 1967 and *pile 1 '68* 1968 are literal definitions of actions and objects linked by process.

Flanagan delighted in the manipulation of materials, and his belief that play led to discovery (the science of imaginary solutions) encouraged him to focus on his own response to materials, which he considered the fundamental constituent of sculpture. While he might select the materials for a given work, he would remove himself, witnessing the effects of physics on the materials themselves. As such, Flanagan shifted the focus of a work's meaning to circumstances beyond the sculptor's immediate control. In *line 3 '68* 1968, for instance, the downward pull of the felt creates a temporary shape in the line of rope. This approach also prompted him to consider the space a work occupies. Early light pieces realised within a studio environment paved the way to a number of multi-part room installations, including projects for the Hayward Gallery and the Museum Haus Lange, Krefeld, which incorporated the use of projected light as a means to explore the two-dimensional beyond the limits of the picture plane, as a 'medium of perception' and as a way to re-frame sculptural form. Flanagan's first multi-part installation *light on light on white on white,*

28 Charles Harrison, 'Barry Flanagan's Sculpture', *Studio International*, vol.175, no.900, May 1968, p.266.

View of Barry Flanagan solo exhibition, Rowan Gallery, London 1968, showing *rack 1 '67/68* 1967/68 (foreground), *heap 1 '68* 1968 (left), *pile 1 '68* 1968 (right)

retrospectively titled *Hayward I*, was created for the exhibition *6 at the Hayward Gallery* in 1969. This consisted of approximately one hundred lengths of rope arranged about the gallery floor, a painted white dado on the walls, with one additional vertical line projection and, in one corner, *light on light on sacks* 1969.

In the same year, for his Krefeld show, he created site-specific works as a direct response to the domestic space of Mies van der Rohe's architecture. The use of simple processes and self-forming materials is again in play here. In works such as *aug 7 '69* 1969 and *aug 8 '69* 1969 sheets of flax were supported in various ways by lengths of bamboo, branches or stretchers. These sculptural objects were leant against walls or propped in corners, playing with the boundaries between the two- and three-dimensional within the architectural space.

In the early 1970s Flanagan continued to deploy these materials and techniques in a number of stretcher and hessian works – materials that are commonly associated with painting. Like the later painted sheet metal pieces, such as *VII 78 as night* 1978 and *VII 78 the corn's up* 1978, these works explore the tension between painting and sculpture. If they can be understood as investigations into the history and convention of the medium, they also challenge the idea that paintings are always two-dimensional, while sculptures are three-dimensional things. Beyond these distinctions, Flanagan seems to insist on the raw materiality of the objects, their palpable presence. For instance, the flat vertical surface of a wall work

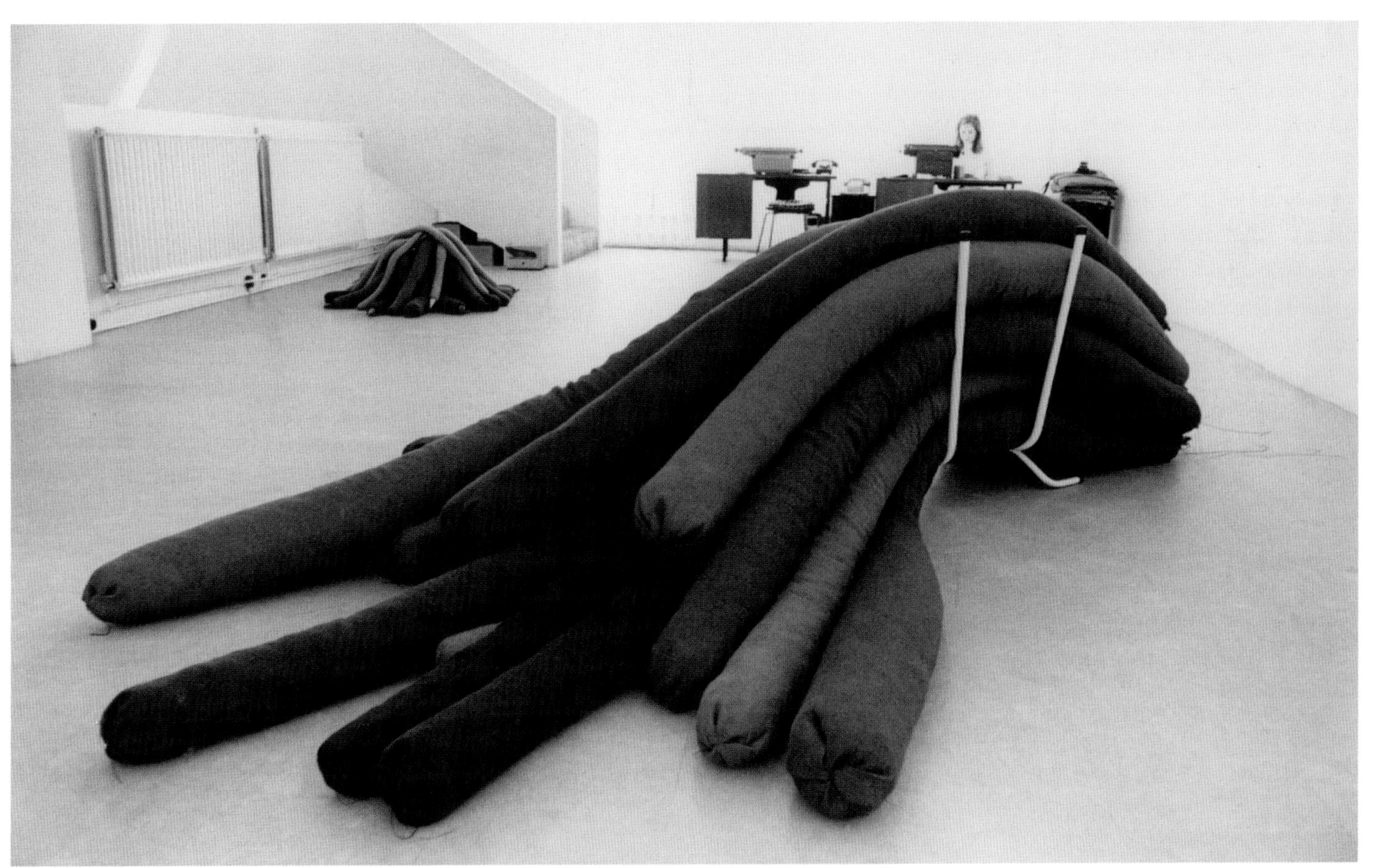

such as *untitled 1* 1972 is disrupted by a semi cut-away spiral. At its simplest, this rupturing of the picture plane raises questions about the experience of looking, about where surface stops and object begins, while also undermining conventional figure and ground distinctions within painting.

This exploration of figure and ground is significant because of Flanagan's interest in the potential openness of all aspects of human perception. This is something he explored in his diagrams and text *Eye-liners* 1968,[29] which examines how we perceive the world. Human perception is both seeing and understanding – literally and metaphorically. The figure/ground relationship in this sense operates in two registers, referring to the intrinsically subjective and perceptual, as well as to objective, physical realities. Flanagan's desire to explore the crossover between the two- and three-dimensional (an interest which also fed into the act of drawing and his approach to carving) is not just the deconstruction of paired opposites that structure art discourse; there are other concerns too. The spiral in *untitled 1* 1972, for example, may be a reference to the *gidouille*, the spiral on the belly of Jarry's monstrous 'pataphysical antihero Ubu Roi.

This fascination with apparent opposites is, however, persistent throughout Flanagan's work. Beyond opposed couplets such as ground/figure, subjective/objective, and so on, Flanagan again and again explores the means to go beyond such dualisms. Thus, Flanagan does not wish merely to indicate the brute physicality of his materials in these works, but rather to use this raw stuff as a *prima materia* that, somewhere between chance and necessity, is transformed to achieve a unity of opposites.

As Hester R. Westley has noted, Flanagan's approach to materials, in fact, poses a fundamental question: 'At what point does a sculptor dictate – or remove himself from the direction of the work?'[30] This question recurred throughout Flanagan's career, not only in his playful but detached manipulation of materials, but also in his relationships with craftsmen. Although the majority of his work from the 1960s deliberately avoided the use of traditional sculptor's materials, he was always interested in the role of the artisan, skilled in the handling of materials. Prior to St Martin's Flanagan was a student at Birmingham College of Arts and Craft, where he studied carving, modelling and casting. He also worked for a while for Robert Savage, a framer on the Old Brompton Road, who introduced him to 'clay bole, gesso and all the medieval recipes'.[31]

As a young man Flanagan had worked as a labourer in the building trade and believed that the carrying, lifting, layering and construction skills he had learned then were also part of 'the role of a sculptor'. In

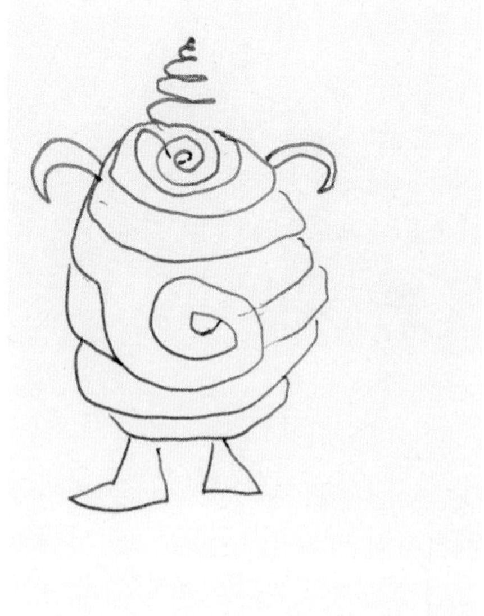

Ubu sketch 3: Pere Ubu 1974

29 Barry Flanagan, 'Eye-liners: Some Leaves from Barry Flanagan's notebook', *Art and Artists*, vol.3, no.1, Apr. 1968, pp.30–3.

30 H.R. Westley, 'Traditions and Transitions: St Martin's Sculpture Department 1960–79', PhD thesis, Courtauld Institute of Art 2007, p.119.

31 *Barry Flanagan Sculpture 1965–2005*, exh. cat., Irish Museum of Modern Art/Dublin City Gallery The Hugh Lane, Dublin 2006, p.63.

works such as *4 casb 2 '67* 1967 his exploration of the relationship between the canvas and the sand was directly based on his knowledge of 'soft shuttering', a process used in building construction to mould concrete while it sets hard, and something he had gained first-hand experience of while working as a site hand in the construction industry. This technique was also used in *soft shuttered sandwell* 1967, sited outside Swiss Cottage Central Library as part of the Camden Arts Centre exhibition *Sculpture in a Civic Setting*. Another work, *one camion sand piece* 1969, literally consisted of a truckload of sand being tipped directly on to the pavement outside the Museum Haus Lange in Krefeld.

Flanagan had a straightforward approach to selling his art: he considered himself a professional who sold the fruits of his creative labours in a simple transaction. This chimed with his interests in trades and craft, but there were times when he found it difficult to make a living, as illustrated by the etching *Appointment book – a struggle with disapointment, to keep the house from falling down* 1972. Here he uses printmaking, a traditional way for an artist to find a market, to reflect on issues of commerce.

His interest in the relationship of the artist to trade prompted him to join the Artist Placement Group, set up by Barbara Steveni and John Latham in 1966 to encourage closer collaboration between artists and industry. By placing artists within industry and government departments

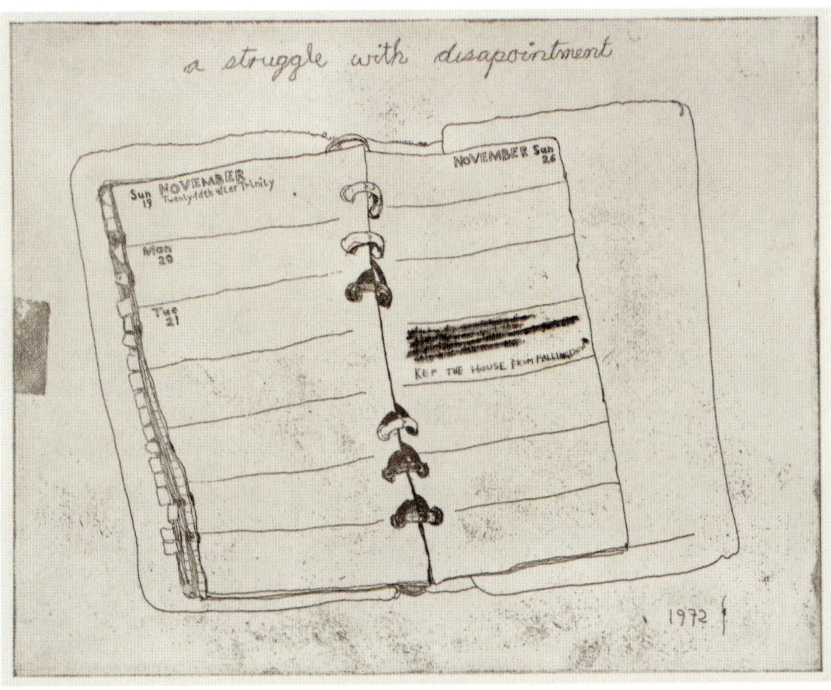

Appointment book – a struggle with disapointment, to keep the house from falling down 1972

and paying them a salary equal to that of other employees, Steveni hoped that they would become involved in the day-to-day work of the organisation, and that in due course their contribution would help reposition the artist within a wider social context.

Flanagan's concern with the social economy of art is also evident in 1969, when he started to print his own money, which he called 'funds'. This lino-printed money (each authenticated by his thumbprint) came in denominations of five, ten, twenty and fifty and, while they could be understood as artworks, they were on occasion used as payment for work or goods. In the mid 1970s Flanagan set up the trading account Rowford Process, under which a number of projects were conceived, including furniture designed for the Hayward Gallery and wooden plinths riveted together for his own work, such as *Hello cello* 1976 and *Soprano* 1981.

In 1973, inspired by a magazine article[32] about the marble quarries of Northern Italy, Flanagan visited the medieval town of Pietrasanta. Michelangelo had used stone from the Pietrasanta quarries and Henry Moore visited and used stone from the same source. Flanagan was impressed by the sense of continuity of artisans and sculptors' skills, making the town a centre of the stone masonry since the mid-thirteenth century. This came with a realisation that 'carving carries seventy five per cent of the traditional business and practice of sculpture'.[33] Pietrasanta had a similarly long tradition of bronze casting, and it may be here that Flanagan began to think about casting as a possible avenue for exploration.[34] Certainly this first trip to Italy must have brought into more pointed contrast the polarities that already concerned him: tradition and anti-tradition, art and craft and so on.

The simple carvings and stone compositions he started to make were in direct response to the particular character of each piece of stone. Selected for their shape and surface, the stones were incised with lines, spirals and rings, which reflect Flanagan's interest in Celtic mark making. Works such as *The Road to Altissimo* 1973 (Altissimo was where Henry Moore went to carve) and *to plough* 1975 were inspired by the Italian landscape. They encapsulate visual or verbal images, whereas other blocks of sandstone are carved with abstract graphic motifs relating to his preoccupation with Jarry's Ubu Roi, whose *gidouille* reappears on a number of other carvings, including *a nose in repose* 1977–9, made from Hornton stone from a quarry near Banbury in Oxfordshire, not far from his studio.[35]

While the spiral may be read as a sign of creativity for Flanagan, it was also suggestive of the umbilical cord, which signified his attachment to the physicality of material and man's attachment to work. The sculpture sits on pit props, demonstrating the artist's interest in traditional,

32 Conversation with Michael-Craig Martin, 12 Jan. 2011.

33 Taken from an unpublished interview with Judith Bumpus, 1982.

34 Flanagan first explored the possibilities of casting as a student in Birmingham. His first bronze work was a portrait of his father-in-law, Emlyn Lewis, modelled from photographs after his death in 1969.

35 See Tim Hilton, 'Less a slave of other people's thinking…', *Barry Flanagan Sculpture*, British Council, London 1982, p.12.

Barry Flanagan 1978

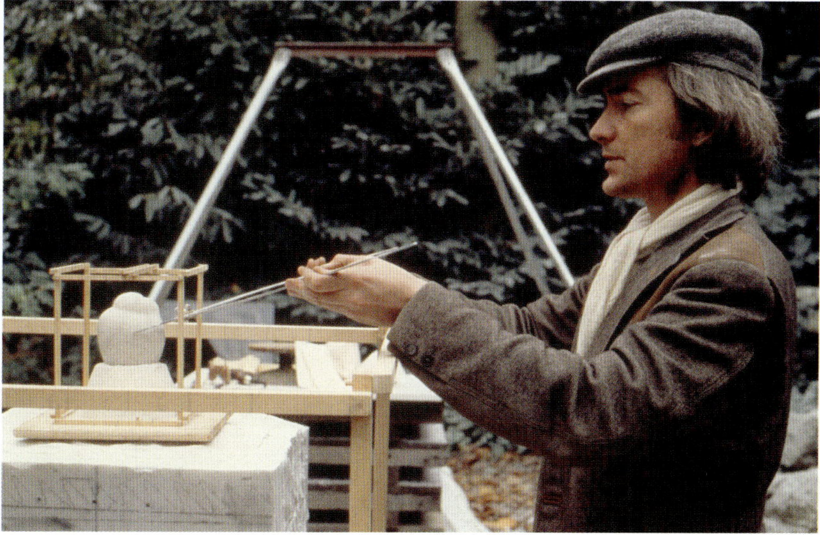

artisanal ways of making and supporting things, an interest apparent elsewhere in the use of ready-made stock items from the mason's yard, such as found pieces of granite shaped for building foundations in *Bollard* 1979 and *Cornish BuB* 1979. In the case of *untitled (3) '73* 1973, different stones and materials are piled up precariously. Flanagan observed how 'the physical world is modelled, re-made, used and appropriated, and that the physical world is the large palette that I work from'.[36] Other works reflect the importance of the rural communities in which he worked during this period – in Northamptonshire in the mid 1970s and Oxfordshire in the late 1970s and 1980s, on several occasions taking a job anonymously in a stonemason's yard.

His reading, too, consolidated this interest. Seamus Murphy's book *Stone Mad* 1966, an account of time as an apprentice stone carver in the 1920s, and D.V. Thompson's translation of *Il Libro dell'Arte* by Cennino d'Andrea Cennini – a guide to methods of painting written in fifteenth-century Florence, which contains information on pigments, brushes, the art of fresco and techniques and tricks, including detailed instructions for painting in egg tempera and the lost art of gilding stone – were both publications he would give as gifts to those working with him.

At the end of the 1970s Flanagan began to commission craftsmen based in Sem Ghelardini's atelier in Pietrasanta to make large-scale carvings in marble from small, hand-sized maquettes of clay. The maquettes were shaped by cupping and squeezing the clay with both hands – in keeping with Flanagan's earlier coil, pinch and squeezed pots – its delicate and exact form clearly bearing the marks of the modelling processes. The

36 *Barry Flanagan Sculpture 1965–2005*, exh. cat., Irish Museum of Modern Art, Dublin 2006, p.59.

challenge for the stone carver was to reproduce or reappraise this form. As Flanagan explained: 'One of these shapes, the size of a hand or formed in the hand, can easily go to stone four times its size. And the significance of four times the size is simply that the hand goes into the arm four times approximately. Therefore, this gives the carver the continuity and the sense of the scaling up.'[37] The marble of *untitled (carving no. 13/81)* 1981 and *untitled (2b × 4)* 1982, for example, was carved to reproduce the shapes moulded by hands, or curved and rolled like dough.

In these works the polarities noted above are put into play: the artisan responds to the artist, who must relinquish control when he hands over the maquette. The small artwork, the fruit of an *avant-gardist* anti-tradition, is transformed into a large object crafted according to immemorial tradition. We can extend the contradictions that Flanagan negotiates in these works to the softness of the clay versus the hardness of the stone and the individual imprint of the artist's hand versus impersonal reproduction.

In an interview with Judith Bumpus in 1982 the artist reflected on the links between authorship and interpretation, artist and artisan, describing his working relationship with craftsmen and the open exchange of skills: 'they're my musicians and I'm the composer'. He goes on to say:

> 'there are understandings which are reached. These understandings are traditional [...] it's very nice to remember that there are places where sculpture is actually made and mutual support and interest and skills, sculptor's skills, are brought to bear by all the individuals as among a group of musicians, all playing different parts but with the actual understanding and willingness to interpret the work in hand objectively and exclusively for the same purpose – to produce sculpture. It can lighten the load.'[38]

However, Flanagan had reservations about the continuing designations of himself as the 'author' and felt that the relationship with the stone carvers never quite worked as he had hoped. They were too literal in their interpretation of his ideas. He wanted more collaboration and interpretation from them, to offer a greater share in the alchemy of creation. This sense of partnership, of being part of a community, was to be of vital importance to Flanagan's long-term way of working.

In 1979 he was invited by his friend Andy Elton to work at A&A Sculpture Casting.[39] Needing to find a subject through which to explore the process of bronze casting, Flanagan was drawn to the book *The Leaping Hare* by George Ewart Evans and David Thompson, which explores the mythological attributes of the hare throughout history. This interest was consolidated by his sighting of a hare bounding across the Sussex Downs, and the *Leaping Hares* were the result. The first *Leaping Hare* was cast on 7 November

37 *Barry Flanagan: Prints 1970–1983*, exh. cat., Tate Gallery, London 1986, p.16.
38 Ibid., p.16.
39 A&A Sculpture Casting was formed by Andy Elton and Henry Abercrombie in 1977.

Large Leaping Hare 1982, installation view
Documenta 7, Kassel 1982

1979, and the foundry in Fawe Street was to become his surrogate studio. From the same mould Flanagan also made *leaping hare, embellished, 2/3 jan '80* 1980, a plaster cast wrapped in gesso. The gesso was sized and gilded 'on the first full moon of 1980'[40] because, according to the Chinese tradition, the full moon and a lake are conducive to the laying of gold. The hare was to prove to be a lasting source of inspiration for Flanagan. As he explained: 'Thematically the choice of the hare is really quite a rich and expressive sort of model; the conventions of the cartoon and the investment of human attributes into the animal world [...] is really quite poignant'.[41] But while the hare can be understood as a surrogate human figure, the sheer richness of its mythology also appealed to Flanagan. The working of myth had been ever-present in his work: the impact of sacred circles can be retrieved in the wigwam forms of *Untitled* 1970; *and then among Celts N. '77* 1977 signals an attachment to elusive home-grown mythologies registered in the land around his studios, while *The stone that covered the hole in the road (the skull)* 1974 and *Cornish BuB* 1979 are suggestive of mythological objects with a talismanic force.

40 Note from Waddington Galleries stock record, 1980.
41 *Barry Flanagan: Prints 1970–1983*, exh. cat., Tate Gallery, London 1986, p.15.

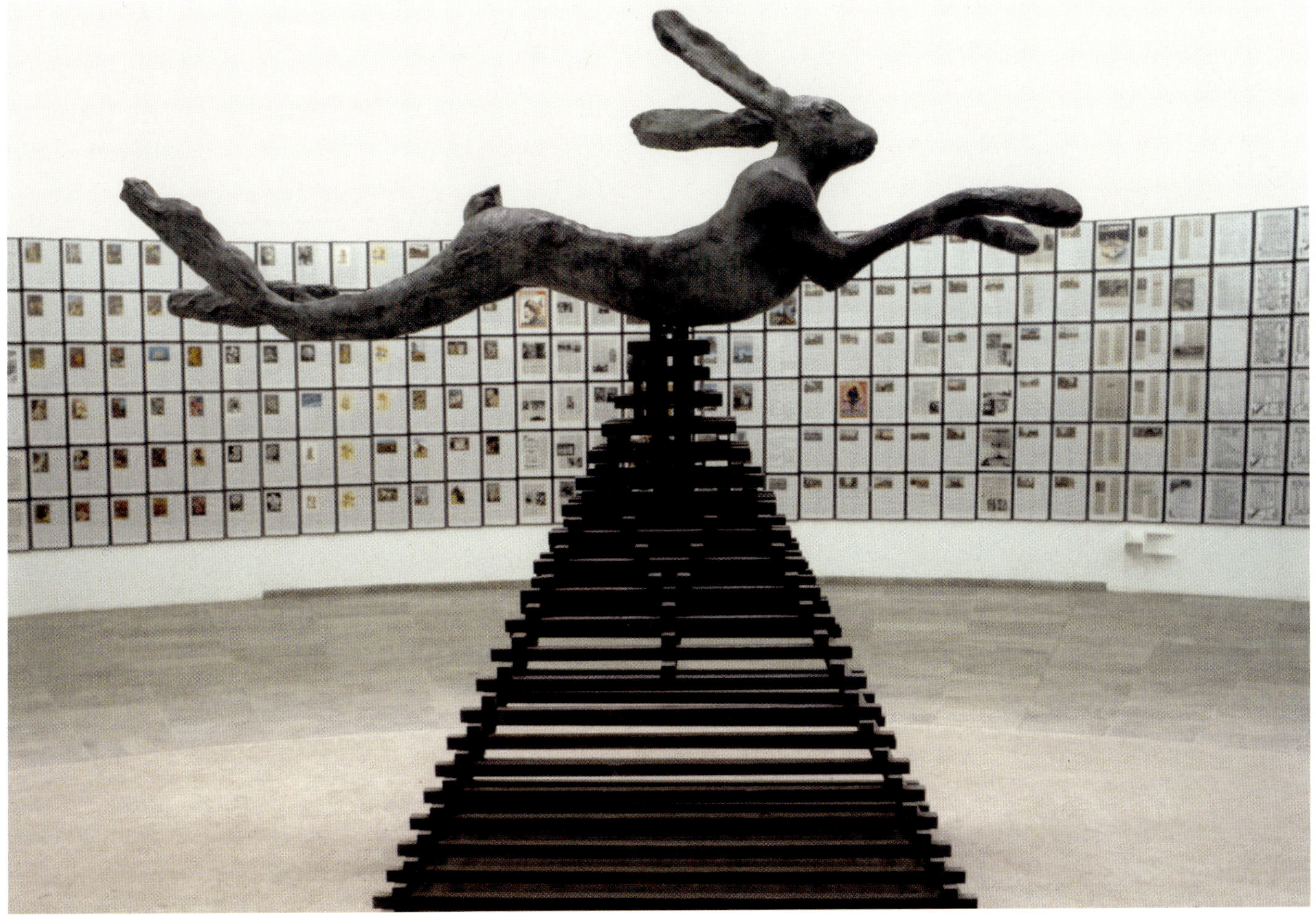

Fables are told across continents of the cleverness, deceit and triumph of the hare, and it is often associated with fertility or celestial phenomena – most often the moon. To give just a few instances of the ubiquitous hare we can look to Egyptian mythology. The hieroglyph 'Wn', represented by a hare on top of a single blue-green ripple, means 'to exist', while one of the avatars of Osiris shows him with the head of a hare and it was in this form that he was sacrificed to the Nile each year. In China the Moon Hare holds a pestle and mortar with which it mixes an elixir of immortality, reintroducing a motif of alchemical symbolism.

Given his interest in alchemy, almost certainly interpreted via Jung, Flanagan would have considered the hare an archetype, and in it he found the perfect metaphor for his own elusive character, personified in Ewart's chapter 'The Hare as Trickster' as mercurial and equivocal. Throughout world mythology trickster figures transgress frameworks of right and wrong, delighting in breaking rules, boasting and playing tricks on both humans and gods. They may also act as messengers between human and

Installation view *Zeitgeist*, Martin-Gropius-Bau, Berlin 1982. Left to right: *Hare on Anvil* 1981; *Acrobats* 1981; *Hare and Helmet III* 1981; *Elephant* 1981; *Soprano* 1981; *Ball and Claw* 1981; *Cricketer* 1981

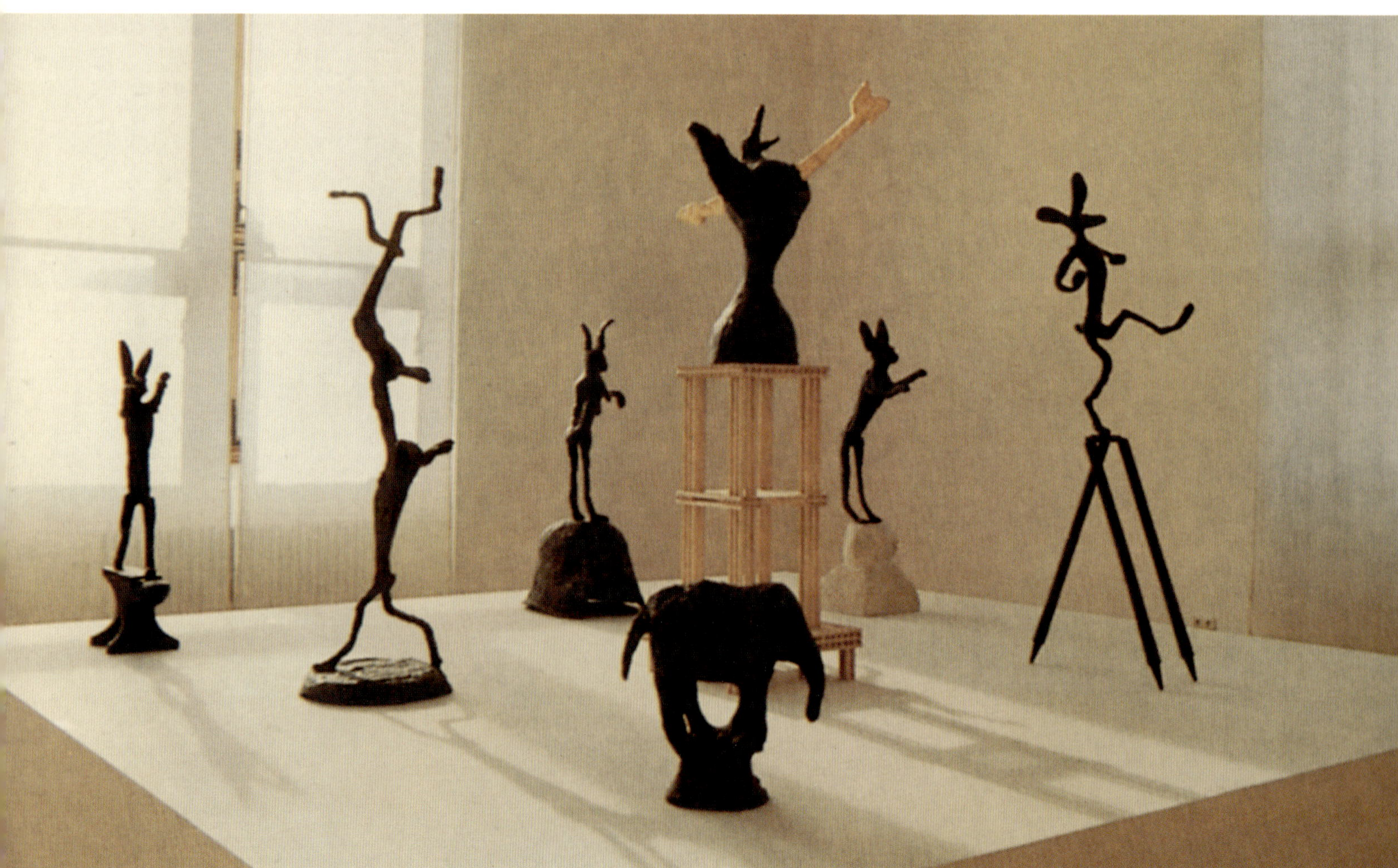

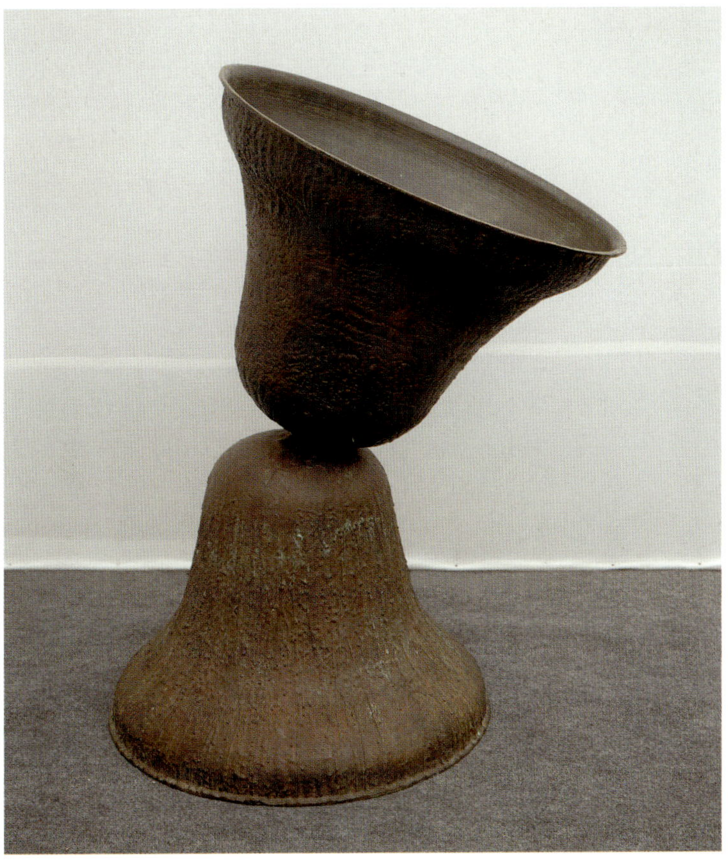
Double Bell 1980

divine worlds, and most tricksters are shape-changers, often appearing as animals, including, of course, the hare.

Flanagan's first hares were supported by pyramid-like structures, fulcrums or points of balance, developed from the Rowford Process bases of the mid 1970s. The link between material properties and processes of placement continued to be explored, most notably in the sculpture of bells. The bell for Flanagan represents continuity and stability of tradition, not only in the tradition of the foundry, but also the regular round of individual and community life. *Hare on Curly Bell* 1980, with the hare capering on top, represents the tension between settled community and the equivocal and possibly dangerously inconstant figure of the hare. Perhaps together they represent a necessary duality, albeit one that may be overcome in the final *coniunctio* or union of opposites of the work itself.

Bells mark the measured passage of time and the course of life, they call to a settled community within earshot of the tower, church or town hall. This is in stark contrast to the madcap, ever-ranging hare who knows no fixed community. Before the appearance of bell foundries, a parish's bell was often cast in the market place or even the church in which it was to be hung, requiring huge communal effort and a massive draw on time, skill and expense. Other bronze sculptures emphasise Flanagan's involvement in communal myths held within the landscape, including *The Long Man of Wilmington* 1981, made after a visit to see The Long Man of Wilmington on the North face of Windover Hill, Sussex. His version of the ancient image of the traveller or pilgrim setting out on a spiritual journey encapsulates a fascination with the many ways in which sculptural form is arrived at. The artist's shifting back and forth between process and figuration is especially apparent, for here the figure is directly cast from wax runners and risers and sprues, with the core for its head – all elements suggestive of the trade and craft of casting, forming a firm link between studio and foundry.

Alchemy, too, was a practical craft that involved labouring over hot furnaces with mercury, sulphur and lead. If Flanagan was drawn to the craft aspect of foundry work, as well as more esoteric matters such as alchemy, he was also interested in Guilds, in particular the Guild of Stone Masons. He commissioned Peter Randall-Page to research the triangulation method of scaling up stone, which at that time was a closely guarded technique and involved the square and compasses – stone masons' tools, but also the most identifiable symbols of Freemasonry – a motif that crops up in various works, including a poster for his exhibition at the Serpentine Gallery in 1979.[42]

This poster may also be a reference to William Blake's *Urizen*, who, within Blake's complex mythology, is a supernatural being that embodies repressive reason and law. Depicted as a bearded old man, Urizen wields architects' tools to constrain the universe within the bounds of his law – the antithesis of Jarry and his followers' distrust of scientific rationalism. For Jarry science cannot fully capture the nature of reality, hence the need for the separate (a-)rationality of 'pataphysics, which has its own logic, causality and laws.

What Flanagan ultimately discovered in the foundry, then, was a place where the magic and alchemy of creation goes hand in hand. In retrospect, we can see that a vital motivation was to define sculptural tradition and work within it, without being trapped by its dead weight. Lewis Biggs captures this succinctly when he talks of Flanagan's 'simultaneous originality and openness to tradition'.[43] It is notable that he found in the A&A foundry a congenial workplace, and it was here that he was able to bring together the interaction of idea and form through an interest in materials and processes, a continuity that continues beyond his turn to bronze. The merging of studio and foundry went some way to finding answers to

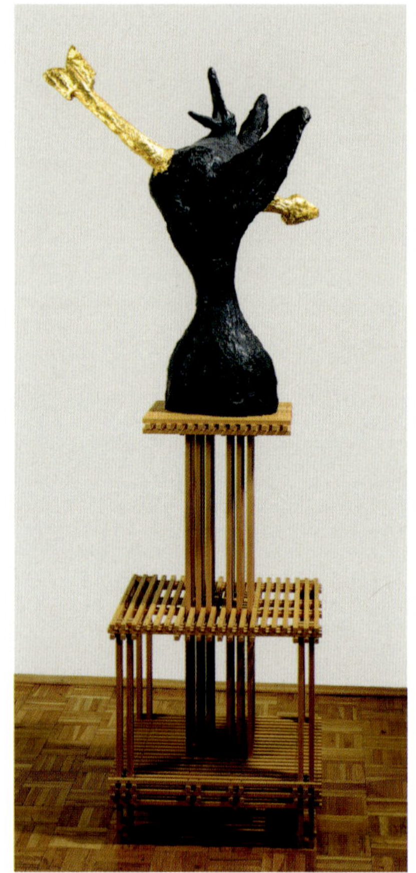

Soprano 1981

42 Conversation with Peter Randall-Page, 7 Mar. 2011.

43 *Barry Flanagan: A Visual Invitation Sculpture 1967–1987*, exh. cat., Laing Art Gallery, Newcastle 1987, p.64.

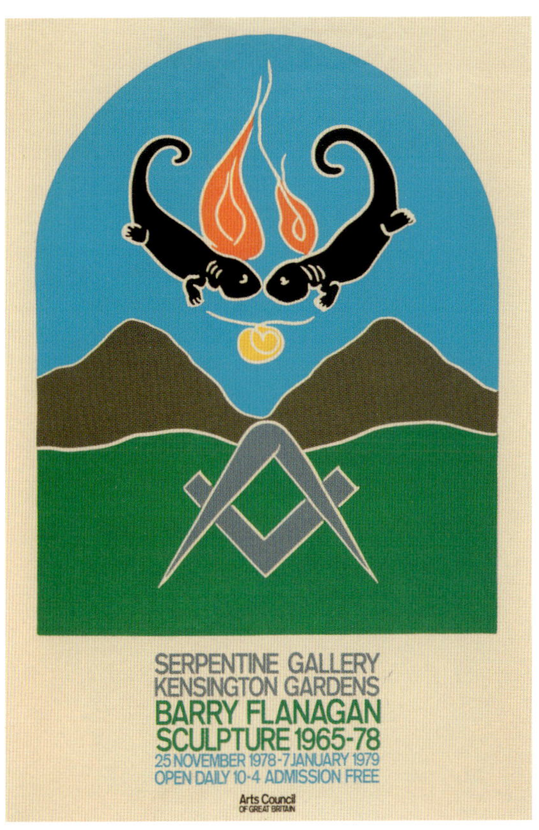

Poster for *Barry Flanagan Sculpture 1965–78*, Serpentine Gallery, London 1978

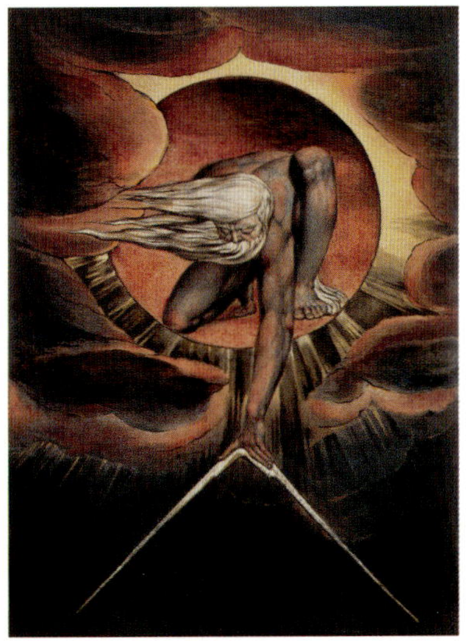

William Blake, *The Ancient of Days*, frontispiece to 'Europe a Prophecy' 1794 University of Glasgow Library, Special Collections

Flanagan's questions about the social nature of art – the tension between artist and artisan, tradition and anti-tradition – issues that consistently preoccupied him throughout his career. Flanagan felt that author and practitioner, like musician and composer, should both have their place, and he ultimately achieved this through close material engagement and an expanded studio practice. The manipulation of materials by hand, eye and mind, coupled with a playful detachment that allowed materials to find their own sculptural form through process, was particularly evident in the works exhibited in Venice in 1982. They collectively highlight the originality and ingenuity Flanagan brought to the evolving nature of sculpture. As he himself explains in straightforward terms:

> 'By the close of the seventies, fashion and aspirations had been continuously qualified by larger external events, and expedients of production put into perspective. The introduction of some concept of trade, drawing on the traditional resources of practice to produce sculpture became necessary. When out of the garret one no longer works alone, but finds a place in a scheme of things.'[44]

44 *Barry Flanagan, Sculptures in Bronze 1980–1981*, Waddington Galleries, London 1981, exh. cat., unpag.

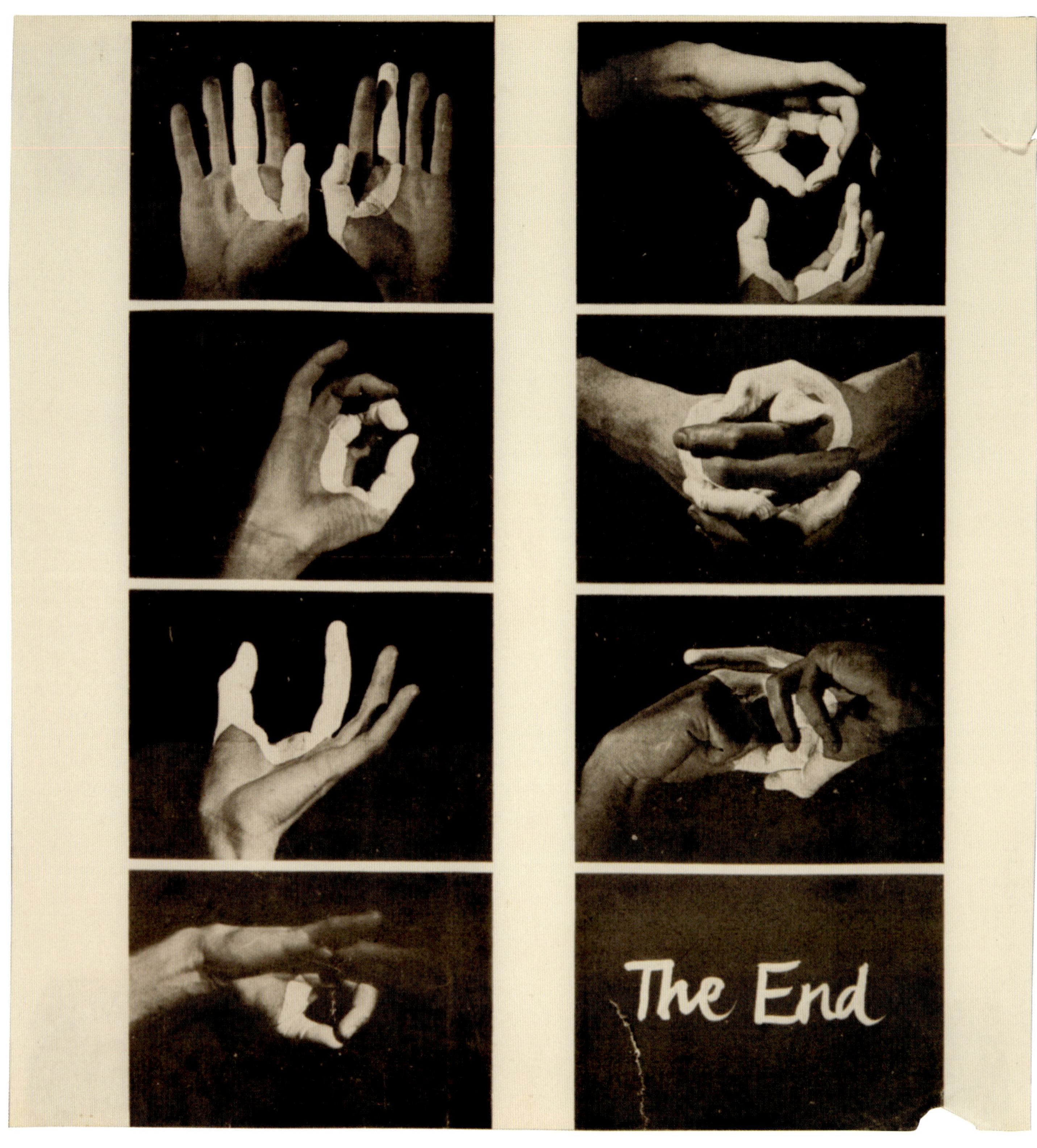

Finger poem performance at the opening event of *Between Poetry and Painting*, Institute of Contemporary Arts, London 1965

'Working towards poem'

Andrew Wilson

Barry Flanagan held that the identity of a sculptor is 'one who "shapes" the things in his life for himself'.[1] As a child he did not speak until he was seven, and so, living primarily in his imagination, he would have constructed internal worlds for himself. The dimensional logic of his sculpture, too, with its shifting state and position in the world, can best be considered in relation to his tendency to reinvent the world – a phenomenon he came to identify with 'pataphysics.

In February 1966, while still a student at St Martin's School of Art, Flanagan wrote that 'poetry is the most economical manifestation of one's "chemistry" – always working towards poem'.[2] The idea of poetry – or more exactly, the sense of 'working towards poem' – occupies a determining position within Flanagan's approach to sculpture. By 1966 this approach had started not with a word, but with the silence that is occupied by the shapes found in the letters that make up words.[3] Flanagan's 'chemistry' uses shapes, discovered through elegant and imaginary solutions, as visual poems – poems that he described as a 'pre-language mark of meaning'.[4] These visual poems took a number of forms: as letters or shapes printed on a page, or performed as lip poems or finger poems derived from Buddhist mudras. Although Flanagan performed these poems on only a very few occasions – notably the lip poem *(O for orange U for you: a poem for the lips) juno965* 1965 at the opening of the *second international exhibition of experimental poetry* at St Catherine's College, Oxford, in June 1965 and a finger poem at the opening event for *Between Poetry and Painting* at the Institute of Contemporary Arts, London, that October – they defined one approach to sculpture.

The poems were not so much written as carved in space by the fingers or moulded by the mouth. One description of the readings at *Between Poetry and Painting* contrasts Henri Chopin's rendering of a Bernard Heidsieck tape poem with the silence of a lip poem by Ernst Jandl and Flanagan's 'space poem, created by the movement of the hands composing letters in the air'. This poem lasted for eight seconds and was 'completely silent – a sort of hand sculpture through space [...] The two hands, developing from separate entities into a complete and natural unit, gave new and direct meaning to a theme often inadequately expressed in words.'[5]

These 'space' or 'O'[6] poems produced sequences of shape that might embody or transmit meaning and divert language to something experienced directly through sight rather than through the process of reading. His hands would carve shapes, capturing shifting volumes in air; or sequences of letters might flow together as a sign language in which letter-shapes were moulded by the hands and fingers, or by the lips. The paradox here lies in the use of letters to make a poem that is not literary and so its meaning cannot be previously known. In 1964 Flanagan similarly

1 Untitled statement, *Barry Flanagan Object Sculptures*, exh. cat., Museum Haus Lange, Krefeld, 1969, n.7, unpag.

2 Untitled statement, *an exhibition of concrete/spatial poetry*, exh. cat., Midland Group of Artists, Nottingham 1966, unpag.

3 In 1966 the poet Dom Sylvester Houédard described concrete poetry in terms of a dissolution of form, as silence rather than sound, and a kinetic poetry of space and interval, especially in terms of destruction – ideas that were encouraged by his involvement in the planning for the Destruction In Art Symposium in September 1966 (see chronology p.135). In his introduction to *Arlington Une* (exh. cat., Arlington Mill, Gloucestershire 1966, unpag.) he positioned Flanagan's silent lip poems and finger poems alongside Ernst Jandl's silent poems, marking them as exemplary of this perspective.

4 From a contribution by Flanagan dated 15 June 1965, in *Silâns*, no.16, June 1965, unpag.

5 Anne Davison, 'Concrete Poetry at the ICA: Silent Poem: Space Poetry', cutting from an unidentified magazine, Frank Martin Papers, accepted by HM Government in lieu of Inheritance Tax and allocated to Tate 2010 (TGA 201014). In a letter, dated 2 September 1965, to the poet Cavan McCarthy, editor and publisher of *Tlaloc*, Houédard describes the impact of Flanagan's performance at the ICA: 'when I saw Barry read a concrete poem in 3-D – shifting position like the printed poem was a score I felt (well I "knew") he was reliable as a creator as I don't think he'll just fold & fizzle out "give in".' Tlaloc Archive, Box 3, University College London, Special Collections.

6 In May 1965 Bob Cobbing described the presentations of concrete poetry at Better Books by listing who he saw as the main practitioners. Apart from himself, Flanagan's 'O poems' are positioned alongside works and publications by John Furnival, Ian Hamilton Finlay, Dom Sylvester Houédard and 'something new every other day, while each day brings its new enthusiasts. Long live poetry OFF the page.' It is telling that Flanagan, still a student, was placed unreservedly in such company. Miles and Cobbing, 'This is not an advertisement this is not an advert this appears to be some notes about Better Books', *Poetmeat*, no.9–10, Summer 1965, p.51.This was written a couple of months after an evening of concrete poetry at Better Books, which Cobbing had organised on 24 March 1965.

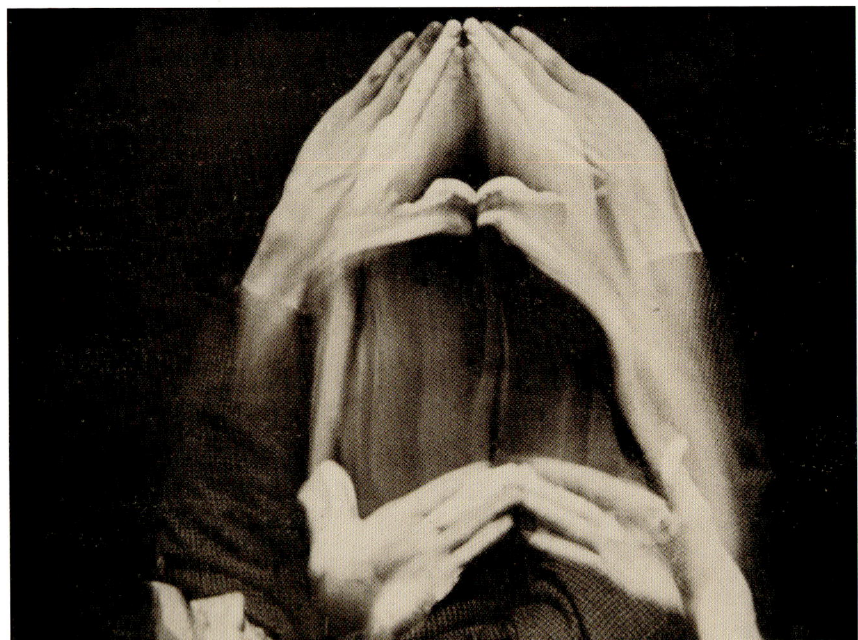

Finger poem performance at the opening event of *Between Poetry and Painting*, Institute of Contemporary Arts, London 1965 (left and opposite)

described sculpture as the origin of language, as it communicated that which had not been known before. He wrote how 'Literary sculpture has been observed. Non-literary sculpture will have to be seen. Once upon a time a human asserted himself in this sculpture form in a non-literary way: the human named the result of his assertion and accompanied it with a group of words.'[7] Flanagan here makes the distinction between a distanced, considered act of observing and the animated immediacy of an engagement with seeing, unfettered by the conventions or operations of language. A literary sculpture describes something already known, it is recognisable; here, however, Flanagan refers to sculpture that is not a representation, but a shape to be experienced for the first time. He would later make a similar distinction between shape and form: 'Form sounds like an educated perception of shape. I don't like to be already educated.'[8]

Arriving at a pre-language state through the world of poetry suggests contradiction, and such paradoxes as this abound in Flanagan's art and were embraced by him. When Flanagan lived in Bristol, between 1962 and 1963, he moved among a group of poets that would later publish the magazine *Resuscitator*. John James and Nick Wayte, both of whom became friends, were searching for a modernism that, they felt, was altogether absent in English poetry. James later recounted that 'little changed in form since Thomas Hardy and it was as if Rimbaud, for example, had never existed. Not only America but also Europe was invisible. Dance,

7 Barry Flanagan, 'Prelude', *Silâns*, no.1, [Oct.] 1964, unpag.
8 Barry Flanagan in discussion with Gene Baro, 'Sculpture Made Visible', *Studio International*, vol.178, no.915, Oct. 1969, p.124.

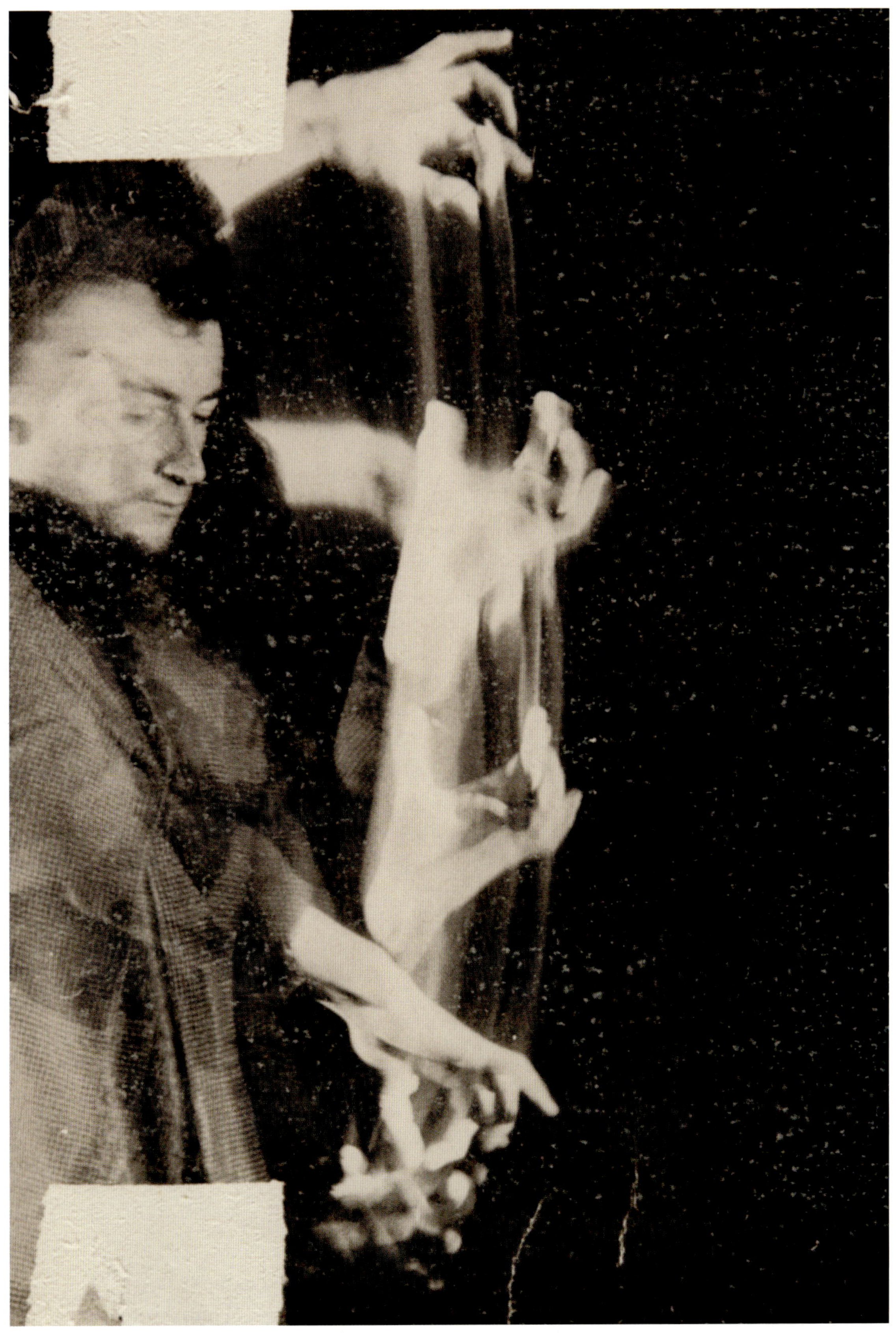

music, painting, sculpture in England had all recognized modernism but writing had turned its back.'[9] It was apt that the title of their magazine came from the first section of Ezra Pound's *Hugh Selwyn Mauberley*: 'to resuscitate the dead art/of poetry',[10] and alongside Pound and James Joyce, the late symbolist provocations of Alfred Jarry were also a topic of conversation and would have a determining effect on the chemistry that informed Flanagan's 'working towards poem'.

In 1963 or early 1964, before his move to London, Wayte gave Flanagan a copy of a special issue of the American literary magazine, *Evergreen Review*, which was devoted to 'pataphysics. The cover asked 'What is 'Pataphysics?', to which the contents page simply answered ''Pataphysics is the only science'.[11] The magazine contained extracts from Jarry's novel *Exploits and Opinions of Dr Faustroll 'Pataphysician* (published posthumously in 1911) as well as additional writing by Jarry and others associated with the *Collège de 'Pataphysique* (founded in 1948). What Roger Shattuck, a Regent of the *Collège*, described as Jarry's absorption into a 'universe of total hallucination'[12] captures well what 'pataphysics might entail. Jarry,

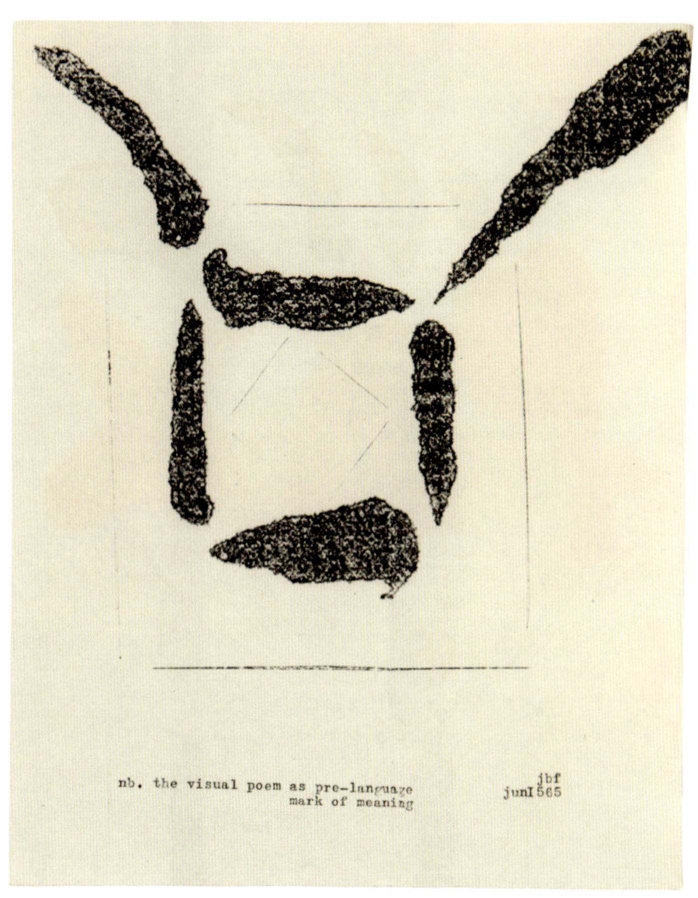

Page from *Silâns*, no.16, June 1965

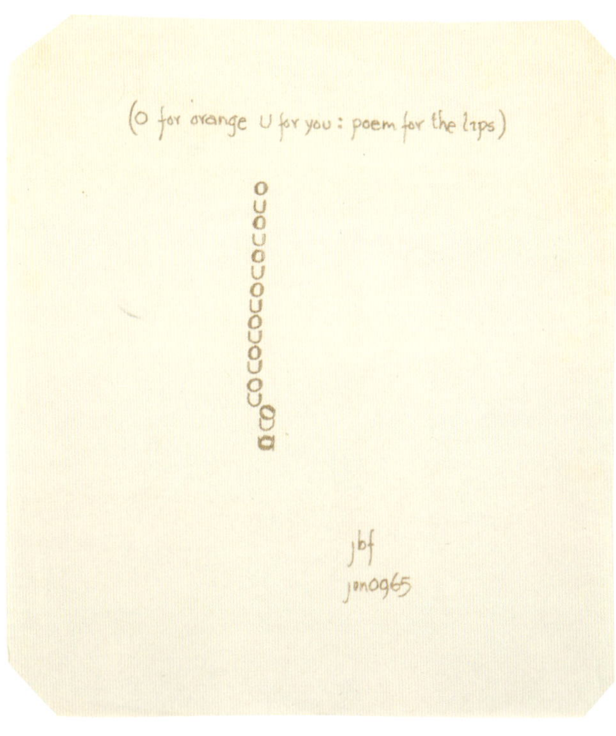

(O for orange U for you: a poem for the lips)
jun0965 1965

9 Letter from John James, 21 February 2011.
10 Ezra Pound, *Personae: The Collected Shorter Poems*, Faber and Faber, London 2001, p.185.
11 *Evergreen Review*, vol.4, no.13, May–June 1960.
12 Roger Shattuck, *The Banquet Years. The Origins of the Avant Garde in France: 1885 to World War 1*, Vintage Books, New York 1968, p.239.

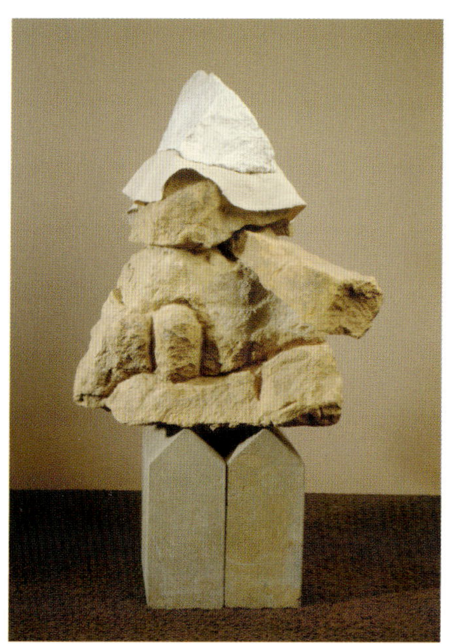

Ubu of Arabia 1976

Shattuck continues, 'refused the contradictions of which he was so keenly aware and asserted the equivalence of all things. "God is the point tangent to zero and infinity," he argued earnestly. No state of being excludes its opposite; everything is not only possible but real. He was learned, and his learning came out backward to prove the preposterous and establish the paradoxical.'[13] Jarry constructed a world-view that transmutes absurdity, by way of a science that 'examines the laws governing exceptions',[14] into an understanding of reality. The world was imagined and constructed as answerable to that imagined new logic; imagination was recognised as real, and lived as such. In this respect 'pataphysics describes 'a universe which can be – and perhaps should be – envisaged in the place of the traditional one'.[15] For Flanagan, drawn to Jarry as a figure he held to be 'emblematic of the individual imagination in revolt',[16] the impact and attraction of 'pataphysics was immediate.

The visual poem as an act of naming and reinventing meaning were motivations at the heart of the magazine Flanagan produced, with Rudy Leenders and Alastair Jackson, shortly after he started the course at St Martin's in the autumn of 1964. Its title – *Silâns*, a phonetic approximation of 'silence' – exemplifies how Flanagan was approaching sculpture by carving out language from silence. Whereas in the first issue Flanagan demonstrated the distinction between a literary and non-literary sculpture, the second issue made clear his allegiance to 'pataphysics. His contribution was signed 'xXHPAPHPAPHPAPHP... silâns' jbf', which, in the following issue, became 'silâns' paphpaph jbf', and such signing – incorporating repetition and shifting apostrophes[17] – continued through each issue of the magazine.

Flanagan identified himself directly with Jarry and adopted his 'pataphysical worldview, which he equated with his own creation of visual poems. However, in his contribution to the March 1965 issue of the magazine Flanagan underlines the difficulties of naming and defining sculpture despite its physical immediacy and presence, which he describes as 'TOUCH IN SCULPTURE'. The tactile experience of a physical object – its reality as material – is then undermined by Flanagan's consideration of the manner of sculpture's existence: 'at best sculpture is unnameable / at least a sculpture may name. / the name betrays the sculpture, even if it could have no other name. / [...] existence is pataphysical (a) / the spirit evades us / the mystery is / superbapa'taphysiful.'[18] Sculpture is not named but names itself, declares itself. It is; and unmediated, as shape, it exists as a visual poem.

The epigraph for each issue of *Silâns* printed on the magazine's front cover – for the first two issues excerpted from Joyce's *Ulysses* and for the

13 Ibid., p.238.
14 Alfred Jarry, *Exploits and Opinions of Dr Faustroll 'Pataphysician*, Exact Change, Boston 1996, p.21.
15 Ibid., p.22.
16 'Barry Flanagan in Conversation with Hans Ulrich Obrist', *Barry Flanagan Sculpture 1965–2005*, exh. cat., Irish Museum of Modern Art /Dublin City Gallery The Hugh Lane 2006, p.59.
17 For instance, in *Silâns*, no.7, Feb. 1965, it is 'silâns' jbf 'paph', in no.8, Feb. 1965, it is 'papphpaphpataphisicspaphpaph ... paphsilâns'paphpaph jbf'. The use of the apostrophe in 'pataphysics is both to prevent unfortunate punning and also to indicate that a prefix is missing.
18 *Silâns*, no.11, Mar. 1965, unpag.

third from Leo Tolstoy's *What is Art?* – provides evidence of the continuation of those discussions around literary modernism in which Flanagan had participated in Bristol. The first of these short quotations is drawn from the 'Aeolus' episode of *Ulysses*, in which Joyce names a sound – the action of a printing press – onomatopoeically: 'Everything speaks in its own way. Sllt.'[19] This occurs within a short section of the book, under the title 'Orthographical', in which Bloom, quite apart from identifying the sound of a printing press as both noun and verb, also presents a conundrum that has kept typesetters on their toes: 'It is amusing to view the unpar one ar alleled embarra two ars is it? Double ess ment of a harassed pedlar while gauging au the symmetry with a y of a peeled pear under a cemetery wall.'[20] Both passages from *Ulysses* are concerned with how language is formed or re-cast as code; they describe an act of naming. Some of Flanagan's poetry plays with a similar dislocating division of words, for instance: 'IN / COURTING / THE / DESTRUCTION / OF / IBITION / feeding / a para root / noic at the / communicable.'[21] But in 1965–6 he devised a way of naming his sculptures that constituted an active element of each visual poem, also suggesting the nature of each sculpture's being as a mystery that is superbapa'taphysiful. These sculptures made up his first solo exhibition at the Rowan Gallery in London in August 1966, shortly after graduating from St Martin's.

aaing j gni aa 1965 was the most imposing work in this exhibition. Although made up of five separate sculptures, Flanagan had decided in June that they should be brought together as one work, a new totality emphasised by the white circle on the floor that surrounded the work and became its sixth element. The title is a palindrome – reading the same backwards and forwards, although the letters are grouped unevenly – with its spine, the letter 'j', standing as a homage to Jarry[22]. The doubled 'aa' might indicate the indefinite article and the doubling underlines the repetition implicit within any palindrome. The letter 'a' can also act as a prefix that reverses meaning (as in asymmetry) or as a suffix that pluralises a word (as in phenomena); or as a letter doubled within the palindrome form, thereby indicating both prefix and suffix operations.[23] The doubled 'aa', as Jon Thompson has explained, additionally designates 'an algebraic negative [. . .] made to cancel itself'.[24] For Jarry, this cancellation held the means of identity: 'A juxtaposed to A, with the former obviously equal to the latter, is the formula of the principle of identity: a thing in itself.'[25] Finally, 'ing' is another suffix used to form a verbal noun (the making of an object, for instance) or when materials are described collectively (sacking, for example). And so the title describes the work as a bundle of opposites that collapses in on itself in a continual state of contradiction

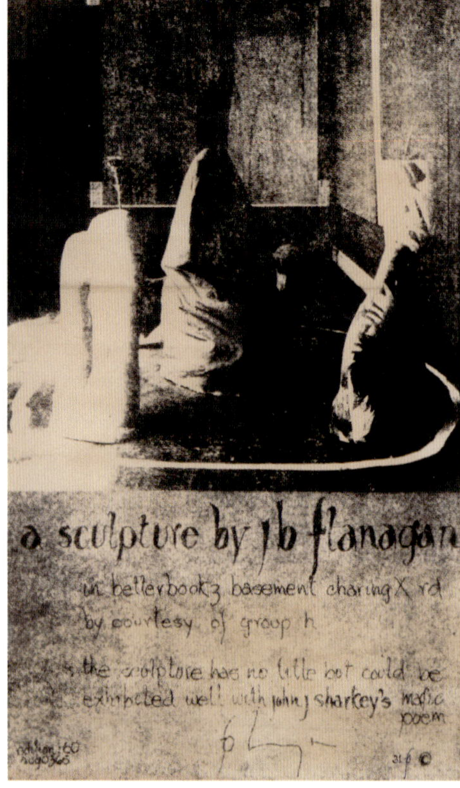

Hand-printed flyer for the display of *aaing j gni aa* 1965 at Better Books

19 James Joyce, *Ulysses, the corrected text*, Penguin, Harmondsworth 1986, p.100.
20 Ibid. This should read, 'It is amusing to view the unparalleled embarrassment of a harassed pedlar while gauging the symmetry of a peeled pear under a cemetery wall.'
21 *Silâns*, no.3, Nov. 1964, unpag.
22 It is also the first letter of Flanagan's first name, reflecting a direct identification with Jarry emphasised by the name he later gave his son – Alfred.
23 Other titles of works in this show – such as *fpre su '65* 1965 and *erpf su '65* 1965 – play further with the idea of the prefix and suffix, both being anagrams of the prefix of 'prefix' and 'suffix'. This play of words was also employed by John Latham, for instance with his use of reversal, as in 'skoob' (for his book reliefs and towers) or 'noit', the reversal of the suffix '-tion', to indicate a way of objectifying abstract thought, especially when read as 'no it'.
24 Jon Thompson, 'Barry Flanagan: Artisan of Unreason', *Barry Flanagan*, exh. cat., Fundación "la Caixa", Madrid 1993, p.35. My interpretation of the titling of this work relies on Thompson's reading given here and also on Michael Compton's in 'A Developing Practice' in *Barry Flanagan Sculpture*, exh. cat., British Council, London 1982, p.18.
25 Alfred Jarry, *Exploits and Opinions of Dr Faustroll 'Pataphysician*, Exact Change, Boston 1996, p.74.

and repetition. These contradictions are unified by the two-dimensional circle that both corrals the five three-dimensional sculptural elements and indicates the work's underlying palindromic identity.

The circle is also a two-dimensional diagram or plan of a mould (like the 'o' shape in Flanagan's lip poem), describing the principle behind the fabrication of each sculptural element. Textiles – predominantly curtain fabric discarded from the St Martin's Fashion School – have been cut, stitched and stapled, then filled with plaster. The action of gravity, along with the peculiarities of stitching of each 'mould' (the generic working with the specific) has helped create monstrous Ubu-esque shapes that are both animal and vegetable in atmosphere. The stitching can be thought of as a type of carving or as a drawn line that creates the character of the mould. Flanagan later confirmed that here he was testing the nature of sculpture as he understood it (and as it was being taught at St Martin's),[26] renegotiating the two- and three-dimensional. Shapes achieved by the coming together of material and action were defined through naming, indicating what something was and how it had come to be as language. They were flagged as both absurd and logical (a logic and a-logical). The chemistry of sculpture was equated with the visual poem, and there was Jarry – the monstrous figure and philosophical equation – standing inside its circle.

That Jarry occupied such a position for Flanagan was explicitly indicated by a statement printed on the private view card for his first show at the Rowan Gallery. Flanagan's statement concluded: 'the business is in the making / of a sculpture / i'm after elegant solutions / elegant in the sense of a theory / being so / "solutions" implies problems – / most likely imaginary ones'.[27] This turn of phrase echoes one of the definitions of 'pataphysics that Flanagan would have learnt from the *Evergreen Review*: ''Pataphysics is the science of imaginary solutions, which symbolically attributes the properties of objects, described by their virtuality, to their lineaments'.[28] The 'solution' for the critic Gene Baro, reviewing the exhibition, was the recognition that works 'appear not so much to have been made as to have happened',[29] that the resulting shape and appearance adopted by each work is inherent in the materials.

One such solution for Flanagan was realised in what was apparently the simplest work in the exhibition: *ringn '66* 1966. This work is the partial result of pouring, from a more or less fixed point, one hundredweight of dry sand on to the floor. Once the designated quantity was used up, Flanagan stood over the resulting cone of sand and, imagining where the four corners of the top of the cone would be (thinking of them perhaps as compass points), took, or carved, four handfuls of sand from each of

26 'Barry Flanagan', *Arnolfini Review*, July–Aug. 1977, p.5.
27 Untitled statement, invitation card for *barry flanagan: sculpture*, Rowan Gallery, London 1966.
28 Alfred Jarry, 'Elements of 'Pataphysics', *Exploits and Opinions of Dr Faustroll 'Pataphysician*, in *Evergreen Review*, vol.4, no.13, May–June 1960, p.131.
29 Gene Baro, 'Animal, Vegetable and Mineral', *Art and Artists*, vol.1, no. 6, Sept. 1966, p.63.

the four corners and then let the sand run down, effectively modelling the side of the cone from which each handful had been taken. *ringn '66*, like much of his work of this period, is concerned with forming sculpture by way of a process, where material characteristics determine its final shape and appearance. For instance, all grades of dry sand exhibit distinct pouring qualities, but the specific sand that Flanagan selected – grade BS19 from J. Arnold Builder's Merchant in Leighton Buzzard – seems to come to rest as if solidifying a molten state; although this appearance of solidity and stability is false, and in fact the resulting poured sculpture is incredibly fragile.

Here Flanagan precipitates a physical process but then intervenes with other more traditional sculpting processes, such as modelling and carving. This is reflected in his use of a utilitarian material, diverting the sand from the building or sand-casting trades and re-siting it in the gallery. And the title *ringn '66* suggests that the work describes a ring, which can be understood in two dimensions or extended into a three-dimensional figure, and that this 'ring' is a noun defining a thing as much as an action or a process.

Alluding to the four carved handfuls of sand taken from the top of the cone of *ringn '66*, Flanagan later remarked that 'The number 4 is an architectural idea'.[30] The ways in which work might be brought together and shown came to increasingly occupy him. With *aaing j gni aa* he had encircled five objects as one work; the following year he proposed that three works should be shown together as part of his contribution to the Paris Biennale. His exhibition in 1969 at the Museum Haus Lange in Krefeld was a direct response to the spaces within the Mies van der Rohe building and its use of light; and between 1969 and 1977 he produced three installations for the Hayward Gallery. One aspect of this decision to group works was to cut the connection with what he saw as a 'literary process' wrapped up in notions of identity: once works are brought together in this way they each cease to have a singular identity. For Flanagan, 'the medium of operation of an object is *actual* space and *anything* qualifying that space. Once liberated from the invested autonomous identity an object operates with *any* object (visually), not just its chosen one (by way of literary mechanics).'[31] By showing these three works – *4 casb 2 '67* 1967, *ringl 1 '67* 1967 and *rope (gr 2sp 60) 6 '67* 1967 – together as one, they make 'claim / to the perceivable space' of the gallery in which they are situated in ways that are demonstrably 'within the auspices / of the phenomena of / sculpture'.[32]

Whereas the titles of the works in Flanagan's first show drew on competing figures of speech, the titles for these three works are a code: four *c*anvas *s*and *b*ags, a *ring* made from *l*ino and a *g*reen *2-sp*ace *60*-foot long rope. The code names things and implies the bringing together of objects and materials to determine process and arrangement. Photographs taken

30 'Barry Flanagan', *Arnolfini Review*, July–Aug. 1977, p.5.

31 Barry Flanagan, 'From notes '67/8', *Studio International*, vol.177, no.907, Jan. 1969, p.37. In this respect the conversation that Dom Sylvester Houédard relates to Cavan McCarthy in September 1965 emphasises the consistency of Flanagan's thinking on this subject: 'Barry (F) is all mixed up he says abt BRIDGES – he doesn't kno if they link separate islands or if in truth there are not & cannot be "autonomous" art.' Letter from Dom Sylvester Houédard to Cavan McCarthy, 2 Sept. 1965, Tlaloc Archive, Box 3, University College London, Special Collections.

32 Untitled text by Barry Flanagan, *Studio International*, vol.174, no.892, Sept. 1967, p.98.

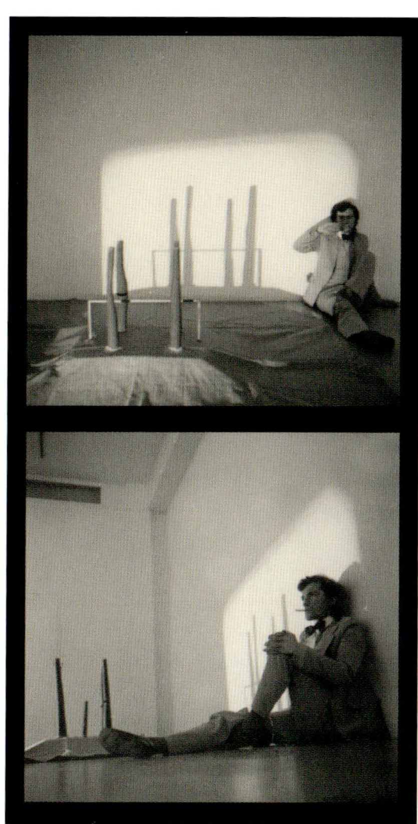

Flanagan with maquette for sculpture made for 1972 Peter Stuyvesant City Sculpture Project, Cambridge, with projection at Rowan Gallery, London 1972

in the studio by Charles Harrison show the elements both individually and ensemble on a 'one-space' sand sculpture, which provided a unifying ground so that Flanagan could work through the relationships between the three works. The four filled bags that make up *4 casb* are shown standing vertically and horizontally (an arrangement that was not repeated).[33] Flanagan's description of them is revealing:

> 'I was interested in typical, general visual configurations that command our attention [...] I don't like to invent an involvement or the terms of an involvement; I prefer to fabricate the sculptures. One of the three pieces consisted of four vertical objects made as a single work. Another was a linoleum ring or perimeter; and the third was a sixty-foot rope, placed linearly on the floor. The three pieces together challenged my assumption that they were autonomous.'[34]

The creation of *casb* was an important step for Flanagan. Rather than the evocative shape of *aaingj gni aa*, derived from the stitched curtain material and the solidity of its plaster fill, each *casb* is a simple tapering conical shape, variously elongated or truncated. Where the plaster filling of *aaingj gni aa* is permanent, the sand within the *casb* is always temporary and intended to be so, its very mobility 'an elegant solution to technical difficulties identified as a problem at that time, at the end of 1966.'[35] Furthermore, the *casb* idea was the result of a successful exploration of the relationship between canvas and sand, with each acting as a support for the other in a 'dialogue between the weight of the sand and the structure of the cloth skin, the modification of the stitched contour making further shape'.[36] The work was about the elaboration of such sets of relationships built from materials and how they act together to create shape, how something that is two dimensional (a piece of cloth) or formless (sand) can together produce shape as a container, vessel, mould and defining skin. Dimensionality was upset in all these works, with *ringl 1 '67* described as a 'perimeter', a border or skin that can be approached as a two-dimensional plan or a three-dimensional boundary. Flanagan identified the 'two-space' rope as something to be experienced as a line, and he extended this approach into the room or gallery. His first 'two-space' rope was made in 1967 – at sixty feet in length it marked the joining or passage between two spaces or rooms; in 1969 he made two 'three-space' ropes, which were 120 feet in length and moved through three spaces.

The Rowan Gallery had moved to new premises shortly before Flanagan's second solo show there in April 1968, and this encouraged him to engage directly with the gallery's interior architecture. Charles Harrison later explained how he was

33 Eight such photographs of 'Developmental Material' were exhibited in *Art in Process IV* at Finch College Museum of Art, New York, in 1969, four of which were reproduced in the catalogue.

34 Barry Flanagan in discussion with Gene Baro, 'Sculpture Made Visible', *Studio International*, vol.178, no.915, Oct. 1969, p.123.

35 Ibid., p.125.

36 Ibid.

'prepared to confront the gallery situation as potentially creative and able to use it idiosyncratically and without compromise. I feel that his exhibition in April 1968 at the Rowan Gallery was partly misunderstood by visitors (or those I've spoken with) who, being aware of his St Martin's background, viewed the work as a series of discrete pieces without sensing that the most exciting and considered contribution was contained in the sum of those parts.'[37]

This sum was formed by the interaction between the works and their various versions, and how they were sited within the space. The repetition of uncomplicated shapes arranged in seemingly unworked ways emphasised the specific qualities of the materials used. The titles equivocally named these works as both noun and verb – *pile*, *rack*, *stack*, *bundle*, *line* – and the doubling of some within the space emphasises how they can be read both as a material entity and as a process or action. As Flanagan wrote in a statement for the gallery, 'structure / process / order / is exactly the way / "sculpture" shows itself / it is real'.[38]

It was through the agency of light that the works were brought together in the gallery, as indicated by the positioning of *one ton corner piece '67* 1967 in a corner under the skylight. Flanagan would continue to focus on how the grouping of works in a given space could underscore a sculpture's material presence. His June 1968 show at Galerie Ricke in Kassel was given the title *Enviroment Skulpturen*; whereas for the October 1968 show at Galleria dell'Ariete in Milan drawings and tearings of architectural plans of the gallery reveal not so much the placement of works but areas of activity.

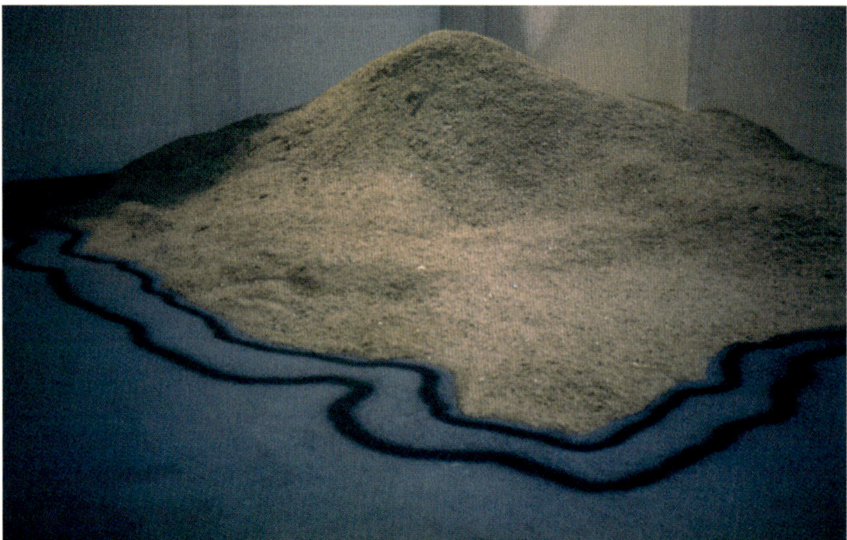

one ton corner piece '67 1967 at the Biennale des Jeunes Artistes, Paris 1967

37 Charles Harrison, 'Some recent sculpture in Britain', *Studio International*, vol.177, no.907, Jan. 1969, p.28.

38 Barry Flanagan, untitled statement, invitation card for *Barry Flanagan Recent Sculpture*, Rowan Gallery, London 1968.

For his exhibition at the Haus Lange Museum in Krefeld in the autumn of 1969 he went a step further, making a number of works in the gallery that were wholly site-specific; and later the same year he made an installation at the Hayward Gallery (the first of three, the other two being for *The New Art* 1972 and the first *Hayward Annual* 1977), which brought together filled sacks and lengths of rope, objects that were revealed through the action of light.

Flanagan's attention to light was a logical development from his interest in film, and especially the films he had been making since 1968, which are concerned with particular ways of looking at his own work, but also document a view on the world – from the window of an aeroplane or a moving bus – that is not so much about 'looking at' but 'seeing', shifting between being more and less attentive. More specifically, his concentration on the material properties of light derives from the way that sculptures can be grouped together and cease to register as autonomous, instead existing within a world made up of real objects, arranged as shape and seen as sculpture. If, as he thought, 'it is not objects themselves or the shapes they are that is visually exciting, but the distances and spaces between them or caught between them',[39] the action of light is how those distances and spaces can be seen. In taking this view he realised that 'my basic assumption has been that light is to be taken for granted. I realised recently that if the light is turned off my whole visual world disappears. My difficulty now with the new interest is to think about and work with light, as a reality and actual phenomenon rather than an "idea about it" or concept.'[40]

Flanagan's concern with materials – how they exist visually and how we may recognise the functional roles they might adopt – is at the core of his work. The play of light (or its absence) categorically alters the way these objects are understood and seen, as do the processes that materials follow to achieve the shapes they adopt. Interestingly, Flanagan understood light to be opposed to colour. Colour as light was, for Flanagan, an idea that belonged to the realm of painting; for him light was inherently white and colour was a property of material.[41] The installation at the Hayward – *light on light on white on white* 1969 – consisted of about 100 lengths of rope (each between three and seven feet long) covering the floor of the gallery, a white freshly painted dado ran around the walls to about a third of the height from the floor; this was punctuated by one narrow, vertical strip of projected light on the wall opposite the entrance, and, in one corner, a wider vertical strip of light was projected on to *light on light on sacks '69* 1969, a pile of sacks filled with polystyrene granules. Certainly light presents a group of objects together in a way that can be compared to the interleaved operations of sand and canvas in *casb*, where the canvas skin holds the sand together as shape and the sand gives three-dimensional

39 Barry Flanagan in discussion with Gene Baro, 'Sculpture Made Visible', *Studio International*, vol.178, no.915, Oct. 1969, p.124.

40 Untitled statement, *Barry Flanagan Object Sculptures*, exh. cat., Museum Haus Lange, Krefeld 1969, n.7, unpag.

41 The only coloured light projection that Flanagan made was an array of disc projections or refractions around a light bulb in his studio in 1969; this was never exhibited.

form to a two-dimensional surface. Light is also revealed as multi-dimensional: it is all around us but it can fall on a flat surface in two-dimensional planes or on an object in three dimensions. It can also shift and change through time like a film projection or daylight – and in these ways light adapts the qualities of the objects it illuminates.

We can watch Flanagan's films as we might experience his sculpture: by not watching but seeing. For Anne Seymour:

> 'the films suggest that slow obsessive kind of seeing which is gazing rather than looking. Often the eye is static with only quite slight shifts like someone sitting in a chair; at other times it is more active. The camera is armature to the film, and always the eye seems to control the events. The camera is Flanagan's bundle in this respect, and everything happens inside it.'[42]

Seymour's assessment raises questions about creativity and the science of seeing, which Flanagan addresses in a sequence of notebook diagrams dated August 1967, four of which were published in the April 1968 issue of *Art & Artists* under the title 'Eye-liners' to coincide with his exhibition at the Rowan Gallery. These diagrams seek to answer the question 'what does the eye look at when seeing?'; the first page comparing the different information to be processed from a surface ('picture plane'), a group of objects ('space plane') and a column ('aesthetic plane').[43] His graphic language here is schematic and technical. He shows how line can delineate section, shape, direction and plan, and how it can enliven a sketch, all of which leads him to suggest that 'on paper the line has nothing to do with sculpture or painting'.[44] 'Eye-liners' is an attempt to provide principles for seeing, but in so doing is a test of the medium of drawing that asks what a line is and what it does, and what the function and essence of drawing might be. Drawing may indeed derive from observation, but for Flanagan observation was more about the drawing itself, its quality of line and material, than the observational transcription of a motif or model. The drawings gathered together in 'Eye-liners' were observational in the sense that the notebook diagram related a play of scientific hypothesis and solution.

Drawing was a consistent part of Flanagan's practice, and in the 1960s this revolved around explorations of additive mark making that included blots, smudges, greasy spots, folding and tearing as much as different qualities of line and material, such as crayon, pencil and ink applied by brush or pen. Drawing becomes like an equation: paper is torn and perhaps arranged in piles or inverted on the page; lines are drawn or torn to define positive and negative spaces; hard and soft, contained or floating free, plan or section, transparent or solid, separated or joined,

42 Anne Seymour, 'Barry Flanagan', *The New Art*, exh. cat., Hayward Gallery, London 1972, p.90.

43 'Eye-liners: Some Leaves from Barry Flanagan's Notebook', *Art and Artists*, vol.3, no.1, Apr. 1968, p.30.

44 Ibid., p.31.

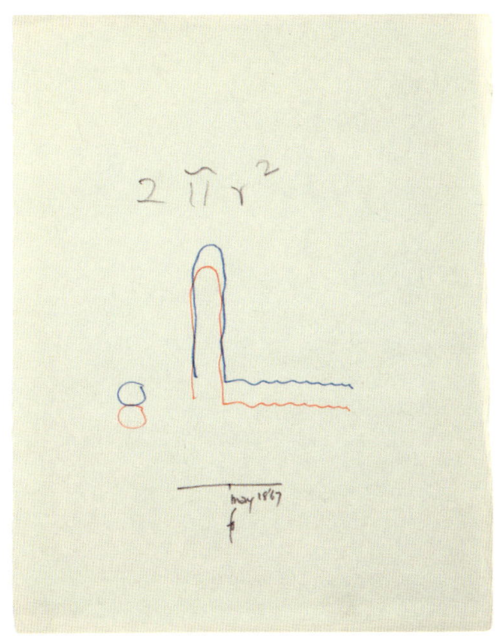

may 18 '67 1967

repeated or singular. These are drawings that search for what the drawn lines might add up to, and are ever conscious of edges, whether created by drawn lines, the sheet of paper or a tear.[45]

Two drawings from May 1967 relate drawn line to the mathematical formulas $2 \pi r^2$ and $E=MC^2$, which respectively calculate the circumference of a circle and express a body's mass as a function of its energy. The drawings do not illustrate the equations but indicate how the logic of Euclidean geometry and Einsteinian physics take their place alongside, or within, a science of imaginary solutions, informing an idea of sculpture that is dimensional, volumetric and energetic: 'superbapa'taphysiful'.

Flanagan might well indicate that the drawn line on paper 'has nothing to do with sculpture or painting',[46] but much of his sculpture plays with shifting dimensions. His rope sculptures, for instance, are solid objects that assume a shape in a room or between a number of rooms, holding, defining and drawing out the spaces they inhabit. The rope, however, also describes a line between two points. What is more, the construction of a rope brings together a number of fibres that are twisted or braided together, with the finished line formed by a number of spiralled lines. The spiral is an important figure for Flanagan. It is 'pataphysical rather than Euclidean and appears in his earliest drawings, as well those from the 1970s of knots, coil pots and of Jarry's anti-hero Ubu Roi. More particularly, the spiral marks a passage between dimensions as well as describing the course a point has taken – as *gidouille*, the mark on Ubu's belly and symbol of his monstrous creativity.

In the late 1970s Flanagan made a number of cut steel works, such as *VII 78 the corn's up* 1978, by cutting a flat sheet of metal into a spiralling circle or triangle and stretching it out, thereby presenting a shift in dimension or, as one notebook drawing of the time suggested, a move from 'closeness' to 'farness'. This dimensional movement and play of positive and negative space corresponds to a number of banner-like wall works in which circles or spirals are cut from cloth hanging from a horizontal bar suspended from the wall by string. These works continue a dialogue between the properties of painting and sculpture, which Flanagan had first entertained in works made for Krefeld in 1969. Here the object of consideration is the banner itself rather than any space of depiction it may support.

'oh! mind how you cross' 1977–8 also articulates space complexly. A stone sculpture is placed to one side of a coiled rope arranged in a figure of eight, as if it were a knot waiting to be pulled. When first exhibited at the first *Hayward Annual* it was accompanied by a number of banner works on the walls, one of which, *Double Eights* 1976, also incorporates the figure of eight motif – a symbol of infinity. The spiral, knot and coil repeat through

45 Jake Tilson, who worked with Flanagan assisting his printmaking between 1977 and 1978, recalls how 'learning to tear paper was something Barry and I did a lot of – rather than cutting it'. Email from Tilson, 22 Mar. 2011.

46 'Eye-liners: Some Leaves from Barry Flanagan's Notebook', *Art and Artists*, vol.3, no.1, Apr. 1968, p.31.

Flanagan's work at various intervals and in different materials, from rope and clay to pen and ink on paper to bronze. They allude to the constant flow and counter-flow within his work and an interplay of opposites as a non-literary state of continual discovery and naming.

ringn '66 is both a circle and a cone, which can register as a triangle in front elevation, or as a spiral if viewed in plan. If the spiral marks a point of creation and its passage dimensionally, the triangle is a fulcrum or a triangulation point – a point of balance and measure. This proposition is there in *a nose in repose* 1977–9, in which line is scored into both sides of the stone: on one side a triangle and on the other a spiral. It is also there in his first scaled-up marble carving made with Peter Randall-Page, *Enlarged Marble Shape* 1978, in which a cone or shell shape emerges from the spiral at the base. The scaling-up process through which this work was made relies on a system of triangulation, and so the sculpture's image of emergent form directly refers to its own creation. Drawing and carving fuse in much of Flanagan's stone sculptures throughout the 1970s, yet few of his drawings refer directly to specific works of sculpture – after all, if a sculpture is made by a material-led process, drawing has very little preparatory role to play. But drawing led Flanagan to etching in the 1970s, where the line drawn into a plate and etched with acid directly correlates with his use of the pointing tool on stone.

The shifting dimensionality of line also features in his light works. In the first Hayward installation in 1969 the change in character between the two projected lines – one falling on *light on light on sacks*, the other directly on to a wall – offers one example of this, contrasting with the very different type of line expressed by the lengths of rope arranged on the floor. Light projections made for Art & Project in 1977 suggest other ways in which this might also be the case. The five projected images each derive from etched copper plates, drawn on with acid to produce a self-portrait, not of the artist, but of light and, more specifically, of the filament of the bulb that projects the light through the copper etched slide. When light shines through each of the five copper slides (the etched lines having punctured the plates) the projected line drawings have a quality that seems paradoxically to have been established independently of being drawn; the quality of line being close to the distinction between a torn or cut edge. For the gallery's publication that accompanied the exhibition, Flanagan made a series of diagrams that present possibilities for looking and projecting, all underwritten by two 'pataphysical spirals moving in opposite directions. Line, in these projections, produces an image that is a symbol of light. It is also descriptive of light's dimensional qualities, carried through space to be caught on a flat wall.

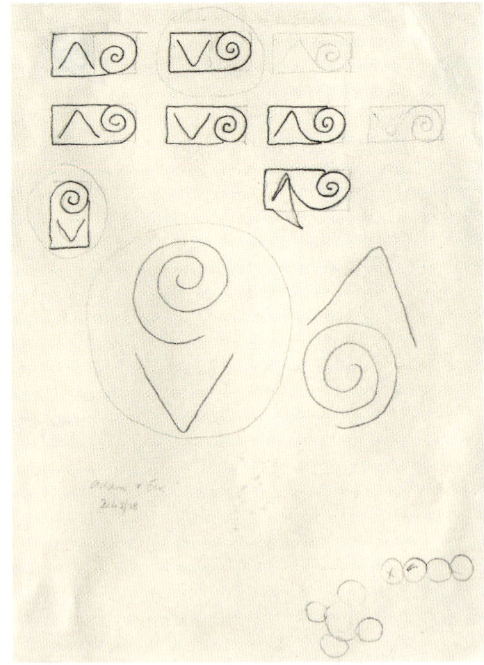

Abstract Adam and Eve theme Feb 3/78 1978

Peter Briggs, with whom Flanagan produced his first cut sheet metal pieces in 1977, has explained how 'the elegance of his solutions consisted in projecting line into space whilst letting the surfaces form themselves. A way of surfaces coming into being automatically, he enjoyed the idea of directing and inventing an operation productive of form from line.'[47] This describes a world subject to generative laws and the slippage between dimensions. It can be recognised in his 1977 light projections, and is also rather like that experienced by Alice, both in Wonderland and through the looking glass.[48] For Flanagan, too, a projection of an enclosed and constructed world corresponds to the properties of dioramas – a subject that occupied him throughout 1978. The diorama is a representation of an enclosed world that moves from a two-dimensional backdrop, through elements of shallow and high relief, to fully rounded three-dimensional representations in the foreground. It is an invented world of shifting scale and dimensionality to be viewed from a particular perspective, and it was this stringent internal, ultimately illogical, logic that attracted Flanagan. His discussion group on dioramas brought together a diverse group of friends from the worlds of art, entertainment, writing and finance to discuss the subject from their own perspective.[49] In these events people from the 'real' world presented models of their worlds (for instance, with regard to space in cooking, or a definition of space in novels)[50] and yet the ensuing discussion was an approximation of a discussion on an elusive subject with a common goal that few among them could fully comprehend, despite Flanagan's insistence on its importance.

Dioramas demonstrate how a concern with the physical world is born of an awareness of place and position within that world. This might

Light Piece at Art & Project, Amsterdam 1977

47 Email from Peter Briggs, 27 Mar. 2011. Briggs, in the same email, suggests that 'the idea of authorship has again to do with the line, letting the surfaces happen. I think this is perhaps one of the keys to understanding his work and attitudes, a conflation of *disegno* in the sense of invention, *dessein* in French and *dessin*, drawing.'

48 Andrew Dipper, who assisted Flanagan between 1969 and 1970, gave him a copy of *The Annotated Alice*, a collection of Lewis Carroll's *Alice's Adventures in Wonderland* and *Through the Looking Glass*, which had been edited and annotated by the scientist Martin Gardiner. Dipper, like Flanagan, was involved with APG. He has recently recalled how he and Flanagan discussed 'the nature of seeing and reality in a fairly profound way [...] I had done a lot of work on perception of objects at the time and had made sense modification experiments to try and elucidate how and why sculptural forms were effective in translating and communicating a purely mental idea. I also was working on tensegrity structures and dimensional manipulations of ordinary objects, so there was much to talk about. Perhaps this is the reason why I gave Barry the annotated Alice by Martin Gardiner since Charles Dodgson also had informed the story by his mathematical ideas and Martin Gardiner had helped me to understand the transference of ideas from one discipline to another. We were, as John Latham so aptly put it "Incidental persons", not completely held within one discipline, but we had realised that through art we were endowed with the potential to bridge the gap between disparate disciplines.' Email from Dipper, 11 Mar. 2011.

49 See Chronology, p.147–8.

50 Paul Levy wrote and delivered a paper, later published in *Harpers & Queen*, 'on how the ideas and practices of the famous historic chefs were outmoded by the French *nouvelle cuisine*', email 28 Mar. 2011; the novelist David Plante talked on the subject of fictional space in the novel and how, when a description of a space is read, each reader can arrange it in a particular way, conversation 28 Mar. 2011.

manifest as a fascination with dimensions and the properties of material that is close to alchemy, but it might also be pursued through shifts in scale, and here one can think of Gulliver as well as Alice. A substance remains the same but is inherently changed: one hundredweight of sand poured in a cone on to a floor, a ton of sand in the corner of a room, a bag containing three tons of sand on a beach, a truckload of sand deposited outside a gallery[51] – all play with shifts in perception and reality through attention to material and scale. Life and function can be given to clay just by pinching or coiling it (another spiral). Similarly, a fist of plaster that has been squeezed or twisted by hand can be scaled up by the ratio of hand to arm and subsequently carved in marble by an artisan in another country, with the accidental nuances of the maquette interpreted as intention; a softly manipulated material reformed as something hard.

A similar approach, structured on opposites that might be made to obey the same alchemical laws, is at the heart of Flanagan's turn to casting and bronze. In the breadth of his work all ingenuity rests on a seemingly arbitrary process that is followed consistently, with artistic creation rooted in the activity of making. Flanagan ceaselessly delighted in the play of materials, and in playfulness itself. Much of his work proceeds from transformation and translation, through shifts of size and scale, or between

Drawing reproduced in *Art & Project Bulletin* no.104, 1977

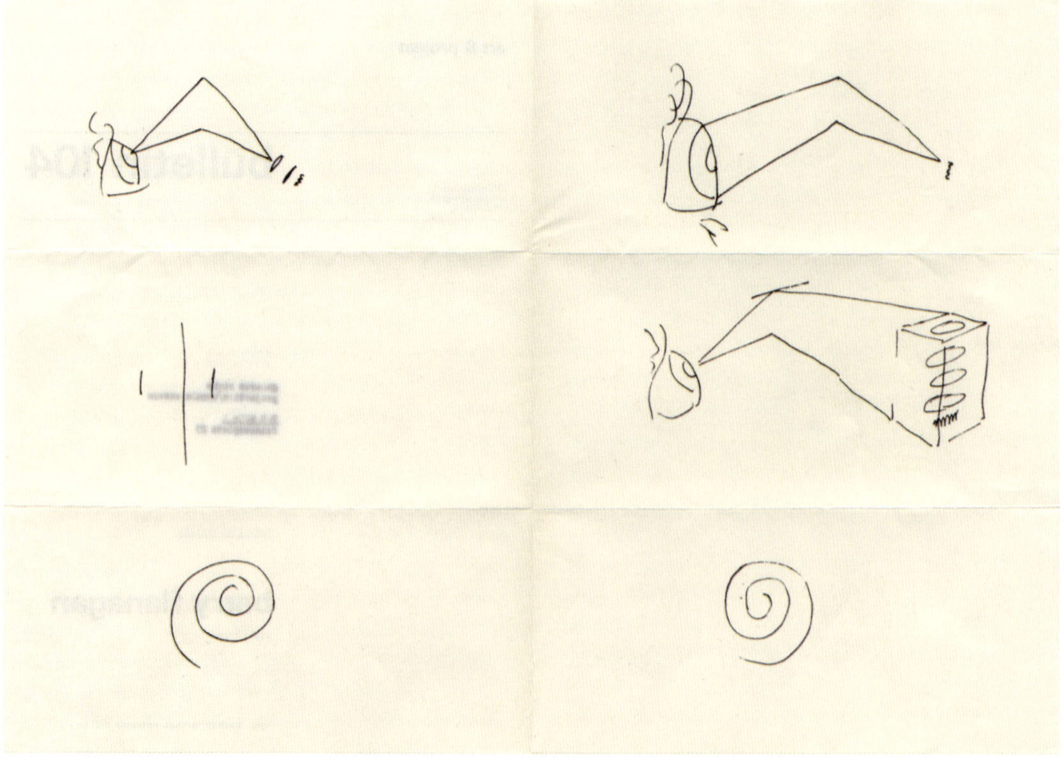

51 These sculptures are, respectively, *ringn '66* 1966, *one ton corner piece '67* 1967, *easter bag '67* 1967 and *one camion sand piece* 1969.

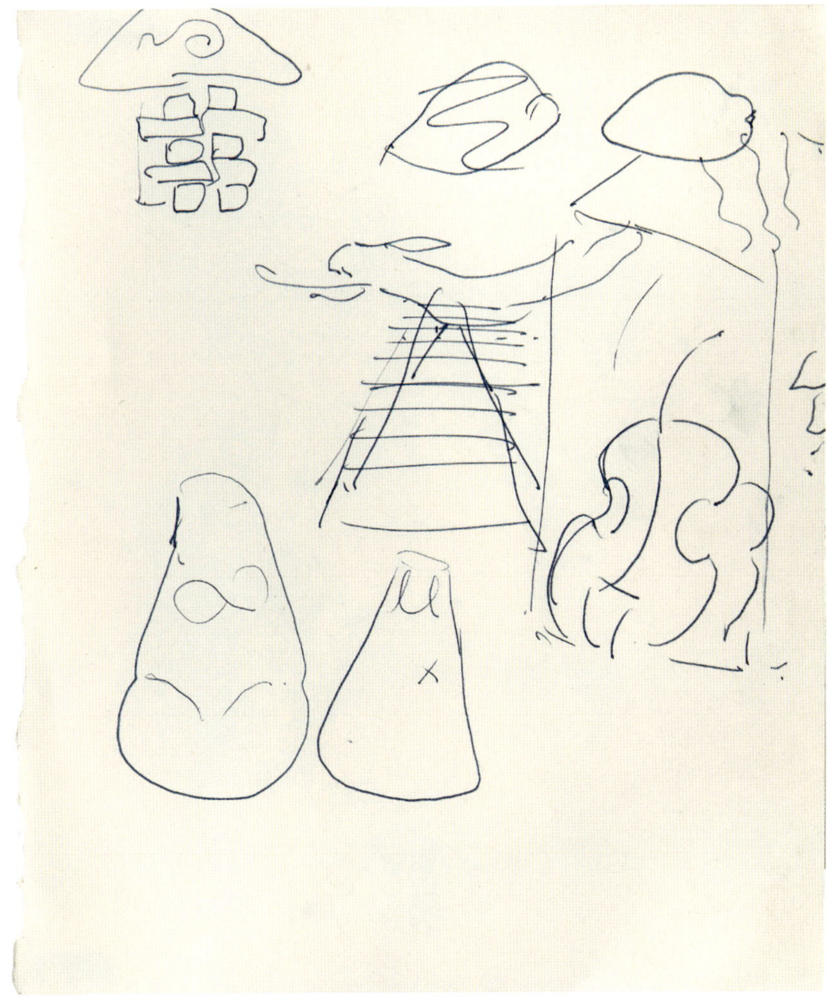

materials, techniques and activities. Relishing all these contradictions, the ultimate translation of material through casting was inevitable, although the idea of the mould had been in his work from the beginning. The emblem with which Flanagan became most identified was the unpredictable spirit of a hare spotted one day in a field on the Sussex Downs. Its impulsive dance presaged how his hare sculptures were often made: clay quickly manipulated over the given line of an armature, providing a spontaneously drawn form that was then rendered permanent in bronze. The anthropomorphism of the hare has often been remarked on, but perhaps it also embodies the *gidouille* or spiral that marks the fat belly of Ubu. As in most of Flanagan's work, metaphysically if not physically, it expresses creation and contradiction, and an equation to be followed both clockwise and counter-clockwise.

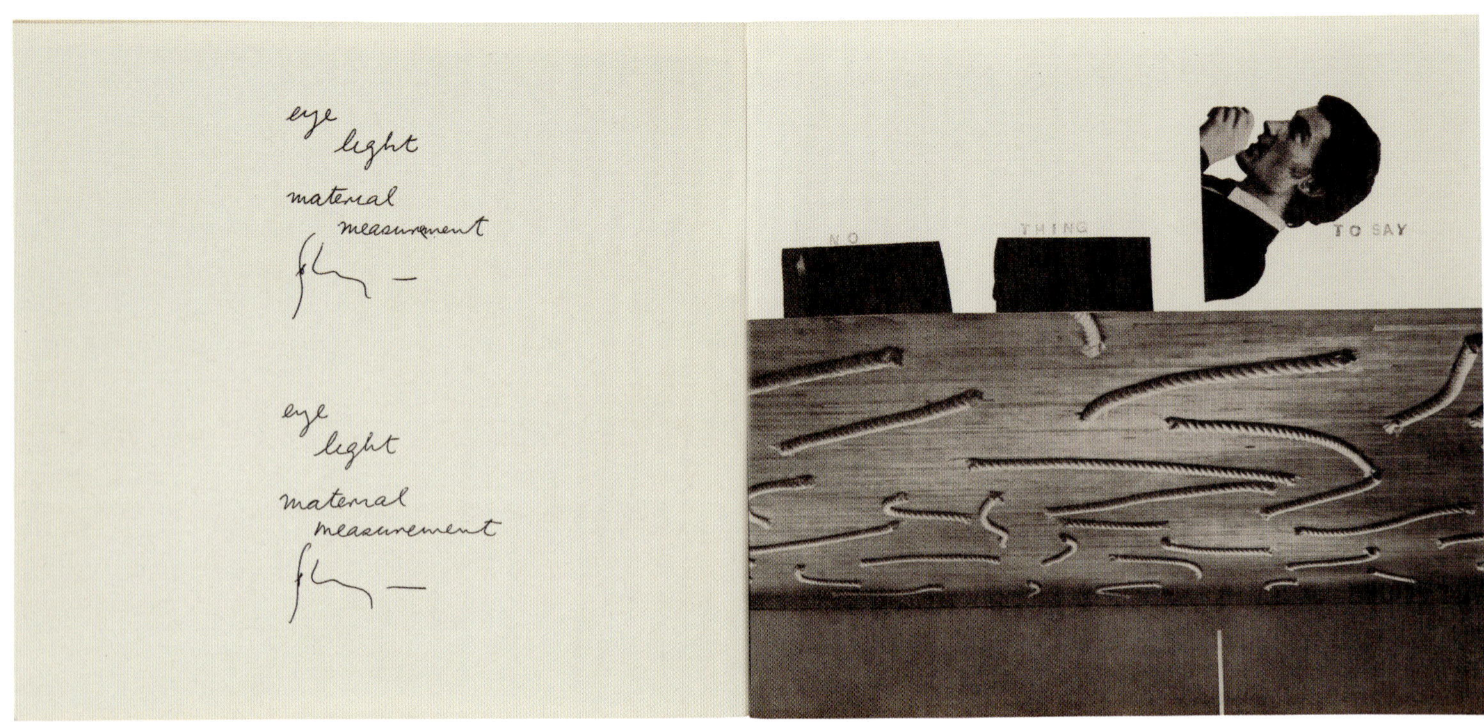

Artist's pages, *Between Mind and Matter, The Tenth Tokyo Biennale*, exh. cat., 1970

'No thing to say'

Jo Melvin

Barry Flanagan's experience of the world was, it seems, perpetually put through a mercurial, but strangely constant, process of filtration, inversion and crystallisation. He would bring light, material and language together in sculptural propositions that were at once serious and humorous, clear and contradictory. A collage of rubber-stamped text, shapes, and photographs parodies the very idea of definitions, of no thing, or nothing. A cut-out photograph of the artist in profile is chopped up, his torso becoming sculptural blocks, while his head, separate and rotated, is open-mouthed as if speaking. The facing page bears the handwritten, emblematic statement: 'eye, light, material, measurement'; in fact it occurs twice and is signed off with Flanagan's signature. The statement is intended as a proposal for both the constituent elements of sculptural experience and communication without speech, and yet, paradoxically, the list is signed, claimed by its author.

The Toyko catalogue was produced in two volumes, the first accompanying the exhibition and the second published afterwards to show the works made in the gallery and its immediate surroundings. The artists were allocated three pages: one for biography, another for their plan for the biennale and the third to treat as they wished, effectively an artist's page with their own layout. The organiser, Yusuke Nakahara, spent two years planning, visiting studios and exhibitions in Eastern and Western Europe, the USA and Japan.[1] He invited forty artists to participate and many travelled to Tokyo to produce their work. Flanagan was the third to arrive, a week after Carl Andre and Sol LeWitt, and two days before Roelof Louw, the other British artist in the show.

Nakahara organised the exhibition to accommodate the radical working methods of artists whose practice was determined by locally sourced materials. This itinerancy was a principle shared by many artists, as it not only reflected current concerns of site-specificity but it removed the need for a dedicated studio in which to make the work. It also reduced transport costs.[2] LeWitt proposed two alternatives for the show, although the first – a pencil wall drawing – was not possible, as the walls were covered by panels with perforations every 4.5 cm. The second proposal was to insert rolled pieces of paper into each of the 65,000 small holes in the walls of his allotted space. This was realised, on his instruction, by thirteen students. Flanagan had intended to make a ten-ton sand sculpture, but the weight exceeded the gallery's structural capacity. Instead he made a work constructed from a hundred rectangular sheets of corrugated cardboard, a large, dense pile of wood shavings and a small amount of sand; its title, *May 1 '70*, was the day it was completed. The work comprised a vertical arrangement of three enclosed cardboard units, with the shavings and

1 The exhibitions he cited as precedents were *Live in Your Head: When Attitudes Become Form (Works – Concepts – Processes – Situations – Information)*, Kunsthalle, Bern 1969, *Op Losse Schroeven (Situations and Cryptostructures)* Stedelijk Museum, Amsterdam 1969 and *Anti illusion: Procedures/ Materials*, Whitney Museum, New York 1969.

2 Flanagan maintained this position throughout his career and his statement for the IMMA exhibition in 2005 referred to itinerant practice.

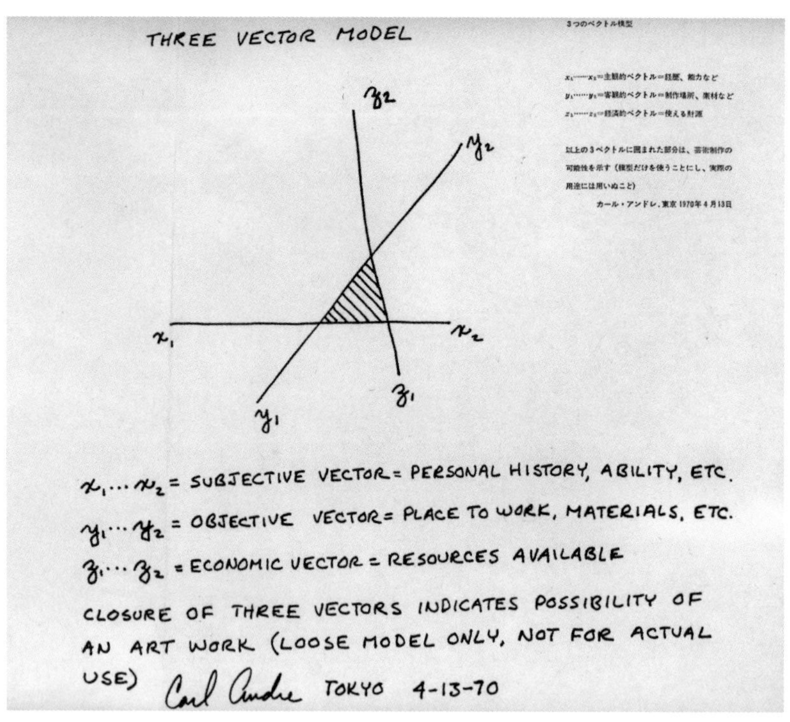

Carl Andre
Three Vector Model 1970
Artist's page, *Between Mind and Matter, The Tenth Tokyo Biennale*, exh. cat., 1970

sand resting on top. The structure was delicately balanced so that the movement and circulation of visitors brought about several stages of collapse. Flanagan considered the sculptural form to be contingent on the situation, and that each stage was intrinsic to the experience of the piece.

Andre found steel rods and wire around the campus of Tokyo University and, after protracted negotiations, used them to make *Rust Garden* 1970. He laid the rods across the floor; they were of different lengths, angular and straight, many had slight curves and formed a series of variegated lines throughout the space.[3] His artist's page shows a 'three vector model', comprising subjective, objective and economic vector elements, where the 'closure of the three vectors indicates the possibility of an artwork'. Andre's incorporation of skills learnt on the building site is well known, Flanagan's perhaps less so, but it is equally significant to his practice. Andre's model was a pragmatic solution to principles both artists shared. And, furthermore, it included a visual engagement with structures of language and concrete poetry. Barbara Reise, an American art critic living in London who was friends with both, told Andre how Flanagan's discussion of Andre's 'ballet poem' with Ann Lauterbach 'blew her mind into comprehension'; in her words, 'she'll never be the same again'.[4] This was during the London showing of *When Attitudes Become Form* at the Institute of Contemporary Arts in 1969, when Lauterbach had, in Flanagan's

3 *Between Mind and Matter, The Tenth Tokyo Biennale*, exh. cat., Tokyo Metropolitan Art Gallery, 1970.
4 Letter referring to an event at the ICA, London, dated 12 Oct. 1969, Barbara Reise Papers, Tate Gallery Archive (TGA 786/5/1/2).

estimation, misrepresented Andre's intention in the work and not understood the relationships between words and form at all.

Flanagan's commitment to the relationships between art, society and institutional responsibility was a constant factor in his attitude to making and showing work, and his statements often assert this. For instance, in Germano Celant's book *Arte Povera* (1969), Flanagan writes, 'Operations grow from the sculptural premise, its exactness and independence is the clue to the scale of its physical, visual, and actual consequence in society'.[5] In a letter published in *Studio International* Flanagan appealed to the 'public communicators and institutions strata to [take] on some creative responsibility, instead of operating within the safe untouchable historic "professional" cocoon'.[6] A few years later, in 1973, he postponed his exhibition at MOMA, New York, in solidarity with the museum staff union, Pasta MOMA, who were striking over better terms for a new contract. 'When it is neither the policy nor the capability of management to give in its leadership, there lurks the bitter ingredient in government [...]

5 Germano Celant, *Arte Povera*, Praeger, New York 1969, p.133.
6 Barry Flanagan, 'An Old New York Letter', *Studio International*, vol.177, no.911, May 1969, p.208.

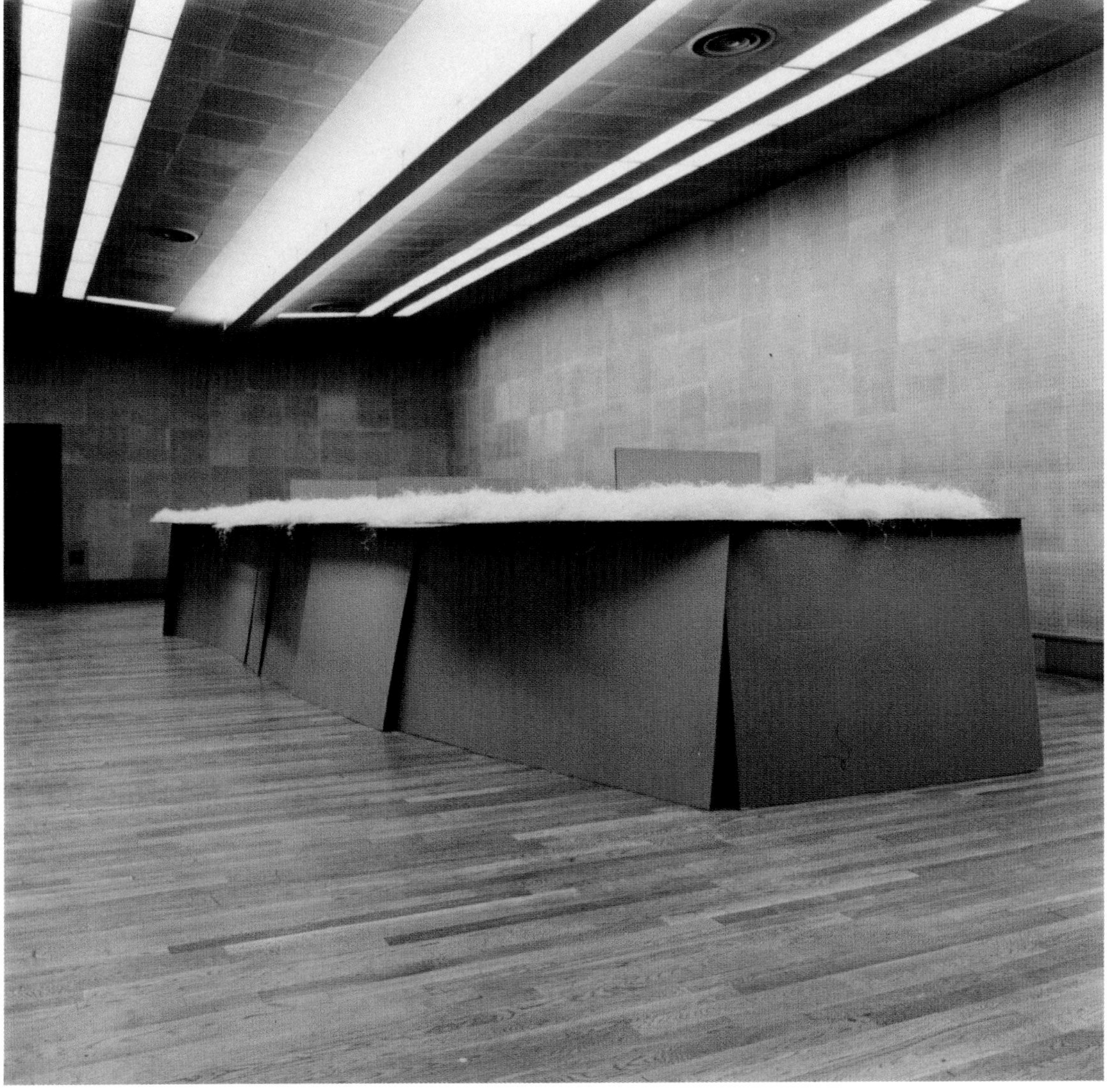

May 1 '70 1970 installation view, *Between Mind and Matter, The Tenth Tokyo Biennale*, Tokyo Metropolitan Art Gallery

my support of this strike action is the proper course of action under the circumstances.'[7]

While in Tokyo Flanagan sent Charles Harrison his contribution for the radical New York dealer Seth Siegelaub's special edition of *Studio International* magazine. Siegelaub's project was to offer six critics eight pages each, in which they were to present a selection of artists without critical or descriptive essays. Effectively, the magazine would be an exhibition site. Initially Siegelaub approached eight critics, but Yusuke Nakahara and Harald Szeemann declined due to pressure of work.[8] Flanagan used the photograph of *light on light on white on white* 1969 that had featured in *Between Mind and Matter*, but the right way up this time, and instructed Harrison by telegram to include with the cable the 'best Hayward photo from Rowan gallery light sight life quite different from Tokyo space interior'.[9] The telegram was addressed to 'straw international' – perhaps an oblique reference to the scarcity of revenue from either the magazine or his art, which was a problem he and Peter Townsend, the magazine's editor, discussed frequently. Flanagan had collaborated with Siegelaub previously: he was one of the thirty-one artists to contribute to *March 1969*, an exhibition in the form of a calendar, with free distribution to anyone on Siegelaub's mailing list or passing by the counter of George Wittenborn's bookshop in New York.

It is interesting that the summer issue of *Studio International* and Celant's *Arte Povera* were in effect exhibitions dependent on printed matter, although Celant did not describe the book as such. Celant's selection has a random order and artists were allocated varying numbers of pages, unlike Siegelaub's publication. And Celant grouped the distinctions that Thomas M. Messer had made within contemporary practice – earthworks, impossible art, actual art and Conceptual art – all under the umbrella of Arte Povera.[10] In 'Impossible Art', published in *Art in America*, Messer described the shared traits negatively, as work not easy to categorise, assess, attract museum attendance or be tax deductible. Celant embraced the paradox expressed by Messer, stating that the book, 'even though it wants to avoid the logic of consumption, is a consumer's item'.[11] Significantly, one of the characteristics that the Hayward curator Michael Compton picked up on in Flanagan's work was the quixotic element, noting, 'I do not know what Flanagan will do [...] but it will be paradoxically very cheap and yet unsaleable, a parable therefore of an ideal art'.[12] The challenge was to maintain the ideal and generate revenue simultaneously – a strategy humorously evoked by the notion of 'straw international'.

On the journey to Tokyo via New York Flanagan filmed the view through the aeroplane window. *Atlantic flight* 1970 was later shown at

7 Letter to Richard Oldenburg, cited in Mark Segal 'Strike! MOMA under pressure', *Studio International*, vol.186, no.961, Dec. 1973, pp.219–21 and pp.241–2.

8 Peter Townsend, *Studio International* editorial papers, July/Aug. 1970 folder, Tate Gallery Archive (TGA 20028).

9 *Studio International*, vol.180, no.924, July/Aug. 1970, p.29.

10 Thomas M. Messer, David Shirey, 'Impossible Art', *Art in America*, May/June 1969.

11 Germano Celant, *Arte Povera*, Praeger, New York 1969, p.5.

12 Michael Compton, *6 at the Hayward*, exh. cat., Hayward Gallery, London 1969. The other artists in the show were Ian Stephenson, Victor Newsome, Michael Sandle, Keith Milow and Stephen Buckley.

The Situation Gallery, London, and in *Prospect 71: Projections*, at the Düsseldorf Kunsthalle in 1971, the first international exhibition entirely devoted to artists' films.[13] Barbara Reise noted the 'long shot of wing (stability) taking off. Then seemingly stationary (wing) with clouds (as film) going past observing vision in time.'[14] As Guy Brett describes, 'The camera was fixed, like the passenger in his seat, staring at the wing and beyond, with time to watch the land slide away, the rain clear from the window and the sun come out above the clouds. There is time to be bored, and the viewer's situation is like that of the filmmaking passenger's, with repetition encouraging reflection on duration and boredom.'[15] *Line on Holywell Beach* 1970 showed the trail left by the camera tripod as Flanagan dragged it from the waterline into the sand dunes.[16] The film is three minutes long and is, in effect, the presentation of a drawing. Like Robert Morris's iconic work, *Box with the sound of its own making* 1961 – where a wooden box contains a sound recording of the time taken and actions performed to make it – the film shows the duration of the drawing of a line on a beach.

There are some parallel intentions apparent in Morris and Flanagan's investigations: both explore the properties of soft sculpture as hanging

13 It was also shown in *The British Avant Garde*, New York Cultural Center, 1971, and *The New Art*, Hayward Gallery, London 1972. *Prospect 71* was organised by Konrad Fischer, Jurgen Harten and Hans Strelow.
14 Handwritten note, Barbara Reise Papers, Tate Gallery Archive (TGA 786/5/2/56).
15 Guy Brett, 'Situation: Films by Artists', *Times*, 18 Sept. 1971, p.9.
16 This was shown in *Prospect 71*, *Film Show*, Situation, London, 1971 and *The New Art*, 1972.

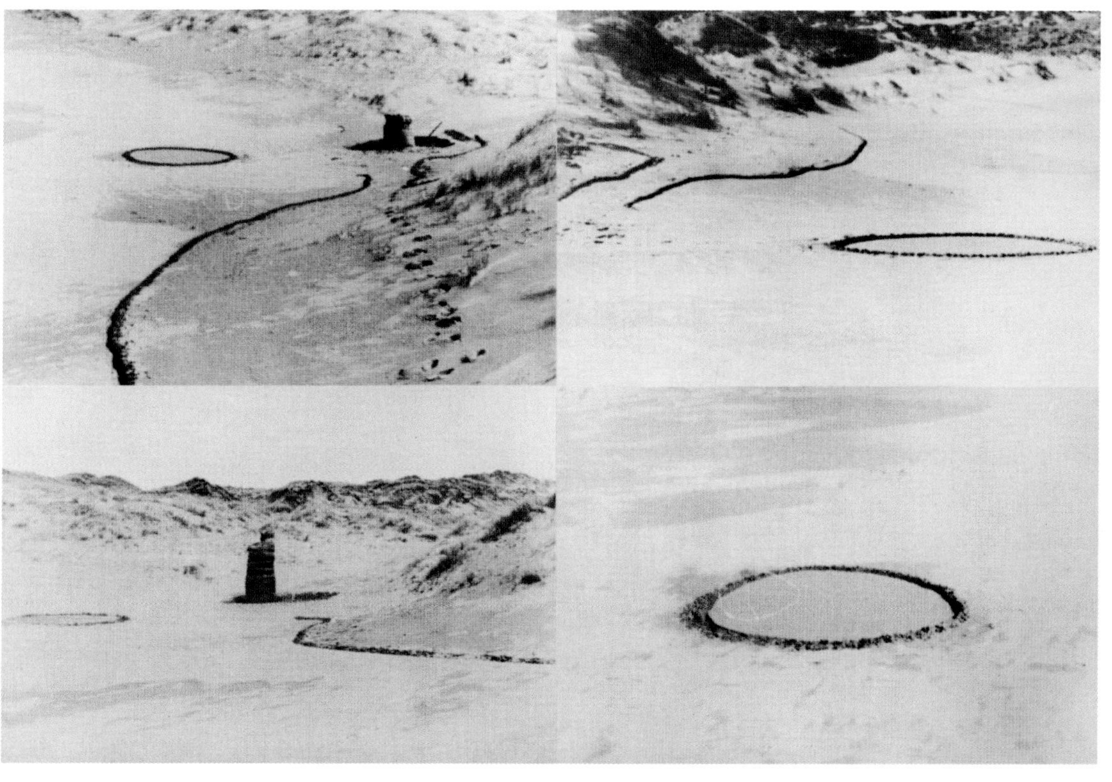

easter bag '67 1967
Holywell Beach, Cornwall, also showing *ring* and *line* sand works, reproduced in *Land Art*, exh. cat., Fernsehgalerie Gerry Schum, Berlin, 1969

works and embrace a humour that sometimes verges on understatement, seesawing between comedy and irony. Bruce McLean, a close friend of Flanagan, made a film called *In the shadow of your smile Bob* 1971, which neatly underscores an attitude that is balanced between acknowledgement and reaction to other artists' practices. McLean was interested in Morris's work and writings on art, particularly the implicit humour. When he saw a photograph of Morris in the catalogue for the London showing of *When Attitudes Become Form* 1969, McLean thought he looked rather glum and serious, despite the humour in his work; and it was this, combined with Brancusi's often-recounted statement that he could not work in the shadow of Rodin, that formed the idea for the work.

In *sand girl* 1970 Flanagan filmed sand falling onto and around a naked woman. There are brief glimpses of the studio's industrial interior and a fleeting shot through the window to the roofs beyond, but the focus remains on the pouring sand as it creates contours and mounds and, like the drawing on the beach, as it presents sculpting in action. Sand, by feel and association, is malleable and when, towards the end of the film, the woman rises, the camera tracks the imprint of her body, relating a moment that is similar to the removal of a cast object from a mould.[17] *a hole in the sea* 1969, a film made in collaboration with Gerry Schum for the *Land Art* TV gallery exhibition, first broadcast in the studio of SFB Berlin, 28 March 1969. It was made in February that year in the North Sea, off the coast of Scheveningen, Holland, where Jan Dibbets had also made his film, *12 Hours Tide Object with Correction of Perspective*, that same month. Flanagan and Schum's film shows the tide coming in to fill a Plexiglas cylinder that stands vertically in the sand, giving the impression of a hole in the sea being filled. It was shot in ten short sequences, with views of the cylinder side-on at ground level as well as a bird's-eye view, achieved by Schum balancing on a fire engine's extended ladder that rested on the sea wall. Just before the end of the film, Flanagan enters the frame to remove the cylinder from the sea, so revealing the construction of the scenario.[18] Unlike Flanagan's other films, where he edits in camera using the on/off switch, *a hole in the sea* is crafted so that the duration of the tide is compressed into a film lasting three minutes forty-four seconds – quite different from *Line on Holywell Beach*, which lasts as long as the making of the line.

Flanagan's second show at the Rowan Gallery was an immediate critical success,[19] and beyond the UK it attracted the attention of Jennifer and Ira Licht as well as Marilyn Fischbach and Donald Droll, the directors of the Fischbach Gallery, New York. The exhibition at Galerie Ricke, Kassel, followed soon after, and amongst the works that had previously

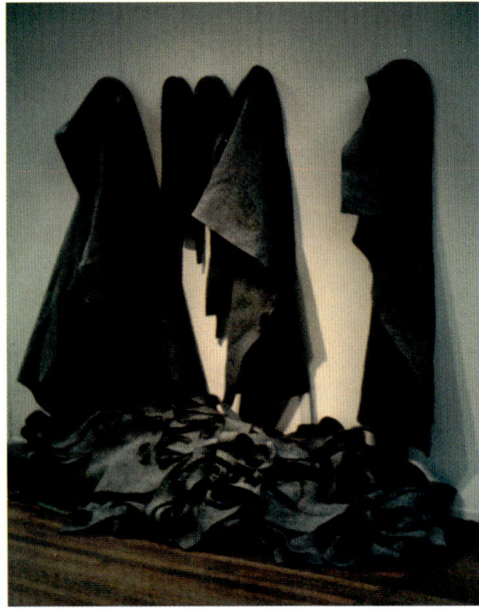

Robert Morris, *Felt piece*, 1967/68 installed at *When Attitudes Become Form*, ICA, London 1969

17 Also shown in *Prospect 71* and *The New Art*.

18 The other artists who worked with Gerry Schum to make films for the *Land Art* TV exhibition were Richard Long, Dennis Oppenheim, Robert Smithson, Marinus Boezem, Jan Dibbets, Walter De Maria and Michael Heizer.

19 Norbert Lynton, 'London galleries: Barry Flanagan and Allen Jones', *Guardian*, 18 Apr. 1968; Guy Brett, 'Sculptural Objects in variety', *The Times*, 22 Apr. 1968; John Russell, 'All for show', *The Sunday Times*, 21 Apr. 1968, p.55; Oswell Blakeston, 'Some New shows', *What's On*, 12 Apr. 1968; Arthur Moyse, 'Around the Galleries', *Anarchist Weekly*, 11 May 1968, p.2; 'The Arts', *Daily Mirror*, 10 Apr. 1968, p.18; James Burr, 'London Galleries: Poetic Eloquence', *Apollo*, vol.LXXXVII, no.74 (new series) Apr. 1968, p.298; Paul Overy, 'Inflations', *The Listener*, 18 Apr. 1968; 'Art', *Vogue*, 15 Apr. 1968; Anthony Fawcett, 'Doubts and Dilemmas', *Arts and Artists*, vol.3, no.1, Apr. 1968, p.42; Oswell Blakestone, 'Barry Flanagan', *Arts Review*, vol.XX, no.7, 13 Apr. 1968, p.193; Charles Harrison, 'Barry Flanagan's sculpture: Claiming attention for objects by statement', *Studio International*, vol.175, no.900, May 1968, pp.226–8.

been shown at the Rowan – including *ringn '66* 1966, which was described by Alex Gregory-Hood, the gallery director, as Flanagan's 'first serious sand sculpture' – were four canvas works that had not been shown before.[20] These canvas works, dated 1966, demonstrate Flanagan's incorporation of painters' concerns with flatness into his practice. The illusion of receding space within the picture plane is negated through the use of layers in actual space, as well as sequences of folds, corner additions and holes for cord to be pulled through and knotted. The lumpy protuberances of *canvas a* 1966 and *canvas b* 1966 – stretchers with cord sewn onto the front, and holes through which to pull and knot the cord – have formal similarities with the anthropomorphic shapes of the soft sculptures. A similar work, *canvas 3 '67* 1967, exhibited in the London showing of *When Attitudes Become Form* 1969, consists of two pieces of canvas sewn together and stretched. The vertical join is a crucial linear element, as are the five cord knots sewn into the surface, which imply the surface must be punctured to allow the cord through.

The knots and thread employ different methods of making the canvas bag sculptures open or closed, tied or sewn together, with the thread showing or not. The floor pieces *canvas floor piece 1* 1966 and *canvas floor piece 2 '66/67* 1966/7 comprise, respectively, a variegated rectangle without mount and nine pieces of canvas strewn on the floor. It was impossible not to walk inside the perimeter of the work, as it was strewn around the gallery and through the doorway into another space, thereby expressing concerns similar to those of Carl Andre's *Scatter Piece*, first shown at the Dwan Gallery, New York, in 1967, although at the time neither artist was aware of the other's practice.

Flanagan accounted for his interest in sculpture by using painting as a hermetic but default position: 'The convention of painting always bothered me. There always seemed to be a *way* of painting. With sculpture you always seemed to be working directly, with materials and with the physical world inventing your own organisations.'[21] Flanagan was preoccupied by canvas: wall-mounting it, stretching or hanging it or leaning it against a wall or in a corner, or balanced with sticks fixed to the floor with plasticine to prevent slipping. An examination of his various uses of knots and threads can continue from the bags to the hanging canvas pieces. These were developed from the canvas bag sculptures (whether open or closed), with material tied or sewn together in pleats or folds, the knotted thread pronounced and hanging freely or not showing at all. And, similarly, sand in a bag behaves differently from a pile of sand directly on the floor. What is more, when *rope (gr 2sp 60) 6 '67* 1967 – sixty feet of sisal rope dyed green and laid out to run through two spaces – is placed inside a hessian bag and retitled *rope/bag (gr 2sp 60) 6 '67* 1967, its qualities are distinctly different,

20 Fischbach Gallery records, 1954–78, Smithsonian American Art Archives, box 5, folder 2.

21 Interview with Flanagan, Gene Baro, 'Sculpture Made Visible', *Studio International*, vol.178, no.915 Oct. 1969, pp.122–5.

even though it is the same rope. These sleights of hand show how paradoxically simple and complex each work is, while presenting its material properties with humour.

Writing to Droll, Flanagan confirmed his participation in the MOMA touring exhibition *Young British Artists – six painters, six sculptors* 1968–9, initiated by Jennifer Licht and presenting new trends in British art. Two artists in the show already had an international reputation: Phillip King and Bridget Riley were that year's representatives at the Venice Biennale.[22] Flanagan exhibited *stack 1 '67/68* 1967/8, *io* 1965, *al casb 4 '67* 1967, *rope (pl corner 12) 2 '67* 1967. Licht had already included Flanagan in a MOMA touring exhibition of British drawings in venues around the US and she was the first American museum curator to identify the radical explorations of his work.

The first time Flanagan's work was shown in New York was at the Theodoran Awards exhibition at the Guggenheim Museum in May 1969. He was already known and respected in America by the group of artists around Seth Siegelaub and Lucy Lippard, and Joseph Kosuth had written to Charles Harrison asking when they could expect to see Flanagan in New York, 'as his arrival was anxiously awaited'.[23] Flanagan had met Lippard the previous year in London and they had immediately become friends. She sent him a note to say how good the works looked in the Guggenheim; in reply he sent her the postcard announcement for *a hole in the sea* and a copy of *(O for orange U for you: a poem for the lips) juno965* 1965, where the letters o and u were arranged alternately in a vertical line. Flanagan had performed this poem at the *second international exhibition of experimental poetry* at St Catherine's College, Oxford, in June 1965 and published it in *Silâns*, the magazine he produced at St Martin's with Rudy Leenders and Alastair Jackson, and where he frequently explored linguistic puns visually. Sending it to Lippard, several years after he had made it, he drew lightly on the implicit connection between her surname and the silent mouthing of letters. It was also a retrospective pun on her role as a critic who is paid to speak. The fact that he arranged the poem's letters vertically rather than horizontally shows his critique of the horizontality of reading left to right, and is similar to his placing of canvases on the floor so that they are experienced horizontally rather than vertically.

Flanagan told Lippard he wanted to make 'photo poems with bodies'.[24] The repetition of the shapes of the letters – o and u formed in the mouth and to be uttered silently – echoes his statement that 'sculpture is always going on', as even a silent mouthing escaping the body's interior is a sculptural process. These letter shapes were two central components of his practice, and are clearly visible in *a hole in the sea*: the letter 'o' being

22 The complete list of artists is David Annesley, Clive Barker, Patrick Caulfield, Barry Flanagan, Paul Huxley, Allen Jones, Phillip King, Mark Lancaster, Peter Phillips, Bridget Riley, William Tucker and Derrick Woodham.

23 Charles Harrison papers, Tate Gallery Archive (TGA 200826).

24 Letter to Lippard, dated 27 June, Archives of American Art, Smithsonian Institute, Lucy Lippard papers, 1940s–2006, box 2, Barry Flanagan folder 1968–75.

the Plexiglas cylinder from above, the 'u' its appearance from the beach as it fills with the tide. The 'o' is also the top of the canvas bag, and the 'u' its cutaway view from the side, since bags too are vessels to be filled.

Edward Fry describes Flanagan's work in the Theodoran Awards catalogue as '"anti-formal" with a surrealist cast, unexpected variations of colour and scale, particularly in his use of erotic imagery'. He observed that its character was in marked contrast to that of the previous generation of artists from St Martin's School of Art. The gallery purchased *four rahsb 4 '67* 1967 from the exhibition and, in 1971, Peter Schjeldahl described the event in retrospect as 'the city's premier show case for new art talent', noting the artists whose reputations had subsequently grown: Barry Flanagan, Bruce Nauman and Richard Serra.[25] It is revealing that he considered Flanagan's international status as important as Nauman's and Serra's.

Flanagan's role as champion for artists is little known. He helped generate interest in the radical practices of his contemporaries, particularly in riposte to the 1968 article in *Time* magazine, 'Art: The Avant-Garde: Subtle, Cerebral, Elusive'. [26] The article presented the new practices of 'antiform', 'process art', 'Conceptual art', 'earthworks' and 'Minimalism' as if they originated in the US, and suggested that the 'fascination for soft cerebral art' had spread elsewhere through the work of three non-Americans: Joseph Beuys and Walter Pichler from Germany and Austria and Lygia Clark from Brazil. It referred to Walter De Maria's filling three rooms of a Munich gallery with eight tons of earth and to Bill Bollinger's remark on rope as sculpture: 'to me, a rope is a simple expression of an idea, a way of conveying information'. De Maria's 1968 exhibition at Galerie Heiner Friedrich, Munich, required viewers to contemplate a three-foot high mound of earth from the doorway but not walk through it. Flanagan had previously made a floor sculpture of sand for the Biennale des Jeunes, Paris, in 1967: *one space sand sculpture* 1967 comprised a room filled with three inches of sand and was installed underneath *4 casb 2 '67*, *ringl 1 '67* and *rope (gr 2sp 60) 6 '67*. The configuration was illustrated in *Studio International* magazine in September 1967 in a special feature on the British artists in the exhibition. Flanagan shortly afterwards became friends with De Maria, putting him up during a visit to London; but by then he had already decided that wall-to-wall sand was unsatisfactory in a gallery context. Nonetheless he was enraged at the blithe assertions of critics, who failed to consider the fluidity of ideas and the context of exchange between artists beyond the US, that it was he who had first covered a gallery floor with matter. In order to set the record straight and demonstrate the breadth of avant-garde engagement amongst British and European artists, Flanagan compiled a documentary exhibition of

25 Peter Schjeldahl, *New York Times*, 17 Oct. 1971, p.25.

26 'Art: The Avant-Garde: Subtle, Cerebral, Elusive', *Time*, vol.92, Nov. 22, 1968, pp.70–7.

practices that significantly contributed to or foregrounded these discourses. He made panels with statements by and photographs of works by Bruce McLean, Richard Long, Roelof Louw, John Latham, Event Structure Research Group and himself. Alan Power contributed £40 towards the costs – a significant sum at the time – and the panels were shown at the Fischbach Gallery in 1969.[27] Flanagan also delivered a series of slide lectures and film screenings, where he showed works by this group of artists. A report on one such event, in the *Nebraska Sun*, noted Flanagan's appearance after Lippard to a capacity audience at Omaha University.[28]

Articles on 'Impossible Art' by Thomas M. Messer and David Shirey, in *Art in America*, May/June 1969, further galvanised Flanagan's determination to rectify matters, as their discussion of radical new practices failed to mention any artist that was not American. This was particularly galling as in March that year the European exhibitions *When Attitudes Become Form*, in Bern, and *Op Losse Schroeven Situaties en Cryptstructuren*, in Amsterdam, had shown new art practices as part of an increasingly international dialogue. Flanagan's advocacy of his contemporaries was predicated on a grassroots desire for action. It was independent of Celant's decision to compile the *Arte Povera* book, although Celant had also used Messer's article as a starting point.

At Museum Haus Lange, Krefeld, Flanagan spent several weeks installing and making works for an exhibition that would interact with the architecture. Designed as a villa by Mies van der Rohe, it had been converted into an art gallery. The publication is unusual – more like an artist's book than a regular exhibition catalogue. Flanagan's photographs

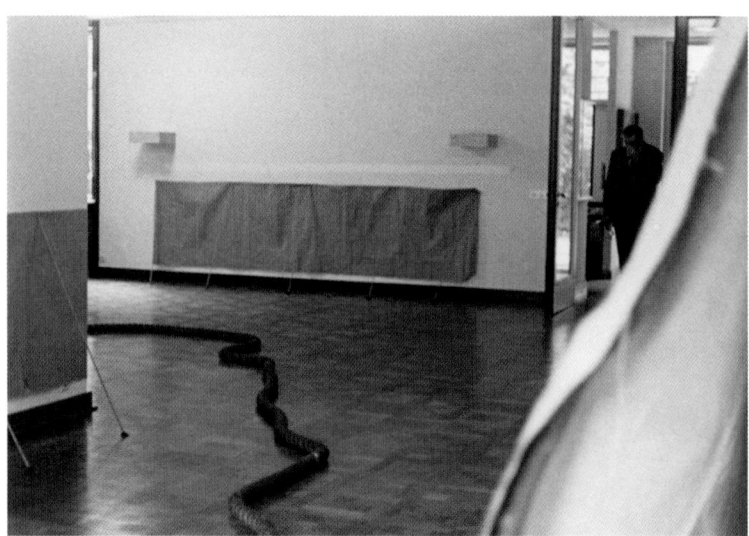

Installation shot Museum Haus Lange, Krefeld, showing *aug 2 '69* 1969 and *3 space rope piece '69* 1969

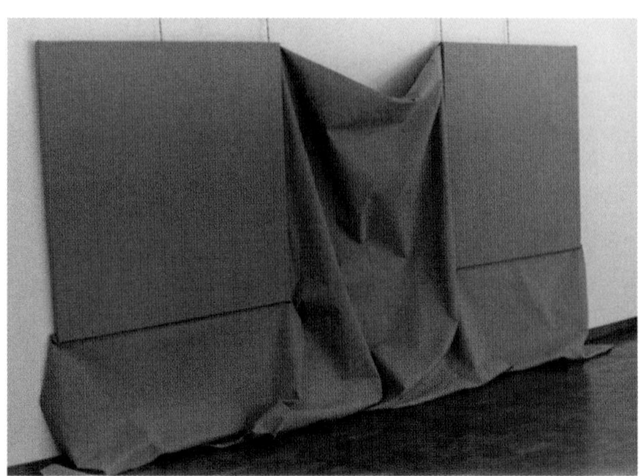

aug 1 '69 1969 at Museum Haus Lange, Krefeld, 1969

27 The articles Thomas M. Messer, 'Impossible Art, Why it is', David Shirey, 'Impossible Art, What it Is', *Art in America*, vol.57, no.3, May/June 1969, pp.30–47 additionally galvanised Flanagan to make and present these panels. Tate Gallery Archive has copies of the original panels, that were deposited by Alan Power in 1974 (TGA 747).

28 *Nebraska Sun*, 1969.

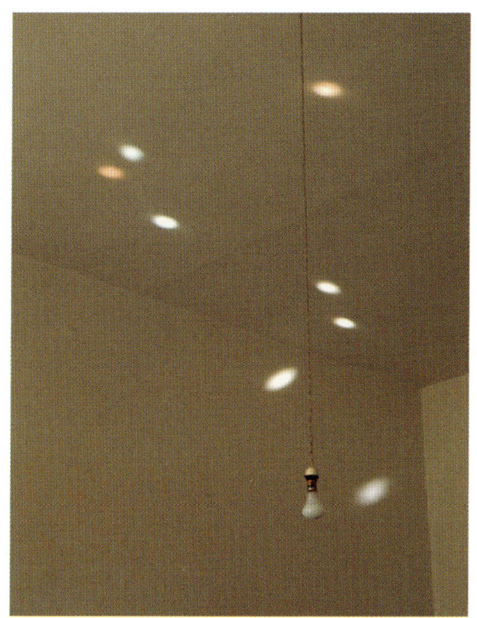

light piece 1969

of the works are printed alongside his written commentaries, which, in the case of *one camion sand piece* 1969, is the builders' merchant's delivery note, signed by Flanagan. Another work in the exhibition, *aug 1 '69* 1969, comprises a large sheet of flax with two sections each tacked over a stretcher, the excess fabric below and between left to sag and drape naturally. As Flanagan stated: 'the use of a stretcher inevitably conforms to the conventional language of paintings, but the emphasis is clearly to do with the materials and substances, it is something to look at rather than to read. My tongue dropped out of my head long ago.'[29] His text on *3 space rope piece '69* 1969 incorporates instructions for its installation:

> 'i don't like people standing on sculpture or kicking it around just because its on the floor. this piece should not be made into any configuration, but placed as rope through 3 rooms. i don't mind other people placing the rope so long as they don't act the fool. if you look at the rope and not in your head for "meaning-full" configurations the visual measurements are vast & interesting. it is a piece for the eyes.'

This exhibition was the first time that Flanagan created site-specific work. Although since his student days he had grouped works in relation to one another, here the experience enabled him to view the exhibition itself as a total work.

While in Krefeld Flanagan was planning the Fischbach Gallery show, for which he asked Donald Droll to source materials and suppliers. As well as works shown previously, he made a second version of the 'three-space' rope, *3 space rope sculpture 2 '69* 1969, and further light pieces. *light corner piece 2 '69* 1969 was a pencil-thin line of light projected into the corner, and *daylight light piece 5 '69* 1969 framed a sheet of brown paper stuck to the wall, evoking a painting. The press reviews described the rope sculpture as 'a kind of indeterminate drawing' and noted the 'fascinating light pieces'. Dore Ashton observed that 'the sensibility working in Flanagan, in spite of his revolutionary intentions is healthily traditional'.[30] The poster for Museum Haus Lange and the invitation card for the Fischbach Gallery both used photographs of his studios and stores: itinerant spaces that debunked the myth of a fixed studio, as had Flanagan's contingent and site-responsive installation at the Tokyo Biennale.

Flanagan discussed the role of light as a separate, but totally sculptural, element and identified it as a key component in many works. The first notable occasion was the exhibition *19:45–21:55 September 9th 1967* at Galerie Dorothea Loehr in Frankfurt. Flanagan's instructions culminated with the participants eating a loaf of bread after having completed a list of other actions: switching the lights on and off for ten seconds at a time, standing

29 *Barry Flanagan Object Sculptures*, exh. cat., Museum Haus Lange, Krefeld 1969, unpag.

30 Dore Ashton, 'New York Letter', *Studio International*, vol.178, no.917, Dec. 1969, pp.23–4; *New York Times*, 4 Oct. 1969; John Perrault, *Village Voice*, 9 Oct. 1969; *Art News*, vol.68, no.7, Nov. 1969, p.16; *Art International*, vol.XIII, Nov. 1969, p.71.

in a queue, then a ring, lighting the gas, and so on. To make a line and then a ring, after being subject to controlled light and dark, all followed by eating bread mixed with salt sounds like a curious way to precipitate aesthetic engagement – yet the processes of orientation and disorientation, and the recognition and subversion of identifiable systems, are established strategies of aesthetic encounter: the interplay of reversals and repetitions are intrinsic to Flanagan's practice. For instance, in an artist's page in a 1970 issue of *Studio International* magazine readers may have puzzled over how to respond to the black advertisement facing the contents page, with white text that stated 'this advertisement will be blacked out for a fee of £2.25n.p.'[31] There would be nothing to stop the reader from blacking out the text themselves to avoid paying the fee, making this a somewhat enigmatic and disconcerting proposition. This is aesthetics in action, disrupting one's normal relations with the world, and it requires a response that is contingent upon 'the willing suspension of disbelief' as succinctly expressed by Coleridge.[32]

Flanagan's sleight of hand can also be applied to entirely serious ends. He made two works for an exhibition at Galerie Ariete, Milan, which were not listed in the catalogue.[33] One used the shredded paper from the crates that had transported his sculptures to the gallery; the other, made from leaves and gravel from the courtyard, was dedicated to Lucio Fontana, who had died the previous month.[34] It was a modest homage, but his regard for Fontana's opening of the domain of painting into sculptural experience by slashing and piercing canvas was clear in his own explorations of canvas and picture plane. As with McLean's reference to Morris, Flanagan's attitude was that practice was part of a dialogue and exchange of ideas, like a handshake, and it can be conducted as much with one's contemporaries as across generations.

Collaboration and participation played an important role in Flanagan's early practice. Reciprocity was central: the sand-filled works rely on bodily actions for completion, the canvas bags need to be held open while sand is poured into them and the rope needs to be uncoiled and held onto. Flanagan would issue instructions when he was unable to install the work himself. For instance, to install *heap 1' 67* 1967 for the exhibition *Art in Process 4*, at Finch College, New York in 1969, he told Naomi Spector of the Fischbach Gallery, 'It takes about four hours when you know what you are doing and you need two people'. These activities are clearly orchestrated by Flanagan, and the later bronze works, too, required teamwork; as he stated, 'I am glad to point out that in the production of these pieces in bronze the work has been done by others, leaving only the modelling bits to me, as author.'[35]

31 *Studio International*, vol.180, no.926, Oct. 1970, p.xix.

32 Samuel Taylor Coleridge, *Biographia Literaria*, ed. H.J. Jackson, Oxford 1985 p.314.

33 As with the Ricke show, some but not all of the works had been shown previously at the Rowan Gallery.

34 Letter from Flanagan to Donald Droll 27 Oct. 1968, Fischbach Gallery Records 1954–78, Smithsonian Archives of American Art, box S, folder l; Flanagan email, May 2009, describing the sculpture of leaves.

35 Artist's statement, *Barry Flanagan*, exh. cat., Waddington Gallery, London 1981, p.3.

It is often thought that Flanagan made a sudden switch to working exclusively in bronze around 1979. This assumption is false on two counts: firstly, his practice was never exclusive in terms of material, since he continued to work with clay, cloth, printmaking, drawing, photography and film throughout his life; and, secondly, he had begun working in bronze much earlier. His first cast was of a portrait of his father-in-law, Emlyn Lewis, in 1969, whose own spectacles were cast for the piece.[36]

This exposure of process and method is something Flanagan performed in any medium. He frequently used casts of objects as components in sculptures and allowed bits of armature to show through strips of clay or plaster, thereby recording the means of its making. The durational nature of his films is also translated into the bronzes, as we bear witness to the processes of casting. It is aptly contradictory, then, that the fleeting hare should become a monument to time and duration, channelling the quixotic and mysterious propositions implicit in the early work. When, in 1979, Flanagan was given a dead hare, he took it to his studio and laid it on paper, tracing its contour with its blood. Later he added the notes: 'they said the hare weighed the equivalent of seven pheasants and was unusually heavy' and 'The hare knows art history, Master Beuys'.[37] Here Flanagan, ever hare-like, doubles back self-referentially, his intention flitting in and out of view, between the pragmatic and the mythical, never allowing itself to rest at a logical conclusion.

36 Henry Abercrombie invited Flanagan to use the foundry at Central School of Art. In 1977 he and Andy Elton formed A&A foundry in Poplar, this later became AB Fine Art foundry, still run by Abercrombie and where Flanagan had a studio from 1982.

37 A reference to Joseph Beuys's performance *How to Explain Pictures to a Dead Hare* 1968, in Flanagan Notebook 1998.

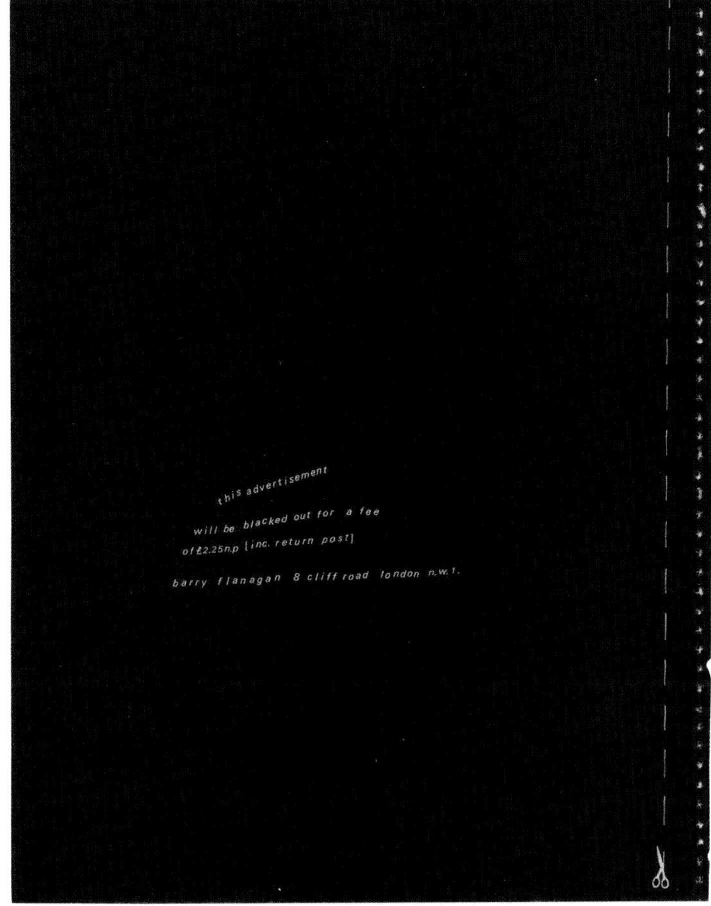

Barry Flanagan Black Advertisement, *Studio International* magazine, October 1970, p xix. The text reads: 'this advertisement / will be blacked out for a fee / of £2.25n.p. [inc. return post] / barry flanagan 8 cliff road london n.w.1.'

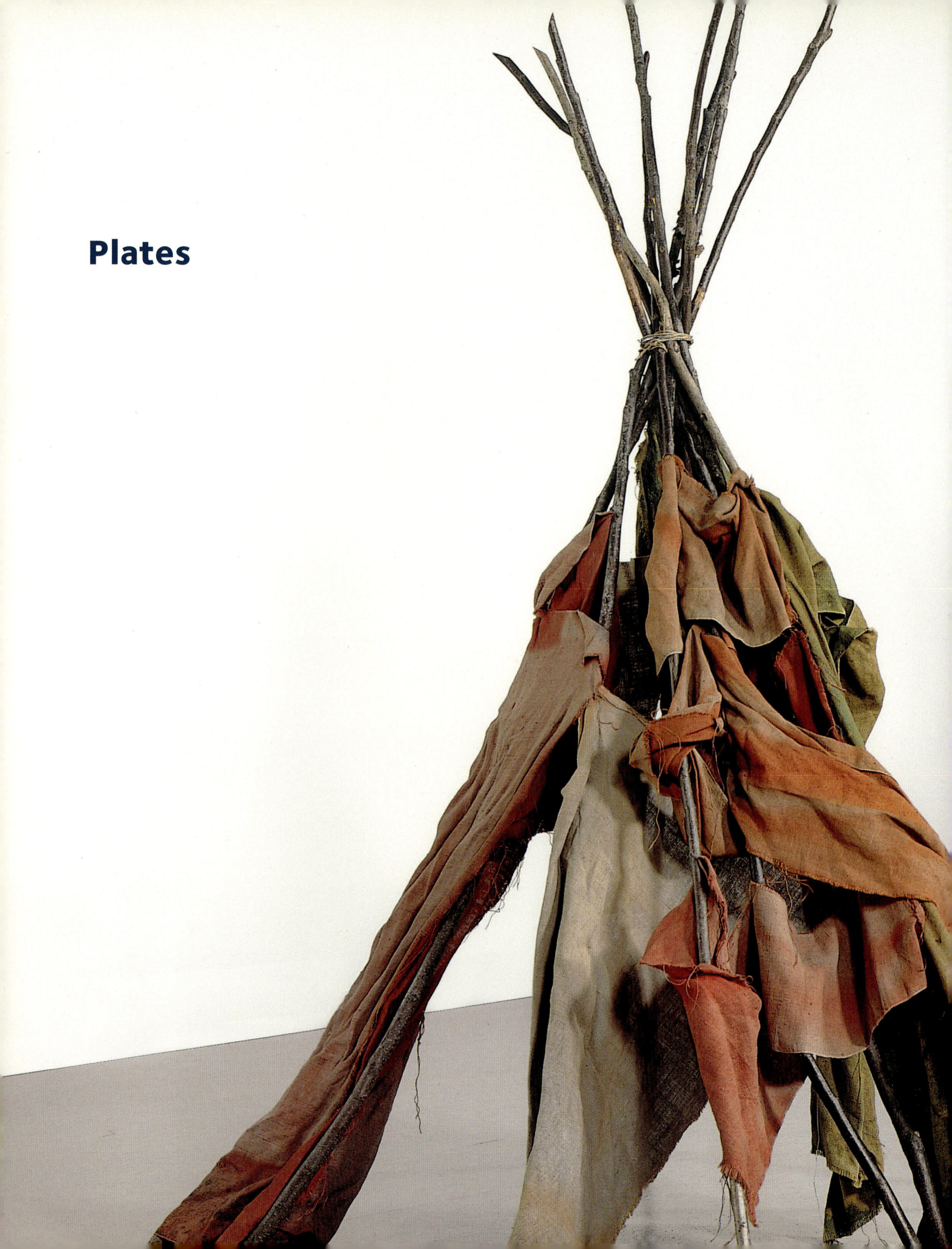

Plates

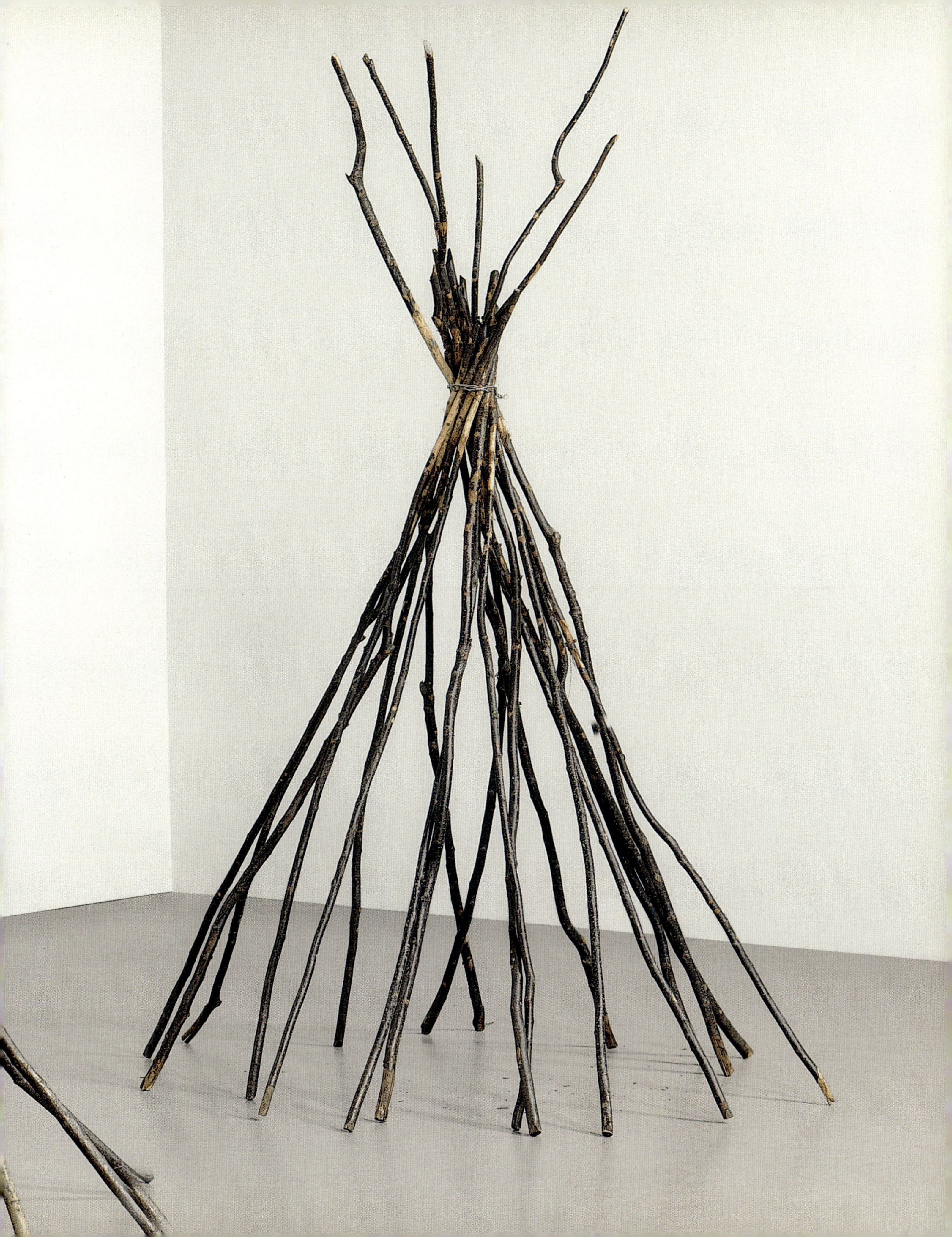

aaing j gni aa 1965

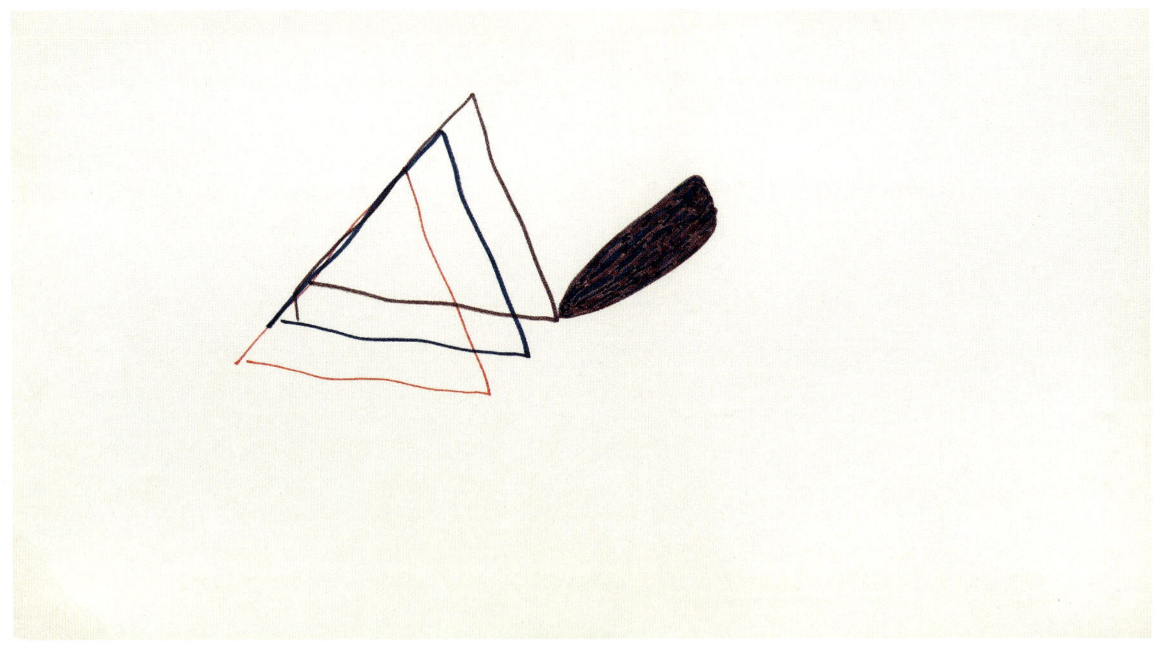

sep '66 ① 6/22 1966

feb '66 1966

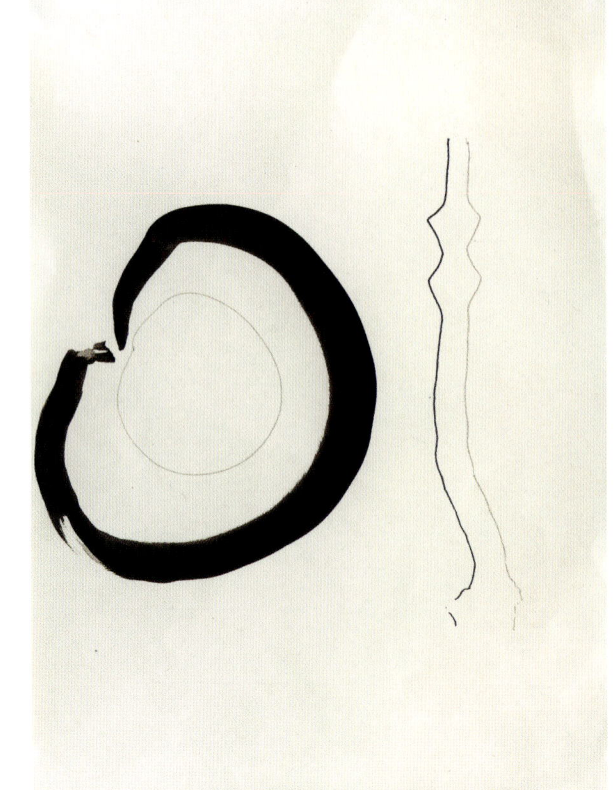

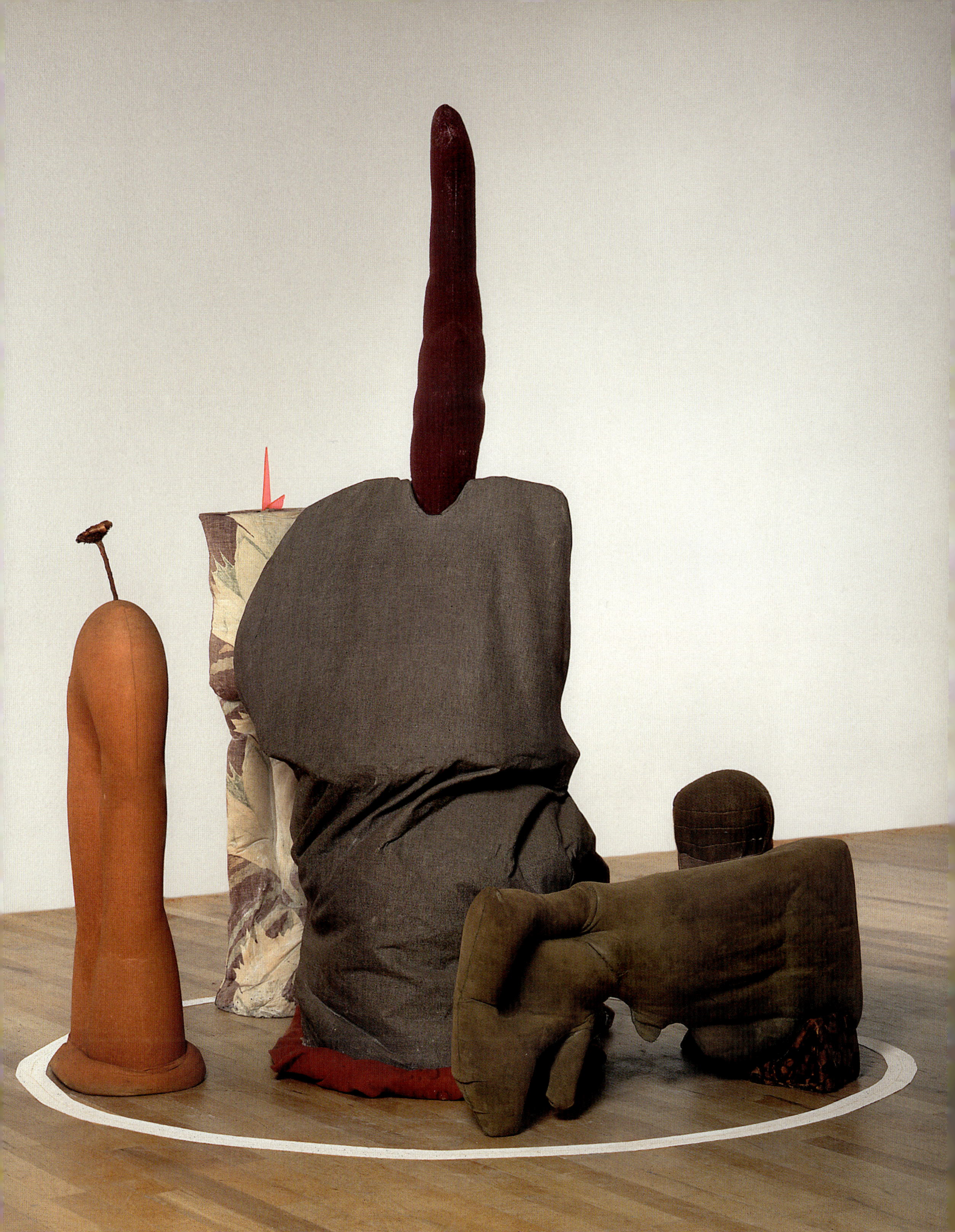

pdreeoo 1965

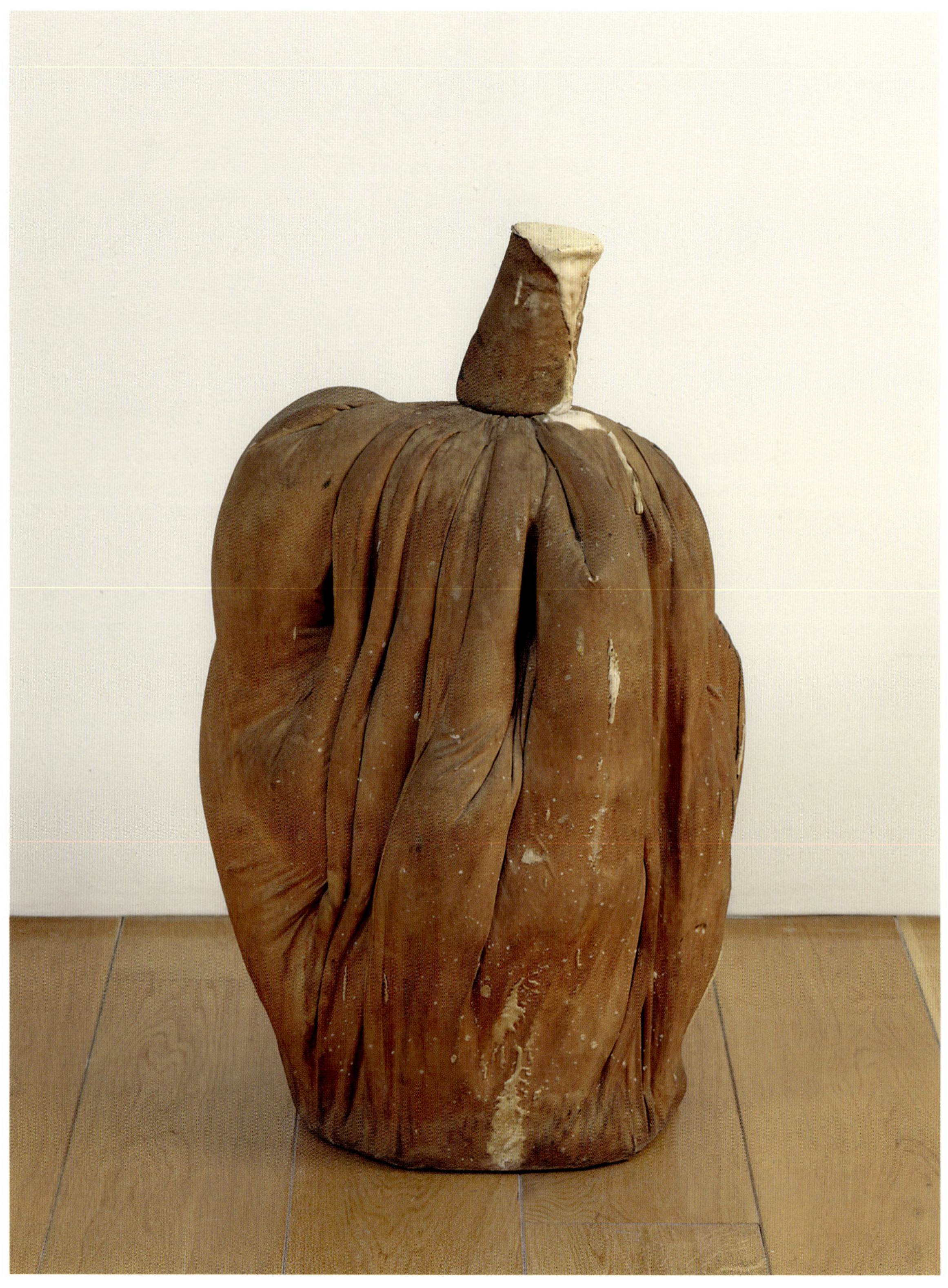

sand muslin 2 1966

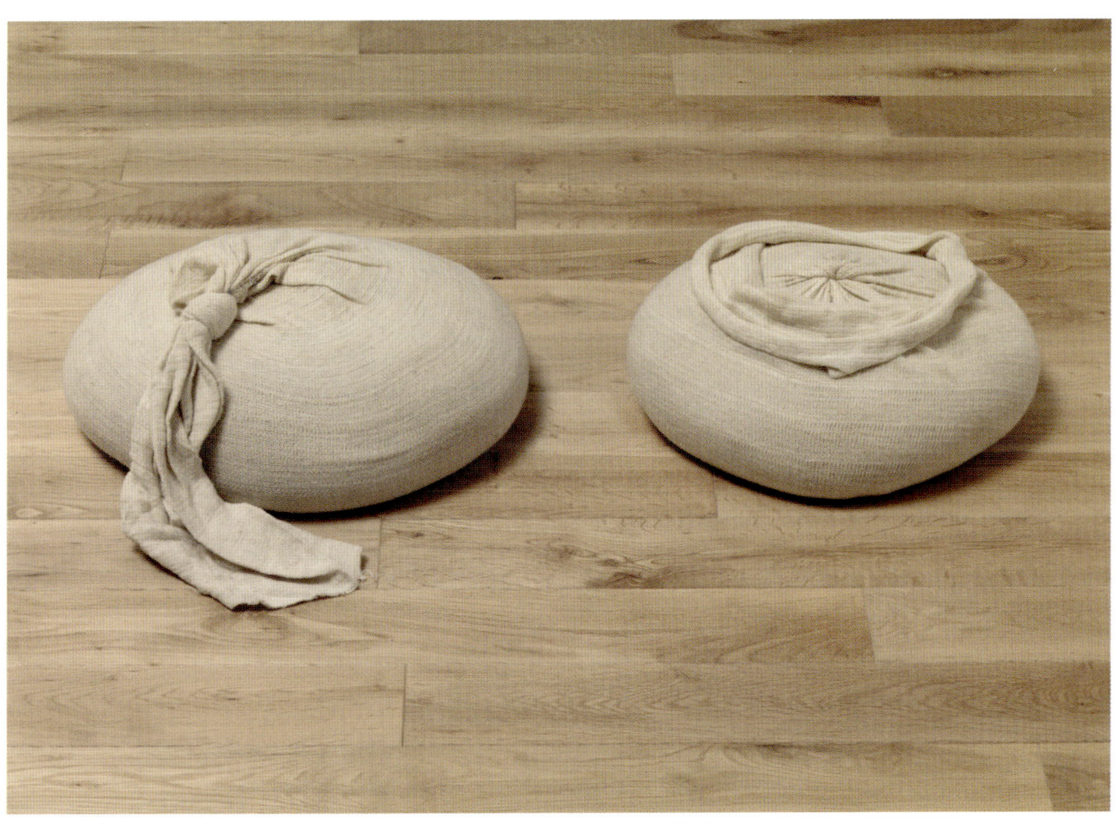

ringn '66 1966

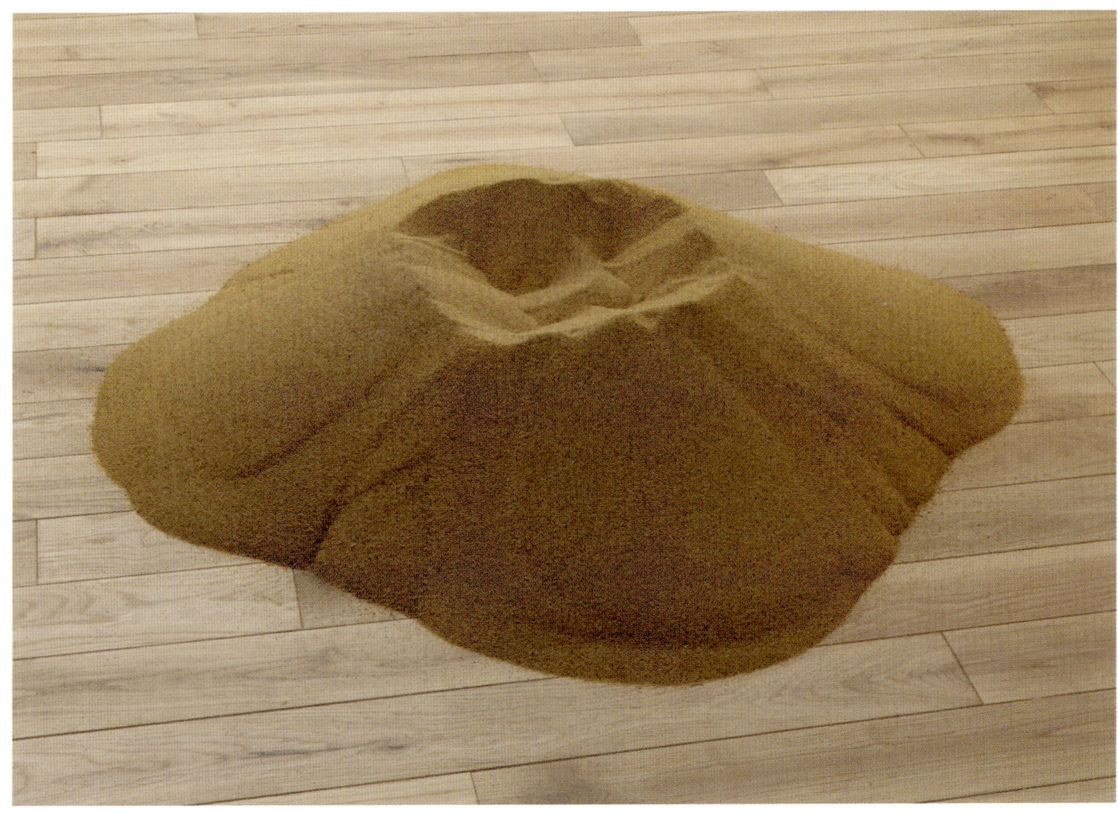

al casb 4 '67 1967 **plant 14** 1971

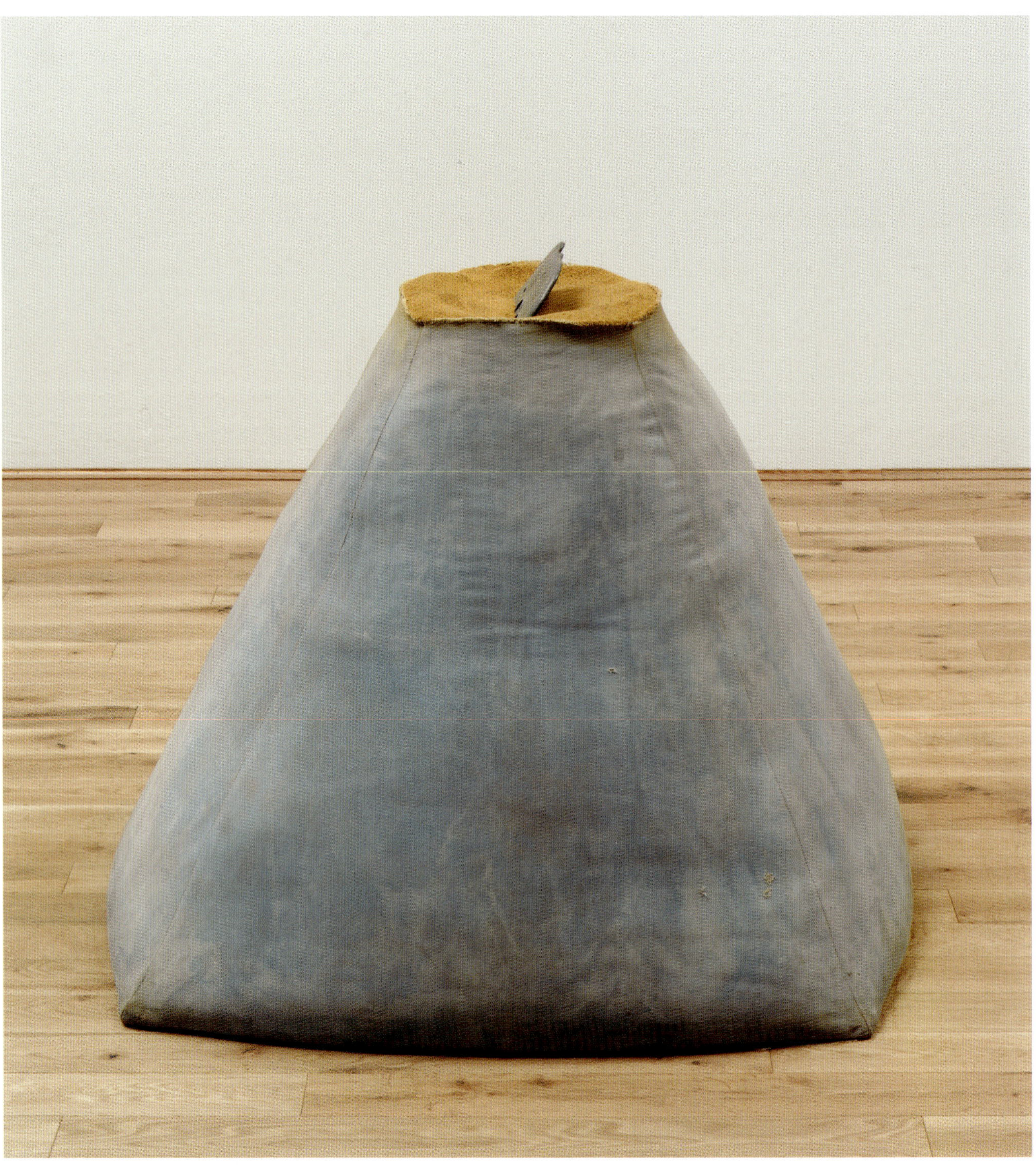

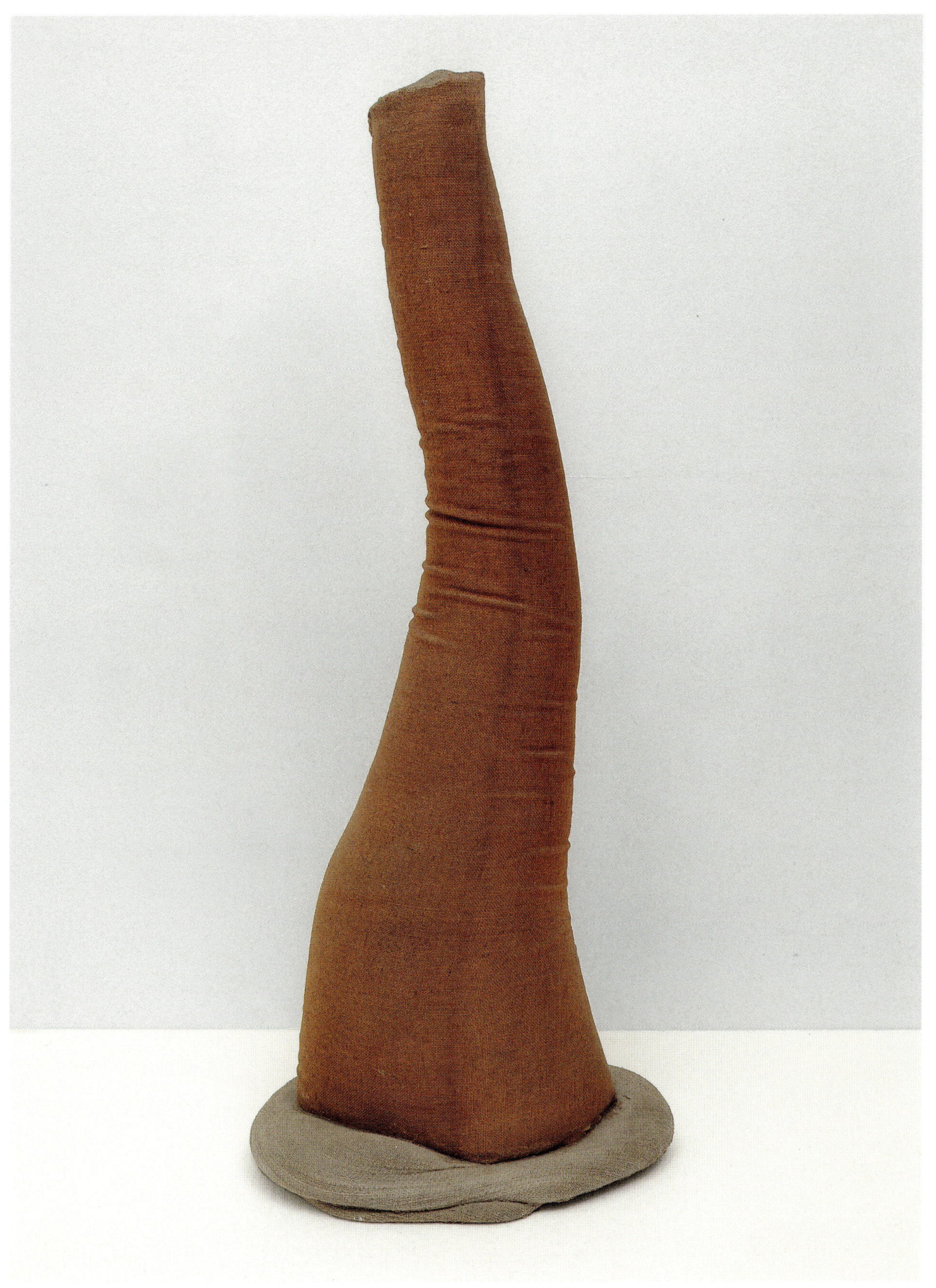

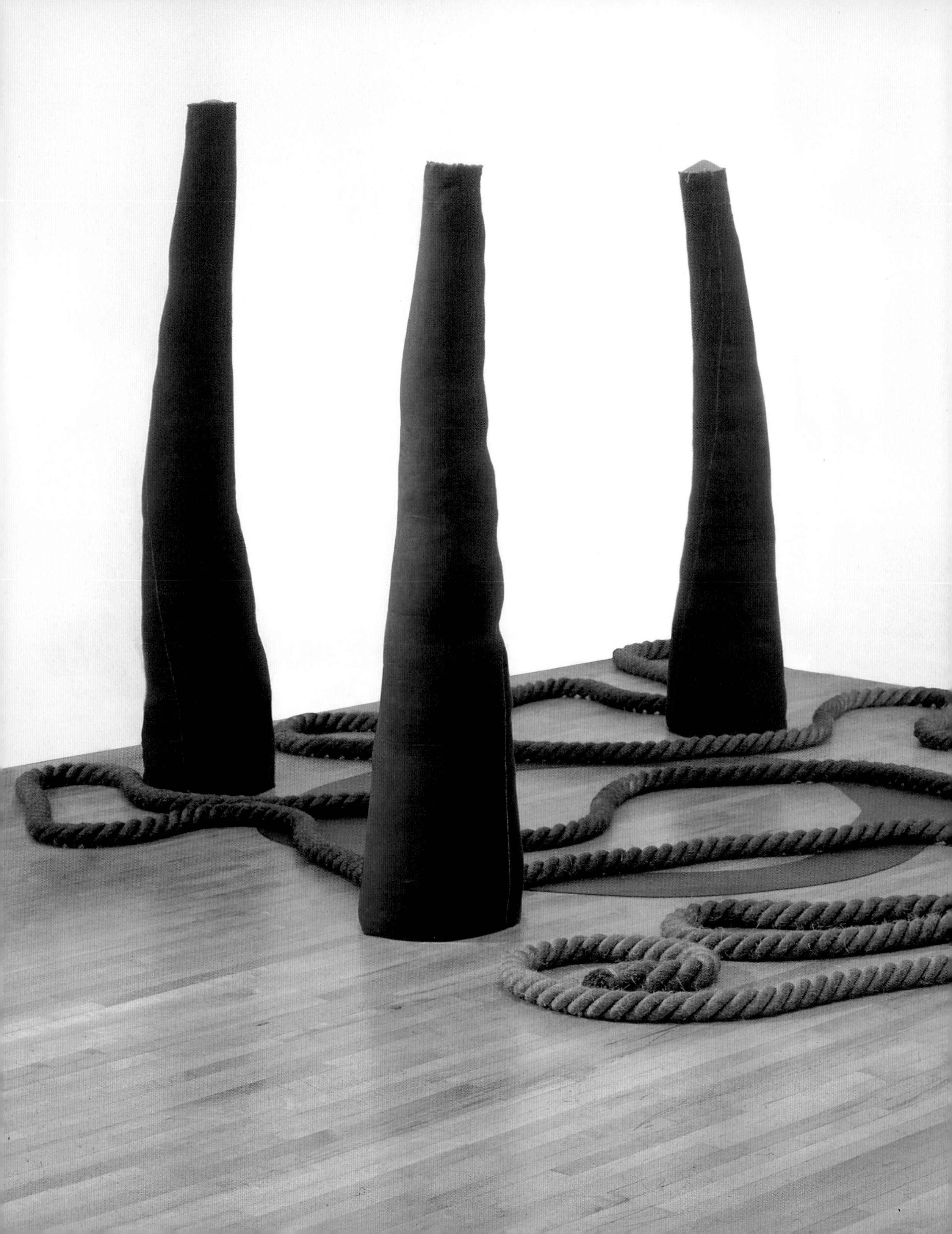

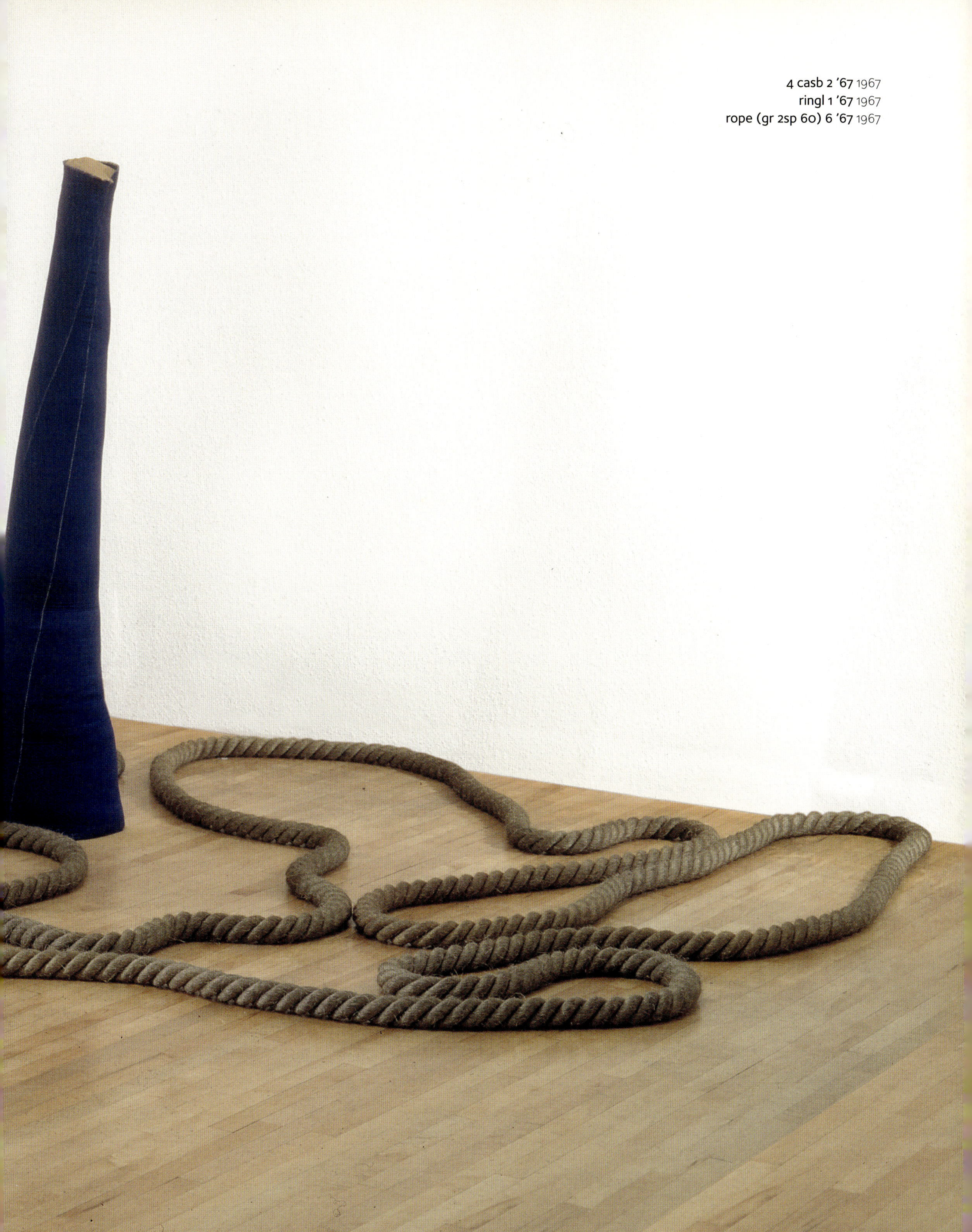

4 casb 2 '67 1967
ringl 1 '67 1967
rope (gr 2sp 60) 6 '67 1967

heap 4 1967   **line 3 '68** 1968

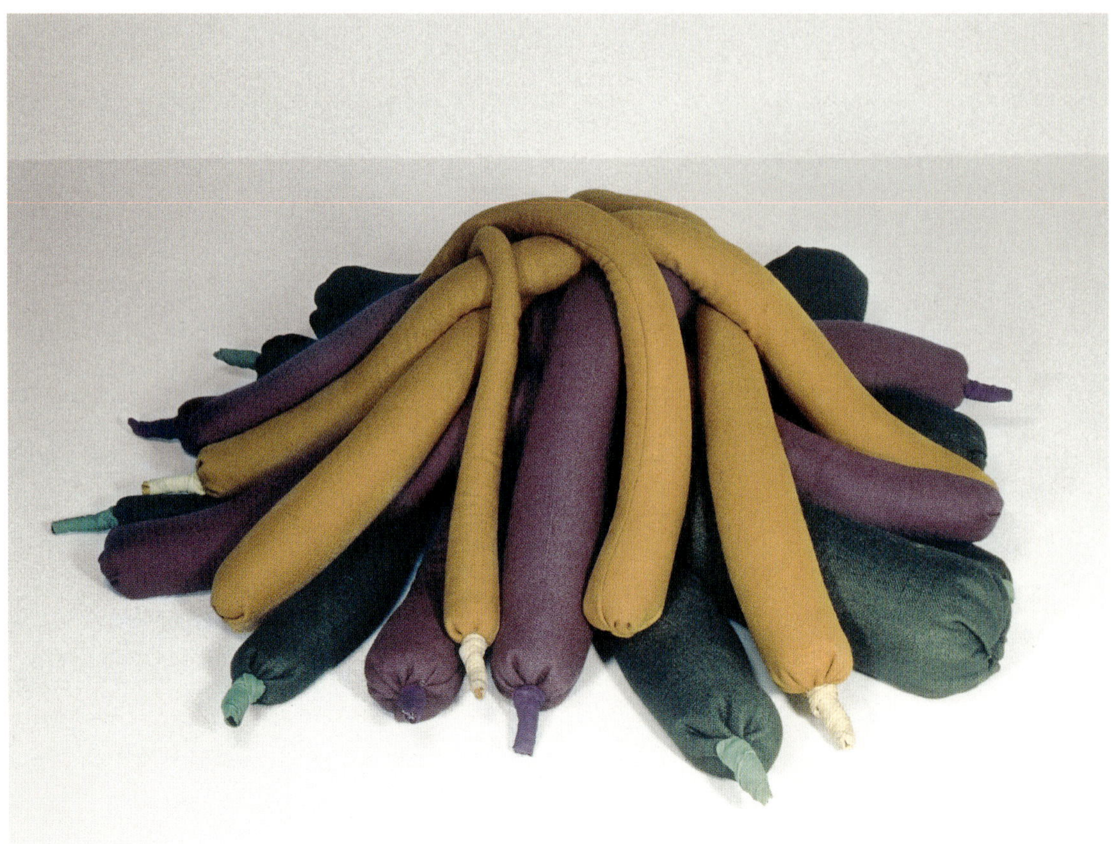

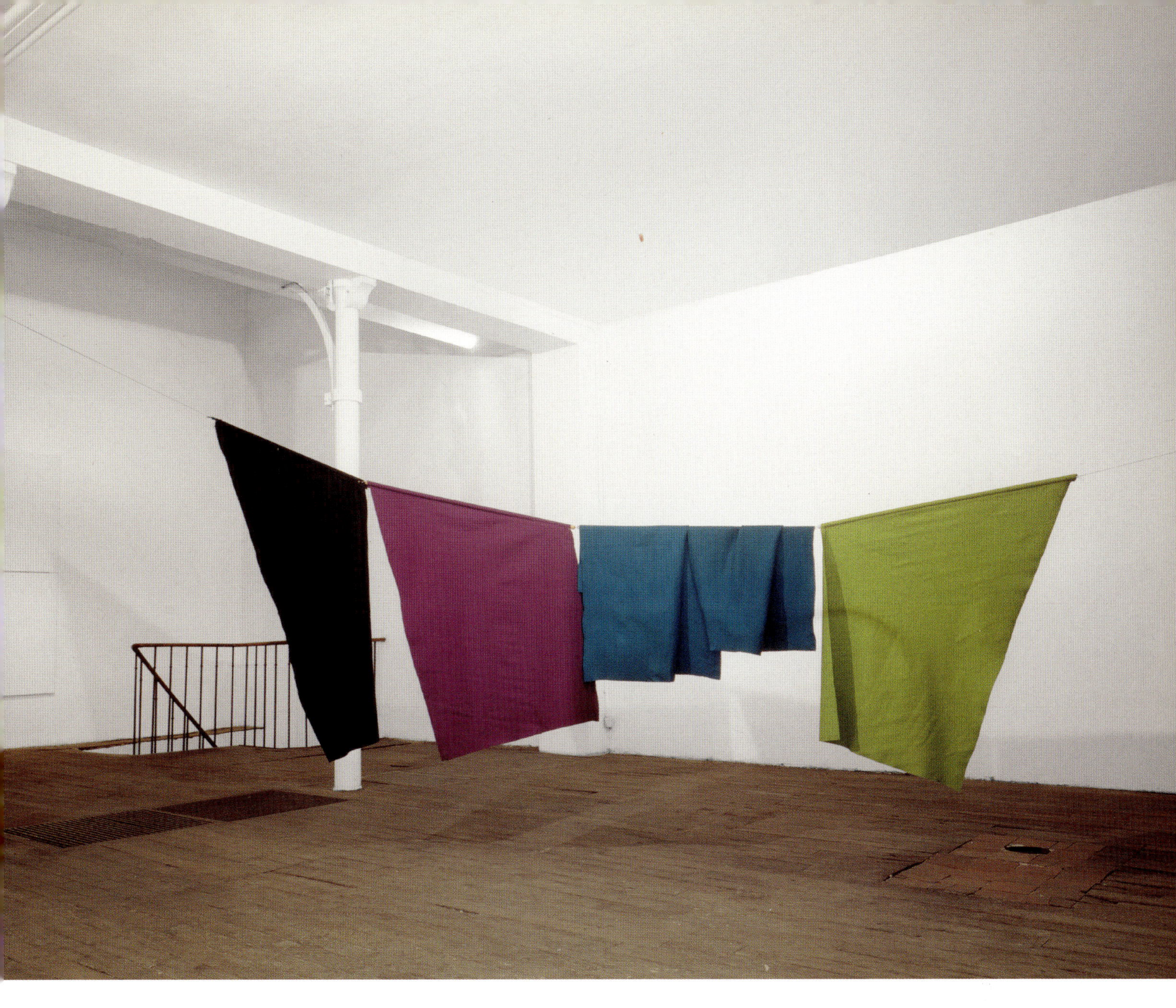

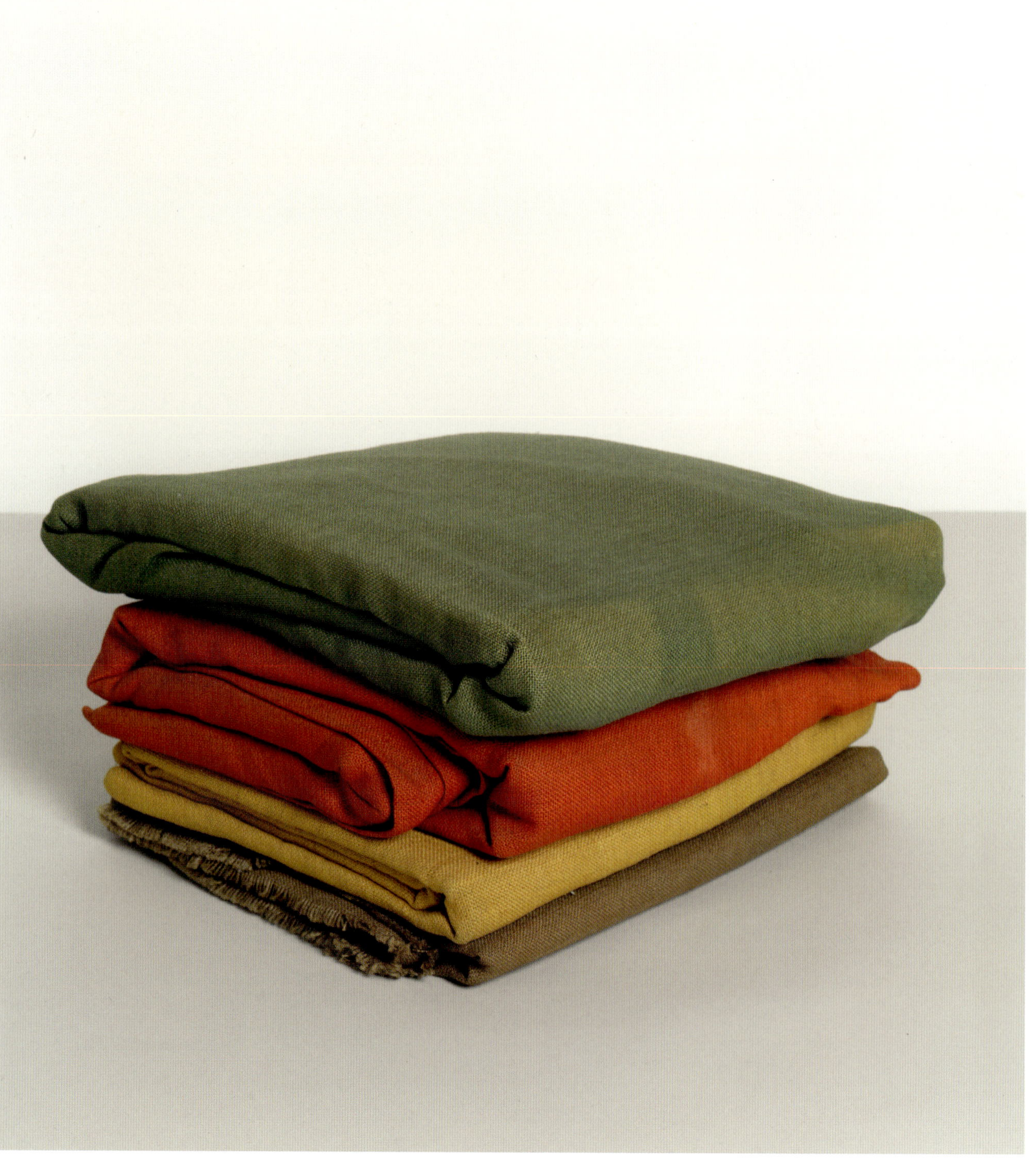

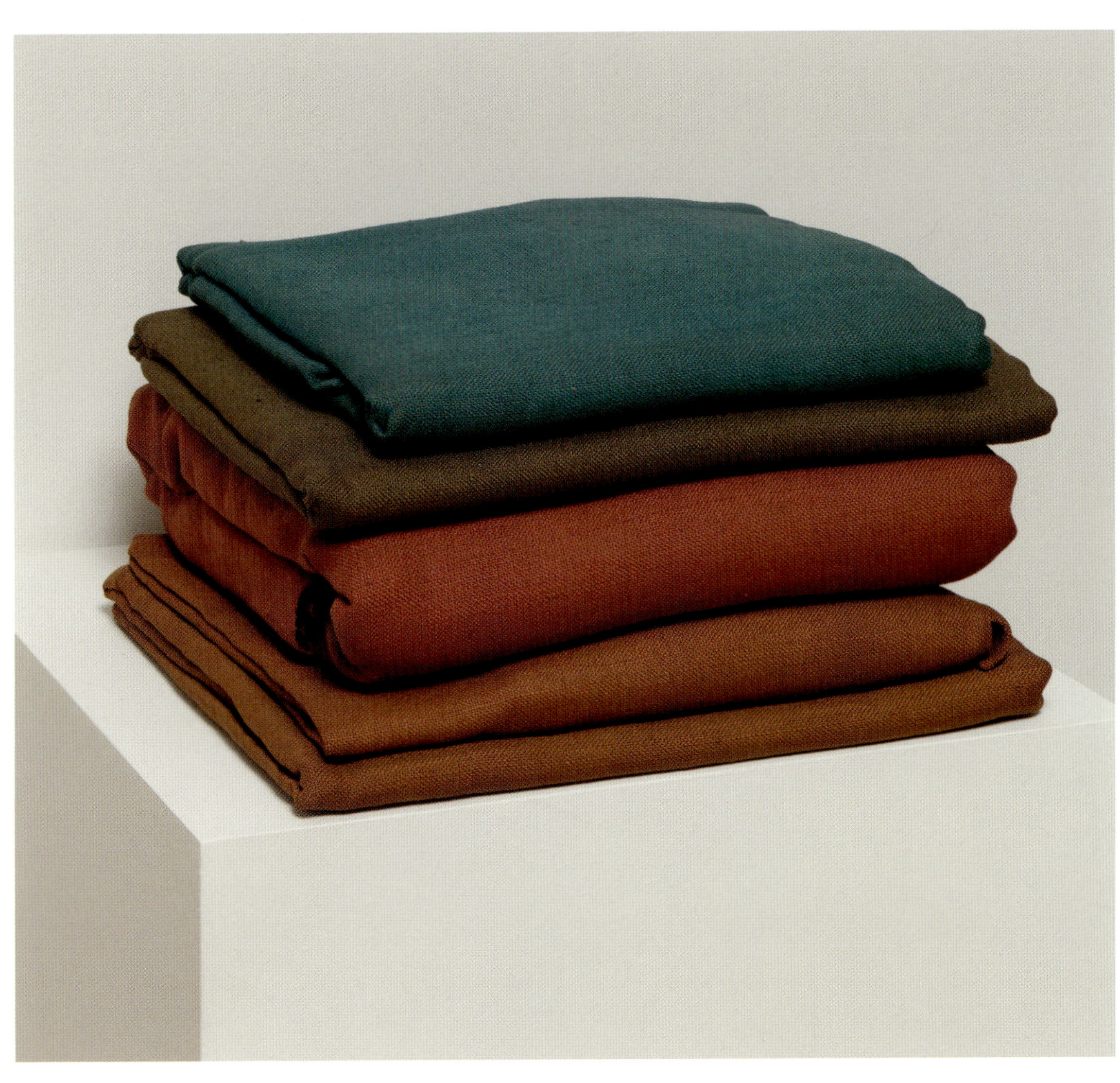

pile 1 '68 1968 **pile 3 '68** 1968/1985

bundle 2 '67 1967

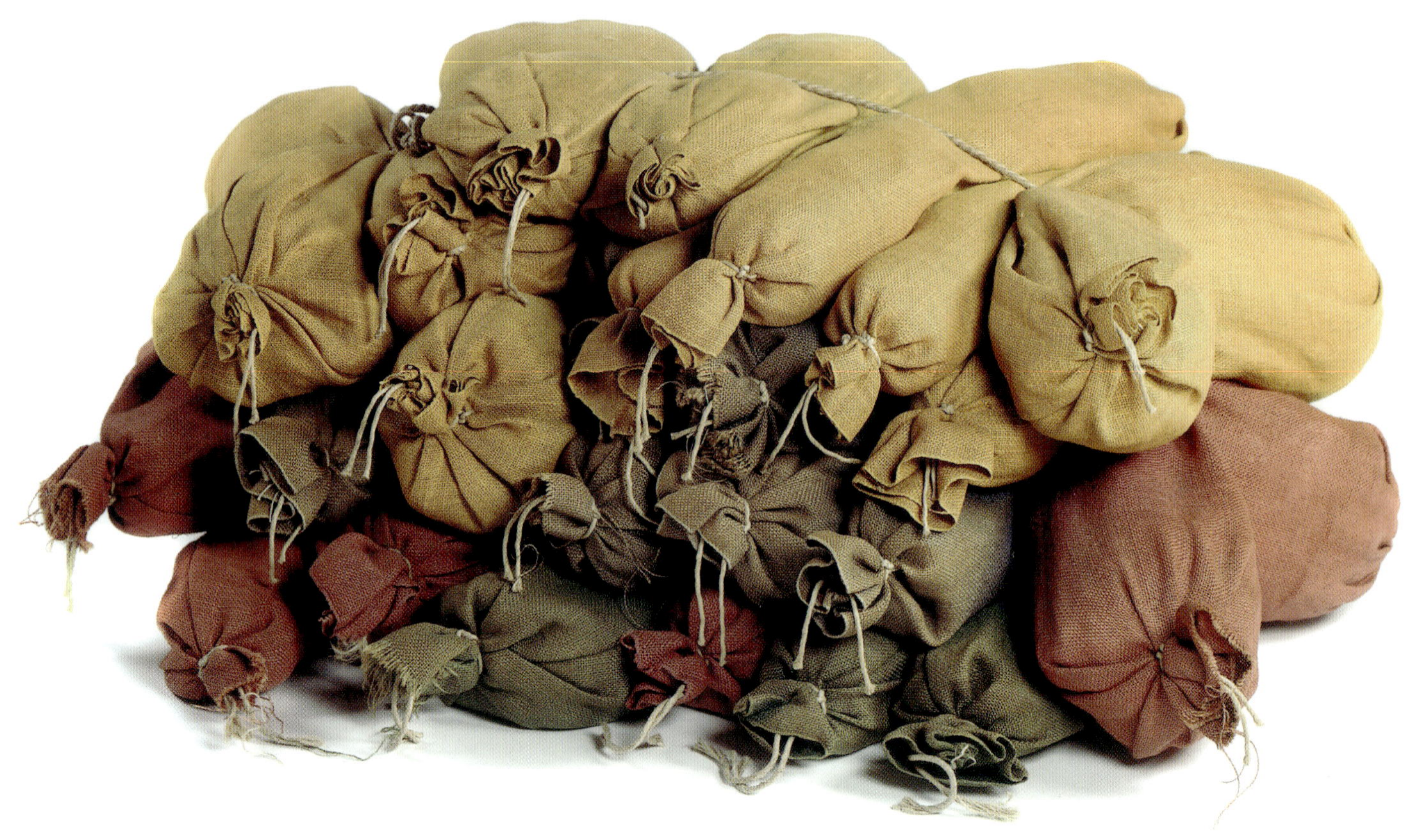

Beutelstuck (bundle) 1967

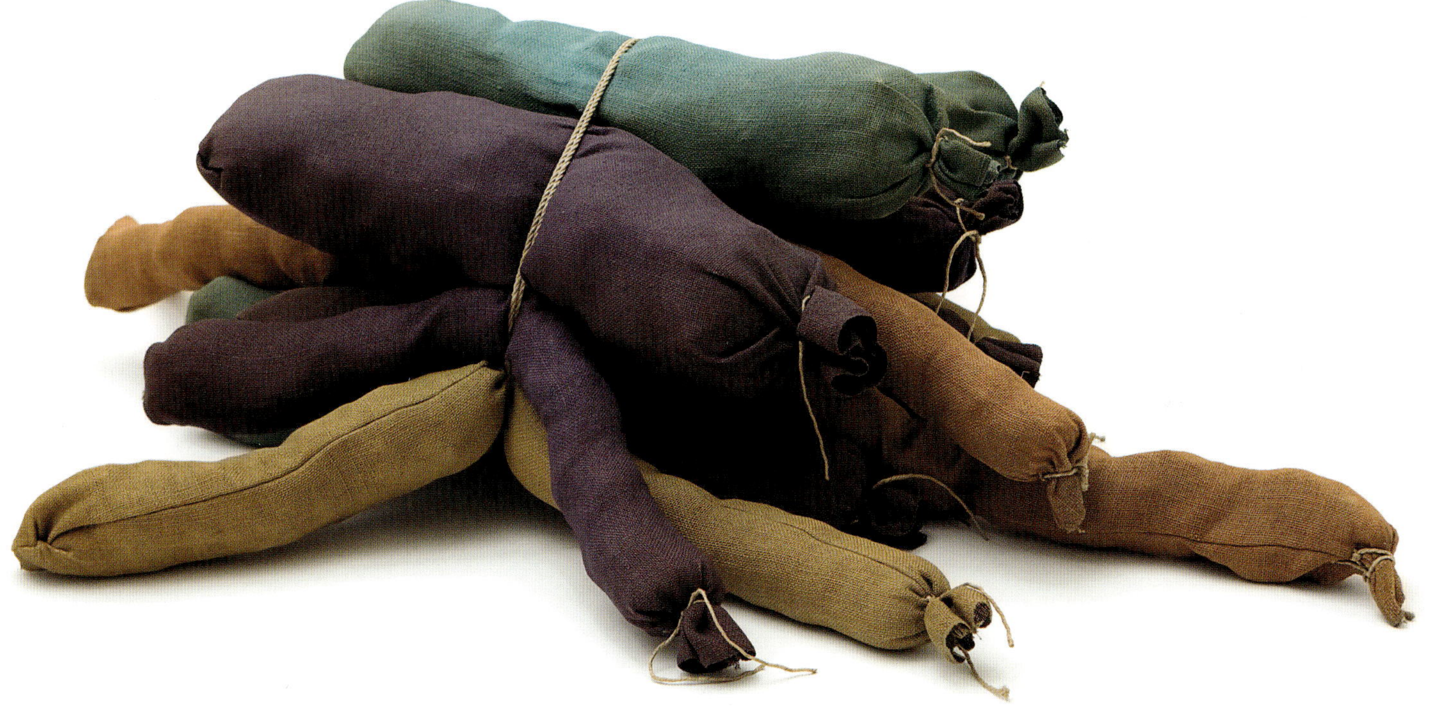

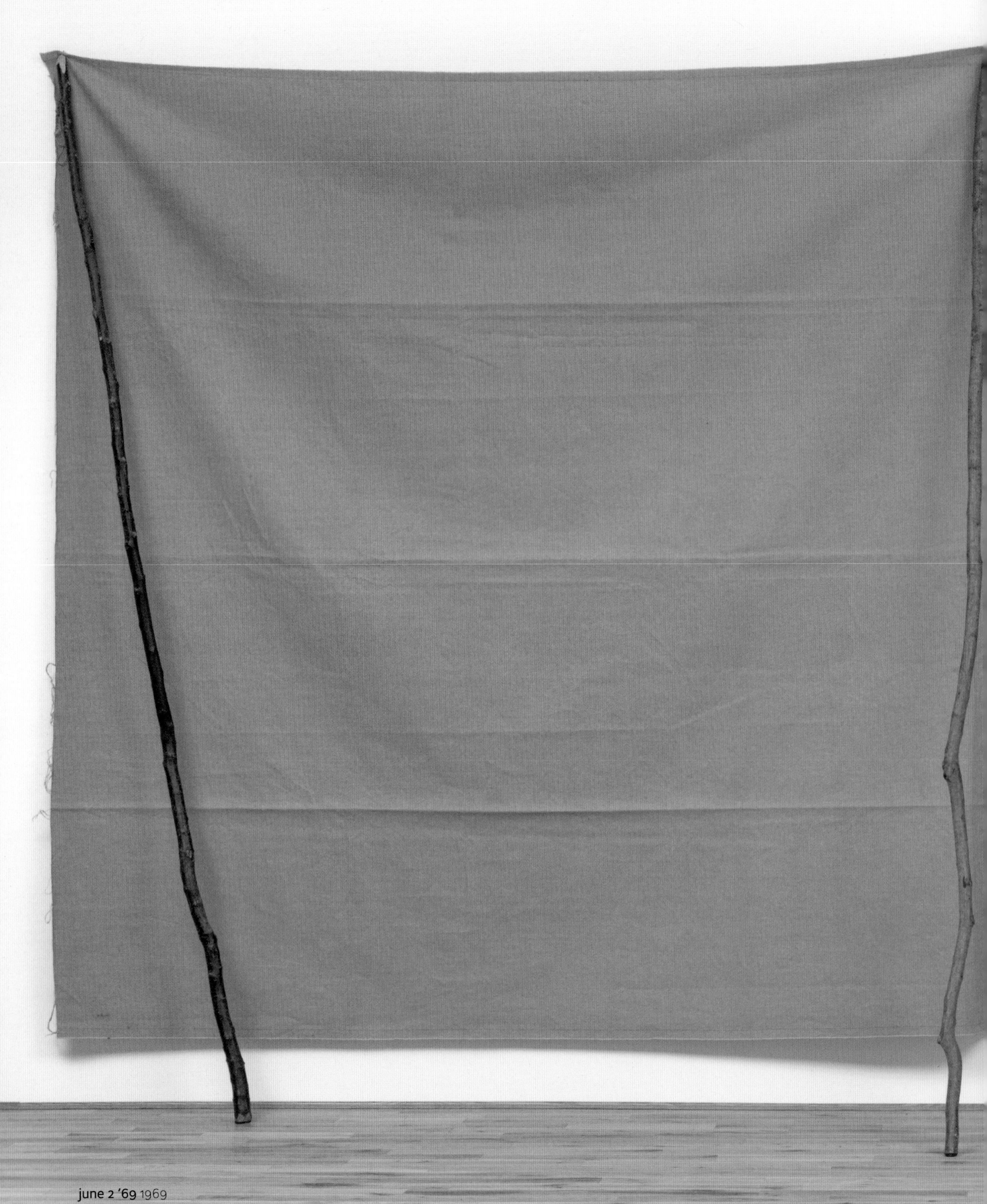

june 2 '69 1969

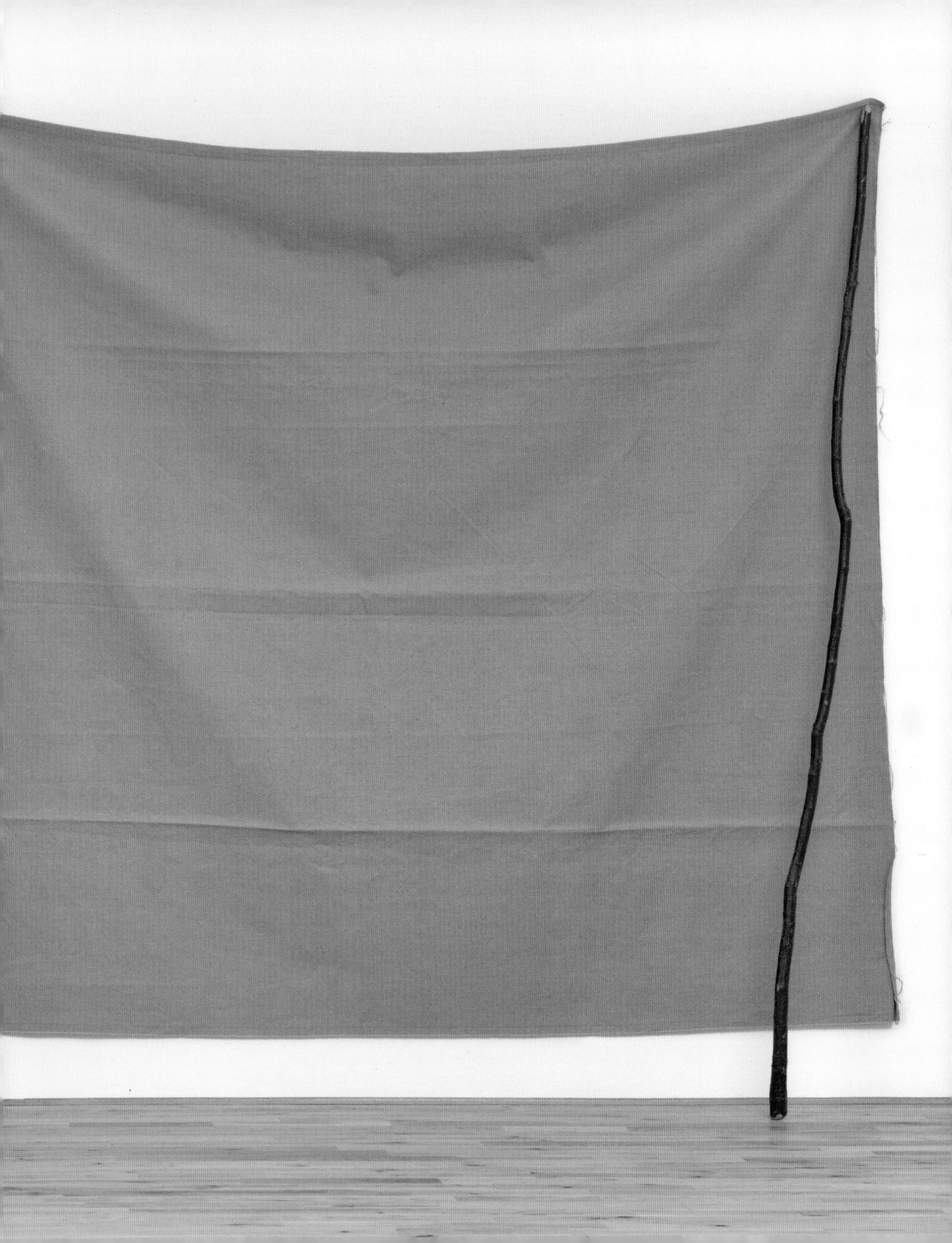

canvas 3 '67 1967

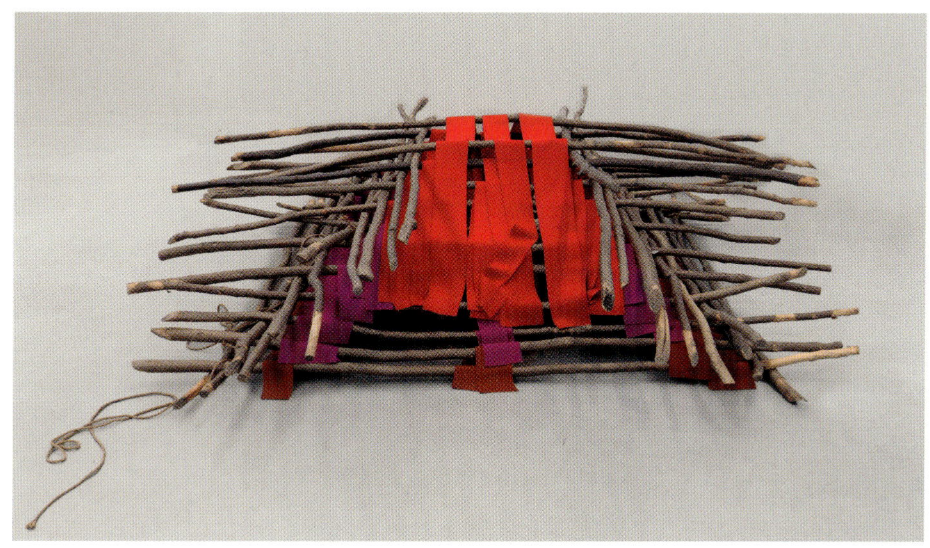

no. 5 '71 1971

Untitled 1970

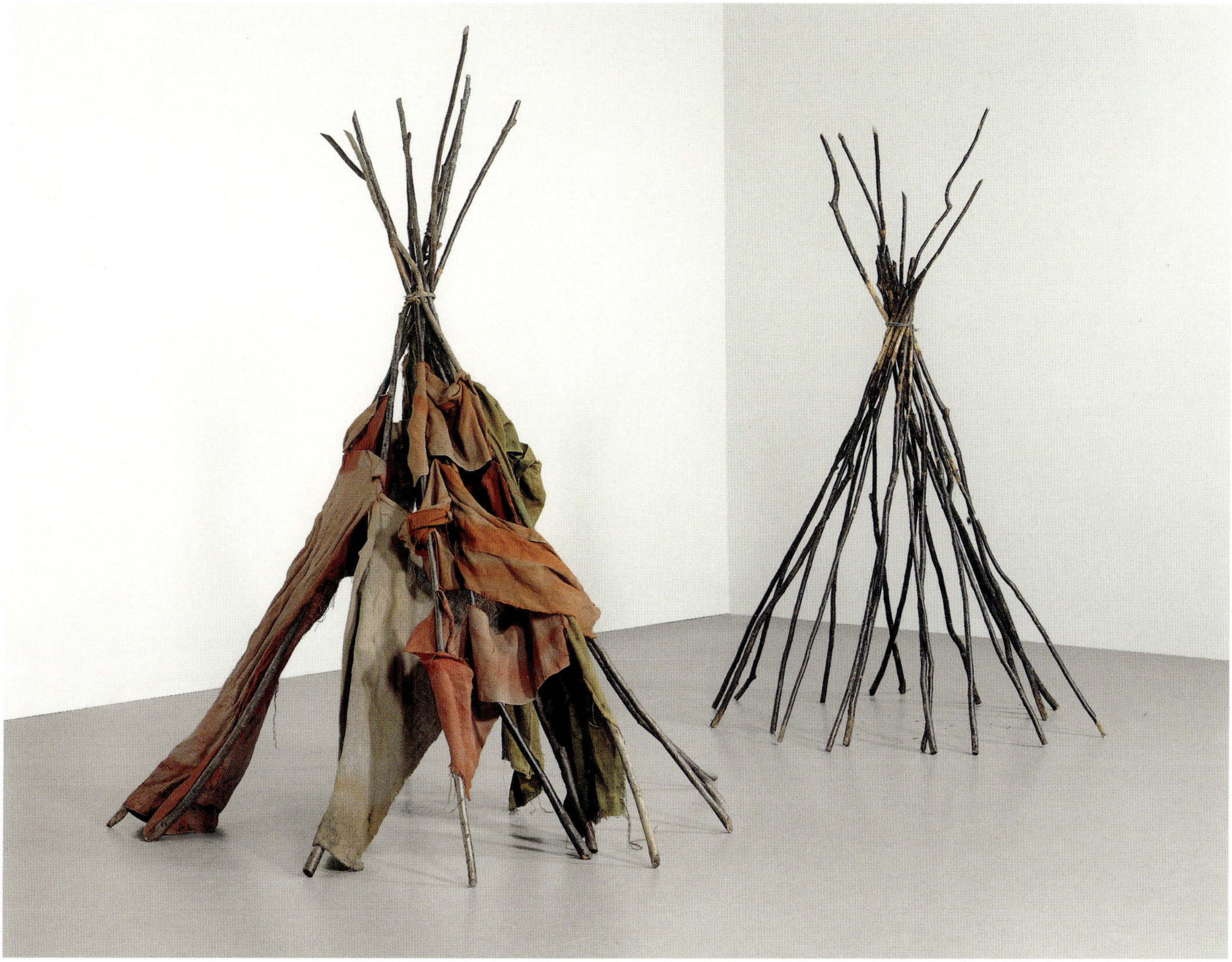

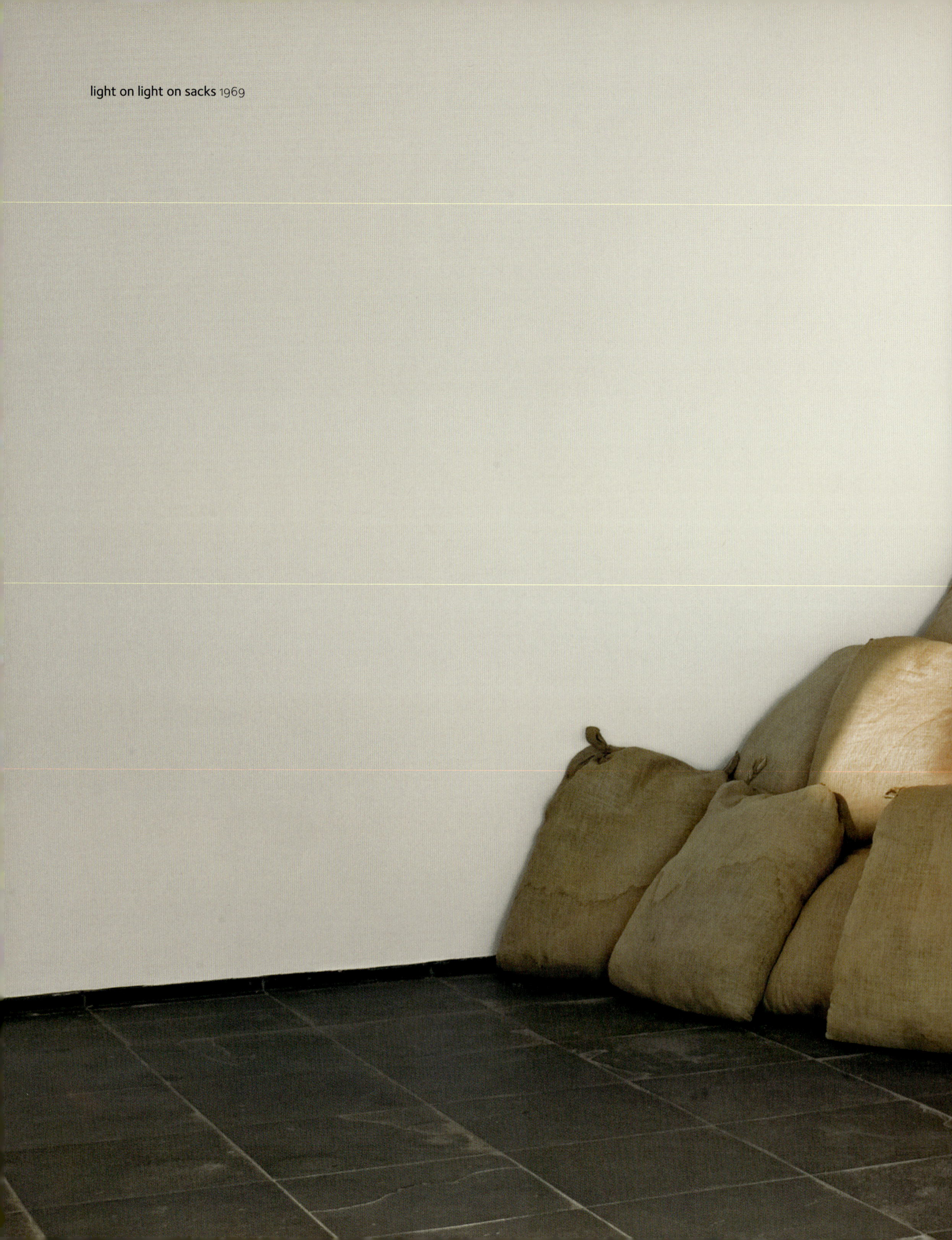

light on light on sacks 1969

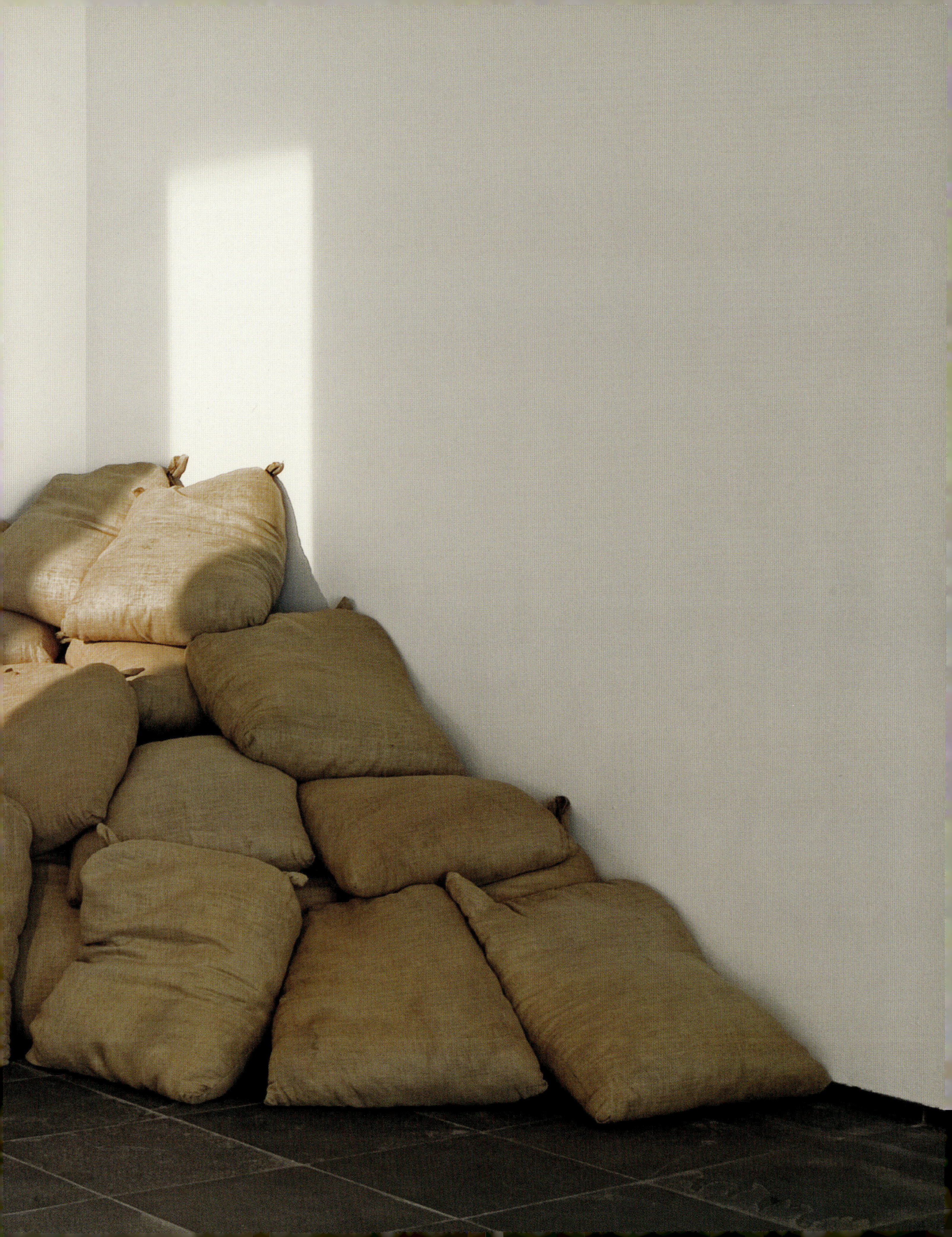

Untitled once 1973

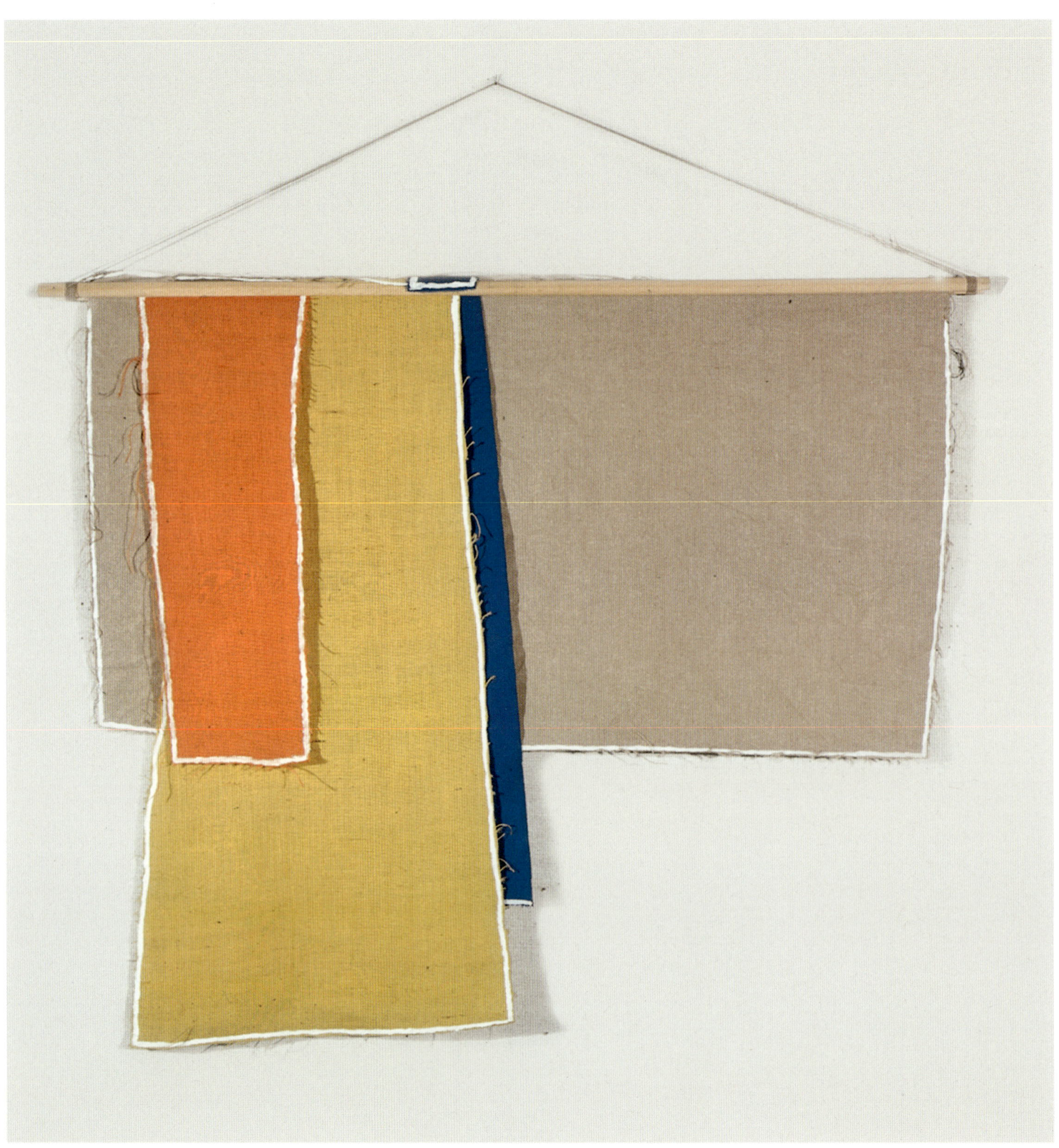

Double Eights 1976

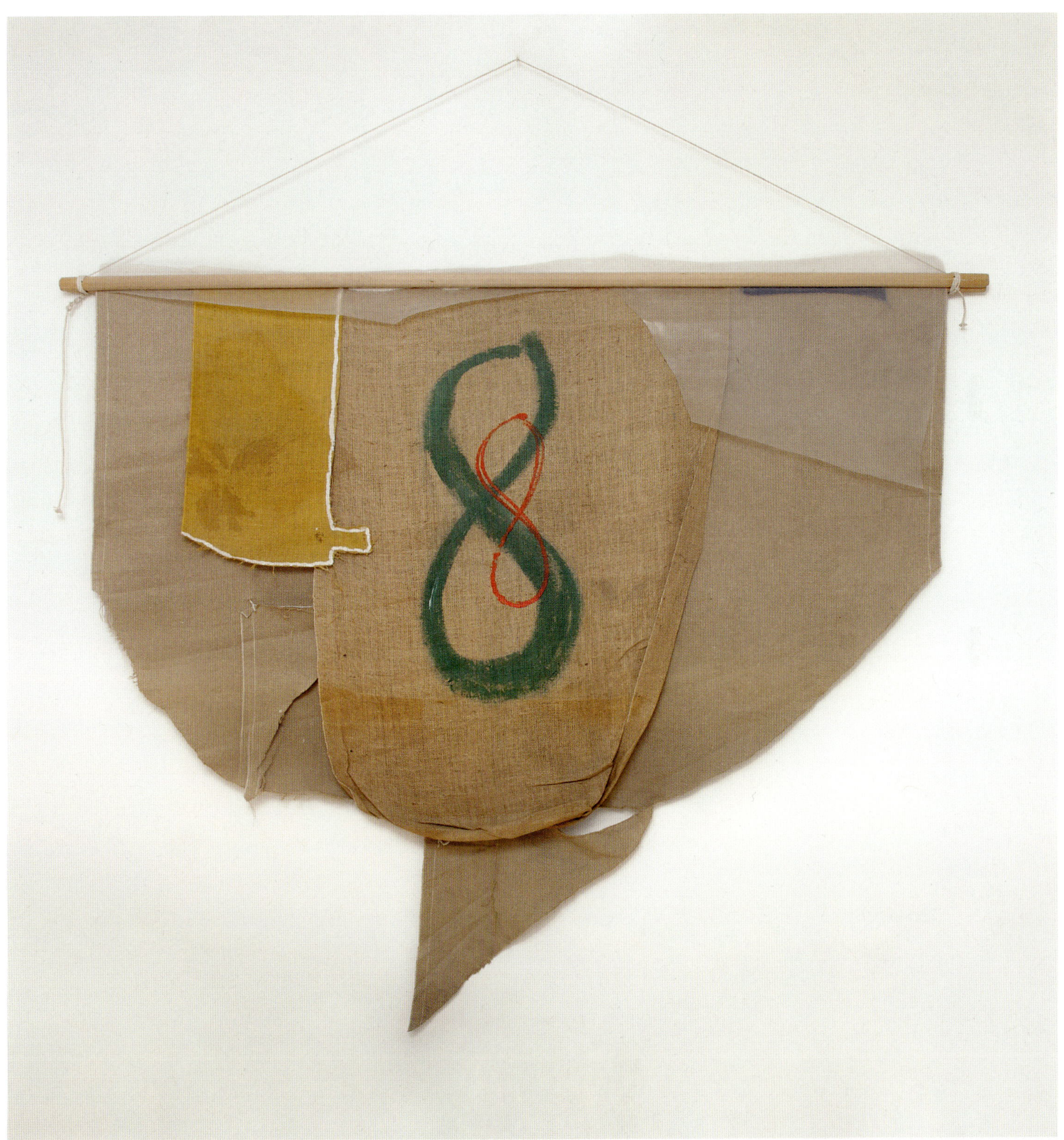

② **feb '73** 1973 ③ **feb '73** 1973

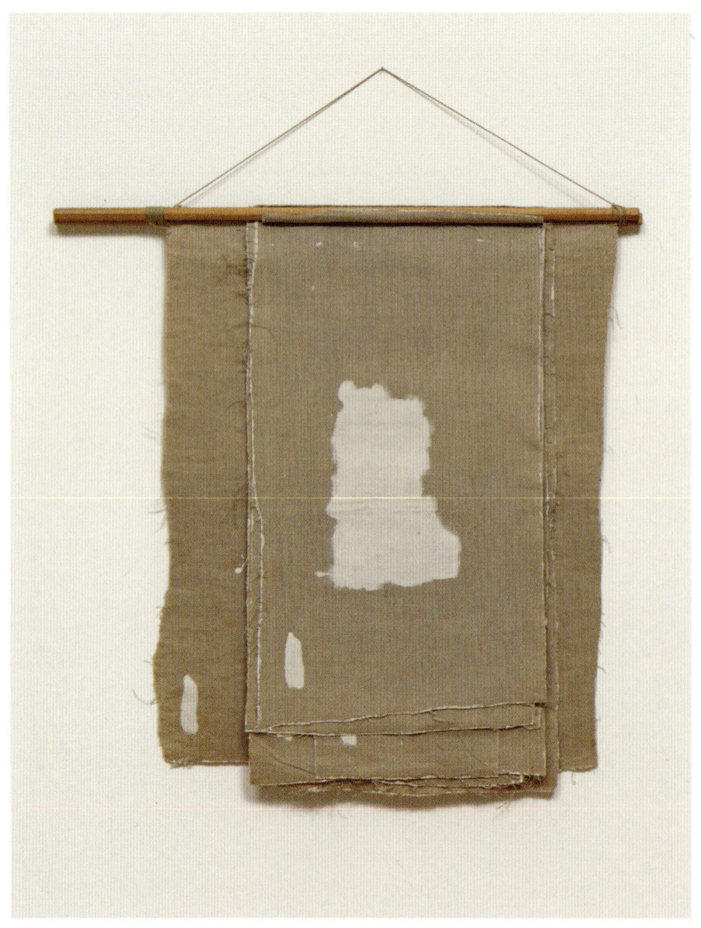

stand '76 1976

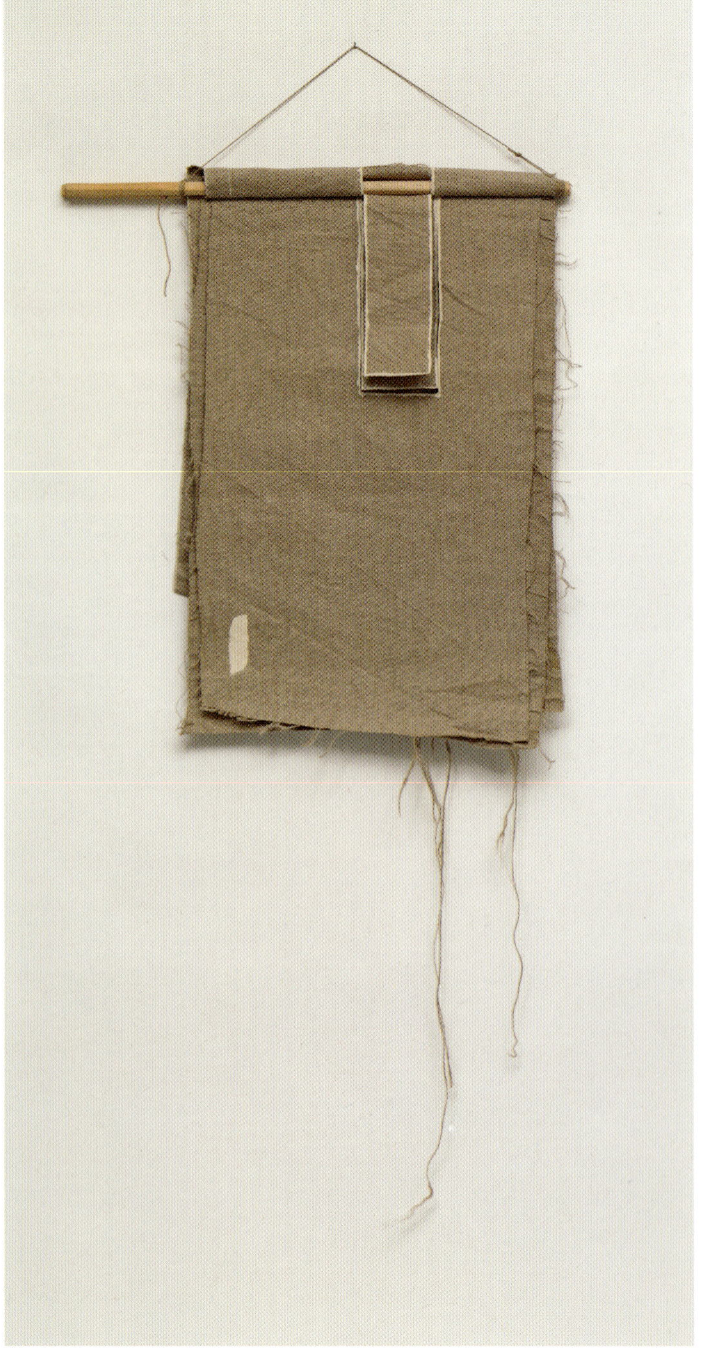

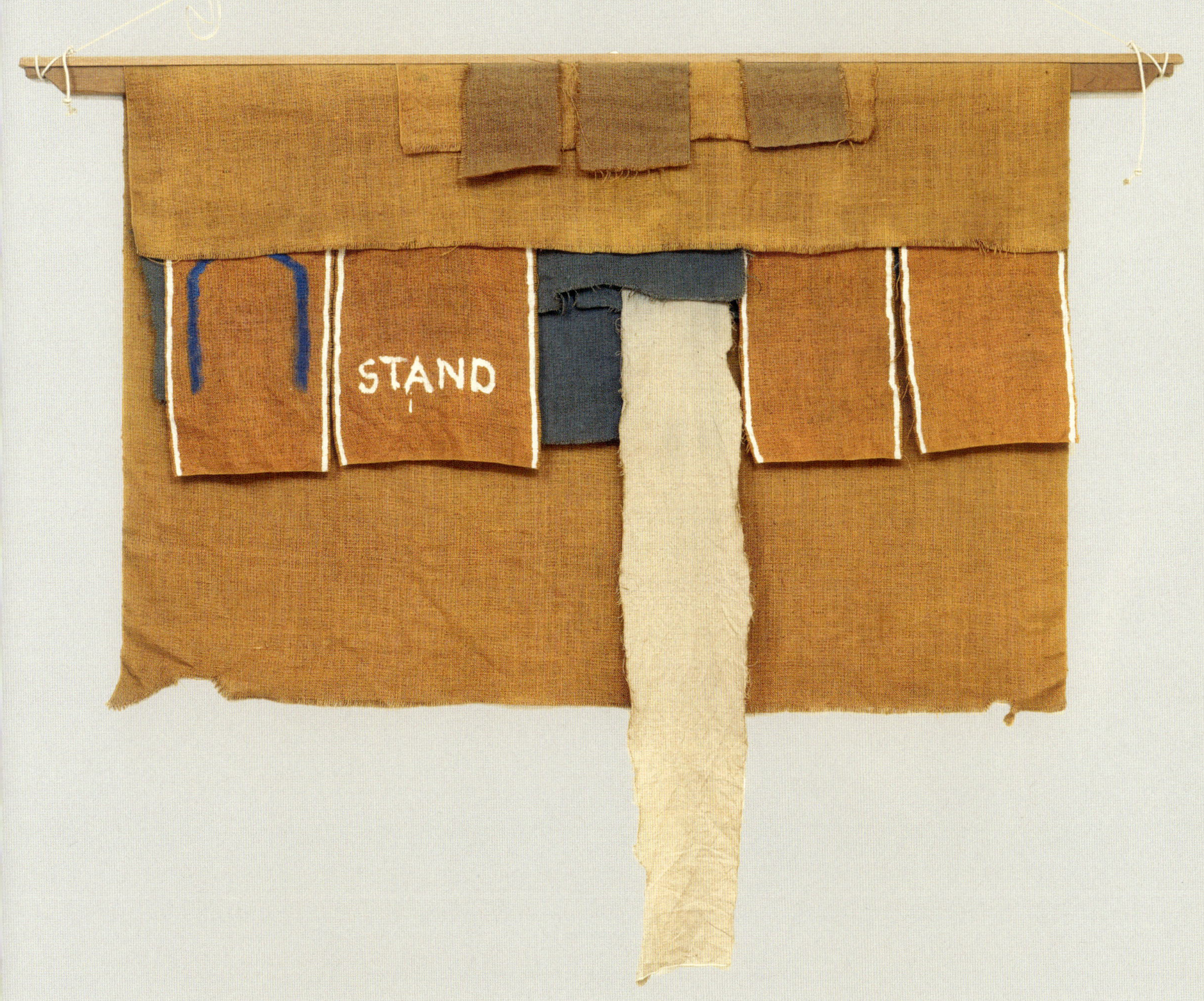
STAND

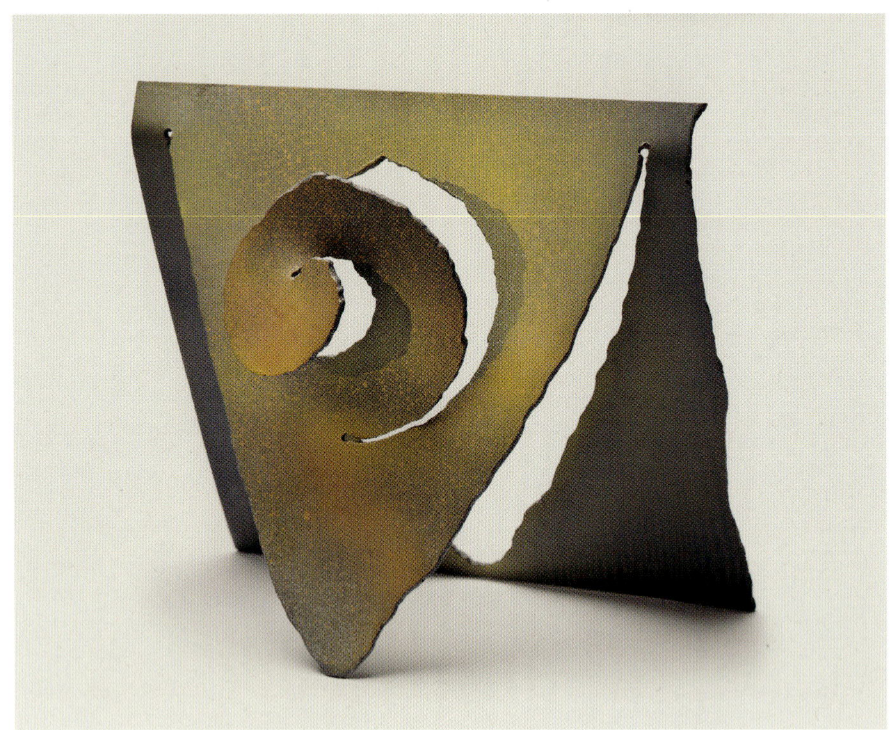

VII 78 the corn's up 1978

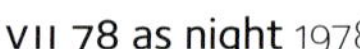

VII 78 as night 1978

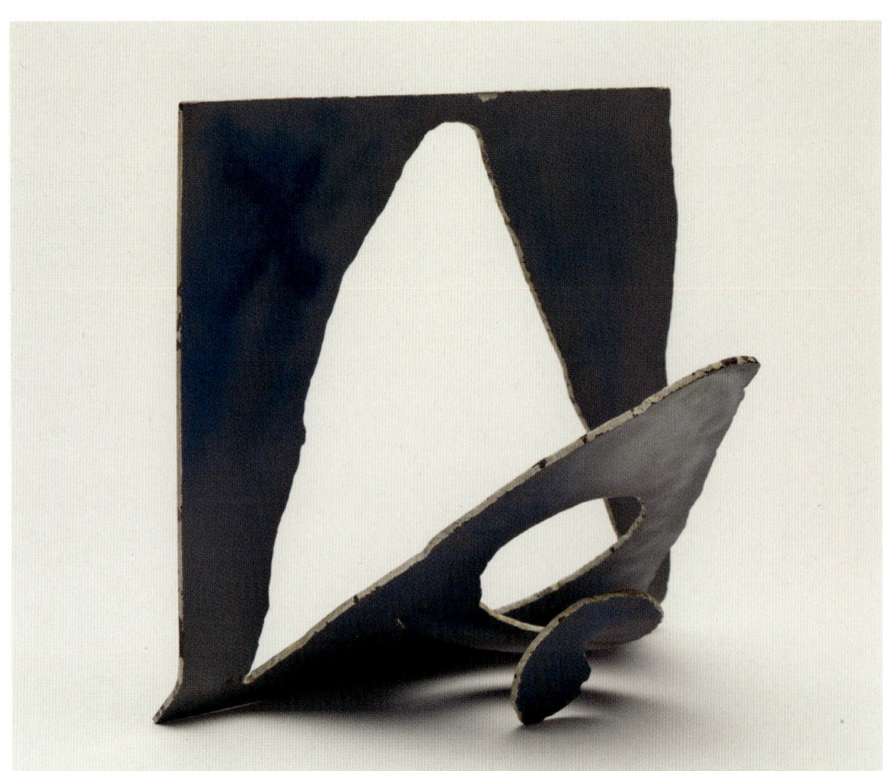

VII 78 moon thatch 1978

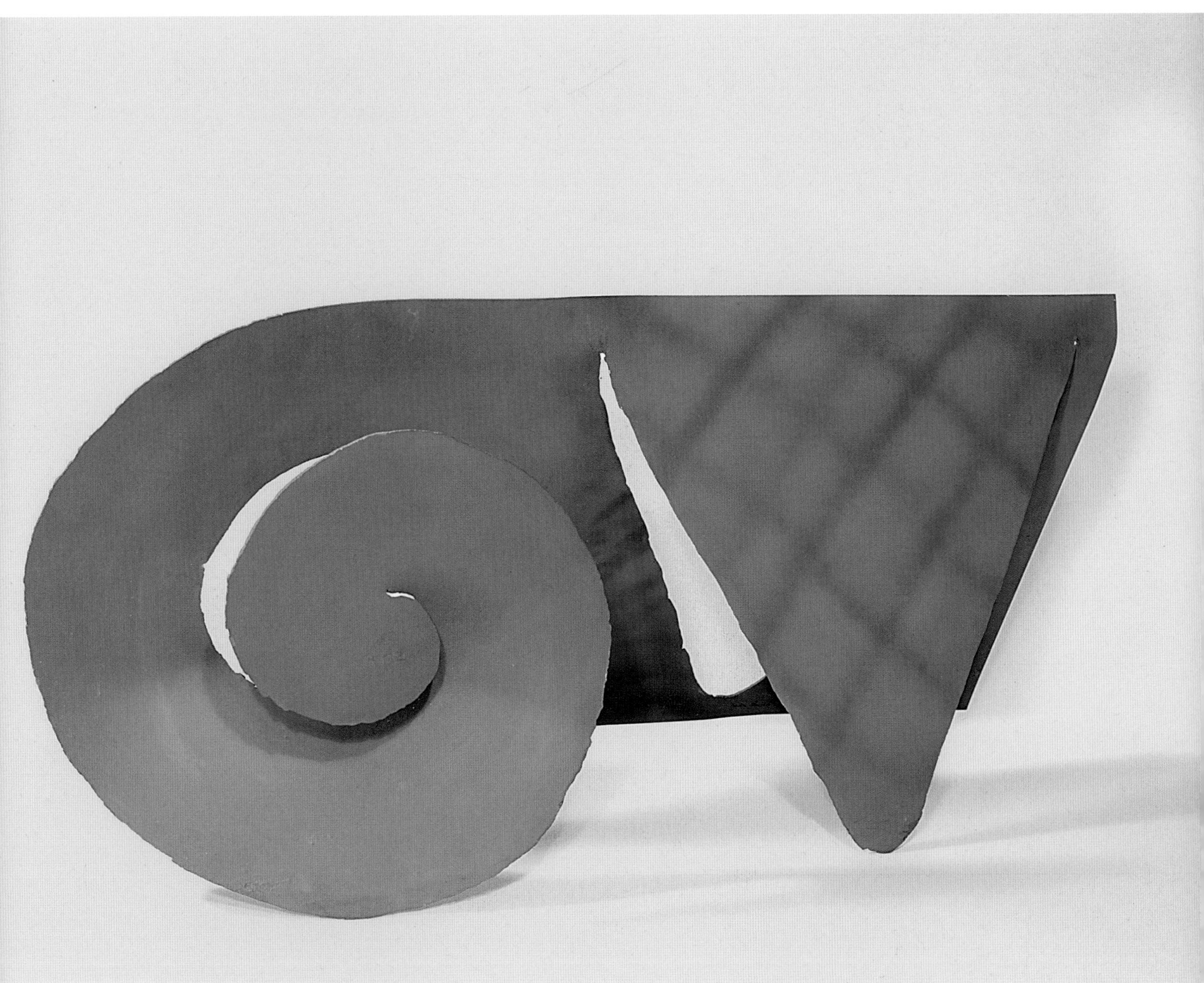

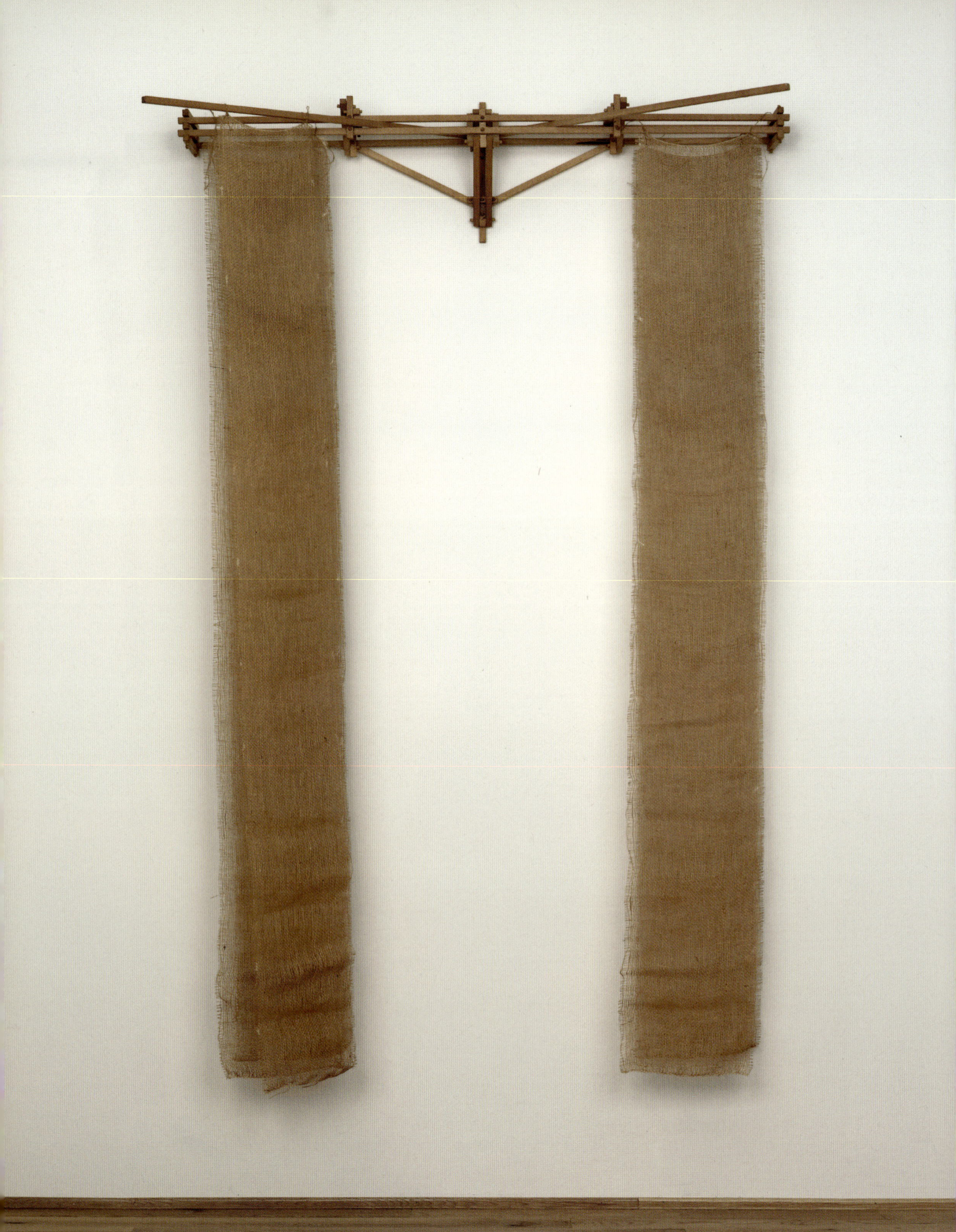

untitled I 1972

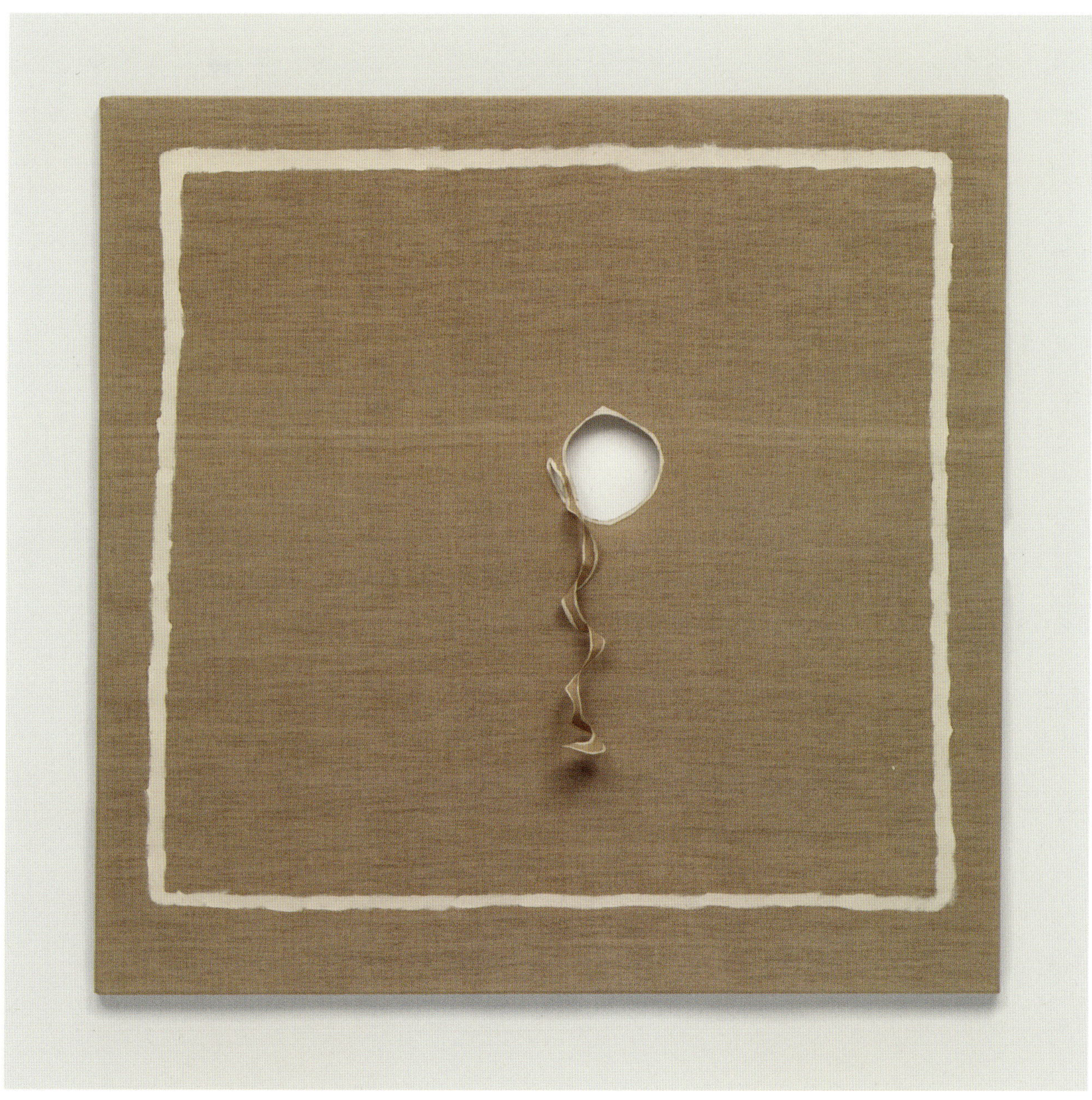

flaming red 1975

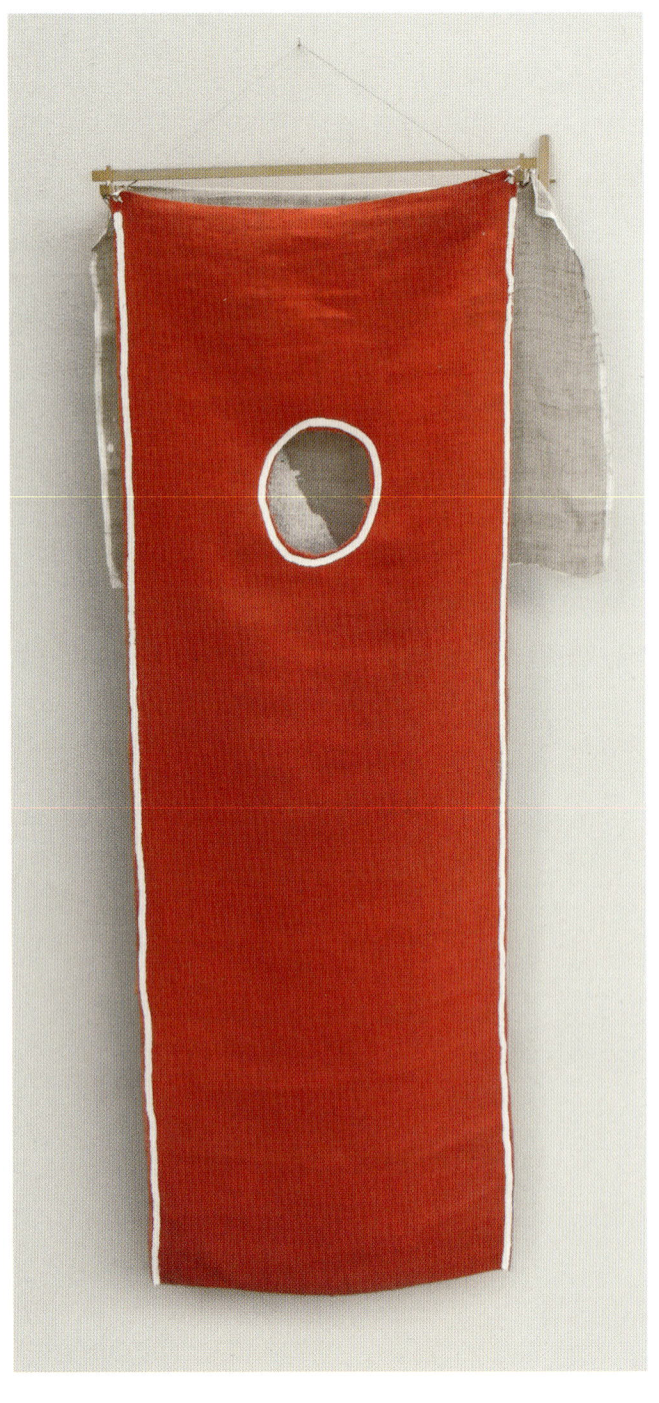

untitled light blue 2 '79 1979

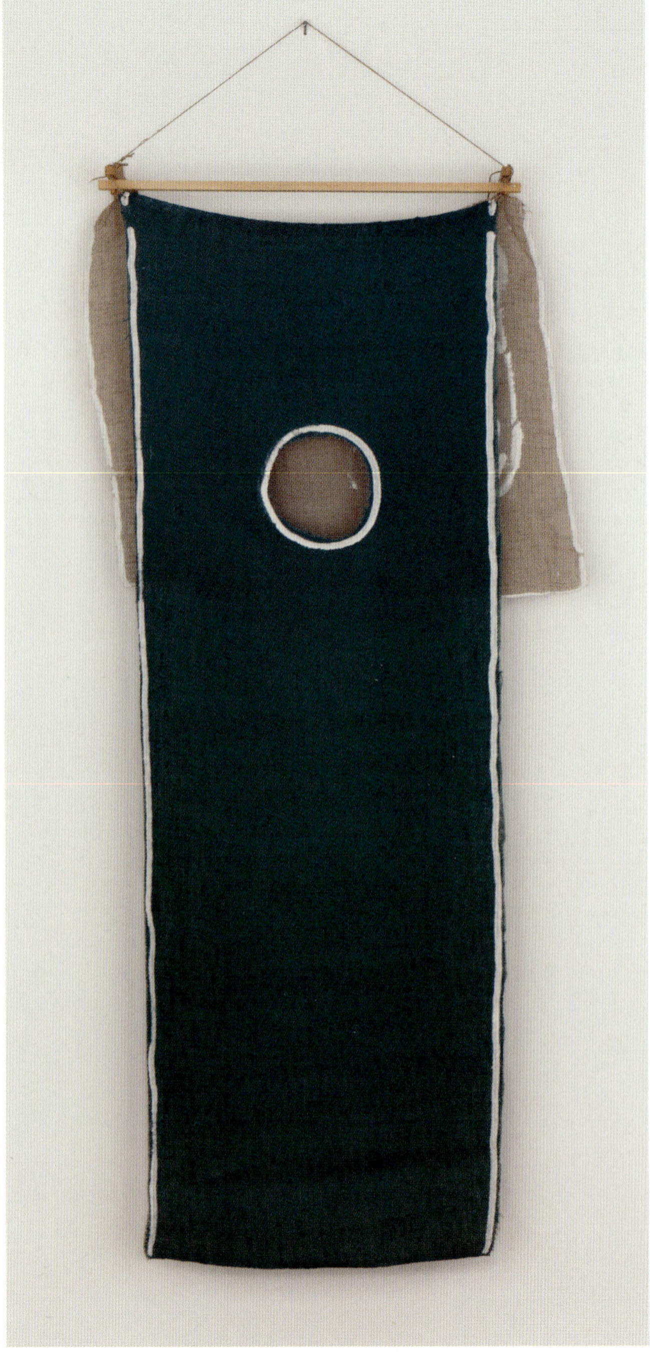

and then among Celts N.W. '77 1977

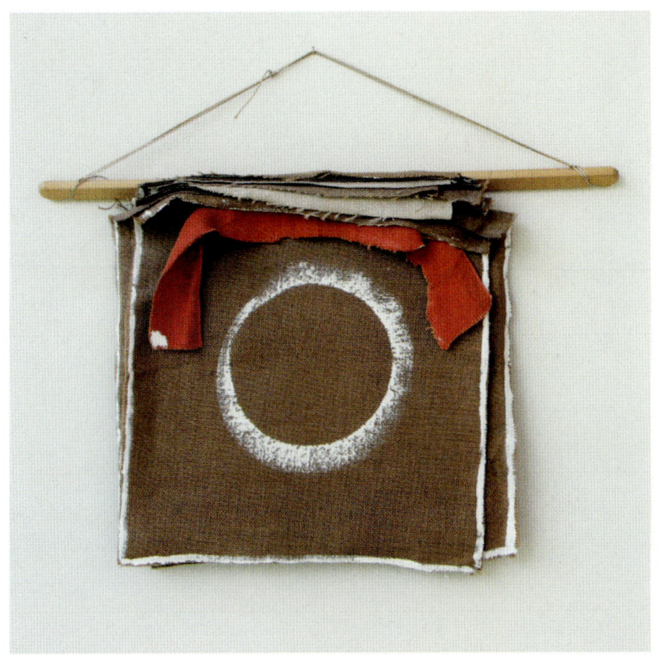

and then among Celts N. '77 1977

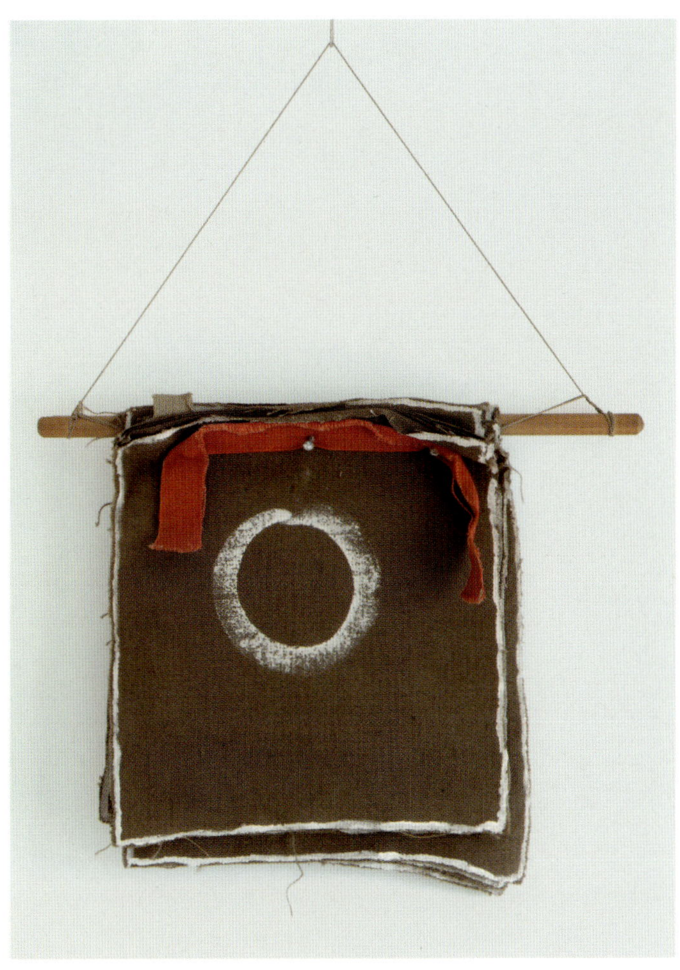

Bye Bye the Elephant 1980 a nose in repose 1977–9

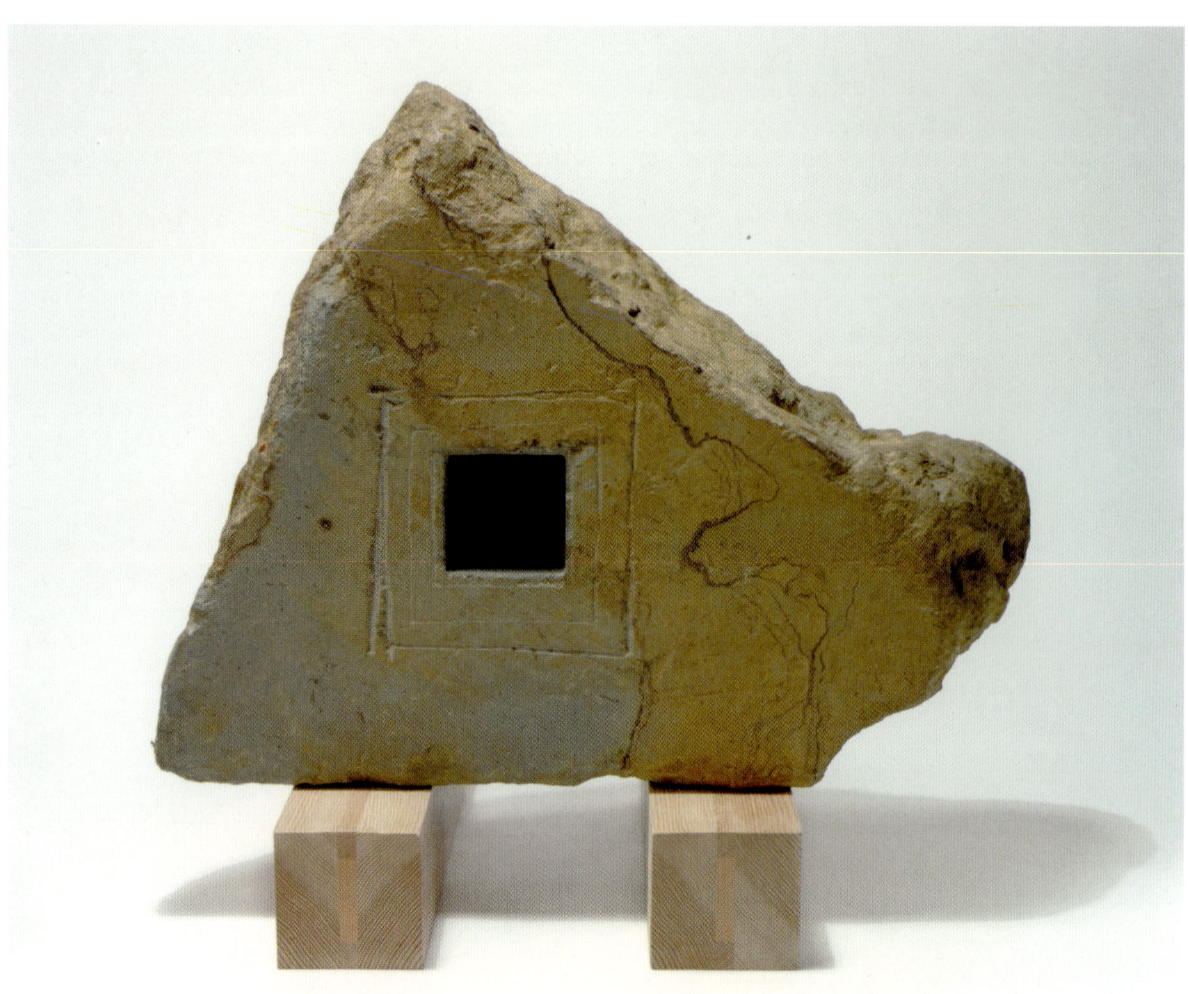

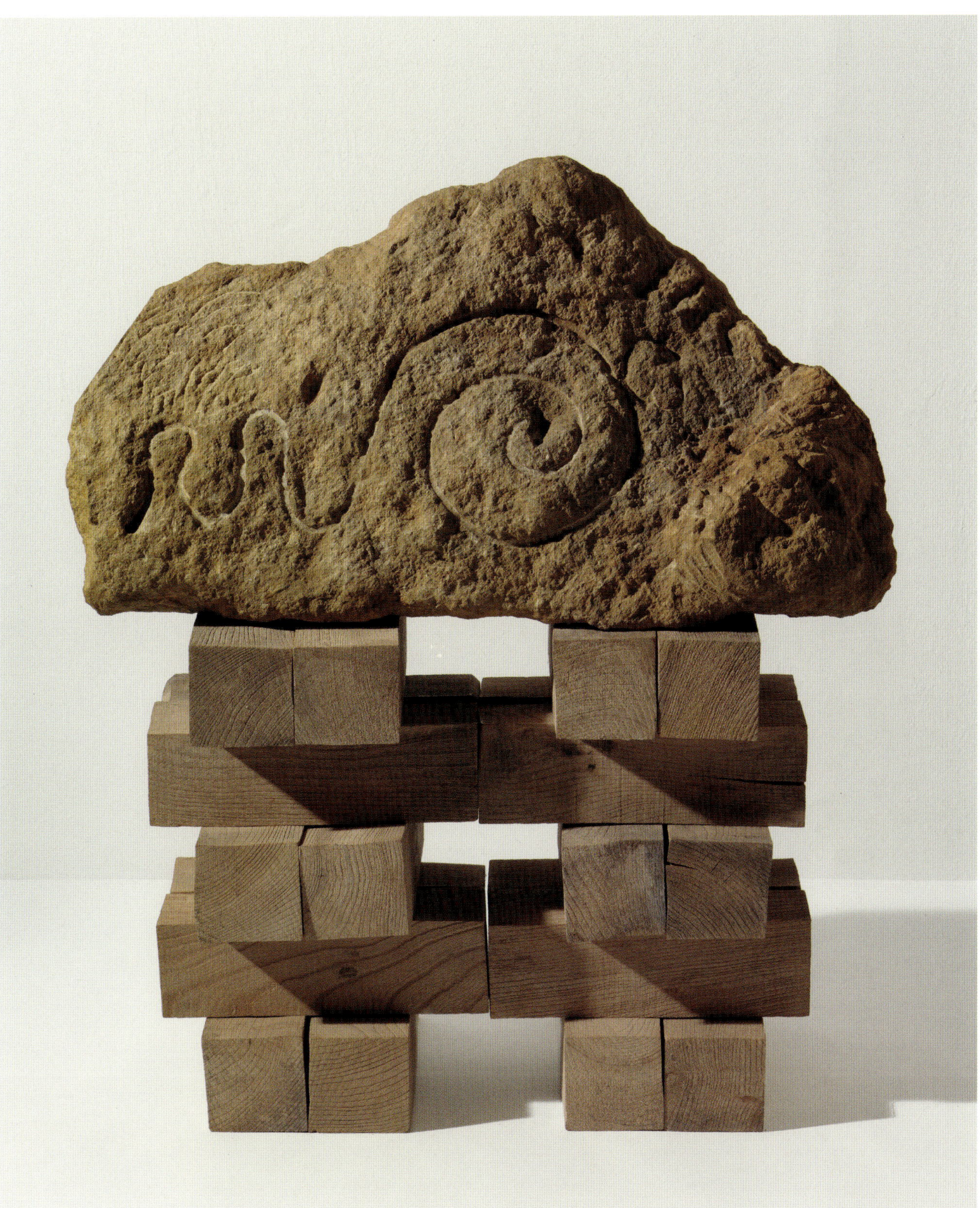

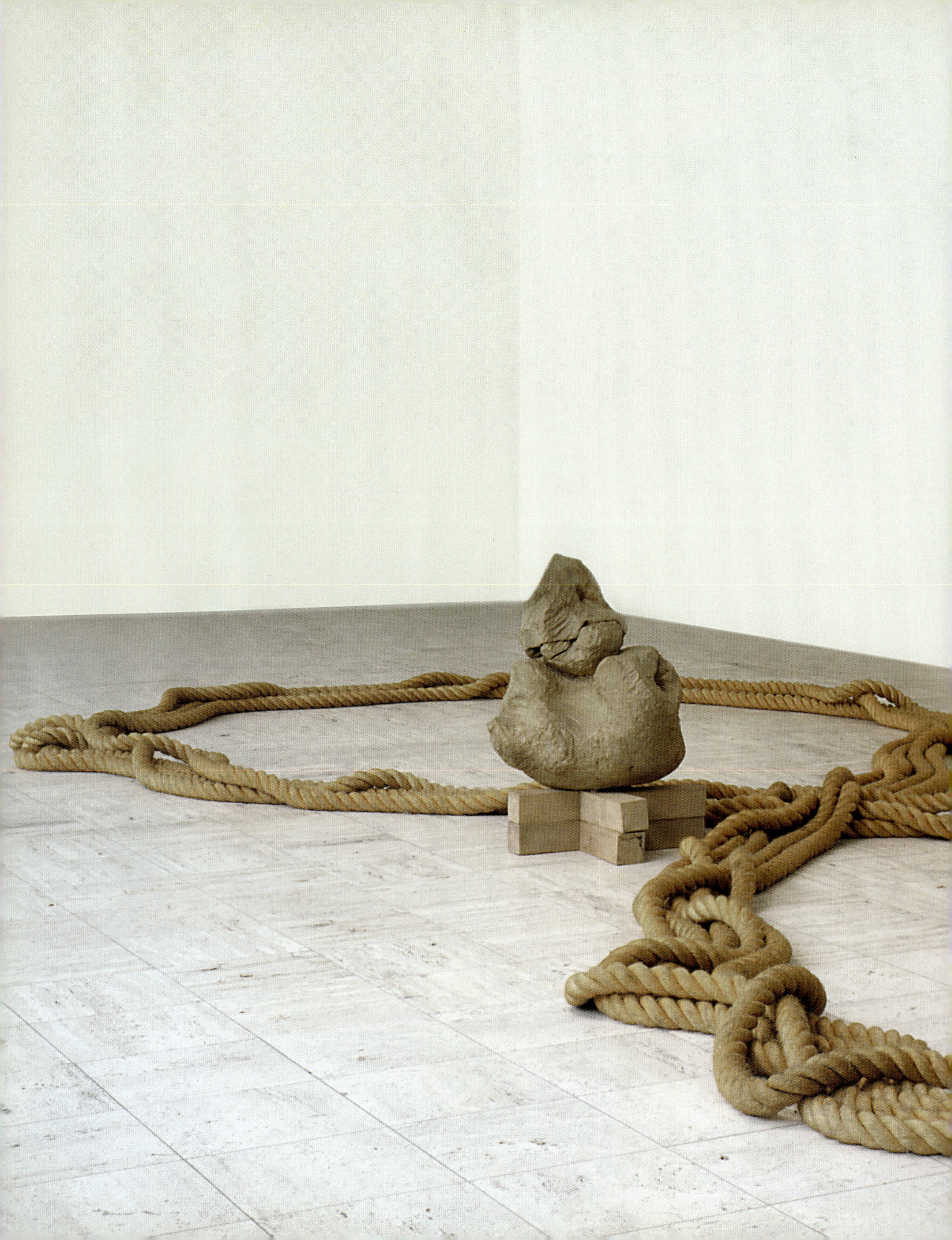

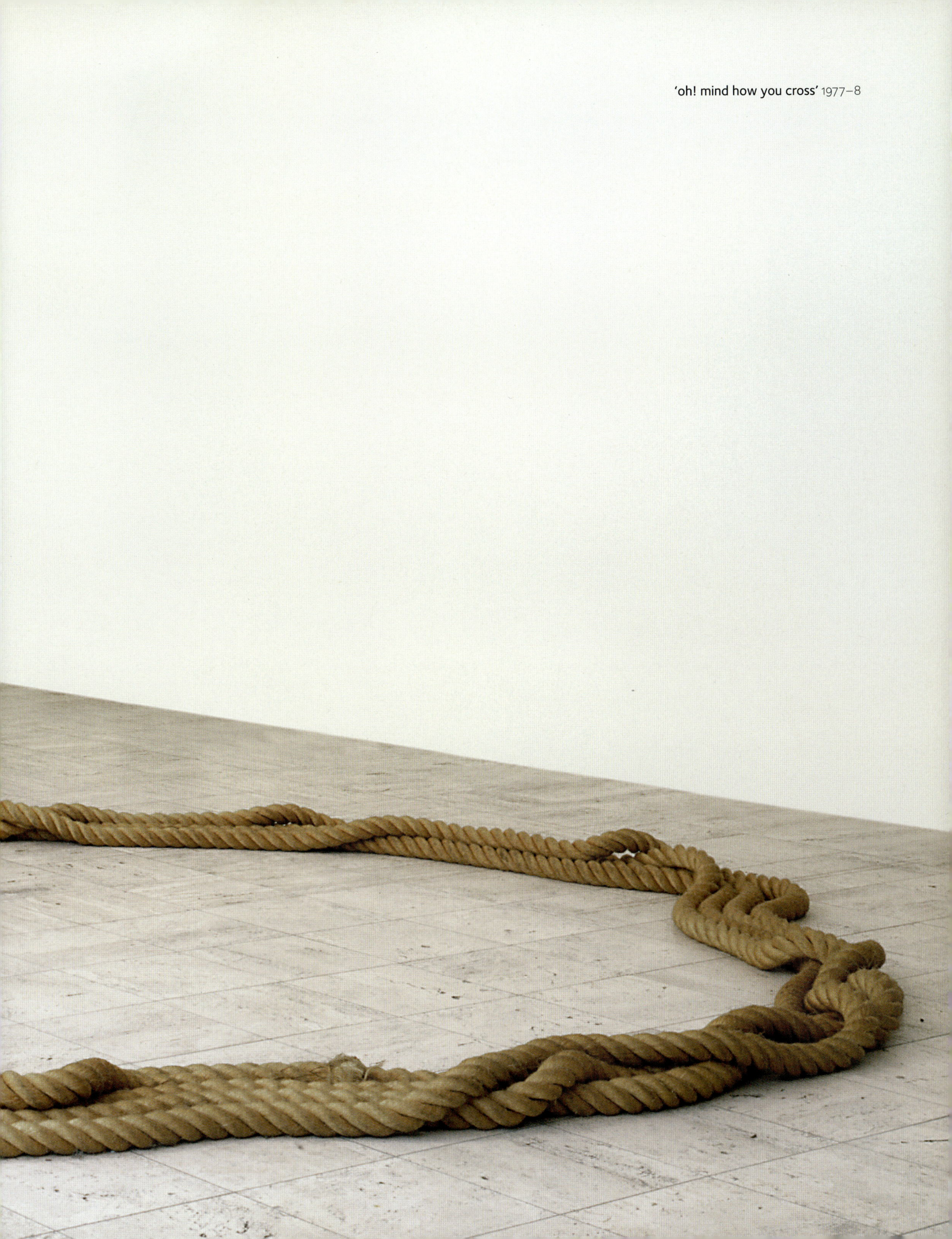

'oh! mind how you cross' 1977–8

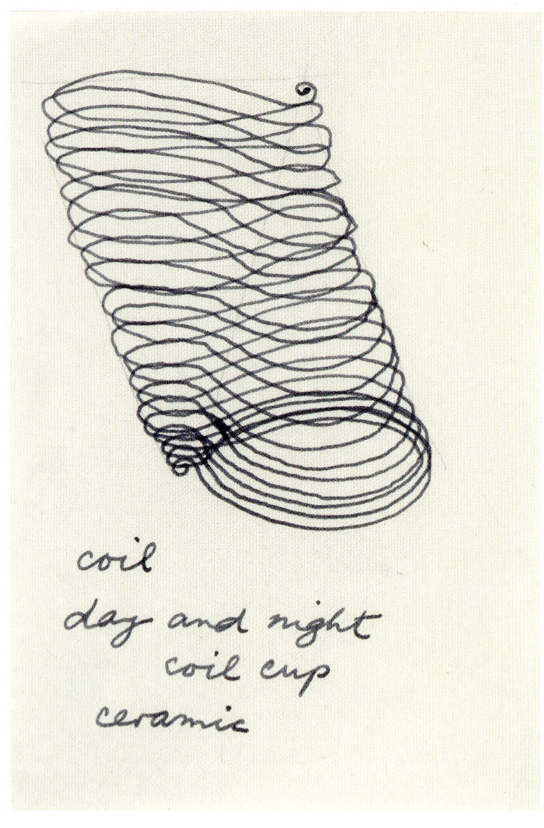

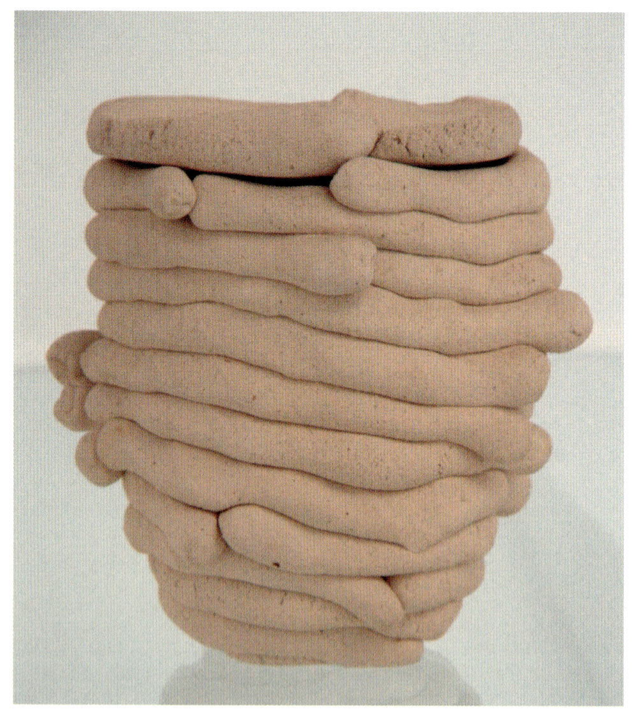

drawing for day and night 1974

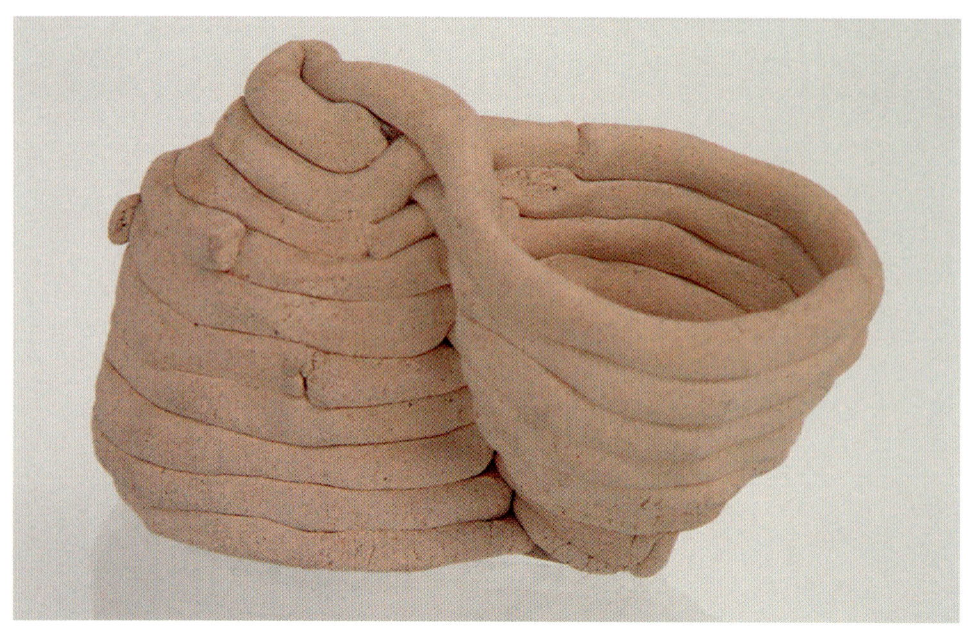

Coil pot 18 (700 grms) 1975

Coil pot 5 (150 grms) 1975

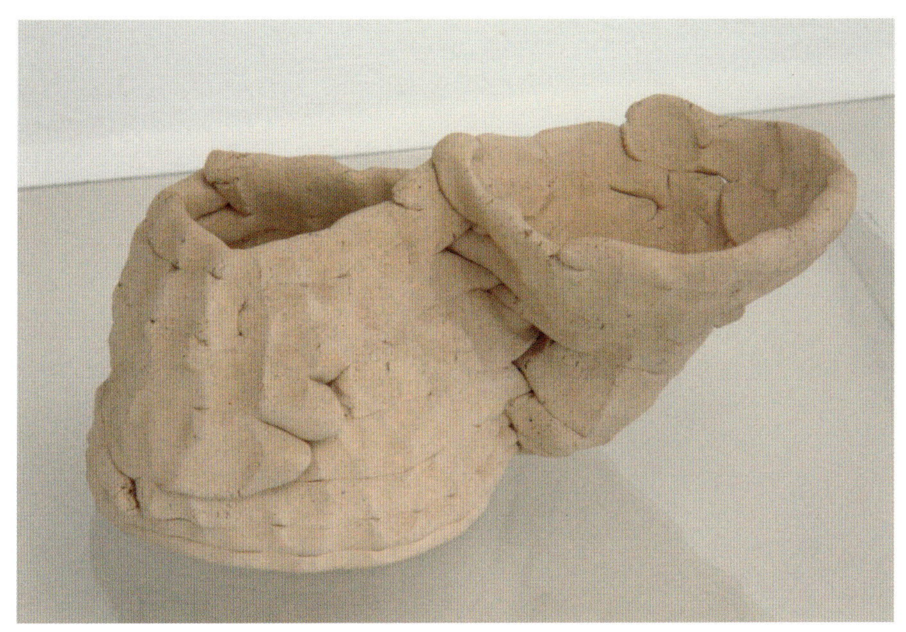

Coil pot 7 (1200 grms) 1975

a selection of five pots,
VII (250 grms) IX (250 grms)
XI (210 grms) X (240 grms)
VIII (190 grms) 1975–1977

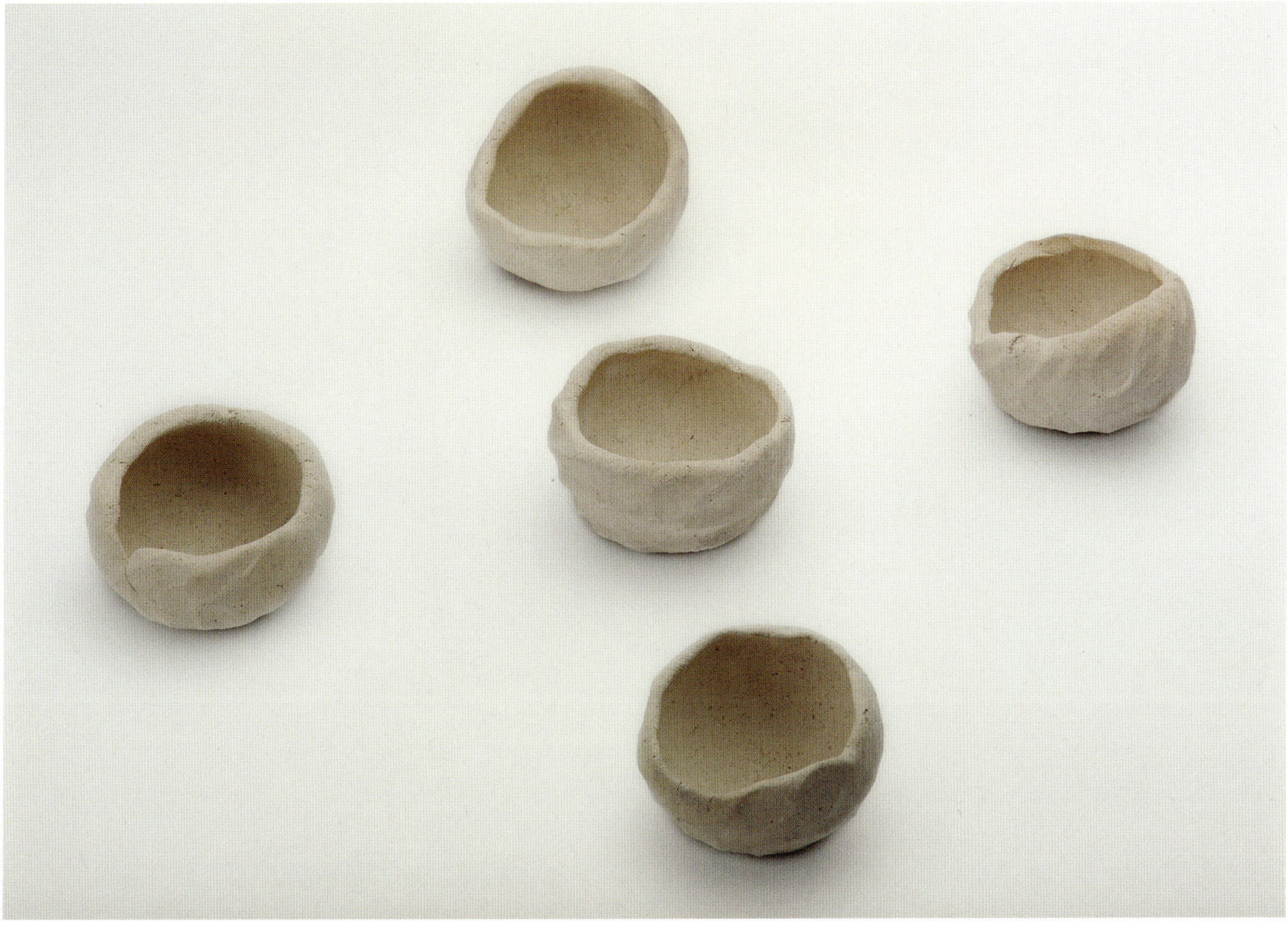

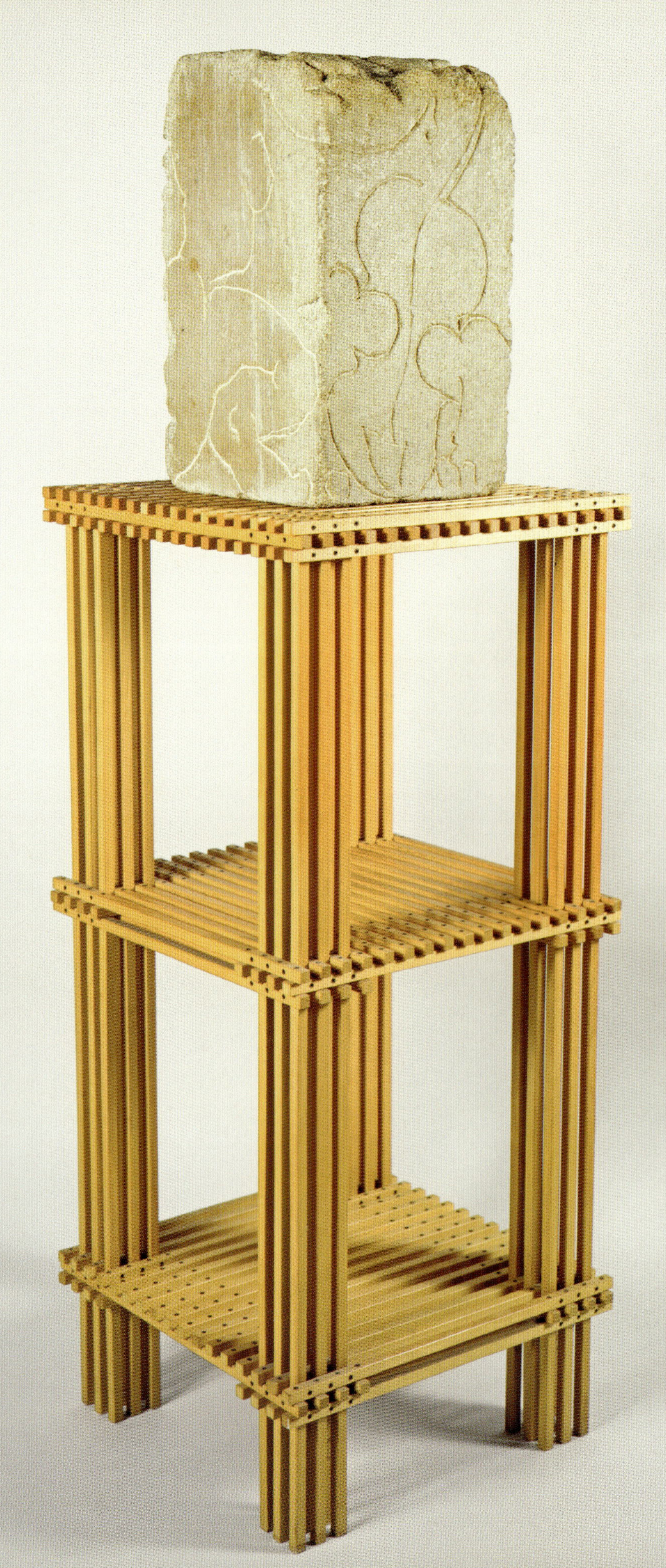

Hello cello 1976

The Road to Altissimo 1973

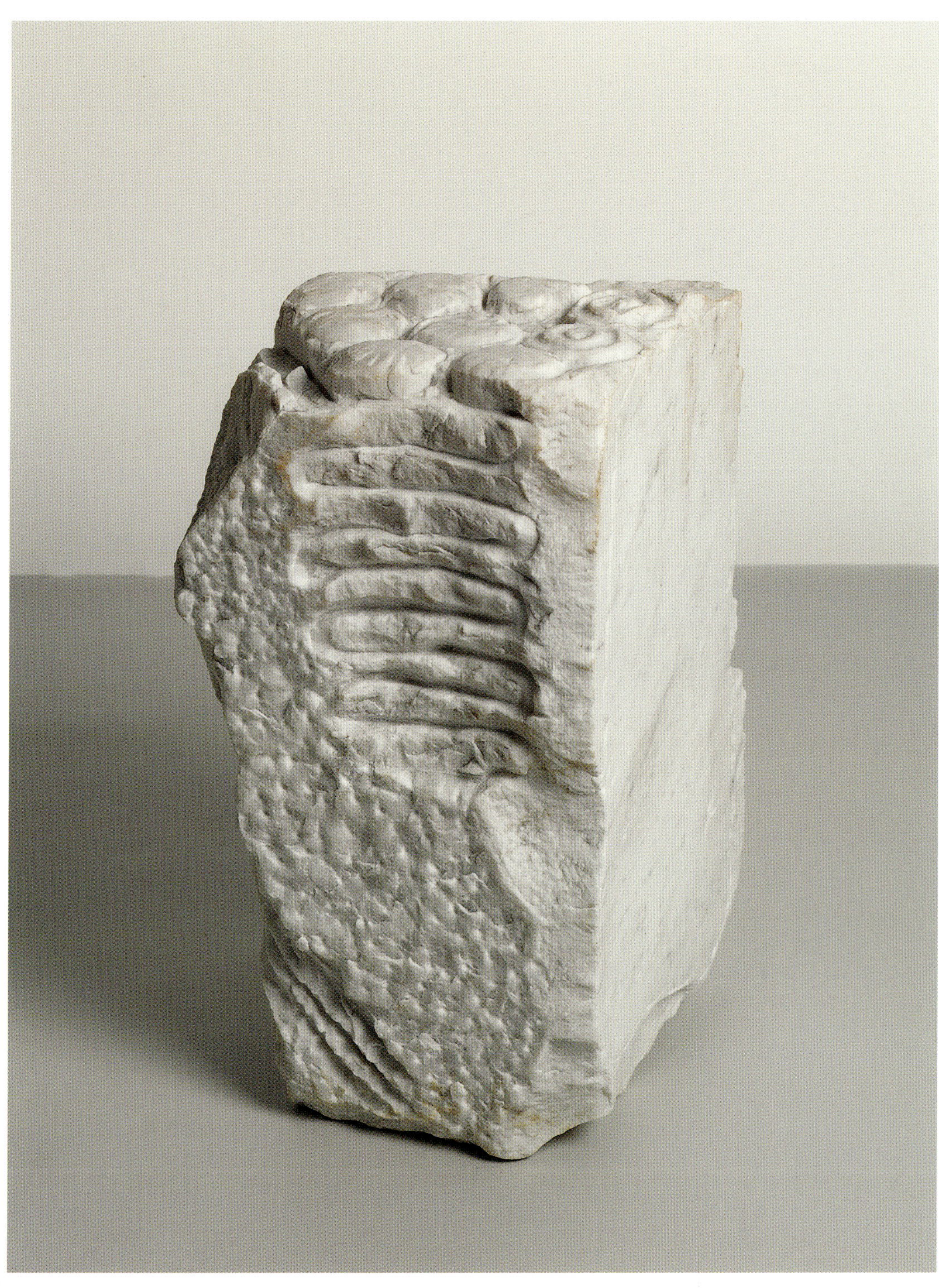

Tantric goddess 1973 Cornish BuB 1979

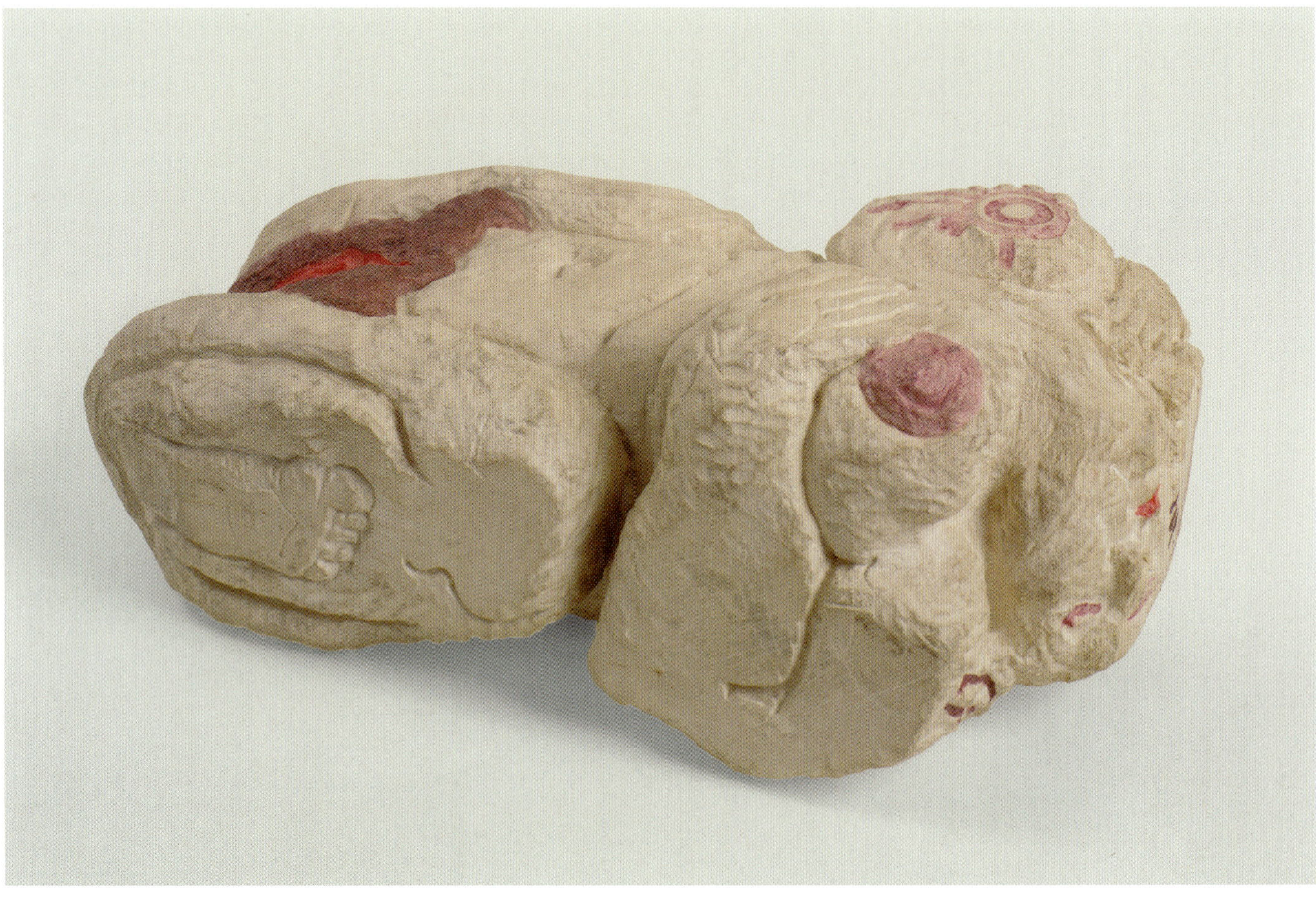

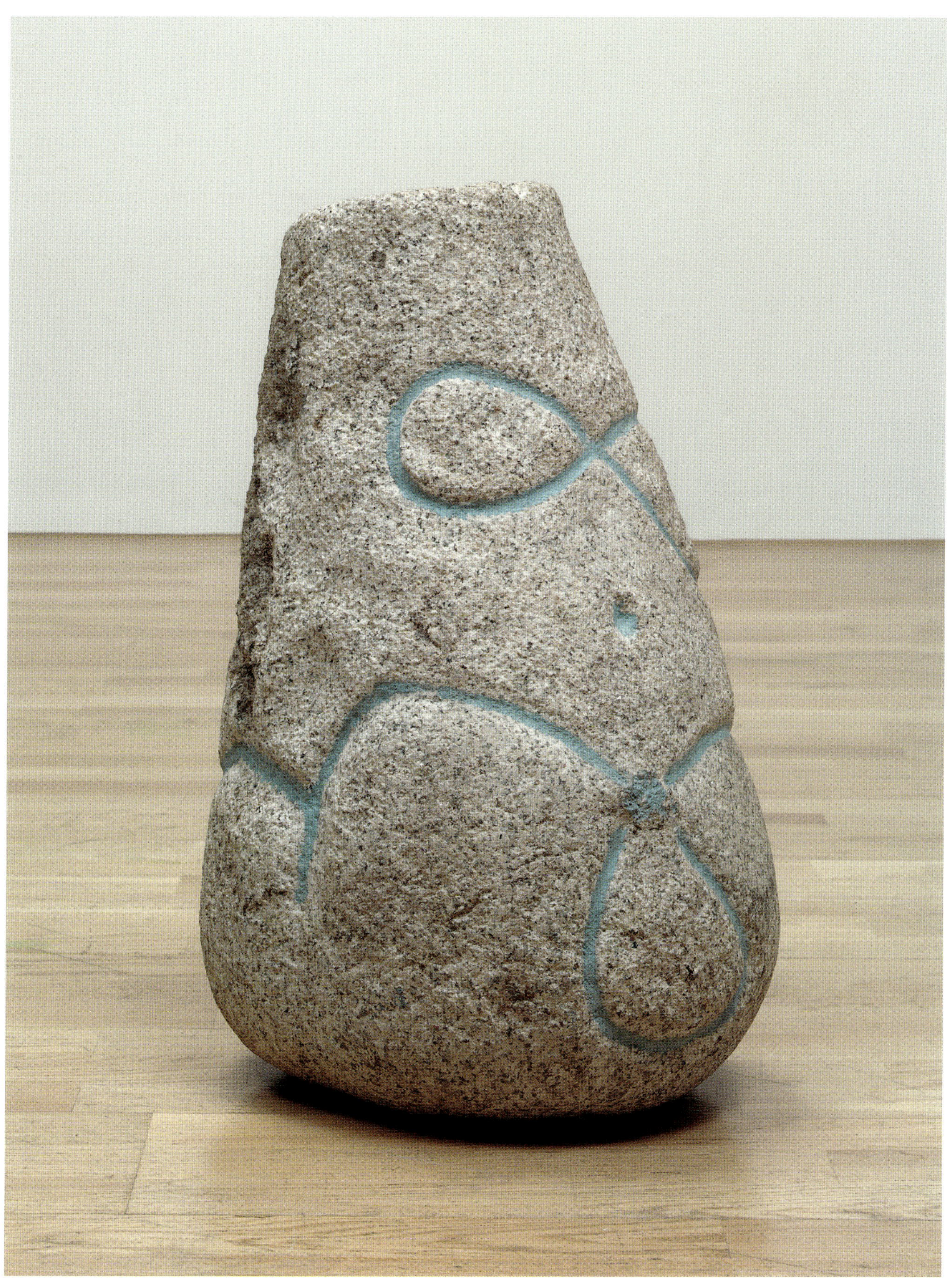

The stone that covered the hole in the road (the skull) 1974

Lamb/Fish 1975

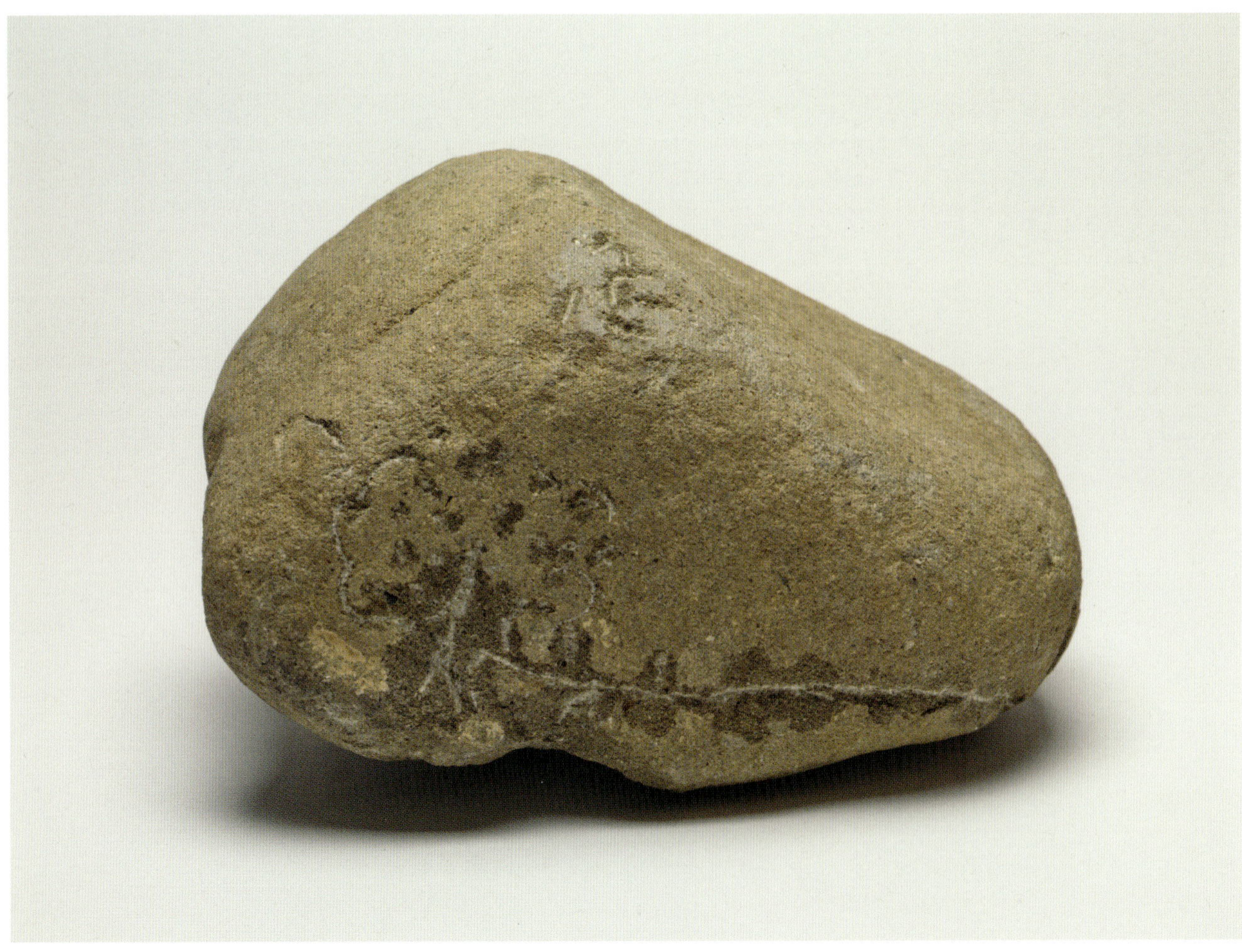

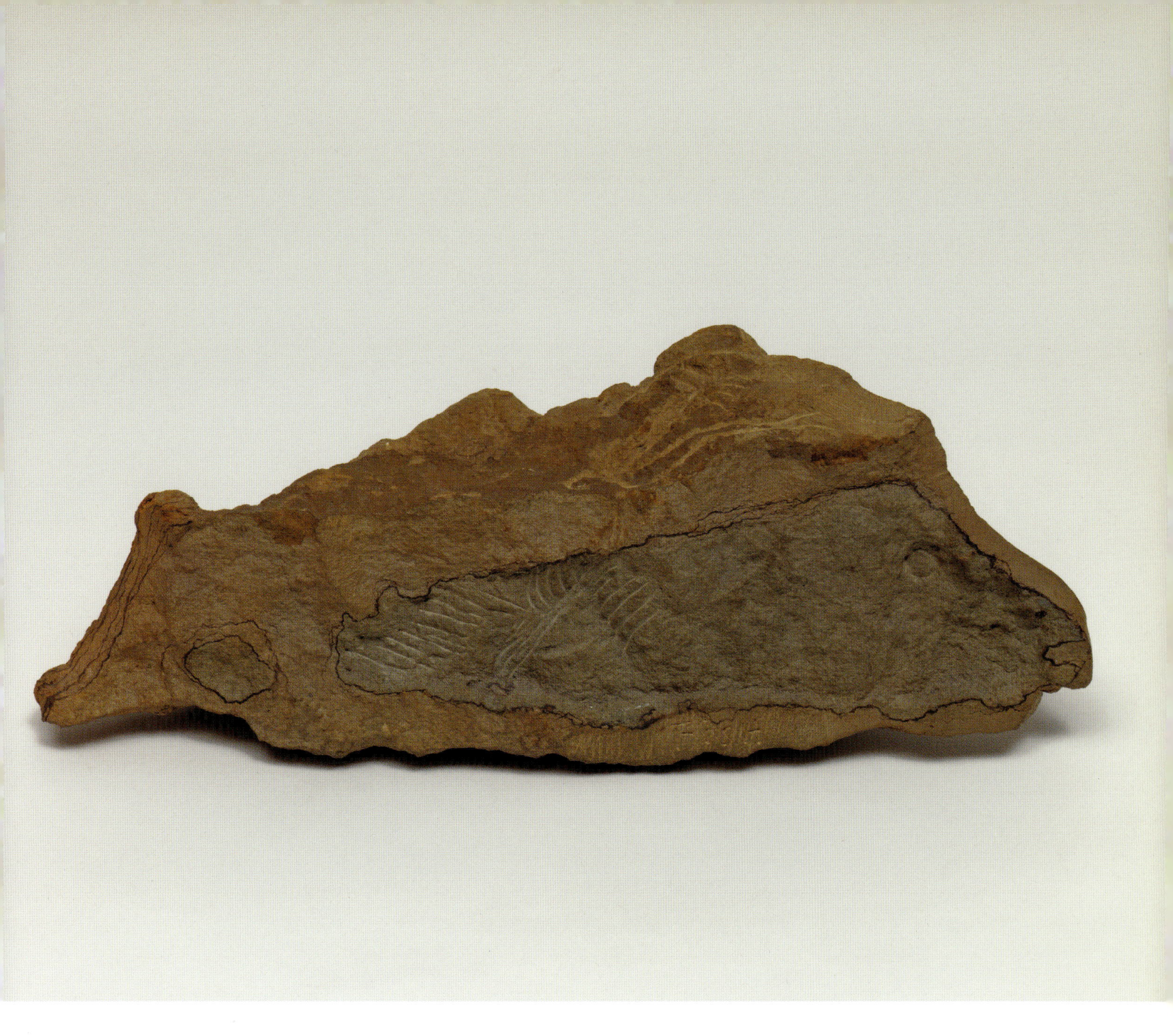

untitled (3) '73 1973

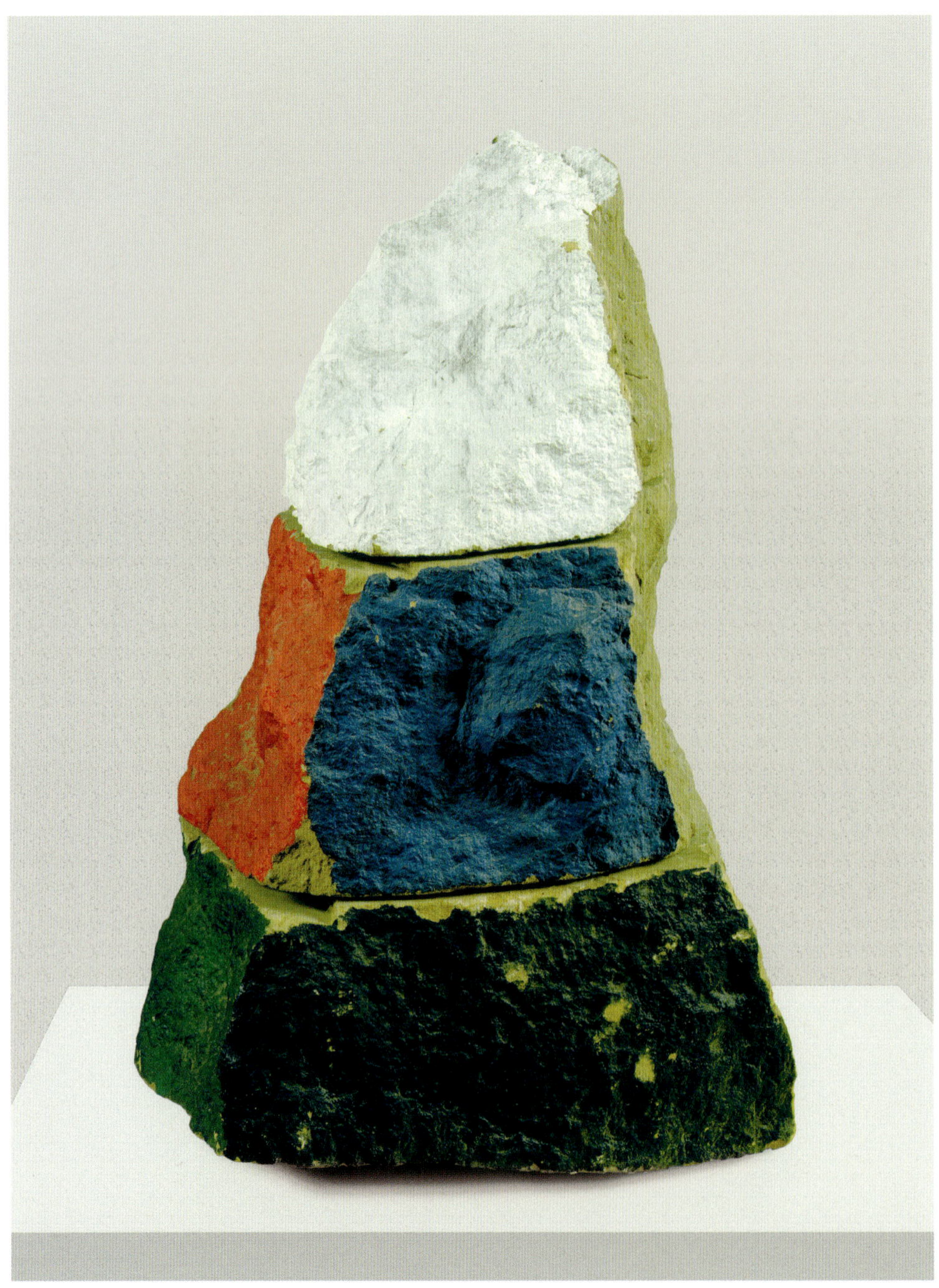

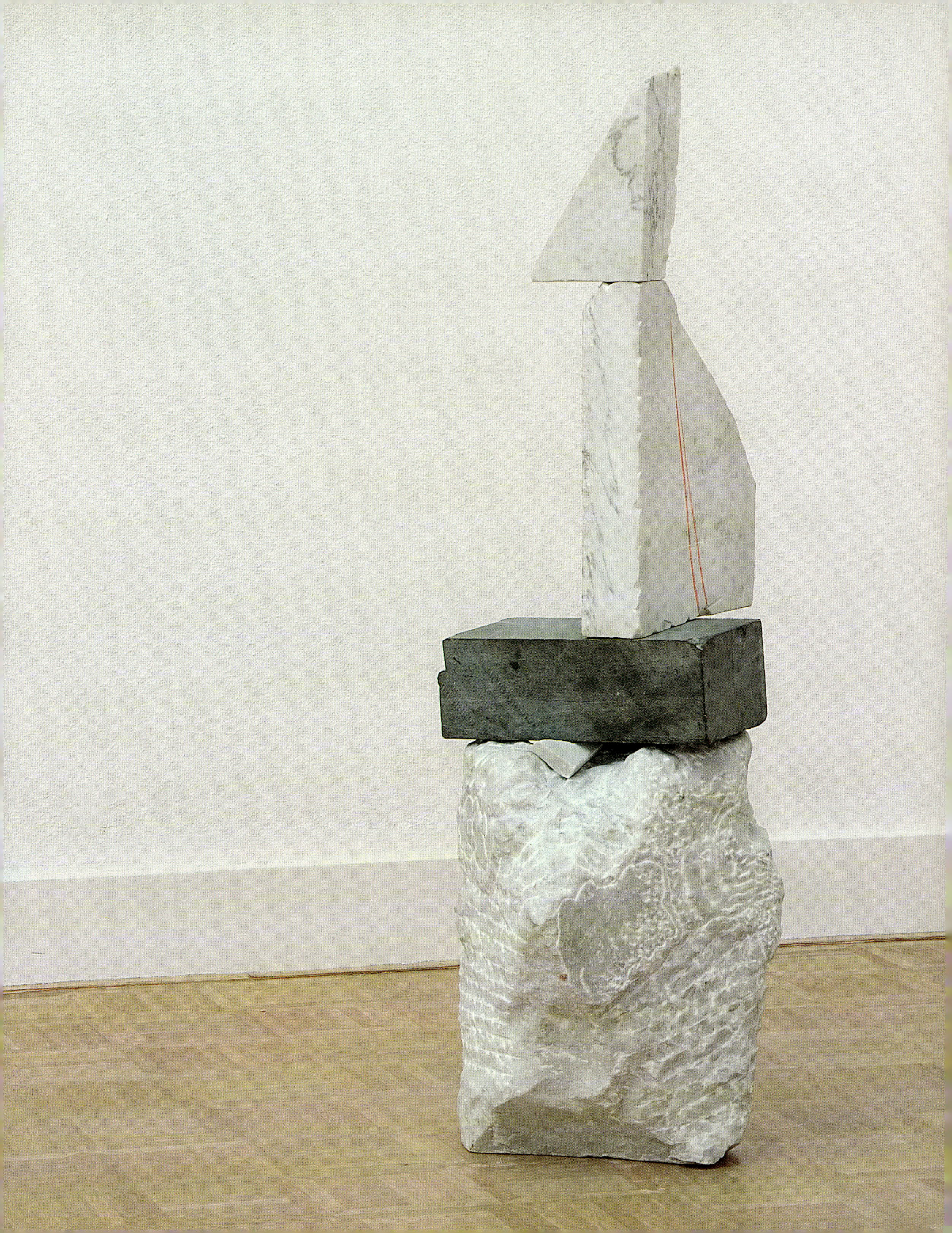

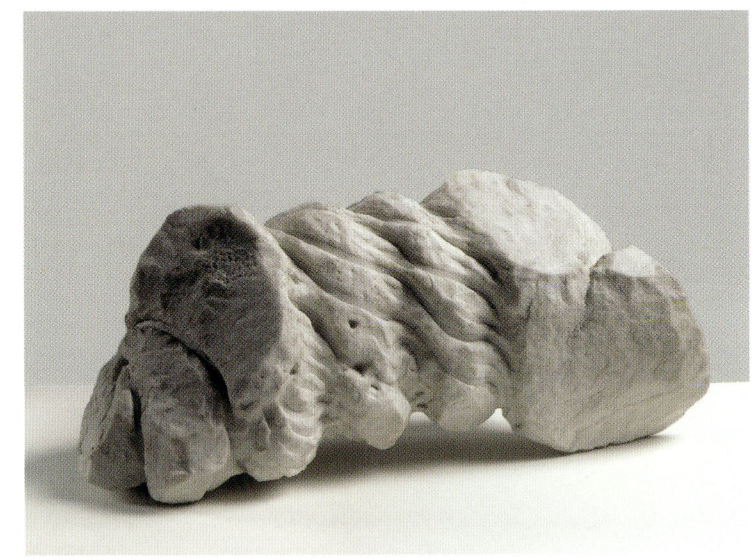

'-if marble smell of spring-' 1978

untitled (carving no. 13/81) 1981

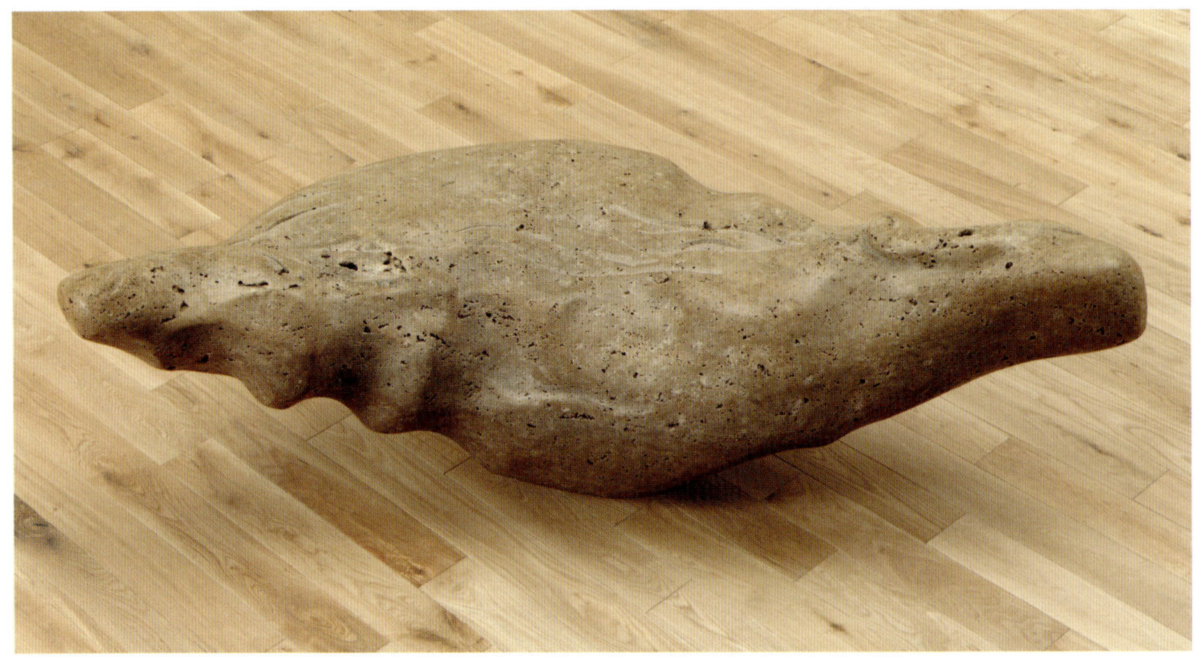

untitled (2b × 4) 1982

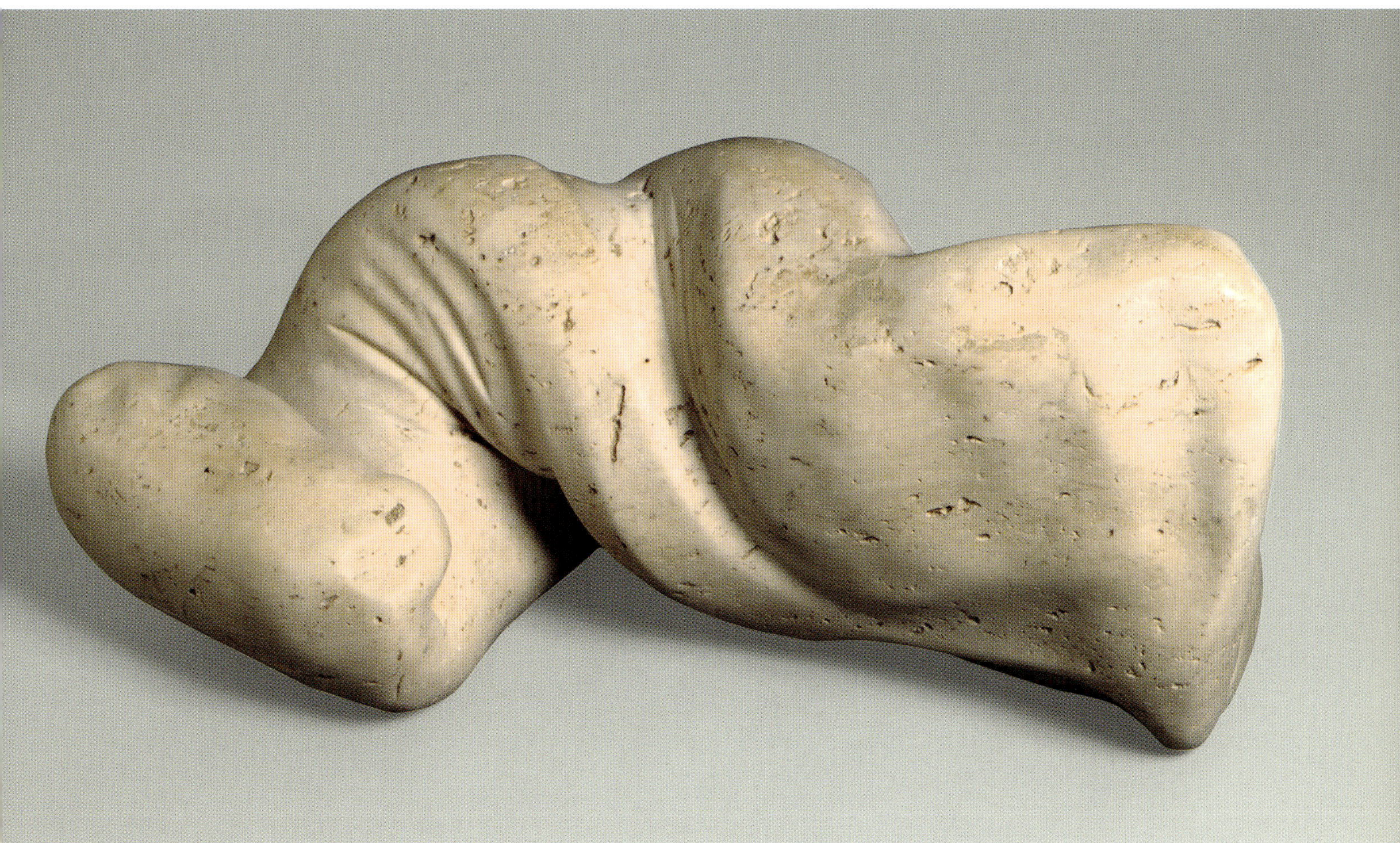

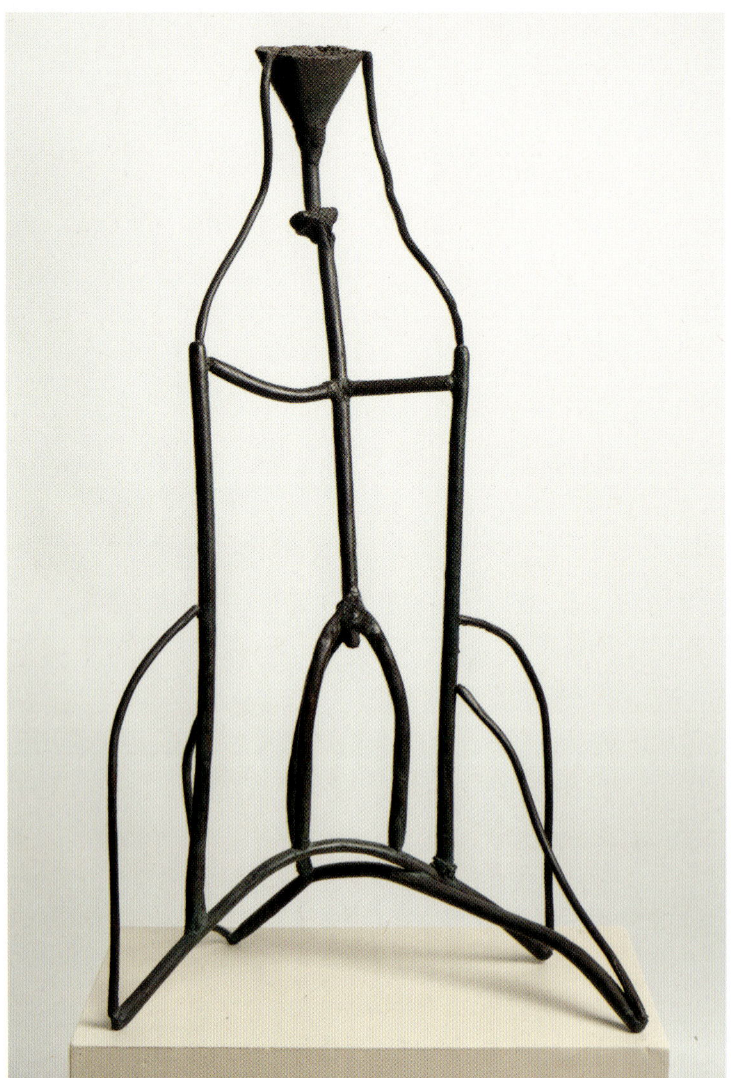

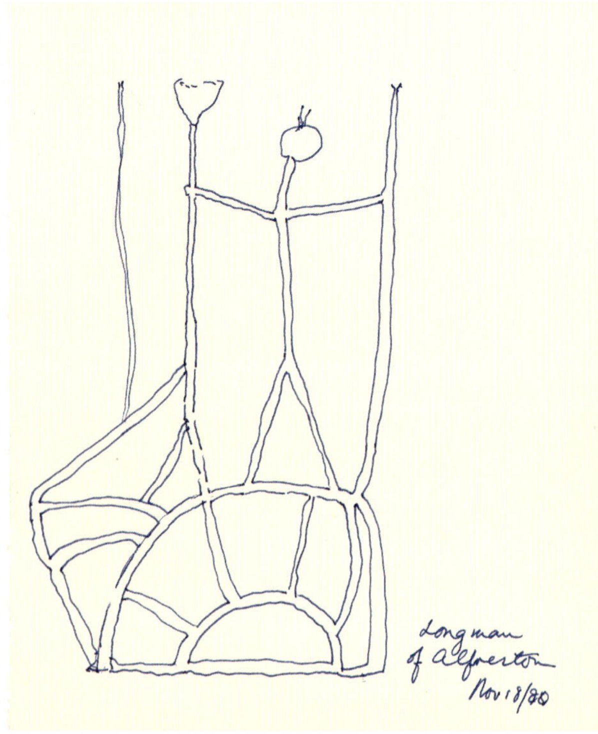

The Long Man of Wilmington 1981

Long man of Alfreston Nov 18/80 1980

Opera Dog 1981

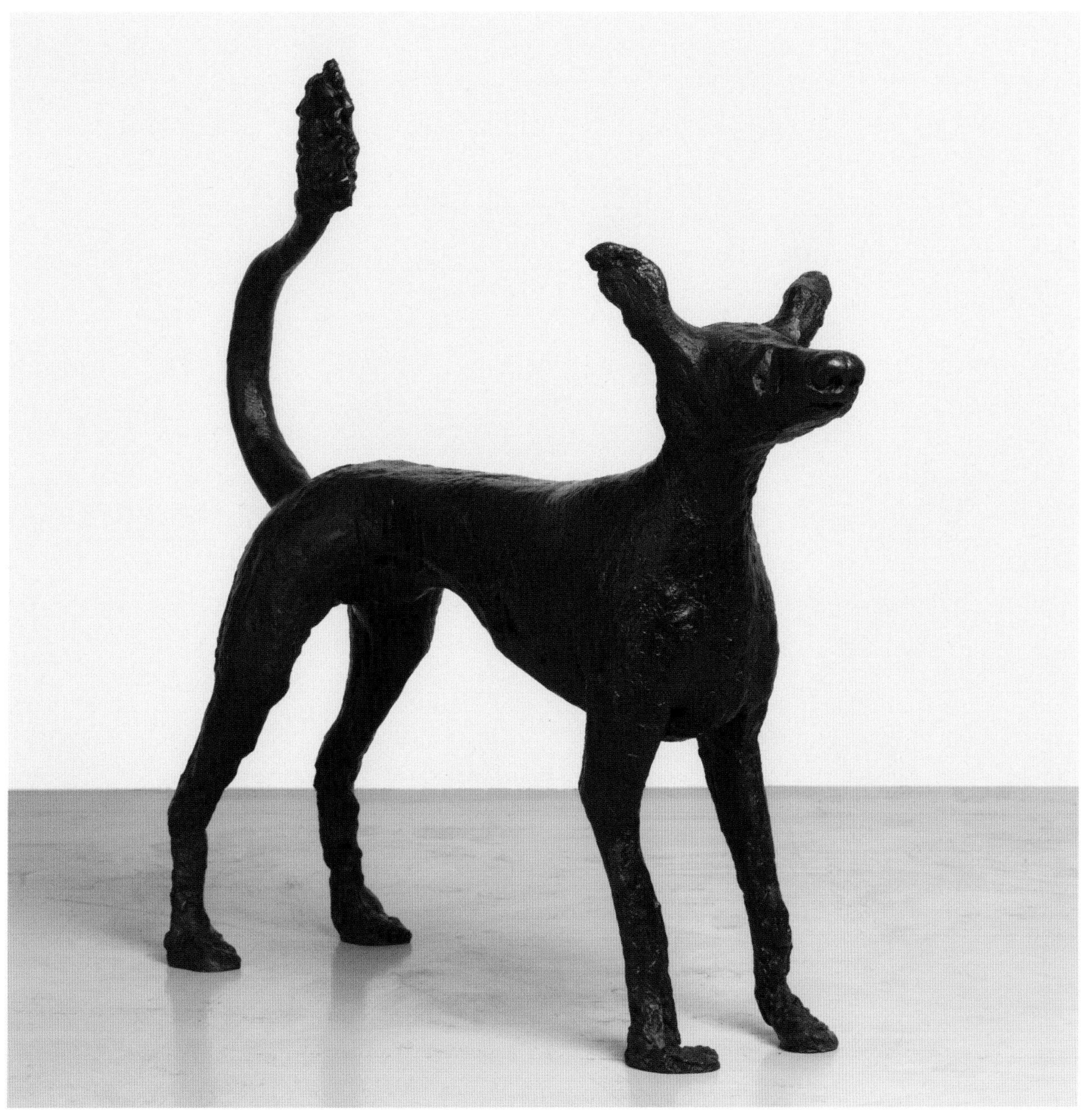

leaping hare, embellished, 2/3 jan '80 1980

Large Leaping Hare 1982

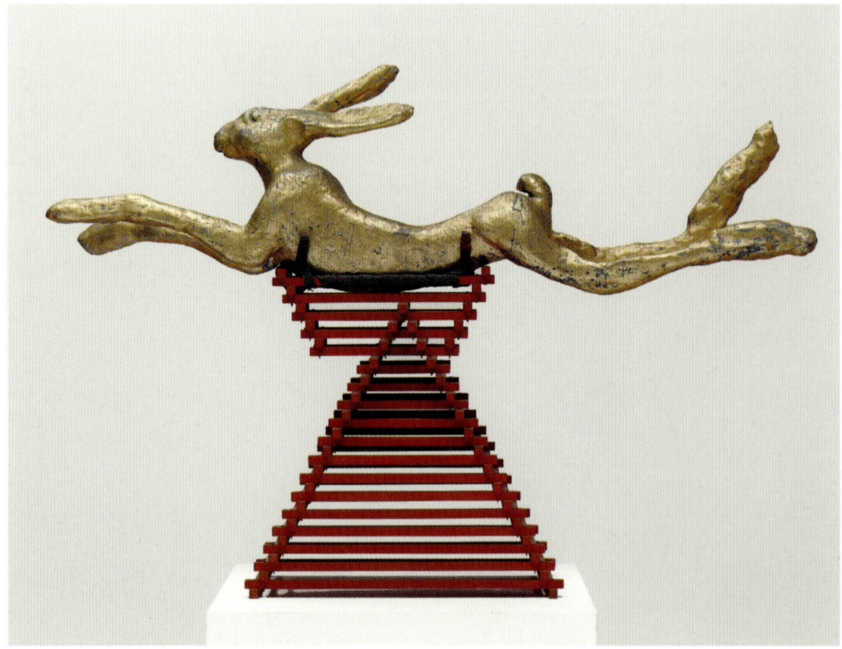

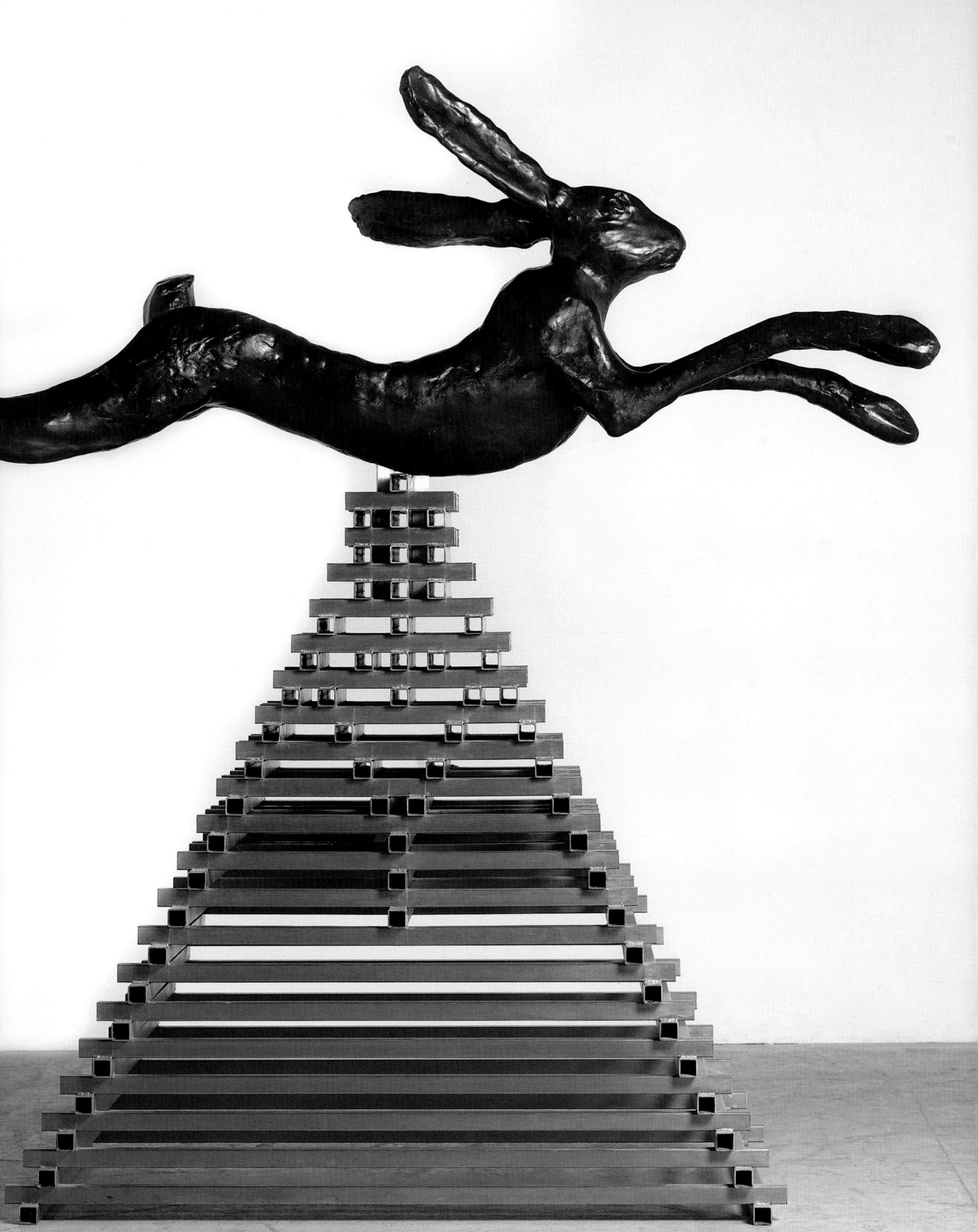

the rate for
the job
wall no 7
@ 10/- (50np) p.y.

.

BARRY FLANAGAN

Selected artist's statements

Untitled statement, *an exhibition of concrete/spatial poetry*, Midland Group of Artists, Nottingham Feb–March 1966

Made sculpture for 8 years: poems for 5 years. Studied architecture 1 year: cello 1 year. " poetry is the most economical manifestation of one's 'chemistry' – always working towards poem." Ink blots: 'Severed Tongue', 'Idea in Mind'.

***with reference to industry*, unpublished response to APG questionnaire, March 1966**

with reference to industry
jbflanagan

ustry

1. yes i would fit in a firm which cld employ my senses as well as my abilities.

   no i would not fit because ind reqrs no industrial ass–ertion(exept whn overqualified), just manpower.

2. a) paid i would be able to dx partisipate,
   b) unpaid i would not be able to partisipate.

3. yes such a system for the availabilit of facilities would apply to me. y

4. min.rate as for top craftsmen, over 10/– ph .. less materials and time at a special rate on a sliding scale for my own work done.

5. yes i would move to a job if worth it

6. I expect to support family on a wage.

7. to do a job of work would be the oblig

8. i would learn a specific skill quickl relevant to the job, workshop, or ind y specific skills are not learnt in school.

9. £15pw to live, av. of I sculpture pm equals £60 per sculpture spent, at the moment.

gallery pays nothing.

the artist seems to be that person with more than one identity, sometime many, conversely he is capable of id- s entifying in more than one area as objectively for each as he will. this is his utilitarian unconvention- ality. the artist will strike a balance maintaining his own, capable of extending in any one area. the artist tapped by industry is capable of fulfilling a roll of a super p r man, he is also capable of numerous specific tasks with unusual corelatio n
it depends on the artist's polit– cal affiliations as to wheather he will be of use to the management or not.
as for myself applied to a task in industry i have no right my own but that of the job. i opperate in my own right at moments in my studio or when at my own work removed from tasks of utility.

Artist's page, *Wall Show*, exh. cat., Lisson Gallery, London 1970

Unpublished end of course thesis 1966, towards the award of a London Certificate in Art & Design (Sculpture) (excerpts)

Perhaps the question is how may I absorb, correlate, assess and continue to do so. How may I spend this accumulation that is absorbed, correlated and assessed. A person may walk, talk, breath, hear, see, eat, feel and he must make sense. The person is aware and accounts.

My hand touched the table for the very first time, for all it knew. My brain seems to have a strange unreel life its own; It will remember many other time, times. Time and times, timing timing times timing timing, and rather overqualify the touch. It's just not good enough, my conduct does not add up to the simple demands of this in digression and wondering situation. The sheer adventure and life of the touch is the only relevancy.

My brain is cluttered; the needle (the thing) remains small but the haystack (information) grows even larger. If the table shrieks "Monday, Shroud, Galapagos", something is wrong.

I must allow my hand to touch and feel, my eyes to look and see, my tongue to lick and taste, my nose to sniff and smell, my ear to listen and hear:

I my
eyes sight
ears hear
hands feel
noses smell
tongues taste
function

sight)
hearing) sense of
touch) direction – instinct
taste) (by agreement)
smell)

One's true heritage is the senses. What use are eyes ears, hands, noses, and mouths without a sense of direction and idea, or trust and patience. Trust and patience are the allies of direction and idea; direction and idea are the objects of trust and patience of necessity. They need each other.

The physical senses need trusting as the body needs trusting to perform. If at one time there is no performance due to breakdown, one promotes conditions for its recovery.

Untitled statement, invitation card for *barry flanagan: sculpture*, Rowan Gallery, London, August 1966

the business is in the making
of a sculpture
i'm after elegant solutions
elegant in the sense of a theory
being so
'solutions' implies problems—
most likely imaginary ones

it is pointless to treat the business
as the tatless commodity
or the object like a prototype

sculpture is without
audience message
communication
comfort diversion
or
good or bad looks

nor does it fall into a time pattern
of history—convenient for the
articulation thereof

the area of sculpture can afford
of its own anonymity
sculpture is without notions
of itself
even

i want art, without its
myth
without its
reputation

'Barry Flanagan Writes', *ICA Bulletin*, London, no.163, November 1966, p.9

if i paint i'd rather paint colour
if i design i'd rather design for a function
if i construct i'd rather construct for a purpose

there is some visual law of distance relevant very much to sculpture.
the way things near to one move faster than those far away when travelling on a train.
the way the cone has emerged as an 'elegant' sculptural unit, in this sense, as its base commands that distance from its apex.

one is forced to see from here to there and perceive its relative distances in depth; the sculpture at points passes itself as the observer moves.

these metal sculptures may best be seen perhaps, the way they were made, ie while walking around and looking.

there's no substitute
for the real thing

there is no way,
no route,
the thing just needs possessing.

without design
without diagram
the drawing
is not
of the duck

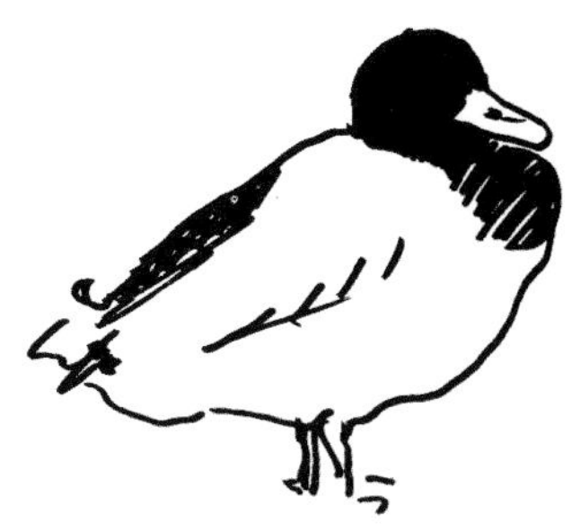

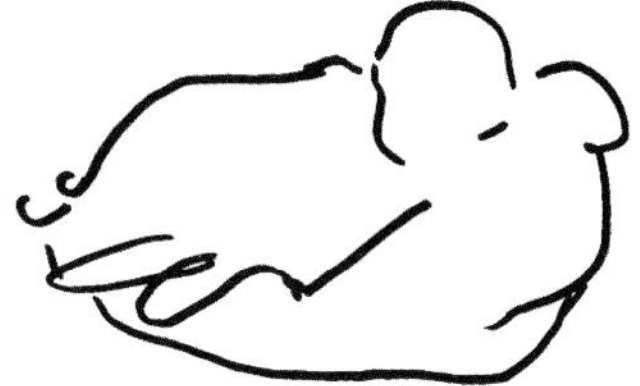

'British Artists at the Biennale des Jeunes in Paris', with artist's statement by Barry Flanagan, *Studio International*, September 1967, vol.174, no.892, pp.98 – 99

invitation   to show three pieces
question   which 3 ?
    as the sculptures are placed for
selection,   a
solution   as to how they may be shown emerges

the sculptures together articulate
and make actual claim
to the perceivable space,
as within the auspices
of the phenomena of
sculpture

i accept none of the
implications within the
thought and demonstrations
of what we already know
of 'environmental' work
or any architectural or
social theses.

there are three sculptures; referred to
as 4 casb 2 '67, ringl 1 '67, rope (gr 2sp 60) 6 '67.
they are seen in the same space;
it is fortuitous or interesting that they
negate their specific identities
and work together in such a way.

within the area of sculpture there are carried its own solutions,
we invest it with problems, ideas and excitements.   one merely causes
things
to reveal themselves to the sculptural awareness.   it is the
awareness that develops not the agents of the sculptural phenomena.

the same two space rope sculpture in its bag takes another form;
as much a sculpture but changed,   possibly better than anything i could
have made or 'invented'.   the sculpture seems to have a life its own,
precocious, like the child we realise has a way its own—precocious.

Untitled statement, invitation card for *Barry Flanagan Recent Sculpture*, Rowan Gallery, London, April 1968

structure
process
order
is exactly the way
'sculpture' shows itself

it is real,

before and beyond
the autonomy
of the object—
its meanings (mine)
and selfconsciousnesses

'Kunsthalle bern', *Live in Your Head: When Attitudes Become Form (Work – Concepts – Processes – Situations – Information)*, exh. cat., Kunsthalle Bern, March–April 1969, unpag.

It's not that sculpture can be seen as more things
and in new ways within an expanding convention,
but that the premis of sculptural thought and
engagement is showing itself as a more sound
and relevant basis for operation in the culture.
feb '69

'An old New York letter', *Studio International*, vol.177, no.911, May 1969, p.208

25 hungerford road london n7
february 1st 1967.
dear k:
i just bought three books published by thames & hudson 'modern movements' covering pop, surrealism & dada. having glued my busted specs to the forehead i'm just ½ the way through pop art, whether or not i make the other two books only time will tell.
you introduced me to claes oldenberg's work virtually, by giving me the catalogue of the show you did for him. i find him most interesting aside from the pop attitude, or in between the propounds of the attitude.
working & making things in the wake of movements (such as pop), characterised by a 'solidarity' and didactic exposure of one sort or another, through the press and large social networks, can be embarrassing when there is reference to it due to a resemblance of a superficial kind, now however, as far as references to oldenberg (i too claim originality, — i invented my whole art thing when in adolescence) concerning my own work, i'm very pleased to detect for myself some quite basic sympathies; in a perspective the references seem quite legitimate.
first and foremost there is a similarity in the 'fondness' or response of materials.
when i saw oldenberg's london show the cigarette butts struck me most of all.
when i had my show there was a pile of sand (nobody reported it or found anything to say about it to my knowledge, although it caused some interest). it was just dry sand poured on the floor, and worked by flattening the top, penetrating the centre and scouping [sic] four times from the centre.
it was actually sand, and worked not to be of any particular shape but worked *with* (subject to my own system, or way, arbitrary by agreement), in a way realistic to the situation with no ambition for the visual to be art, or to have any historic/social dialogue therein. the working of it was the real art dialgoue in itself.
with these notions about that kind of thing in mind one may understand my response to the butts as i tell it.
i saw oldenbergs butts, simply, saw them, and they were really beautiful; for them (the art diolague rendered obsolete) simply beautiful.
the pop attitude (as reported in the book) aside, perhaps even then there is a fundamental difference as i would rather introduce sand into the real world rather than seperate it as art, as perhaps oldenberg did with his butts.
anyway my rather british and questionable isolation has been dented or even penetrated and i think oldenberg the most regular of sculptors subject to characteristic qualifications. i'm learning to understand his work and only my admiration may be unqualified—i admit to only one forebear and he is my father, my 'adolescent' art movement challenged him we fought and parted, as is the pattern, fight no more and have mutual regard.
these mere words form a skeleton of a communication to you, who has seen fit to have a piece of sculpture of mine, it seemed a jolly good thing to do, and i was absolutely in favour of the transaction!
barry flanagan.

while regurgitating this unanswered letter and while thinking on the difficulties which surround the autonomous art activity, i am amazed now at this last paragraph—coy/flattered and ingratiatingly british; within the terms of the letter not able to put myself over with any seriousness and confidence in the literary form, then, at the time indeed a reflection of the london malaise. for home readers i make reference to nigel gosling's observer column, march 30 'creative doldrums'—and suggest the creative bit goes on if only it can be seen and put over, after all the shape of his words has no bearing on the state of the economy. that professional non sound is yet another vote of no confidence the london artist must get through on his own account, and it reflects badly right the way through. with all the art schools geared to the creative potential of its entire intake these last years there is a lot coming on. the creativity thing is more to do with ideas and less to do with economy and no middle man has any business blaming by implication the creative participants as well as the economy of a locality because he sees nothing to report on. things do not come along blessed by a generation of age, style, new york or dusseldorf any more; smothered by the convenience of the father-son credit role which is the first and often the only thing understood by london observers.

'A literary work', *Studio International*, vol.178, no.913, July/August 1969, p.4

things happen in the realm of ideas and action which promotes turnover, the balance of which is your economy with or without your decimal system/common market or whatever the hell makes the headache better. the art creative thing is catered for here at source, the next thing is to plant a crop of new shape cantolds to give the talkers better people to talk to (and someone tell me who they save their pearls of wisdom for while out for safety and a comfortable ride?). this place is a bad situation for artists and i'm interested in turnover (after some faulty starts) and not takeover, and i wonder what tactical genius lies behind the gallant studio's move to cause action in these pages from new york placed artists, literary trained and anxious to expound, and trace the historic trail for themselves. well so long as referees are not needed, failing the wit of london based observers, and a further invitation and opportunity is extended to new york observers to sort out the winners, and hand out the bon bons. if it can be done within some turnover of ideas from the correct premise and be an art growth situation within the bankrupt literary culture.

and political blood and thunder aside (i'm reminded of the local cultural sunday press having tired, through their own lack of structure and professional content, and gone through angry young men, satire from the ½ world of entertainment), swinging london (from the avaricious world of p. r.) empty stuff when the tub is empty of ideas can only carp at the creative nature of a community, one eye somewhere else, on whom they can lean needing to be fed. its about time the public communicators and institutions strata took on some creative responsibility, instead of operating within the safe untouchable historic 'professional' cocoon. it is creative participation in these areas that is problematic not the economy.

signed in general

barry flanagan.

london nw3

recently more than one artist has thrown in his meal ticket on the international circuit to structure literary articulations, in an effort to contact the other side of the literary curtain that is fabricated round what is haplessly known as the 'art world'.

my own effort of a few thousand words adhering closely to the common language structure (with their meanings only slightly obscured due to the nature of the general purpose behind their fabrication), may well remain lost, as public literature has a habit of being, forever to travel from terminus to terminus—north and south via charing cross in the bowel of the london underground, condemned never to be freed from the tracks on which it was inadvertently deposited. i had intended to be more explicit with more words having been driven to a journalistic mode in response to a bad public noise the visual arts are in the habit of suffering in london.

however—the shortcomings and dangers of a visual artist doing this sort of thing aside—i do not accept the general notion that the visual artist is the 'dumb' object of the grand-patronage, to be cornered by nationalism (despite the miniscule 1.5% of the arts council budget available), and smothered in the unmoving petticoats of anglophile well-bred liberalist gestures—at very best wrapped up in heroic literary fantasy. nor do i accept the notion that the artist is outcast from his society, as in new york; the plaguist bandit with tax relief licence to operate in integrated dialogue within the cultural literary fabric of purpose and idea. and again it is unacceptable that the artist be obliged to uphold extremes within political thought, to effect an identity and purpose within his locality, as on the continent. or that he be available to exploit as anarchist clown. one may well conclude from these generalizations that the visual man is driven from pillar to post by the past literary master whose shape the culture is.

the literary mechanism for thought is indeed the past master of the visual arts, and the means by which civilizations have had a use for them.

despite the heritage of the western culture—its language incested with its tumbling debate, moralities, conducts and consequences both local and global (the outspokenness and dicentres making its atrocities and deterioration

possible under the threat of its ultimate deterrent)—it is time the guardians and observers of the culture recognized as fact a basic operative drive in all men to think, structure and organize their existence in a visual way. understanding and thought-process can have foundation in another and particular premise, and it is the job of affiliates to seek that out wherever it shows itself. the visual arts maintained by the vested interests of the industrial machine in new york, education in london, and politics on the continent, solely maintained to these purposes, cannot make any genuine contributions of their own to the culture. it is to trap a whole thought-process servile to particular and local literary priorities of conduct and aspiration, still with their differences, and still people starve and bombs drop while the brain with its habitual training is outstripped and compromised by centuries of its own speculative investment.
the visual arts—their premise for operation, their purpose—must no longer be ignored by literary wizz-kids, like for instance mcluhan, and de bono, the visual arts must no longer be called to order by their literary affiliates because they are not known to solve, entertain, articulate, or demonstrate the perversities and difficulties (social and semantic) the culture has invented for itself, so that it knows its ugly face a little better. with a self-respect established and made available for the visual arts in this culture, the life we know now may then be illuminated, coloured, shaped and ordered with more beautiful consequence on the human life style, semantic stalemate cut through.

Untitled statement, Germano Celant, *Arte Povera*, New York 1969, p.133

Operations grown from the sculptural premise; its exactness and independence is the clue to the scale of the physical, visual, and actual consequence in society.

'Toy', *Play Orbit*, exh. cat., Royal National Eisteddfod of Wales, Flint Institute of Contemporary Arts, London, August 1969, p.116

A toy is an object invented in play so that the game may be played again.

Untitled statement, *557,087*, exh. cat., Seattle Art Museum, September 1969, unpag.

dear bernhard

the future of art carries with it no precedent available in my literary thought mechanisms to appraise or solve it.

barry

may 27, 1967

Untitled statements, *Christo Barry Flanagan*, exh. cat., CAYC, Buenos Aires, November 1970, unpag.

Actually, I don't tend to make the interpretation of shape. There is no personal way of seeing it, only a personal way interpreting it. In the case of three-dimensional work the thinking procedure is at all times to enhance the particular identity of personality of the piece involved. I have become less interested in the autonomous object. If you don't have an autonomous object, the most tempting thing to do is to apply some system of order. But this might well have more to do with the systems themselves than with the nature of the physical existence of the materials.
I think the visual experience of the materials has been central to my interest in sculpture.
Objects and their roles in the world, and their configurations, are part of the interest as well.
The issue is light. Without light, this worldceases to exist. In fact, maybe it is not objects themselves or the shapes they are that is visually exciting, but the distances and spaces between them or caught within them.
I have taken light absolutely for granted and have always standardized its presence in the proximity of any objects, when obliged to think about it; and I also remember excluding any light play from the surface of my objects, as a matter of course. After all, if light is being reflected from the surface, it is not the surface you see but the blinding description of it.
what I like to do is to make visual and material inventions and propositions. I don't think about making sculpture, and I don't think whether or not what I'm making is sculture.
I don't like the idea of inventing a rationale to accompany the work. The tradition is only a collection of rationales.
I don't like to invent an involvement or the terms of an involvement; I prefer to fabricate the sculptures.
I was interested in typical, general visual configurations that command our attention. This for me was the fabrication of a formal involvement.

I prefer working with the essential stuff of sculpture rather my own "ambitions" for it. This way I hope to find things. HEAP practically made itself. In reference to it after the fabrication it was a heap; *that* is *it*. Then I got the "idea" about stacks & racks etc. By then I had made what I knew would be a bundle. Then made up stack & rack, the line was somewhere else from the start but it was something I don't know about yet.
Then there was the pile of hessian, made all the time, I carried from the suppliers. I had been on a whole trip. The last piece was as good as the first for me. Sculpture itself set the standard.

'SCRIPT', exh. cat., *Art Spectrum London*, Alexandra Palace Great Hall, London, August 1971, unpag.

On the other hand
Art still
thinks it's
special

I got 'on the other hand'
from my father.
He would say 'on the
other hand' then, very
soon in his conversation
he would say 'on the
other hand'—like
the hands of a boxer
about my ears.
I was afraid of him,
but I inherited the tactic.
It's like putting a ½ pound
butter dab into shape.
It's how I play.

What could I possibly
have done?

NOTE Fill out script
with those impossible
letters from people
apparently hoodwinked
into a fantasy relationship
with radio or TV.

Untitled statement, *Road Show: A New English Enquiry*, exh. cat., Museu de Arte Moderna, Rio de Janeiro, January 1971, p.18

When I was a child I wanted to be a film star and make people laugh.

Untitled statement, *Studio International*, vol.181, no.933, May 1971, p.219

The operation of the sculpture is between the crust and the idea.

'Bronze Sculptures', *Barry Flanagan Sculpture in bronze 1980–1981*, Waddington Galleries, December 1981, p.3

BRONZE SCULPTURES

When I attended Birmingham College of Art, students were taught modelling, casting, and carving. Mr. Bridgman and Mr. Bridgwater arranged the week so that Saturday morning was shellacking day. We did everything ourselves, and those of us who enjoyed a Friday night would receive quite a charge from the pungent mixture, patinating the plaster casts.

The future lay in the use of modern materials, far more obnoxious, for casting sculpture. However the course I chose later on, while completing my studies at St. Martin's School of Art, was to work direct in manageable materials in a relatively inexpensive way.

By the close of the seventies, fashion and aspirations had been continuously qualified by larger external events, and expedients of production put into perspective. The introduction of some concept of trade, drawing on the traditional resources of practice to produce sculpture became necessary. When out of the garret one no longer works alone, but finds a place in a scheme of things.

I am glad to point out that in the production of these pieces in bronze the *work* has been done by others, leaving only the modelling bits to me, as author. Thank you.

Barry Flanagan

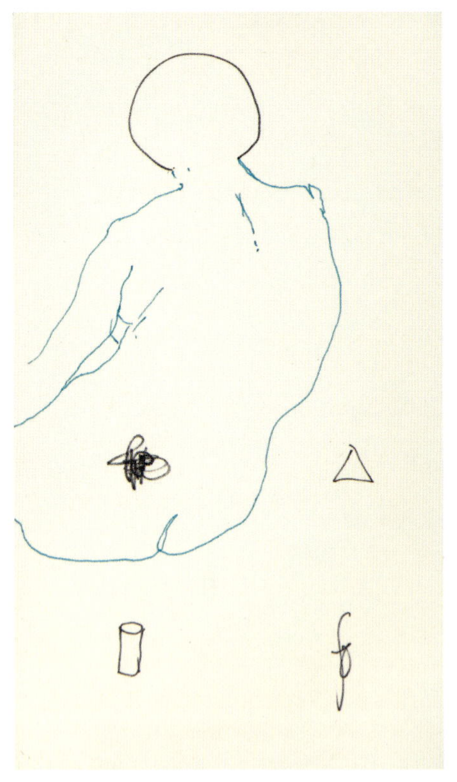

jan 19 '67 15 ⑮ 1967

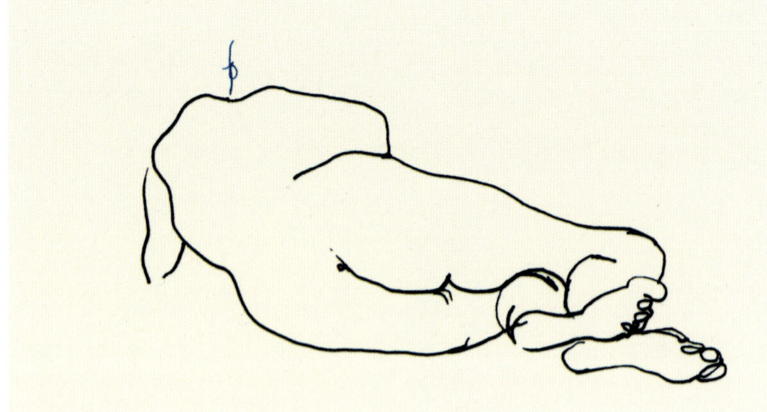

jan 19 '67 2 ⑮ 1967

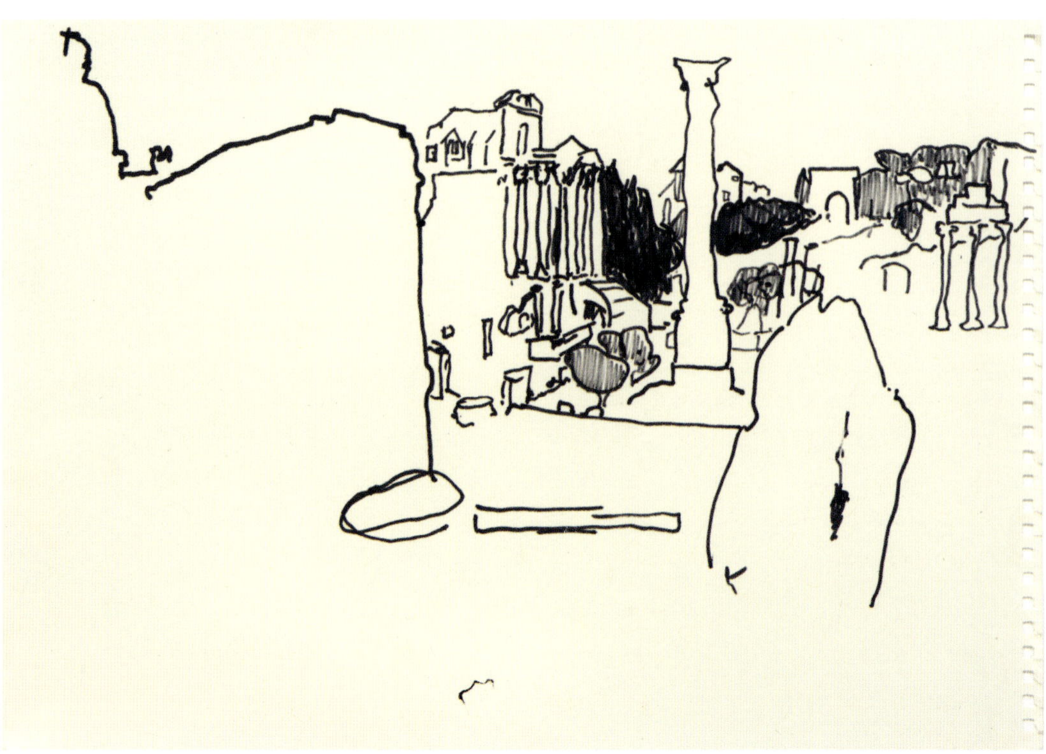

Rome 1974

Trumpeter Swans 1976

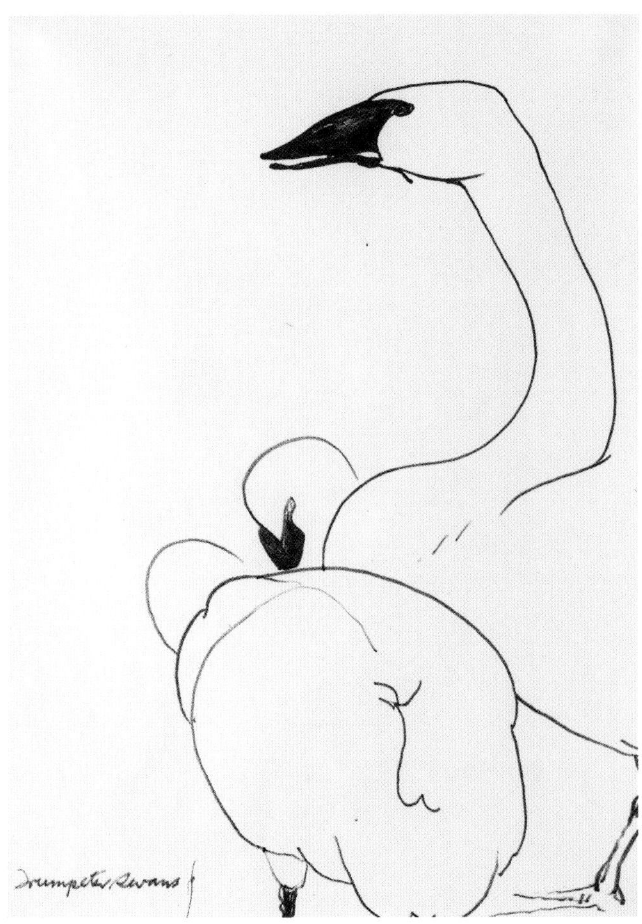

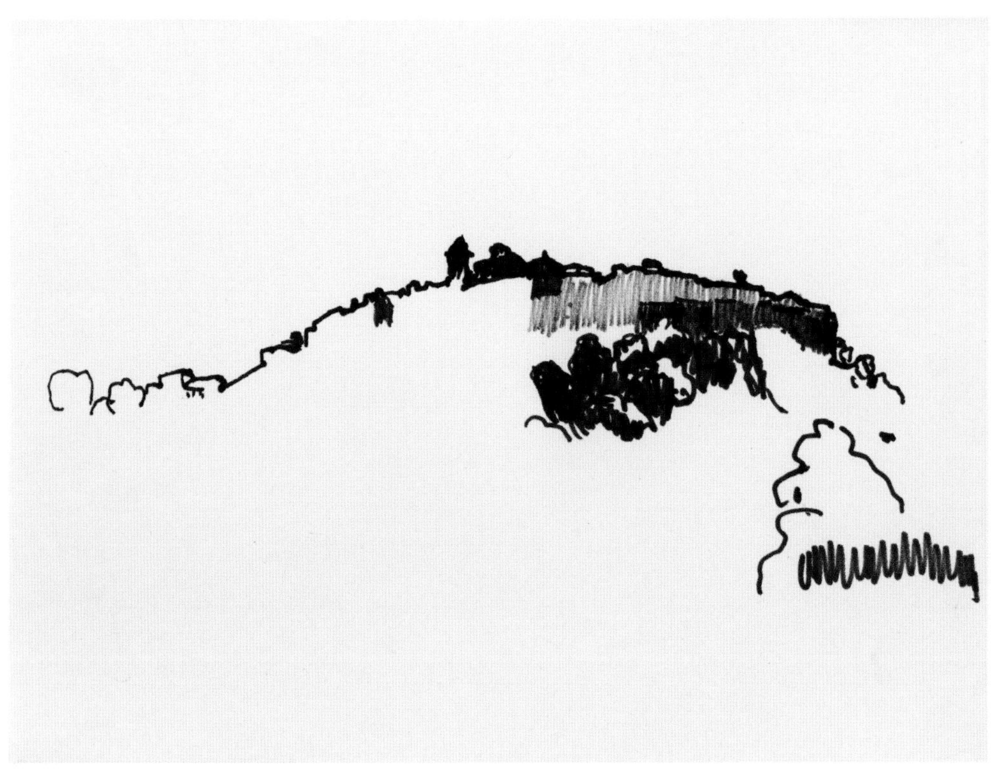

Landscape 1974

Chronology 1941–1982

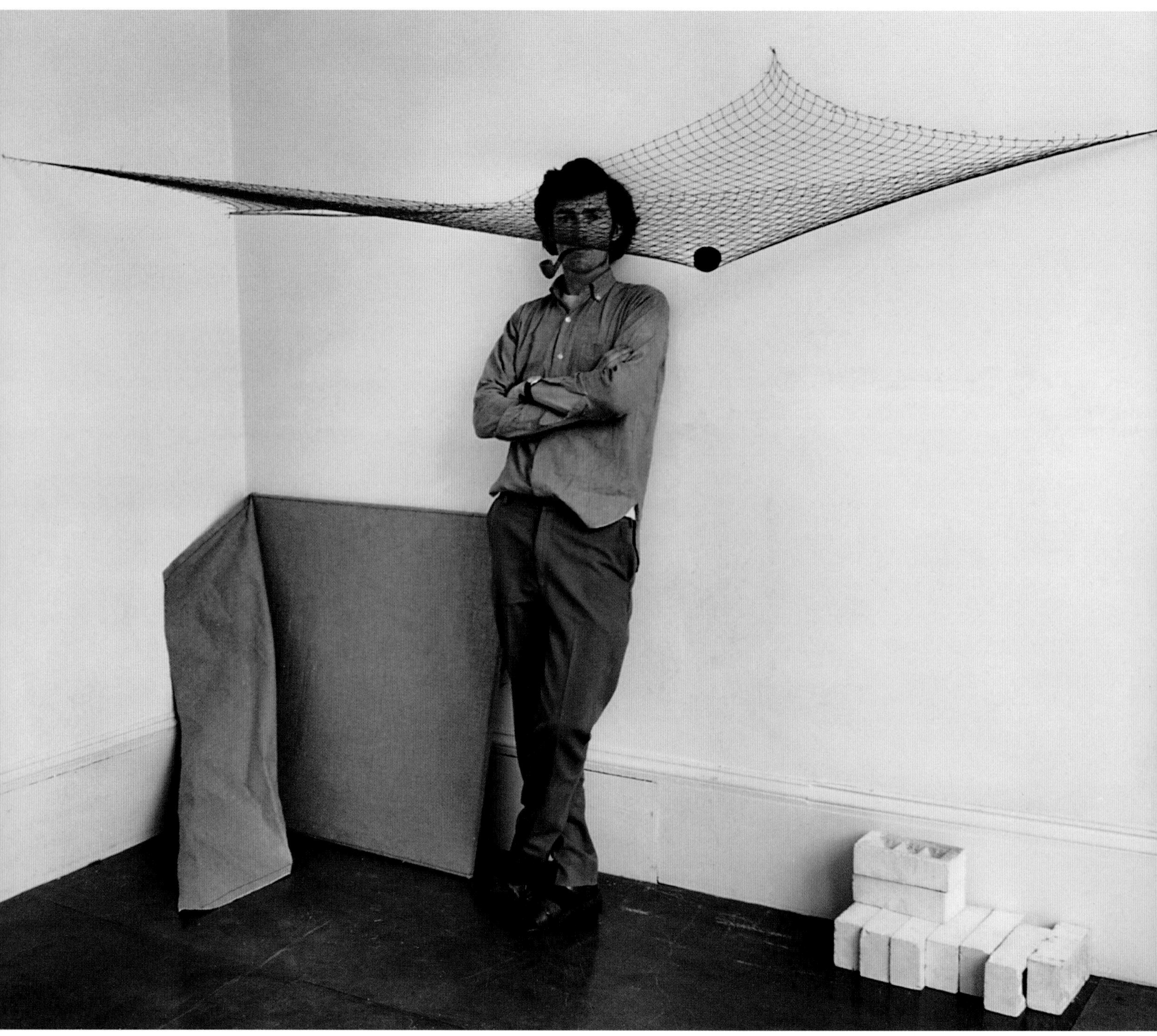

Flanagan in his studio with *net 3 '69* 1969
and (in corner) *3 '66/69* 1966/69

1941–8

James Barry Flanagan was born on 11 January in Prestatyn, North Wales, the son of Bill and Monica Flanagan (née Mullins). Bill was a stage manager when they met, and Monica had run away from home to go on the stage (although her mother was a costume seamstress). She was in the chorus line as a mermaid in *Water Extravaganza*, a show that was managed by Bill and toured England. One of the tour venues was the Hackney Empire, where Monica swam in a tank onstage. For a short while the couple ran the Blue Post public house in Soho and, with music hall giving way to film, Bill became a runner for Warner Brothers. Bill's uncle Bert had been a high-wire artist and his sisters were the musical star Ella Retford and Hannah who used to dress Ella and later ran Hannah's Bar on the Strand, London. Among Ella Retford's hits were *Take Me Back to Blighty, Take Me on the Flip-Flap, Hello There Little Tommy Atkins* and *Under the Honeymoon Tree*. Retford, the family's theatre name, was adopted by Ella because there was a popular comedian with the surname Flanagan. Bill used the name Retford from the mid-1920s until he was enlisted in the RAF in 1941, by which time he reverted to Flanagan. He had volunteered immediately war was declared, only to hear that volunteers were not being accepted and he would have to wait until his age group was called up. In 1943 he was assigned to fighter command in the Middle East, stationed in Cairo.

Barry was the youngest of four children: Patricia, born 9 September 1932; Michael, born 4 January 1934; John, born 13 April 1936. In 1940 the three children had been evacuated to America through a company evacuation plan, whereby children of Warner's British-based employees could be sent to the United States and cared for by staff there for the duration of the war. Barry and his mother, meanwhile, lived in Piggery Nook, a small cottage in Prestatyn. The other three children returned from the US in September 1945, and several months later Bill was able to obtain leave from the RAF, when the family was finally reunited.

1949–57

Flanagan was educated at the School of St Edward the Confessor, or Foxhunt Manor Preparatory School, in Waldron, East Sussex, run by the Xaverian Brotherhood to prepare children for admission to the nearby Mayfield College, which Flanagan also attended. During this period the family moved homes frequently.

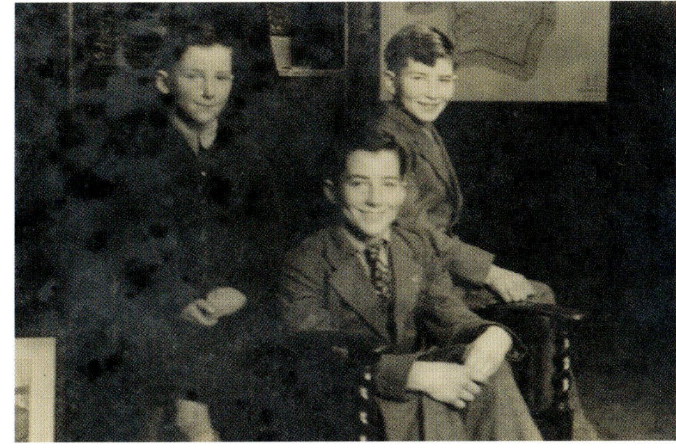

1

In 1949 they rented the ground floor of a large Victorian house in Wooton-under-Edge, Gloucestershire, from Beatrice McCartney, a painter, raconteur and frequent traveller. When he was home from school she would invite Barry to her painting classes. Some school holidays were spent at the Severn Wild Fowl Trust at Slimbridge (later the Wild Fowl Trust), living in caravans next to the Tudor Arms, beside the canal. This was the village's focal point and was where Monica was manager of a longboat, the trust's accommodation for special guests. In 1953 Flanagan joined the chef at the Tudor Restaurant in Birmingham, Gerald Hibler, in a 'balloon dance' to entertain children from the Birmingham Infantile Paralysis Group at their Christmas Party (*Birmingham Gazette*, 13 Jan. 1954, p.5).

At sixteen Flanagan enrolled at the Birmingham College of Arts and Crafts to study architecture.

1958

Flanagan progressed to the second year of the Intermediate Course in Art and Design at the Birmingham College of Arts and Crafts. His Record Card for 1958–9 shows that he studied life drawing, lettering, lino craft, sketching, 'complementary studies' (history of art) and modelling. His tutors on the modelling course included John Bridgeman, Bryan Blumer and Alan Bridgwater, who, according to that year's prospectus, provided instruction in composition, life modelling, carving, letter cutting, waste-piece and slip-mould processes, as well as casting in plaster, concrete and terracotta. Flanagan did not work in bronze while at college. Despite being proposed for the vice-presidency of the college's student union, he left for London.

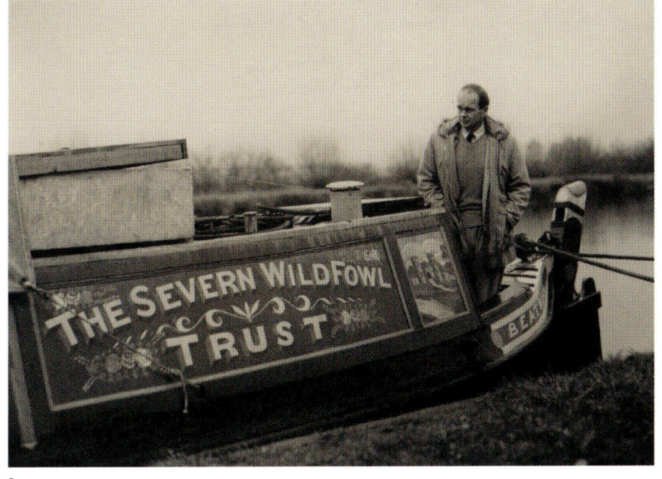

2

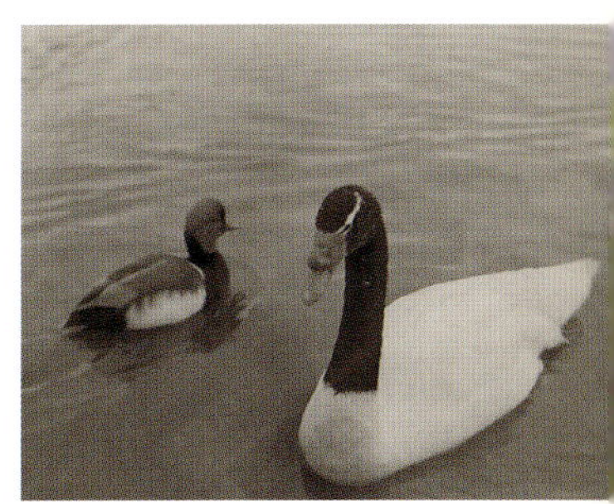

3

1 Flanagan aged about four, with brothers Michael and John
2 The Severn Wildfowl Trust canal boat
3 Water birds at Slimbridge

1959

During a short stay in Devon he met Fred Newton on the beach at Beer. Newton had once been a mason at Beer Quarry and he gave Flanagan work as a beach-hand. (Throughout the 1970s, Flanagan would return with his family for holidays in the area around Beer.) Later in the year Flanagan moved to Bristol, where he took on a number of jobs as a driver and labourer on building sites. He visited Bristol City Art Gallery, where he particularly admired the works of the French-born sculptor Henri Gaudier-Brzeska. It is likely that he saw Brzeska's bronze bust of *Horace Brodzky* 1913, which was purchased by the gallery in 1951, and the two drawings *Reclining Deer* 1913, acquired in 1953, and *Woman on Horseback* 1913, acquired in 1956. He later bought a number of works by Brzeska: the sculpture *Three Monkeys* 1912 and several drawings of animals, birds and figures.

1960

Back in London Flanagan worked at Pinewood Studios on the sets for the film *Cleopatra* 1963, directed by Joseph L. Mankiewicz and starring Elizabeth Taylor, Richard Burton and Rex Harrison. Flanagan started buying antiques from Church Street Market, London, and selling them in Crawford Street – a business he would continue for several years. As well as kitchen jobs (for short periods at Nick's Diner on the Fulham Road and Le Meridian Hotel, Piccadilly) he also gained experience as a gilder – where he was introduced to using clay, bole and gesso – while working for the frame maker Robert Savage on Old Brompton Road.

For three months Flanagan attended Friday evening drawing classes at St Martin's School of Art, taught by Anthony Caro in the sculpture studio. Caro had begun teaching in the Sculpture Department in 1956 and encouraged students to take an experimental approach to life drawing, employing modelling in order to think about the life model in three dimensions.

1961

Flanagan spent three months at Flintshire Technical College, North Wales.

Over the summer he visited his brother Mike in Montreal, who was working as an engineer on the Place Ville-Marie building project for the headquarters of the Royal Bank of Canada. During this short period Flanagan found work as

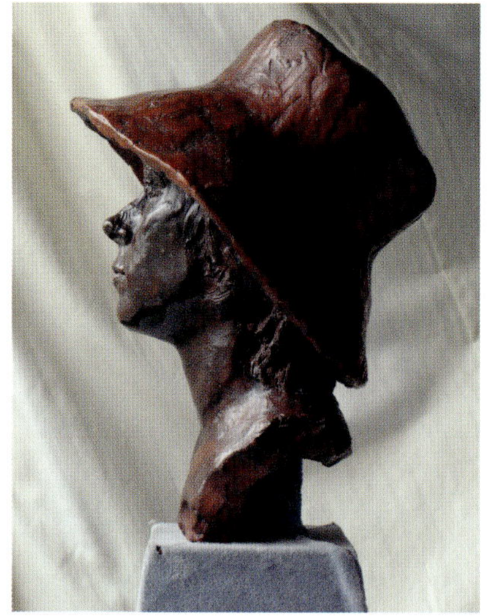

4

a picture framer, a site hand with his brother – where he learned to pour concrete – and in The Place coffee shop on Stanley Street, which was owned by the poets Bryan McCarthy (of whom he also modelled a portrait bust), Joe Sage and Milton Acorn.

He met Judith Wayte before going to Canada, and later modelled her head, wearing a hat, making a false patina on the clay to give it the appearance of bronze (a process that he had learnt at Birmingham).

1962–3

Flanagan settled in Clifton, near Bristol, in a basement flat at 9 Cornwallis Crescent. He and his friends would frequent local cafés and pubs, such as The Blackboy Café, The Greyhound, The Artichoke, The Mauretania, The Ostrich and The Quinton in Clifton and the Cotham Porter Stores. He consequently became friendly with the poets John James and Nick Wayte, who had both been students at Bristol University. Other writers in this circle, were Peter Armstrong, John Sharkey, Chris Torrance and Ian Vine, as well as the painter Peter Swan and Mike Rowlands, a neighbour of Flanagan's. Conversations would focus on the modernist writers Ezra Pound and James Joyce, and Alfred Jarry.

Flanagan modelled a head of Rowlands and gave Judith and Nick Wayte a lino-print, dated 1962, in exchange for the use of an iron and the help they gave with entertaining. He also modelled the head of his landlord Tony Crofts's infant son in lieu of rent. He experimented with powdered clay and *ciment fondu* pieces shaped from various moulds, including used condoms, which Wayte recalls being 'like droll little fish with webbed tails, hanging on a line using clothes pegs'. For a while, Flanagan worked the night shift in Parkers Bakery with John James, and as a van driver for a wallpaper company. Later he was employed as an antique restorer for Hall and Rowan and sat as a life model at the West of England Academy (RWA).

On 27 April 1963 Flanagan married Sue Lewis, a student of theatre and costume design at the Bristol Old Vic Theatre School. Later that year they moved to the small village of Cambridge in Gloucestershire, where Flanagan worked in Kilcraven Antiques and the couple lived above the shop. It was from this address that Flanagan wrote to Anthony Caro – the letter he was later to publish in *Silâns* no.6 (January 1965) and which has been frequently quoted from as an early statement. In the autumn he saw Caro's solo exhibition at the Whitechapel Art Gallery, London. This encouraged him to move to London and apply to St Martin's College of Art.

1964

Flanagan moved to London and enrolled as a full-time student at St Martin's, having received a grant from Gloucestershire County Council. His allocated tutor was Phillip King, with whom he became close friends. Other tutors included David Annesley, Adrian Montford and Isaac Witkin; Caro was present only for short periods, as he spent much of his time between October 1963 and July 1965 in America. Visiting tutors during this period included, among many others, John Latham and Alexander Trocchi. Flanagan met the concrete and sound poet Bob Cobbing, probably as a result of frequenting Better Books bookshop on New Compton Street, near St Martin's. Between January 1965 and November 1967 Cobbing worked in the paperback department, which was managed by Barry Miles from about December 1964 until September 1965, after which time Cobbing took over (the hardback department was at 92 Charing Cross Road, next door). Cobbing and Miles co-organised events and poetry readings in the basement, continuing to use it as a venue for exhibitions and performance events, as Cobbing had started to do a few months earlier, along with Jeff Nuttall and others, and which Flanagan and his fellow students attended regularly.

While at St Martin's Flanagan started a magazine entitled *Silâns* with Rudy Leenders and

4 Clay bust of Judith Wayte 1961

Alastair Jackson, which included poems, articles and illustrations by Flanagan and others. Copies were duplicated and distributed at St Martin's and at Better Books. The magazine ran to sixteen issues and was produced every other Monday during term time between October 1964 and June 1965. Contributing artists, writers and poets, besides the editors, included David Bainbridge, Stanley T. Brobyn, Shirley Cameron, Henri Chopin, Douglas Jeal, Phillip King, Bruce Lacey, John Latham, John Sharkey, Ian T. Spence, Wendy Taylor and Stefan Themerson; it also included short pre-existing texts by Jean Arp, James Joyce, Leo Tolstoy and Georges Vantongerloo. Flanagan used to send copies of *Silâns* to John James and Nick Wayte in Bristol, where they edited the poetry magazine *The Resucitator* (seven issues in the first series, 1963–6, a further four issues, in three parts, were published from Cambridge 1968–9). Flanagan published two poems by Wayte in *Silâns*. During this time Flanagan encountered concrete poetry at events at Better Books and the ICA. One particularly important event featured the sound poet Henri Chopin as part of 'An Evening of Concrete Poetry, Audiovisual and other poetry' at the Institute of Contemporary Arts, with Dom Sylvester Houédard and others on 15 May.

Flanagan had already become interested in 'pataphysics the previous year, following Nick Wayte's gift to him of a copy of the special issue of the *Evergreen Review* devoted to 'pataphysics ('What is 'Pataphysics?', *Evergreen Review*, vol.4, no.13, May–June 1960). This contains extracts from Alfred Jarry's novel *Exploits and Opinions of Dr Faustroll Pataphysician* (published after his death in 1911) and other writing by Jarry and those writers who were associated with the Collège de 'Pataphysique

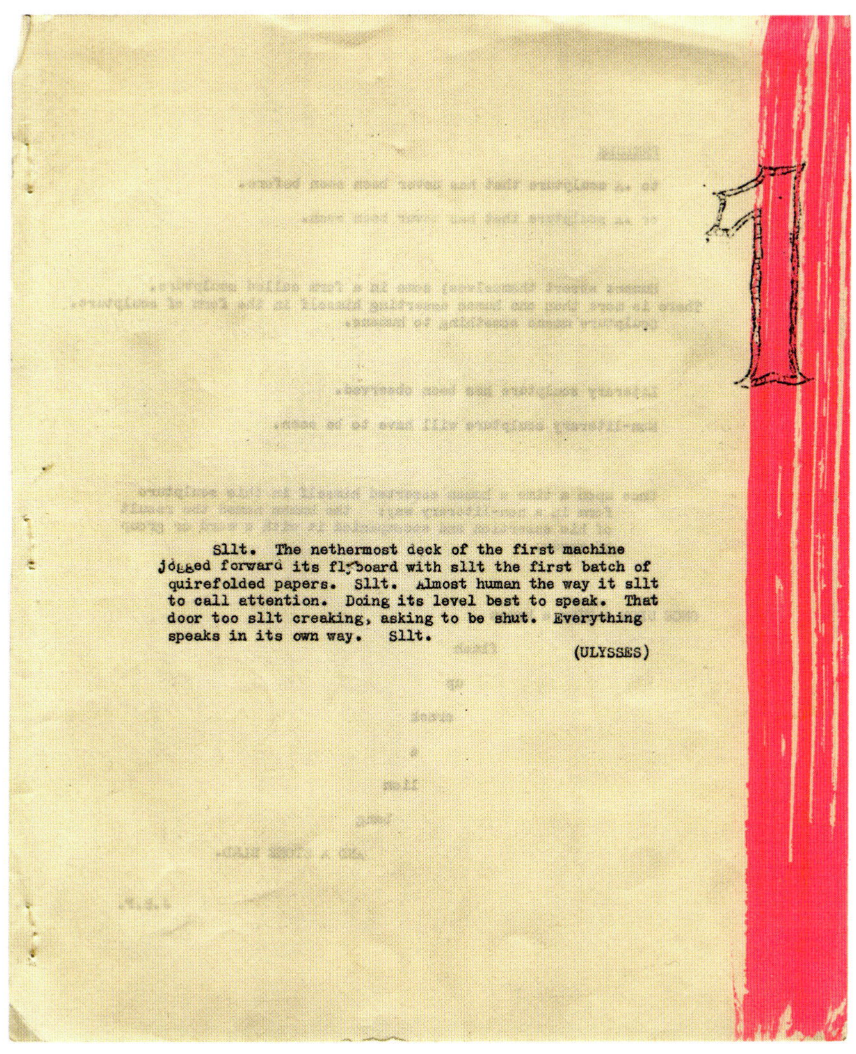
Sllt. The nethermost deck of the first machine jogged forward its flyboard with sllt the first batch of quirefolded papers. Sllt. Almost human the way it sllt to call attention. Doing its level best to speak. That door too sllt creaking, asking to be shut. Everything speaks in its own way. Sllt.

(ULYSSES)

5

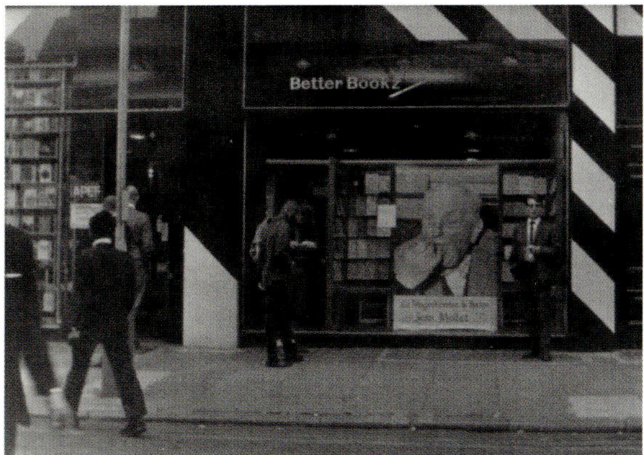

6

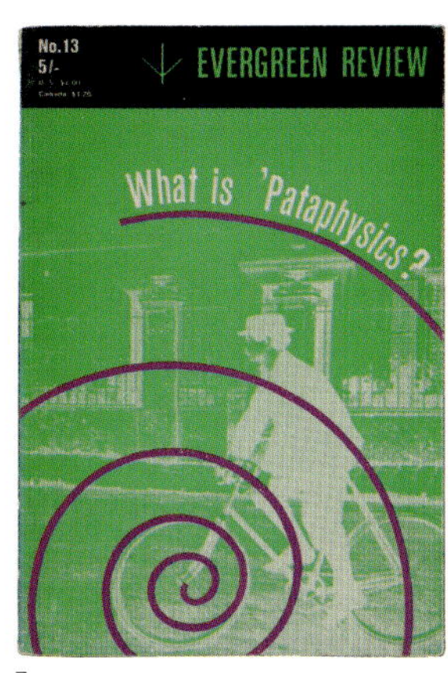

7

(founded 1948). His involvement with the ideas surrounding 'pataphysics and Jarry's 'science of imaginary solutions' grew while at St Martin's; many of his contributions to *Silâns* directly indicate the profound impact that 'pataphysics had.

Flanagan studied the cello part time (one and a half hours a week) at the Guildhall School of Music for one year, securing an additional grant from Gloucestershire County Council, the application supported on the grounds of complementary study by Frank Martin, the head of Sculpture at St Martin's. Flanagan visited Sadler's Wells (where Sue Flanagan worked in the costume department) to see the Merce Cunningham Dance Company, in London for the

5 *Silâns* no.1, October 1964
6 Better Books ('pataphysical window display) 1965
7 *Evergreen Review*, 1964

first time and premiering *Cross Currents* (music by Conlon Nancarrow, arranged by John Cage) and *Winterbranch* (music by La Monte Young and art direction by Robert Rauschenberg, who was present at the London performances). The show opened on 31 July 1964 and starred the ballerina Carolyn Brown. It was so successful that after a week at Sadler's Wells it ran for an extra three weeks at the Phoenix Theatre. Sharkey recalled how the opening night 'was a total uproar as half the audience jeered and tried to leave the theatre while the rest of us clapped, stamped our feet and cheered'. Flanagan described the dance company as 'art in motion' and this encounter marked the first of many with the dance world.

Having joined the ICA specifically so that he could attend private views at the Tate Gallery, Flanagan met Joan Miró at his retrospective exhibition there, *Joan Miró: painting, sculpture and ceramics*, 27 August – 11 October, 1964.

During this year Flanagan moved to 25 Hungerford Road, London N7, a top-floor two-room attic space with a shared bathroom.

1965

Daughter Samantha, later known as Flan, was born. She would become an artist herself, and worked for her father between 1988 and 1998.

Flanagan met Edward Wright and the co-directors of Gaberbocchus Press, Franciszka and Stefan Themerson, who had published the first English translation of Jarry's play *Ubu Roi* in 1951. Franciszka was an artist and writer and Stefan a poet, novelist, filmmaker, composer and philosopher. In April Flanagan wrote to Stefan asking for material to make up a Gaberbocchus bookstore at the exhibition *Three Painters Two Sculptors* in Birmingham; sample pages of the imprint's publications were supplied. Flanagan also met Jasia Reichardt, Assistant Director of the ICA from 1963 to 1971, and renewed his acquaintance with John Sharkey, ICA Gallery Manager from 1965 until 1970/1. Although Sharkey and Flanagan had little contact during this time, two of Sharkey's poems had been published in November 1964 in *Silâns* nos.3 and 4.

To celebrate the publication of the Methuen edition of the *Selected Works of Alfred Jarry*, Miles organised a reading and window display on 'pataphysics at Better Books. The window display featured rare first editions of Jarry's publications surrounding a four-foot circular photograph of His Magnificence The Baron Jean Mollet of the Collège de 'Pataphysique eating a cherry. The portrait revolved once an hour.

Flanagan delivered a silent lip-poem at the opening of the *second international exhibition of experimental poetry* at St Catherine's College, Oxford. This was reproduced as *(O for orange U for you: poem for the lips) juno965* 1965 in *Silâns* no.15, June 1965. The exhibition included Ian Hamilton Finlay, John Furnival, Kenelm Cox, Henri Chopin, Jirí Valoch, Jasia Reichardt, John Sharkey, Bob Cobbing, and Dom Sylvester Houédard. It was organised by Charles Cameron with the help of Gloucester Gloup (which included Cox, Furnival, Houédard and Sharkey). Houédard became a friend of Flanagan, sending him a typestract on a sycamore leaf wishing him 'best thoughts' when he was unable to attend Flanagan's exhibition at the Rowan Gallery the following year. Flanagan also delivered a finger poem at the exhibition *Between Poetry and Painting* at the ICA later in the year.

Flanagan witnessed the first *International Poetry Incarnation* at the Royal Albert Hall, London, on 11 June. The event was attended by at least 7,000 people, and performers in the nineteen-strong programme included Gregory Corso, Lawrence Ferlinghetti, Andrei Voznesensky, Allen Ginsberg, Harry Fainlight, Alexander Trocchi (the event's compère and one of its organisers), Adrian Mitchell and Michael Horovitz. The event included sculptures by Bruce Lacey (which malfunctioned), and Jeff Nuttall and John Latham failed to perform *Film*.

Latham started teaching part time in the painting department at St Martin's, and from 1966–7 he also lectured in the sculpture department. Flanagan later recalled that he and Latham 'were both lateral thinkers (Flanagan in conversation with Hilary Gresty, cited in Gresty 'Sculpture in Britain in the early '70s',

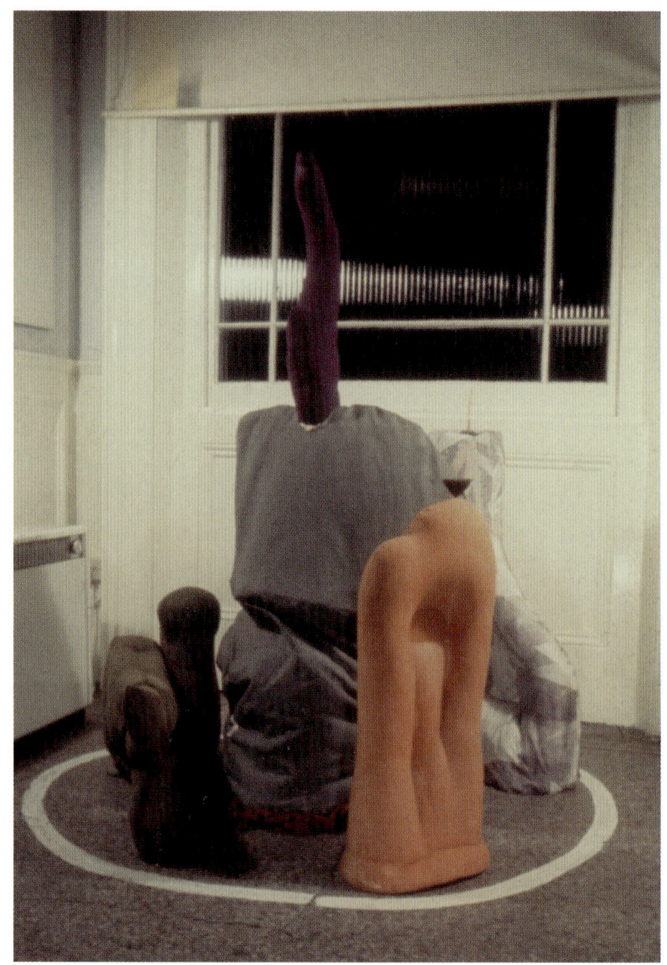

8

8 *aaing j gni aa* 1965 installed in the hallway of Jasia Reichardts's house: covering the window is a 1965 *Roller Painting* by John Latham

MPhil thesis, Courtauld Institute, University of London 1983, p.43).

Flanagan's sculpture *aaing j gni aa* 1965 was exhibited in the basement space of Better Books in July as part of the 35th exhibition of Group H, an art society that Cobbing had founded in Hendon in 1950 as part of Arts Together, and which also included Writers Forum and a Film Society, later to become the London Filmmakers Co-op. By 1965 Group H included artists not living in Hendon, such as Flanagan, Lacey and Nuttall. Flanagan only exhibited twice with Group H: at Better Books and in 1966 at the Drian Gallery. The Better Books exhibition also included work by John Latham and Franciszka Themerson, as well as more regular members of the group. In August Flanagan produced a handbill as a print, suggesting that his work could be exhibited alongside John Sharkey's *Magic Poem* 1965, which, in the event, it was. Sharkey wished to extend poetry, releasing it from the restrictions of the printed page. *Magic Poem* was made up of arcane and alchemical symbols printed on a foot-wide strip of paper about twenty feet in length and had been shown in the exhibition at St Catherine's College, Oxford, the previous year. Sharkey explained how 'The poem surrounded Barry's sculpture which was set out on the floor, so that people could walk in and around and through the combined work'.

GROUP EXHIBITIONS

London Group, Federation of British Artists Galleries, London, 18 Mar. – 9 Apr. (exh. cat.); *Three Painters and Two Sculptors* (or *Five Artists*), RBSA Gallery, Birmingham, 26 Apr. – c.10 May; *second international exhibition of experimental poetry*, St Catherine's College, Oxford, June (exh. cat.); *Group H 35th exhibition*, Better Books, London, July; *Between Poetry and Painting*, Institute of Contemporary Arts, London, 22 Oct. – 27 Nov. (exh. cat.).

SELECTED READING

Gene Baro, 'Britain's Young Sculptors', *Arts Magazine*, vol.40, no.2, Dec. 1965, pp.13–17

1966

Flanagan graduated from St Martin's School of Art with a Vocational Diploma in Sculpture with honours. The diploma had been marked as a pass but the external assessor Brian Wall argued for the grade to be raised to a first.

Latham exhibited at Bangor Art Gallery in the summer and invited Flanagan to show with him. Flanagan showed three sculptures and a group of fifteen drawings, Latham a group of twelve *Skoob* works. In August Flanagan helped to organise, with Latham, the *Still and Chew* event, for which he also designed and printed the invitation. The two artists invited Latham's students from St Martin's, as well as some of the part-time tutors such as Trocchi and other friends, to take part in this event-based work in which they chewed pages of Clement Greenberg's book *Art and Culture* 1965 as a mark of protest against the critic's formalism and his comments on British art. The chewed pages were then spat out, collected and fermented. The event took place from 9pm on 12 August until breakfast the following morning. When Latham received an overdue notice for the book in May 1967 the liquid was distilled and sealed in a glass phial and returned to the library. Latham's contract was not renewed. Records of his action, along with the phial, bottles of liquid and powder used in the fermenting process, as well as the remains of Greenberg's book, were placed in an attaché case and entitled *Still and Chew: Art and Culture* (Collection of MOMA, New York, acquired in 1970), by which time Flanagan had distanced himself from the event.

Flanagan participated in the *Destruction in Art Symposium*, 9–11 September 1966, organised by Gustav Metzger and Sharkey at the Africa Centre, Covent Garden. The programme ran from August to September and comprised readings, lectures, performances and happenings around London, with a three-day symposium at its heart. It aimed to focus attention on the element of destruction in Happenings and other art forms, and relate this to destruction in society. International artists, philosophers, scientists and psychoanalysts took part; Cobbing, Houédard, Sharkey and Miles all served on the organising committee, and the basement of Better Books was used as venue for some of the events. Flanagan contributed a work described as *Sand Sculpture* to the symposium's *Final Event*, which was held at the Mercury Theatre on 30 September. Throughout September Flanagan looked after Yoko Ono and her husband, the filmmaker Tony Cox, driving them around London and effectively acting as their roadie. He recalls collecting Biba dresses for Ono's *Cut Piece*, which was presented at the symposium. Although not announced in the programme, and for one presentation only, Flanagan accompanied *Cut Piece* by riding slowly around the room on a white racing bike with drop handlebars, his shoulder leaning against the wall.

Flanagan joined the Artist Placement Group, set up by Barbara Steveni in 1966 to encourage closer collaboration between artists and industry, commerce and government. Flanagan, Latham and Jeffery Shaw formed the original core of the APG (noit) group – the artists' division – and were soon joined by David Hall and Stuart Brisley and followed by other artists. Flanagan was one of a number of young artists initially interviewed to determine the feasibility of placing graduates

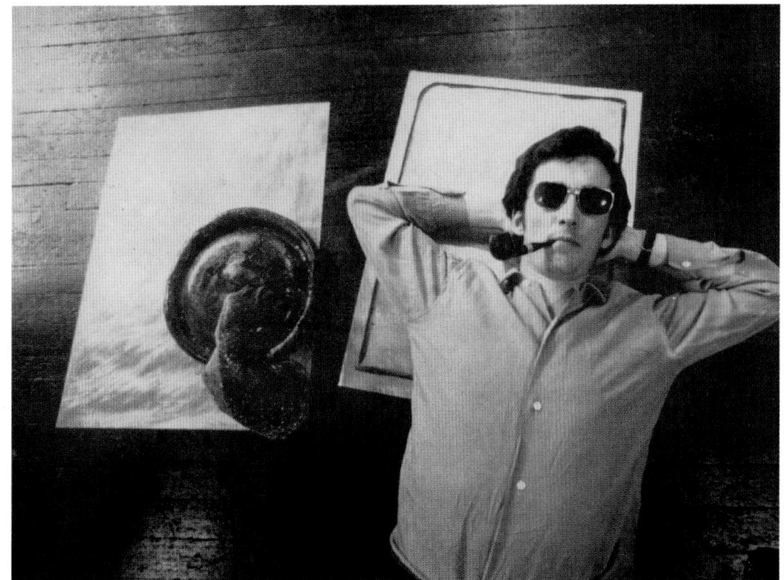

9

9 Invitation card for Flanagan's first solo exhibition, Rowan Gallery, London 1966

in industry. The group's aim was to examine 'the potential activity of a "fine artist" relative to industrial and commercial organisations, to investigate the circumstances of their professional segregation, and to look into ways in which the two might be brought closer together' (APG Research Limited, *The Individual and Organisation*, Tate Gallery Archive 8430.37). For Flanagan, his interest in APG revolved around the relationship of the artist to trade, as he observed in relation to APG that 'not to plan practical occupations for each other to be economically involved in the future is surely revolting' (Ibid.).

Flanagan held his first one-man exhibition at Alex Gregory-Hood's Rowan Gallery, 25a Lowndes Street, Belgravia, London. Phillip King had previously introduced Flanagan to the gallery while he was studying at St Martin's. John Russell concluded 'Processes of Renewal', his review in the *Sunday Times*, by advising readers that rather than an August sleeper show, this debut foretold of new developments: 'If Clement Greenberg is correct in seeing Caro as today's spokesman for the English Sublime, then Flanagan is shaping up to be spokesman for the English Picturesque: for a wayward, shaggy, impulsive and cryptic form of art, an art of calculated incongruity – and, what is equally important, an art the process of renewal.' Gene Baro, a writer of short stories and poetry (one of his poems had been included in the first issue of *Resuscitator*), devoted an entire article, 'Animal, Vegetable and Mineral', to Flanagan in *Art and Artists* vol.1, no.6, Sept. 1966, p.63). Opposite a full-page illustration of *pdreeoo* 1965, he described works with 'no over-riding formality . . . principally, they come out of intuition and process'. Baro continued to write about Flanagan after his return to the United States, where he worked for the Brooklyn Museum, the Carnegie International Museum of Art and the Corcoran Museum of Art.

SOLO EXHIBITIONS

barry flanagan sculpture, Rowan Gallery, London, 5 Aug. – 1 Sept. (artist's statement on private view invitation).

GROUP EXHIBITIONS

an exhibition of concrete/spatial poetry, Midland Group of Artists, Nottingham, Feb. – Mar. (exh. cat. with artist's statement); *Barry Flanagan and John Latham*, University College North Wales Arts Festival, Bangor Art Gallery, 5–26 Mar. (exh. cat.); *Young Contemporaries*, Federation of British Artists Galleries, London, undated (exh. cat.); *Arlington Une International Exhibition of Concrete Poetry*, Arlington Mill, Bibury, Gloucestershire, summer (exh. cat.); *Winter Exhibition*, Rowan Gallery, London, 5 Aug. – 1 Sept.; *group H*, Drian Gallery, London, 4–28 Oct. (exh. cat. with artist's statement); *"New Dimensions": Exhibition of Sculpture*, Hampstead Arts Centre, London, 9–30 Oct. (exh. cat.).

SELECTED READING

Conroy Maddox, 'Barry Flanagan', *Arts Review*, vol.XVIII, no.19, 6 Aug. 1966, p.371

Gene Baro, 'Animal, Vegetable and Mineral', *Art and Artists*, vol.1, no.6, Sept. 1966, p.63

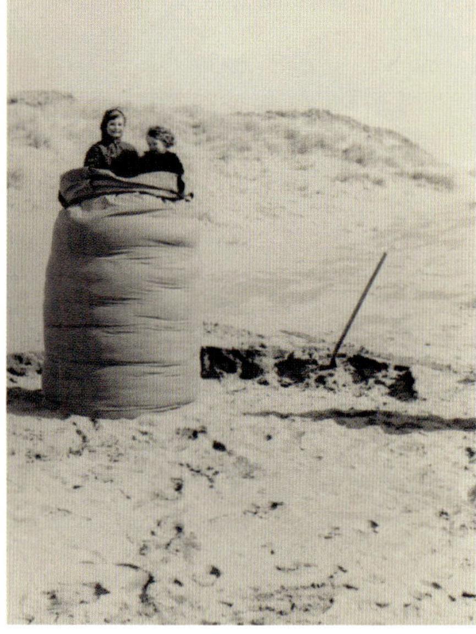

10

1967

Flanagan and Sue's daughter Tara was born.

Flanagan drew in dance classes at the Ballet Rambert. He started teaching for one day a week at the Central School of Arts and Crafts in place of Menashe Kadishman, while he was away in Israel. On Fridays Flanagan also taught on the second year DIP. A.D. sculpture course at St Martin's and would continue teaching at the school in one capacity or another until 1971.

Flanagan worked in Alan Gouk's (painter and teacher at St Martin's 1967–90) studio in Kilburn to prepare and photograph works for the Paris Biennale de Jeunes. The photographs were taken by the critic Charles Harrison, who became a close friend and supporter of Flanagan's work.

Over Easter, Flanagan created *easter bag '67* on Holywell Beach in Cornwall – a ten-foot high, three-ton bag of sand placed in relation to a line drawn and a ring dug into the sand. This was the first of two works made on Holywell Beach, the other being the film *Line on Holywell Beach* 1970. Views of the sculpture were reproduced, with an artist's statement, in the June *ICA Bulletin*, and also in the publication for *Land Art* (Fernsehgalerie Gerry Schum, Berlin 1969). The work was destroyed by soldiers training on the beach soon afterwards. In June he made the smaller *soft shuttered sandwell* as part of the Camden Arts Centre exhibition *Sculpture in a Civic Setting*, which was also vandalised. The work was sited outside the Swiss Cottage Central Library, designed by Sir Basil Spence and housing the

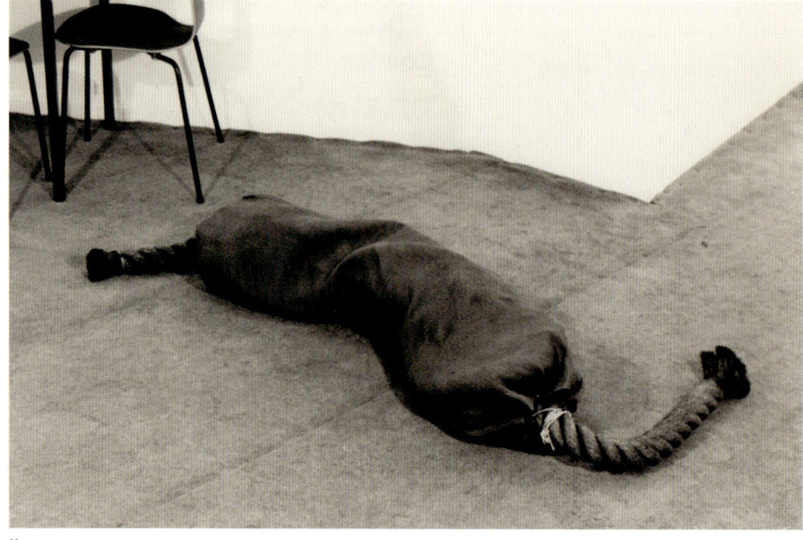

11

10 *easter bag '67* 1967 on Holywell Beach in Cornwall, with Flanagan's niece Sarah and daughter Flan on top

11 *rope/bag (gr 2sp 60) 6 '67* 1967

library that had, until 1964, been held in the Camden Arts Centre building.

The Nagoka Museum exhibited *casb 3 '67* 1967 in the International Art Exhibition of Japan and subsequently purchased the work (the first of Flanagan's work to enter a museum collection).

GROUP EXHIBITIONS

«*Ventures*, Arts Council Gallery, Cambridge, 25 Feb. – 18 Mar., toured to the Art Gallery Oldham, 25 Mar. – 15 Apr.; New Metropole Arts Centre, Folkestone, 22 Apr. – 6 May; Museum of Modern Art, Oxford, 13 May – 3 June; City Art Gallery, Birmingham, 10 June – 2 July; Round Tower, Portsmouth, 8–30 July (exh. cat. with artist's statement);» *Trade View*, Maida Vale, Easter*; *Sculpture in a Civic Setting*, Hampstead Artist Council, Hampstead Arts Centre, London, June (exh. cat.); *Premier Inventaire Internationale de la Poésie Elémentaire*, Galerie Denis Davy, Paris, 20 June – 13 July; *Tribute to Robert Fraser*, Robert Fraser Gallery, London, 5 July – 8 Aug.; *British Drawing Today*, Brighton Arts Festival, summer*; *The Ninth International Art Exhibition of Japan*, (Tokyo Biennale), Tokyo Metropolitan Art Gallery, summer*; *19:45 – 21:55*, Galerie Dorothea Loehr, Frankfurt, 9 Sept. (exh. cat. with artist's statement); *Cinquième Biennale de Paris. Manifestation Biennale et Internationale des Jeunes Artistes*, Musée d'Art Moderne de la Ville de Paris, 29 Sept. – 5 Nov. (exh. cat.); «*British Drawings: The New Generation*, organised by Museum of Modern Art, New York, toured to State University College, Oswego, New York, 8–29 Oct.; Wells College, Aurora, New York, 15 Nov. – 13 Dec.; Phillips Collection, Washington DC, 20 Jan. 1968 – 10 Feb. 1968; Municipal University of Omaha, Nebraska, 4–31 Mar., 1968; Moorhead State College, Minnesota, 19 Apr. – 12 May, 1968; State University of New York, Albany, 1 July – 11 Aug., 1968; University of Manitoba, Winnipeg, Canada, 13 Sept. – 6 Oct., 1968; Saint Cloud State College, Minnesota, 25 Oct.–17 Nov., 1968; Edinboro State College, Pennsylvania, 2–23 Dec., 1968; Kresege Art Centre, Michigan State University, East Lansing, 10–31 Jan., 1969; University of Georgia Museum of Art, Athens, Georgia, 24 Feb. – 1 Mar., 1969; State University College, Brockport, New York, 4–25 Apr., 1969, (brochure).»

SELECTED READING

Christopher Finch, 'British Sculpture Now', *Art and Artists*, vol.2, no.2, May 1967, pp.20–3

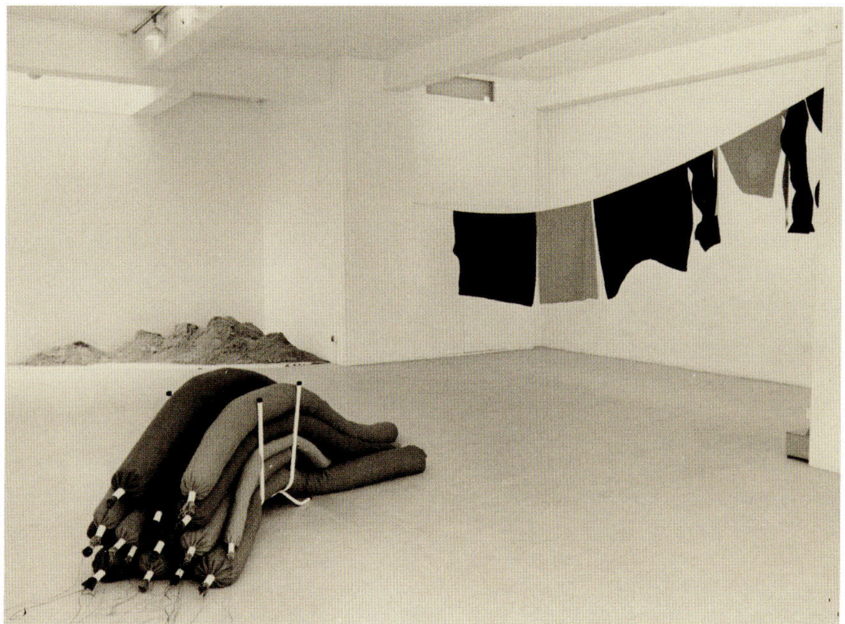

12

1968

Flanagan moved with his family from Hungerford Road to a raised ground-floor double-fronted flat at 44 Belsize Park Gardens, London NW3, which also housed his studio.

He was a founding faculty member of the Anti-University of London, initiated on 12 February in response to what was seen to be the 'intellectual bankruptcy and spiritual emptiness of educational establishment both in Britain and the rest of the Western World'. Other faculty members included Cobbing, Latham, Trocchi, R.D. Laing, Juliet Mitchell and Cornelius Cardew. Flanagan is listed in the original programme as offering a course on 'Space'.

In the autumn Flanagan made the 16mm film *film light shape short*. His interest in film began in Caro's evening classes in 1960, and from then on he often carried a camera as a matter of course.

His second solo show at the Rowan Gallery was in its new space at 31a Bruton Place, where the work engaged directly with the architecture. A similar group of works was also exhibited in the autumn in his first show at Galleria dell'Ariete, Milan, and a group of drawings made on top of the gallery floor plans show that he was thinking of this exhibition in a similar way to that at the Rowan Gallery. Beatrice Monti della Corte ran Galleria dell'Ariete 1958–77, showing Italian avant-garde art, particularly by Boetti, Giulio Paolini and Piero Dorazio, as well as international artists like Robert Rauschenberg, Jasper Johns, Kenneth Noland and David Hockney.

SOLO EXHIBITIONS

Recent Sculpture, Barry Flanagan, Rowan Gallery, London, 5–25 Apr. (artist's statement on private view invitation); *Barry Flanagan Enviroment Skulpturen*, Galerie Ricke, Kassel, 27 June (date of private view); *Barry Flanagan*, Galleria dell'Ariete, Milan, Oct. (exh. cat.); Christian Stein, Turin*.

GROUP EXHIBITIONS

Summer Exhibition, Rowan Gallery, London*; «*British Artists: 6 Painters, 6 Sculptors. An Exhibition Circulated by the Museum of Modern Art New York*, (*Young British Artists*), toured to State University of Albany, New York, Albany, 1 July – 11 Aug.; Munson-Williams Proctor Institute, Utica, New York, 8 Sept. – 6 Oct.; Rose Art Museum, Brandeis University, Waltham, Massachusetts, 15 Sept. – 13 Oct.; Herron Museum of Art, Indianapolis, 3–24 Nov.; University of Texas Art Museum, Austin, 15 Dec. – 15 Jan., 1969; Colorado Springs Fine Arts Centre, 3 Feb. – 3 Mar., 1969; High Museum of Art, Atlanta, Georgia, 24 Mar. – 21 Apr., 1969; University of South Florida, Tampa; Krannert Art Museum, University of Illinois, Champaign; Hopkins Centre Dartmouth College, Hanover; Rose Art Museum, Brandeis University, Waltham, Massachusetts, (finished 26 Oct. 1969) (brochure).»

12 Installation view of Rowan Gallery exhibition 1968 showing (left) *rack 1 '67/68* 1968, (right) *line 1 '67/68* 1967/68, (background) *one ton corner piece '67* 1967

SELECTED READING

Piero Gilardi, 'Da Londra', *Flash Art*, no.6, Jan.–Feb. 1968, pp.1–2

Barry Flanagan, 'Eye-liners; Some Leaves from Barry Flanagan's notebook', *Art and Artists*, vol.3, no.1, Apr. 1968, pp.30–3

Oswell Blakeston, 'Barry Flanagan', *Arts Review*, vol.XX, no.7, 13 Apr. 1968, p.193

Paul Overy, 'Inflation', *The Listener*, 18 Apr. 1968.

Charles Harrison, 'Barry Flanagan's Sculpture', *Studio International*, vol.175, no.900, May 1968, p.266

Piero Gilardi, 'Microemotive Art', *Museum Journal*, no.4, 1968, pp.198–203

1969

Flanagan's first bronze work, a portrait of Emlyn Lewis modelled from photographs, was cast by Henry Abercrombie at the Central School of Arts and Crafts foundry. Lewis was Flanagan's father-in-law and a consultant surgeon in charge of the Plastic Surgery Unit for Wales at St Lawrence Hospital, Chepstow, Gwent. The sculpture took Flanagan two years to complete, finishing it after Lewis's death in May; it was in the possession of St Lawrence Hospital and was recast in 1987 in an edition of three.

Flanagan started to print his own money, called 'funds', in denominations of five, ten, twenty and fifty. Although these prints could be understood as artworks, they were also intended to be used by Flanagan as payment for work undertaken or goods received, and on occasion were accepted as such. They highlight Flanagan's own lack of money at this time. His assistant Andrew Dipper was paid in 'funds' rather than Pounds Sterling, having been asked how he would prefer to receive his wages. Each note was marked, and so authenticated, by the artist's blue thumbprint. Dipper had been Flanagan's student in his final year at Central School (1969–70) and subsequently worked for Flanagan on a number of projects for six or more months between 1970 and 1971. While still at Central he had helped Flanagan carve foam rubber with a wire brush, making a foam version of a Magritte's *Le Viol* 1934 – *The literary observer* 1969 – which was reproduced in the July/August 1969 issue of *Studio International*, alongside his text 'A literary work'.

Flanagan visited New York on a number of occasions. His first solo exhibition in New York opened at the Fischbach Gallery, and he gave a number of lectures at American university galleries as well. At the end of September he was introduced to Eva Hesse by Lucy Lippard, and visited her studio on the Bowery. During this period he became acquainted with Carl Andre, Richard Artschwager, Mel Bochner, Chuck Ginnever, Michael Heizer, Joseph Kosuth, Sol LeWitt, Walter de Maria, Dennis Oppenheim, Seth Siegelaub and Lawrence Weiner.

During his exhibition, at two separate events – one at the Fischbach Gallery and the other at Lucy Lippard's loft in Prince Street – Flanagan showed, to an audience of New York artists, critics and curators, a portfolio of British Conceptual Art comprising seven sheets of photographs of works and artist's statements by himself, Roelof Louw, Bruce McLean and the Eventstructure Research Group (Theo Botschuiver, Jeffrey Shaw and Sean Wellesley-Miller). It was compiled by Flanagan the previous year and published by Alan Power (who covered the costs), prompted by the *Time* magazine article 'The Avant-Garde: Subtle, Cerebral, Elusive' (22 Nov. 1968, pp.70–7), which addressed primarily minimal, anti-form and process sculpture, but only named two European artists – Joseph Beuys and Walter Pichler – among the fourteen American artists. Flanagan's aim was to show that such work was also being made independently in Britain.

On another occasion, during a lecture tour in the US, he gave a separate slide lecture one evening at Lucy Lippard's loft, attended by, among others, Carl Andre, Richard Artschwager, Michael Heizer, Sol LeWitt, Walter De Maria and Michael Compton.

Flanagan's first institutional solo exhibition was at the Museum Haus Lange, Krefeld, under the direction of Paul Wember. Influenced by the effect of light in the Mies van der Rohe architecture, he created site-specific works, some of which used light as material – both projected and natural light – and featured two films, *film light shape short* 1968 and *the works*, made that summer. The films, along with a photograph of *ringn '66*, were included in the group show *Information* the following year at MOMA, New York; *the works* was subsequently acquired by the museum.

Flanagan's first multi-part room installation, *light on light on white on white*, retrospectively titled *Hayward I*, was created for the exhibition *6 at the Hayward Gallery*. This consisted of about 100 lengths of rope (each between three and seven feet long) arranged about the gallery floor, a white painted dado around the wall, one vertical light projection and, in a corner, *light on light on sacks*.

Flanagan provided the cover image (taken from the sequence of *Grass* prints of this year) for *Oppo-Hectic*, a collection of poems by Douglas Oliver (published by Ferry Press in September). John James's poem 'October 27 1969' is dedicated to Flanagan and is a response to his work (James had witnessed Flanagan's works in *Op Losse Schroeven* at the Stedelijk Museum, Amsterdam and *When Attitudes Become Form* at the ICA). It was published in *The Curiously Strong* (vol.3, no.1, Sept. 1970) and in James's 1975 collection *Striking the Pavilion of Zero* (published by Ian McKelvie, London).

aaing j gni aa was acquired by the Tate Gallery, London; during the previous three years the sculpture had been lent to Jasia Reichardt, who had displayed it in the hallway of her house in Belsize Park Gardens.

Flanagan made two films, *the works* and *a hole in the sea*, the latter made on Scheveningen beach in Holland that February with Gerry Schum (whom he had met through Konrad Fischer and

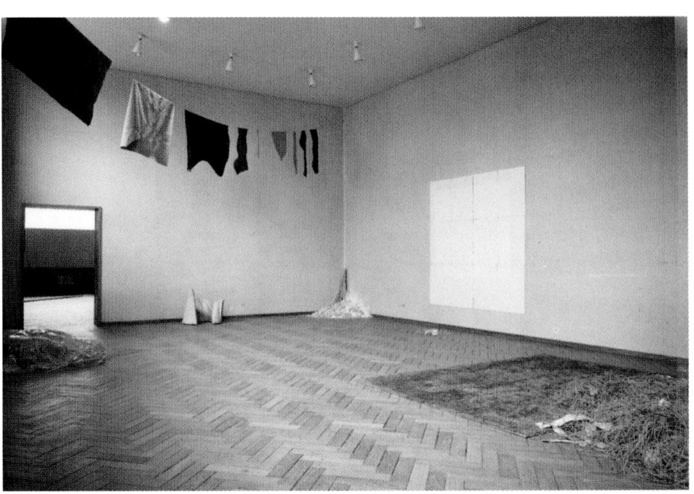

13

13 Installation view of *Op Losse Schroeven*, Stedelijk Museum Amsterdam, showing *line 1′ 67/68* 1967/68 and (underneath) *kope* 1966. Also on display: Alan Saret *Untitled* 1968 (corner); Robert Ryman *Classico V* 1968 (wall), directly beneath which is Carl Andre *Scatter Piece in Five Elements* 1968; Frank Viner *Containers* 1968/9 (at left); and Olle Kåks *Process* 1969 (right foreground)

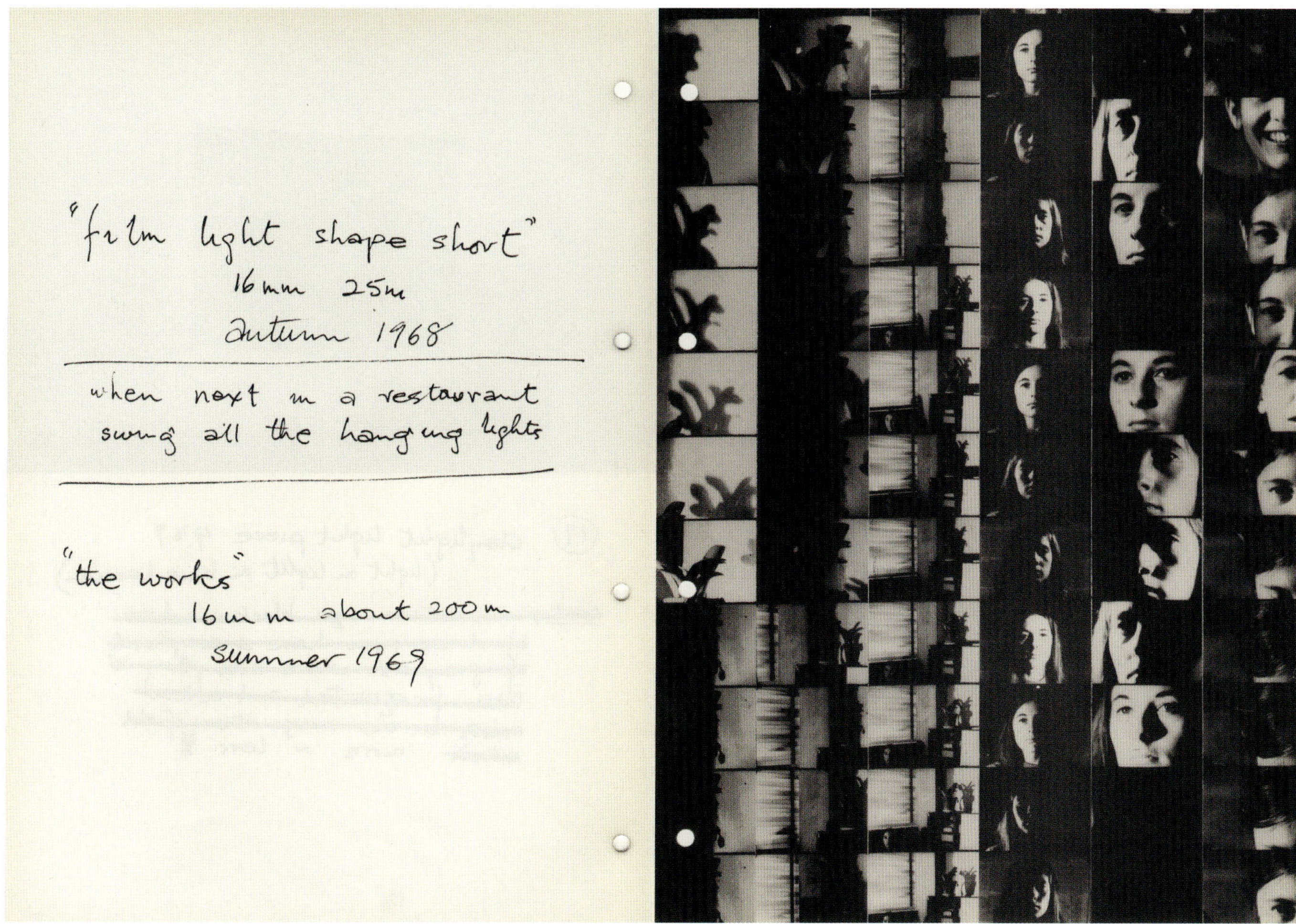
"film light shape short"
16mm 25m
autumn 1968

when next in a restaurant
swing all the hanging lights

"the works"
16mm about 200m
summer 1969

14

Paul Maenz) for his *Land Art* programme. Jan Dibbets also made a film for the project. Shortly after making it Flanagan showed the film to Andrew Dipper, explaining that 'one of the driving forces behind the work were the lyrics of the Lennon/McCartney song *Fixing a Hole*. At this time Flanagan was in touch with Eventstructure Research Group in Amsterdam through Jeffrey Shaw, who was also part of APG and a friend of John Latham.

SOLO EXHIBITIONS

Barry Flanagan Object Sculptures, Museum Haus Lange, Krefeld, 7 Sept. – 12 Oct. (exh. cat. with artist's statements); *Barry Flanagan*, Fischbach Gallery, New York, 27 Sept. – 16 Oct. (press release with artist's statement).

GROUP EXHIBITIONS

One Month, Seth Siegelaub, New York, 1–31 Mar. (publication with artist's page); *Op Losse Schroeven (Situations and Cryptostructures)*, Stedelijk Museum, Amsterdam, 15 Mar. – 27 Apr., (exh. cat. with artist's page); «*New Media: New Method*, Trinity College, Austin, Texas touring to Robertson Centre, Binghamton, New York, 16 Mar. – 13 Apr.*; *Live in Your Head: When Attitudes Become Form (Works – Concepts – Processes – Situations – Information)*, Kunsthalle, Berne, 22 Mar. – 27 Apr., toured to Kaiser Wilhelm Museum, Krefeld, 10 May – 15 June; ICA, London, 28 Aug. –28 Sept. (exh. cat. with artist's statement)»; *Land Art*, Fernsehgalerie Gerry Schum, Berlin, 15 Apr. (exh. cat. with artist's pages); *Verbogene Strukturen*, Museum Folkwang Essen, Ausstellung, 9 May – 22 June (exh. cat.); *Nine Young Artists Theodoron Awards*, Solomon R. Guggenheim Museum, New York, 23 May – 29 June (exh. cat.); «*Play Orbit*, Royal National Eisteddfod of Wales, Flint, 4–9 Aug., toured to ICA, London, 28 Nov. – 15 Feb. 1970 (exh. cat. with artist's statement);» *557,087*, Seattle Art Museum Pavilion, Seattle, 5 Sept. – 5 Oct. (exh. cat. with artist's statement); *Kunstmarkt Koln*, Galerie Ricke, Cologne, 14 Oct. – 9 Nov. (exh. cat.); *Survey 69 New Space*, Camden Arts Centre, London, 24 Oct. – 23 Nov. (exh. cat.); *6 at the Hayward Gallery*, Hayward Gallery, London, 13 Nov. – 21 Dec. (exh. cat.); *John Moores Liverpool Exhibition 7*, Walker Art Gallery, Liverpool, 26 Nov. – 26 Jan., 1970 (exh. cat.); *Art in Process IV*, Finch College Museum of Art, New York, 11 Dec. – 26 Jan., 1970 (exh. cat. with artist's statement).

SELECTED READING

Charles Harrison, 'Some recent sculpture in Britain', *Studio International*, vol.177, no.907, Jan. 1969, pp.26–33

14 A Page spread from *Barry Flanagan Object Sculptures*, exh. cat., Museum Haus Lange Krefeld, 1969, showing stills from *film light shape short* 1968 and *the works* 1969

Germano Celant, 'La Natura è inserta', *Casabella*, Aug.–Sept. 1969, p.107
Charles Harrison, 'Against Precedents', *Studio International*, vol.178, no.914, Sept. 1969, pp.90–3
Dore Ashton 'New York Commentary', *Studio International*, vol.178, no.917, Dec. 1969, pp. 230–1
Barry Flanagan in discussion with Gene Baro, 'Sculpture made visible', *Studio International*, vol.180, no.926, Oct. 1969, pp.122–5
Germano Celant, *Arte Povera*, Praeger, New York, 1969

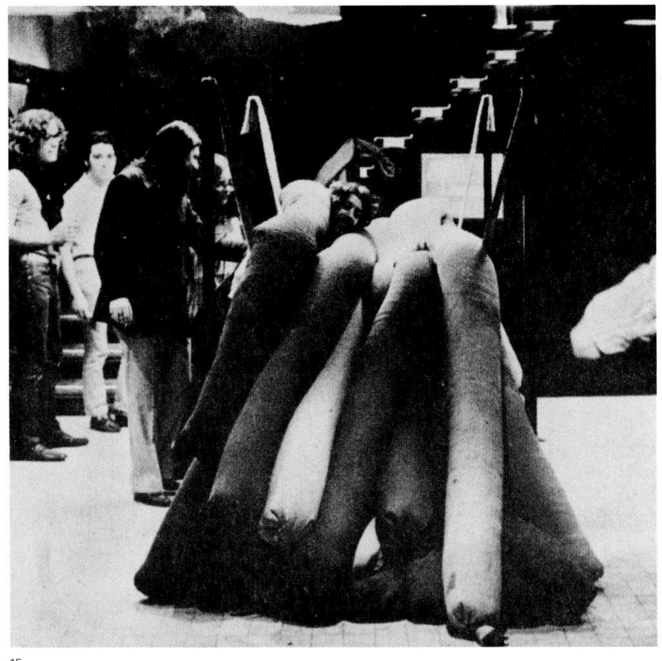

15

1970

Flanagan moved with his family from Belsize Park Gardens to a house at 8 Cliff Road NW1, which had been bought by Sue Flanagan. While working on the house Flanagan, who was short of money, worked as a labourer for the builder Jock Murray, who the Flanagans had employed; also working on the project were a number of friends, including engineer Jonathan Park as project manager, music journalist Paul Winstanley as a chippy and Paul du Feu as labourer. The house was over four floors with an open-plan basement as living area, a raised ground-floor area for Barry and Sue, a first-floor studio and a top-floor office and room with kitchenette, which was sometimes let out (for a while to art dealer Anthony Stokes). Flanagan described the arrangement of the house as a 'four-drawer system'.

Flanagan continued to play the cello and at this time his daughter Flan remembers him 'teaching himself by listening to Pablo Casals on the record player and playing'. He visited Japan for the exhibition *Between Man and Matter*, and during this visit he mainly socialised with Carl Andre and Roelof Louw.

Flanagan wrote an obituary for Eva Hesse, published in the July/August issue of *Studio International*, in which he states that 'it was my fortune to meet her and see some early pieces last year, also new pieces more recently. Her maturity and courage are reflected completely in the strength of her work; the loss of such an artist is acute.'

He initiated a portable sculpture project around Camden and Islington for which he rented an open-bed truck with a cement mixer, wheelbarrow, a mounted worker's hut and a sewing machine. Pulling up to a location, Flanagan and his assistant Dipper would sew the dark blue canvas bags, mixing the cement and filling the bags in situ, anchoring them to the spot by hammering rebars into holes in the paving. Flanagan's canvas-covered concrete bollards were a protest against council plans to erect a large number of permanent bollards on such sites as the corner of Agar Grove and Murray Street in Camden.

Flanagan was regularly invited back to St Martin's by Frank Martin, Alan Gouk and Rudy Leenders to teach on the Advanced Sculpture Course and, alongside Caro, Tim Scott and Phillip King, to assess the students' work. Gouk recalls that he did not favour the group teaching ethos that was followed at St Martin's, preferring to teach on a one-to-one basis. Flanagan ran the course for only one year (September 1970 – June 1971), after which Gouk took over his post.

Flanagan produced his first etchings at St Martin's, notably *O'Rembrandt*, a study of the feet of Eve from Rembrandt's etching *Adam and Eve* 1638, and *Some of a young Turk*. He also made five films: in April *Line on Holywell Beach*, which followed the trail in the sand left by a camera tripod as it was dragged from the waterline to the dunes; in May *Atlantic Flight*, the view of the Atlantic out of a Boeing 747 window en route to Tokyo; *Works II; Bus Ride*, shot from a bus from the airport to the city on his first visit to New York, and *sand girl*, showing sand from a sack suspended from the ceiling pouring and trickling onto a naked woman.

SOLO EXHIBITIONS

Barry Flanagan recent work, Rowan Gallery, London, 10–30 Apr.

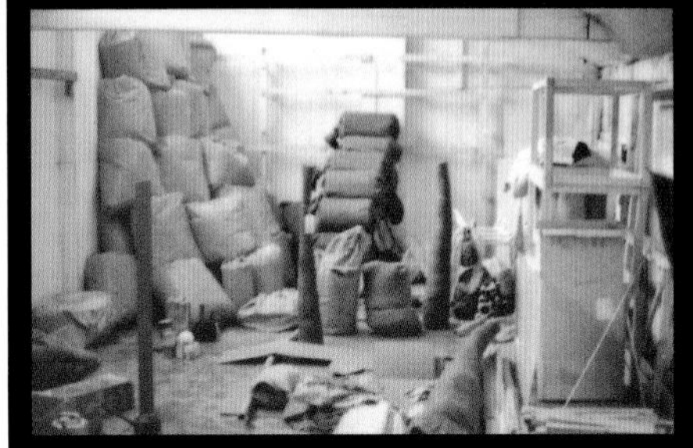
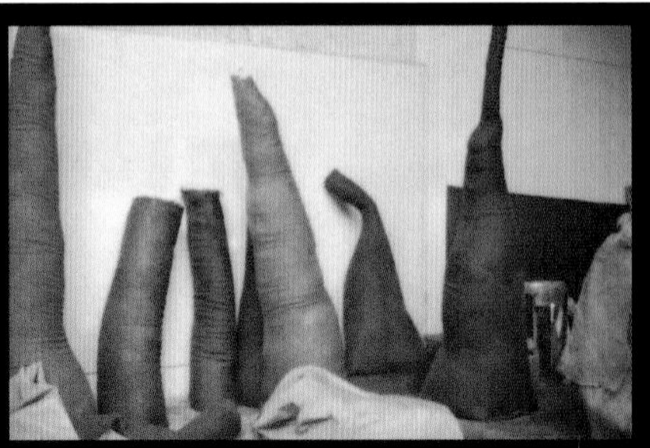

16

15 Installation view of CAYC, Buenos Aires 1970, showing *rack* c.1970
16 Flanagan's studio/store, London 1969

GROUP EXHIBITIONS

String & Rope, Sidney Janis Gallery, New York, 7–31 Jan. (exh. cat.); *Some Recent Art in Britain*, Leeds City Art Gallery, Leeds, 10 Apr. – 17 May (exh. cat.); « *Between Man and Matter: The Tenth Tokyo Biennale*, Tokyo Metropolitan Art Gallery, Tokyo, 10–30 May toured to Kyoto Municipal Art Museum, Kyoto, 6–28 June; Aichi Prefectural Art Gallery, Nagoya, 15–26 July; Fukuoka Prefectural Culture House, Fukuoka, 11–16 Aug. (exh. cat. with artist's pages); » *Drawings and Projects of 16 British Sculptors*, Galería Bonino, Buenos Aires, organised by CAYC, 11–27 May (exh. cat.); *July/August Exhibition Book*, within the pages of *Studio International*, vol.180, no.924, July–Aug., 1970 (exh. cat.); *Information*, Museum of Modern Art, New York, 2 July – 20 Sept. (exh. cat.); *British Sculpture out of the Sixties*, ICA, London, 6 Aug. – 27 Sept. (exh. cat. with artist's statement); *Contemporary British Art*, National Museum of Modern Art, Tokyo, 9 Sept. – 25 Oct. (exh. cat.); *Christo, Barry Flangan*, CAYC, Buenos Aires, Nov (exh. cat. with artist's statement); *Wall Show*, Lisson Gallery, London, 10 Dec. – 30 Jan., 1971 (exh. cat. with artist's page).

SELECTED READING

Peter Fuller, 'Barry Flanagan', *Arts Review*, vol.XXII, no.7, 11 Apr. 1970, pp.217 and 231

Barry Flanagan and Peter Fuller, *Connoisseur*, vol.174, no.701, July 1970, p.210

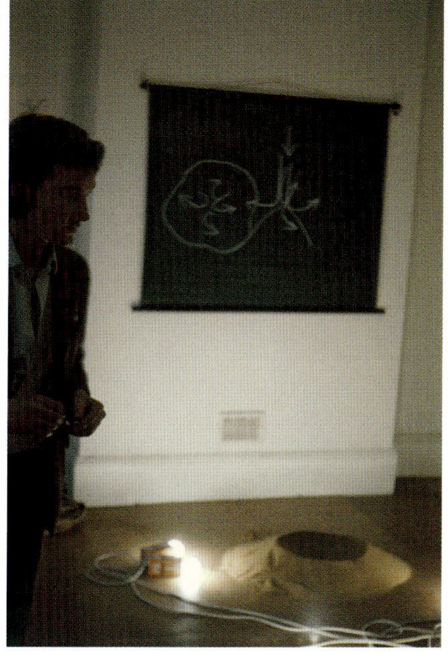

17

1971

Flanagan took part in the *Wall Show* at the Lisson Gallery with *wall no. 7*, for which he painted the gallery wall for 50p per yard and signed it. His contribution to *Art Spectrum London*, at Alexandra Palace in August, took various forms: a statement in the catalogue, a film screening and the distribution of his own fee amongst the other participants. He wrote to the organisers requesting the maximum amount available without revealing his intentions, but stated it was essential for the realisation of the work. Although reluctant to release funds without the purpose explicitly declared, the organisers eventually agreed and Flanagan distributed the amount to the artists in the form of postal orders to be exchanged for the newly minted 50p pieces at the opening of the exhibition. (50p pieces had only recently been issued; Flanagan, however, would not adopt the metric system of weights and measures until 1977.) He also made an unprogrammed performance: he drew a chalk line about ten paces long, had his wife jump on his back, he picked up his daughters, one under each arm, and then walked along the line.

Flanagan made Hessian armbands marked with 'pataphysical spirals for a football match of artists versus poets at Charlton Athletic football ground. The artists (largely drawn from the studios at Stockwell Depot) beat the poets 10–0.

Flanagan visited Burleighfield House, Loudwater, the arts centre established by the stained glass artist Patrick Reyntiens and his wife, the painter Anne Bruce, under the auspices of the Burleighfield Trust. Here his etchings *60's Dish*, *Joke ink blot* and *Grate* were printed by David Harding, who worked as a printmaker there. Subsequently, Flanagan started to produce the majority of his etchings in his own studio, where he set up a printing press. He was assisted first by Harding and then, between 1971 and 1972, by Peter Briggs, a student in his final year at Hornsey School of Art who proofed most of his etchings in these years. The relationship with Burleighfield continued and in 1976 a foundry was established there, where Flanagan's 1969 portrait of Emlyn Lewis was recast in 1987.

Flanagan worked with Alan Sekers at the Scott Bader Company (a manufacturer of polyester resins for glass reinforced plastics, but described by Flanagan as a 'paint company') to produce a film that was presented at the APG's *Inno 70* exhibition at the Hayward Gallery, London, in December. Flanagan describes how Sekers 'came along with me with a stills camera and I carried the tape recorder. After he had taken the still photographs, we filmed the photographs using a Super-8 camera which had been developed by birdwatchers. A voice-over accompanied the film of the photo stills.' ('Barry Flanagan in conversation with Hans Ulrich Obrist', *Barry Flanagan Sculpture 1965–2005*, Irish Museum of Modern Art, Dublin 2006, p. 57).

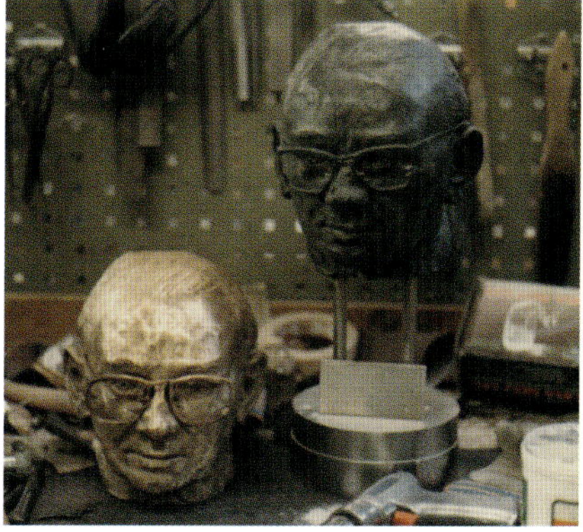

18

Flanagan made the films *The Phantom Sculptor* and *The Lesson*, the latter the result of a conversation with Charles Harrison, who had wanted to include the work *ringn '66* in *The British Avant Garde* at the New York Cultural Centre. Both were interested in the procedural aspect of the work but Flanagan thought its durational nature would be best documented by a film, which could also become a work in itself. In the autumn *Atlantic Flight* and *Line on Holywell Beach* were both included in *Prospect 71: Projection* at the Düsseldorf Kunsthalle, the first major survey exhibition of artists' film in Europe. Most of the British artists had previously shown their films at Situation Gallery. In September *Atlantic Flight* had been shown at Situation and reviewed by Guy Brett in the *Times*:

'Barry Flanagan's *Atlantic Flight* at Situation is a film made through the window of a plane. The camera is fixed, as the passenger is fixed in his seat, staring through the window at the wing and the air beyond. This is time to watch the land slide away, the rain clear from the window, and the sun come out above the clouds. There is also time to be bored, but the situation of the watcher of the film and the passenger on the plane is so akin than he can, in a sense, examine his boredom. It is not whisked away by a change of scene.' (*Times*, 18 Sept. 1971).

SOLO EXHIBITIONS

Barry Flanagan, Rowan Gallery, London, 2–29 Apr.; Galleria del Leone, Venice *.

17 Flanagan filming *The Lesson*, 1971
18 *Emlyn Lewis* 1969, with new cast 1987

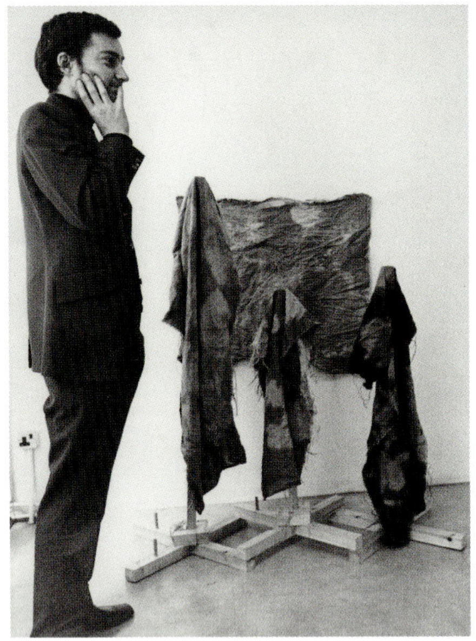
19

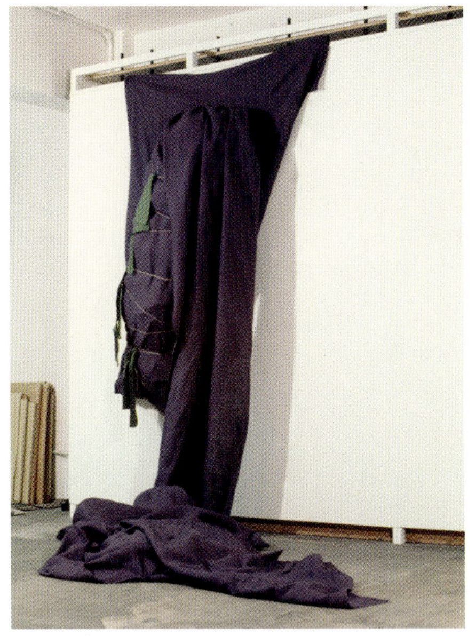
20

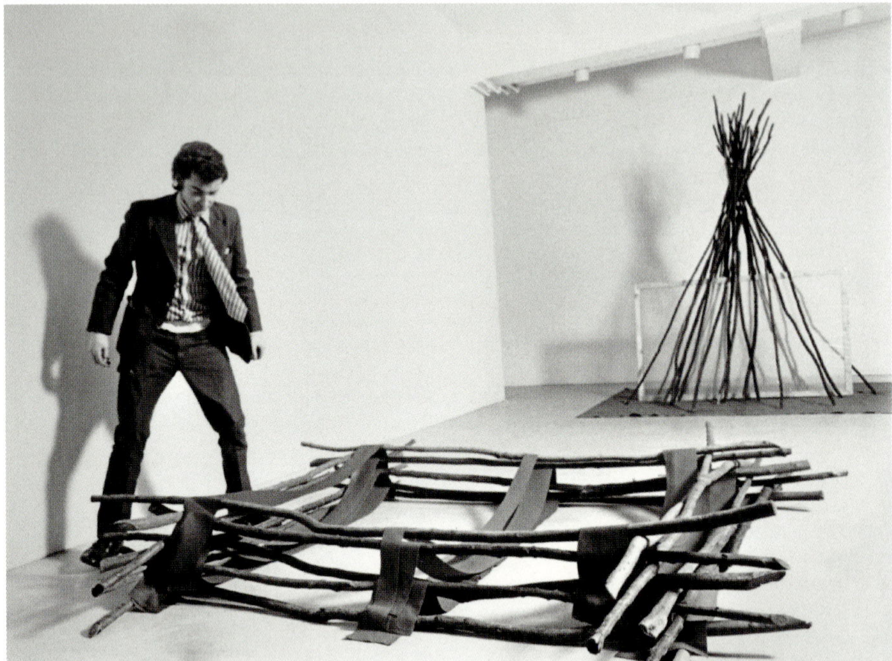
21

GROUP EXHIBITIONS
«*São Paulo Bienal – Road Show: A New English Enquiry*, British Council exhibition, toured to Museu de Arte Moderna, Rio de Janeiro, 26 Jan. – undated; Museu de Arte Moderna, São Paulo, 4 Sept. – undated; Museo de Artes Visuales, Montevideo, Uruguay, 12 Apr. – 25 July, 1972; Museo Nacional de Bellas Artes, Buenos Aires, 29 June – 25 July, 1972; Museo Nacional de Bellas Artes, Santiago, 16–31 Aug., 1972; Museo Nacional de Arte Moderno, Mexico City, 24 May – 8 July, 1973; and subsequently to Spain in 1974/1975 and to the Netherlands 1975/1976 (exh. cat. with artist's statement);» *Films by Artists*, Situation, London, through April; *At the Moment*, Frankopanska 2a, Zagreb, 23 April 1971; *The British Avant Garde*, New York Cultural Centre, 19 May – 29 Aug. (exh. cat.); *Sonsbeek 71: Sonsbeek buiten de parken*, Park Sonsbeek, Arnhem, 19 June – 15 Aug. (exh. cat.); *Arte de Sistemas*, CAYC, Buenos Aires, July (exh. cat.); *Art Spectrum London*, Alexandra Palace Great Hall, London, 11–30 Aug. (exh. cat. with artist's statement); *Film Show – Barry Flanagan, Hamish Fulton, Bob Law, Bruce McLean, David Tremlett*, Situation, London, 7 Sept.; *In another moment*, SKC Gallery, Belgrade, 15–20, 22–27 Sept., 29 Sept. – 3 Oct. (exh. cat.); *Prospect 71: Projection*, Städtische Kunsthalle, Düsseldorf, 8–17 Oct., (exh. cat.); *Inno 70: Art & Economics*, Artist Placement Group, Hayward Gallery, London, 2–23 Dec. (various documents); «*Eight Individuals*, Arts Council of Great Britain exhibition toured to Derby Museum and Art Gallery, 4 Dec. – 15 Jan., 1972; Southampton City Art Gallery, 29 Jan. – 11 Mar., 1972; Folkestone Arts Centre, 25 Mar. – 6 May, 1972; Billingham Art Gallery, 20 May – 1 July, 1972; Graves Gallery, Sheffield, 15 July – 26 Aug., 1972 (exh. cat.).»

SELECTED READING
Caroline Tisdall, 'Barry Flanagan Exhibition in London', *Guardian*, 22 Apr. 1971, p.8

1972

Flanagan was awarded a Gulbenkian Foundation grant to work with the dance group Strider in London during its first season. He worked with the company for six months, choreographing two short pieces in collaboration with them. In preparation he also attended dance classes at The Place (the London School for Contemporary Dance) under the tutelage of American-born teacher, dancer and choreographer Carolyn Carlson. For *Hundreds and Thousands*, choreographed with and performed by Sally Potter, Jackie Lansley and Diana Davies, Flanagan arranged a ton of sand in a heap on the stage and shovelled it from one side to the other with the help of a collaborator (for some performances this was artist John Hilliard, for others Paul du Feu). The visual rhythm of the movement, the recorded sound of the shovelling and the accompaniment of the Portsmouth Sinfonia's rendition of the *Sugar Plum Fairy* provided a foil for the dancers to react to. For the second piece, *Counterfoil*, Flanagan choreographed and performed a dance that related to the idea of traversing reality and focussed on the four corners of the room. The two pieces were performed at The Place Theatre, the Edinburgh

19 Flanagan beside *bleach 1 '70*, 1970
20 *purple hanging piece* 1969
21 Flanagan building *no. 5 '71* in the Rowan Gallery 1971

Festival, in *Body as Medium of Expression* at the ICA and the *British Festival of Art* in Oslo.

Flanagan created a sculpture in Laundress Green, Cambridge, for the *City Sculpture Project*, sponsored by the Stuyvesant Foundation. Eight cities were involved in the project and Phillip King and Stewart Mason were on the selection panel. Two sculptors were chosen to create works for each city, with Flanagan and Brower Hatcher selected for Cambridge. Flanagan's sculpture, made with the assistance of Andy Elton and Roger Moss, was attacked, and eventually destroyed, by students attaching washing lines and hanging clothes from it before removing the piece completely (some fragments were later found outside Peterhouse junior common room). Later this year in his *Homework* exhibition at the Rowan Gallery, Flanagan showed the maquette he had made for Laundress Green. Slides of the site were projected onto the work so that it appeared in the setting and would cast shadows. Flanagan had initially tried to make a work out of glass-fibre for the project, but he did not favour this medium, and instead adopted a resin surface hardener. When he spoke about the Stuyvesant project in a *South Bank Show* interview with Melvyn Bragg (broadcast in 1983), he said he found the material used to strengthen the sculpture unsatisfactory, and the experience made him 'take off to Italy to chew it over a bit'.

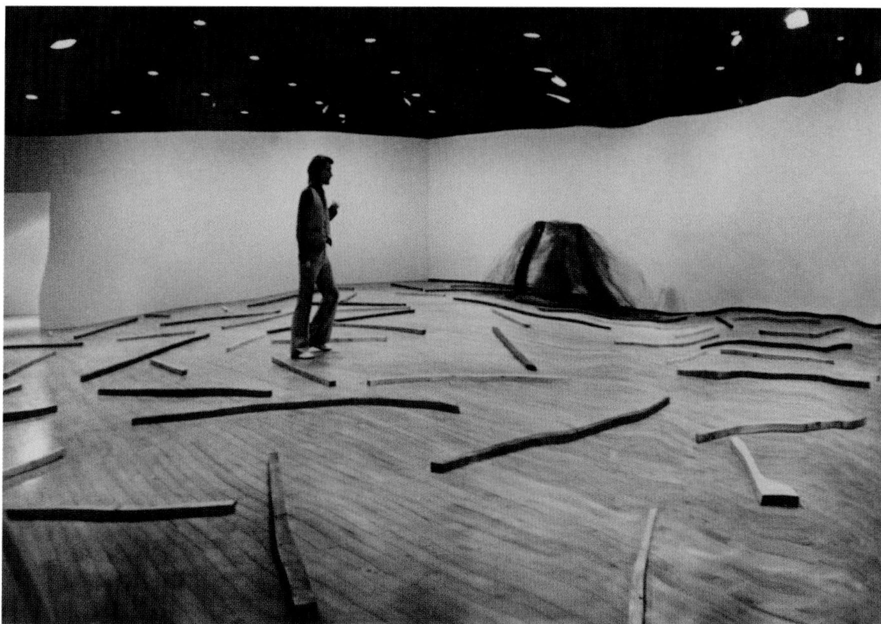

22

As his contribution for *The New Art* at the Hayward Gallery Flanagan revisited *Hayward I* and made *Hayward II* – a smaller room installation made up of lengths of wood (the same length as the ropes in the earlier installation), scaffolding, stuffed-cloth columns and a wall covered in a reflective and distorting mirror foil. He also showed three films – *Line on Holywell Beach*, *Atlantic Flight* and *sand girl* – for three hours each Tuesday and Thursday in his space. Between 1968 and 1972 Flanagan made ten films, and his interest in filmmaking continued well into the 1970s. When asked by the critic Barbara Reise if he would like to make films for TV he responded: 'I'd like to work w[ith] other people'. Reise asked whether this was in terms of subject, technique or technicians and Flanagan responded: 'In terms of [a] job, I'm tired of my job as a sculptor' (undated notebook page, Tate Gallery Archive, TGA 786/5/2/56).

Flanagan left the Artist Placement Group, though wrote supportively in a letter to Robin Campbell at the Arts Council in 1973, stating that the 'APG is a good idea to me, a fine NOTION, there will always be an element of potential in it . . .' (Tate Gallery Archive, TGA 20042. 1.2a).

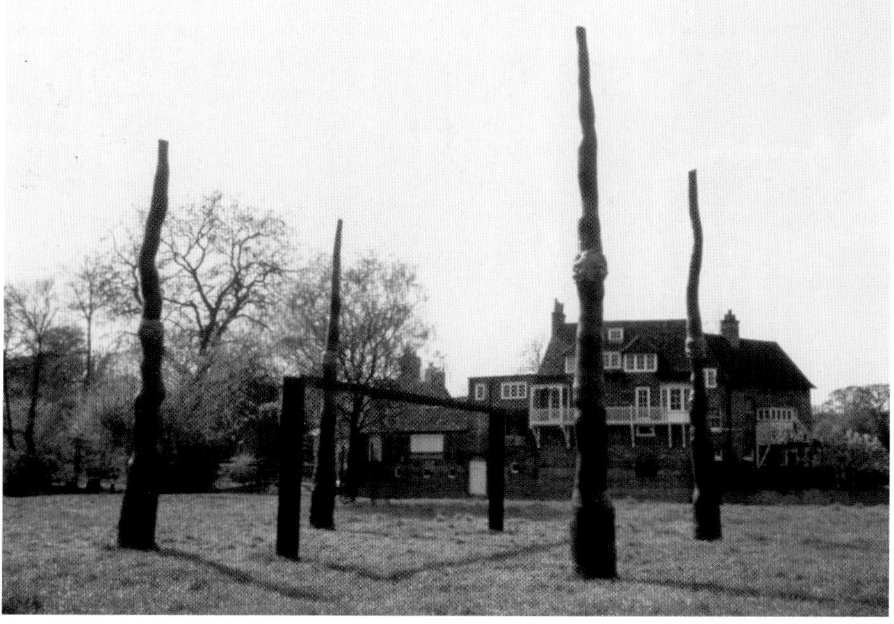

23

SOLO EXHIBITIONS

Barry Flanagan: Homework, Rowan Gallery, London, 10 Nov. – 7 Dec.

GROUP EXHIBITIONS

Peter Stuyvesant Foundation City Sculpture Project, commission for Laundress Green, Cambridge, Apr. – c.Sept., « the accompanying exhibition *City Sculpture*, ICA, 13–30 Apr., toured to Laing Art Gallery, Newcastle, 25 May – 9 June; Graves Art Gallery, Sheffield, 21 June – 7 July; Walker Art Gallery, Liverpool, 19 July – 4 Aug.; City Museum and Art Gallery, Birmingham, 16 Aug. – 1 Sept.; National Museum of Wales, Cardiff, 13 – 29

22 *Hayward II* 1972
23 Sculpture for Laundress Green, Cambridge 1972

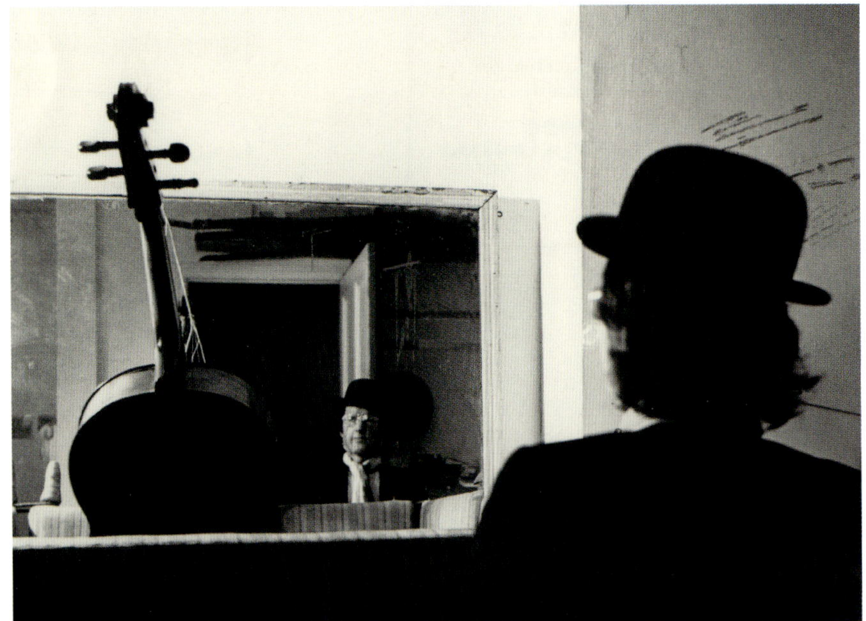

24

Sept.; City Museum and Art Gallery, Plymouth, 11–27 Oct.; City Art Gallery, Southampton, 8–24 Nov. (exh. cat., artist's statement contained in the accompanying publication *City Sculpture. A special issue of Studio International in collaboration with the Peter Stuyvesant Foundation City Sculpture Project 1972*); *Contemporary Prints*, Ulster Museum, Belfast, 5 July–10 Sept. (exh. cat.);» *Burleighfield Printing House at the New Art Centre*, New Art Centre, London, Aug. 1972*; *The New Art*, Hayward Gallery, London, 17 Aug. – 24 Sept. (exh. cat.); *Festival of British Art – "British Thing"*, organised by the British Council, Henie-Onstad Foundation, Høvikodden, Norway, 21 Sept. – 16 Oct. (exh. cat.); *Drawing*, Museum of Modern Art, Oxford, 18 Nov. – 23 Dec. (exh. cat.).

1973

Flanagan visited Pietrasanta, which led to a commission from Stewart Mason, an art patron and director of Leicestershire Education Department, for Rawlins School, Quorn, Leicestershire. The commission was a direct result of Flanagan's work for Laundress Green the previous year, Mason having been one of the selectors for the *Peter Stuyvesant Foundation City Sculpture Project*. The resulting work, *portoro 1* 1973, is a group of large naturally shaped stone blocks of Portoro marble standing or lying on the ground, suggestive both of the stonemason's yard and prehistoric standing stones. Barry met the potter Ann Stokes, editor Nikos Stangos and poet and novelist David Plante while in Italy that summer.

Some of Flanagan's prints were used to illustrate Tom Raworth's collection of poetry, *Act*, published by Trigram: on the cover *A Pound Note, by a Governed Imagination* 1972, portrait of *Tom Raworth* 1972 for the frontispiece, and *60s Dish* 1971 and *When Attitude Offend Form* 1971 inside.

SOLO EXHIBITIONS

Barry Flanagan, Rowan Gallery, London, 13 July – 3 Aug.

GROUP EXHIBITIONS

Graphics, Rowan Gallery, London*; «*11 British Artists*, British Council touring exhibition to Kunsthalle, Baden Baden, 4 May – 10 June; Kunsthalle, Bremen, 1 July – 5 Aug.; Koninklijk Museum voor Schone Kunsten, 15 Sept. – 14 Oct. (exh. cat.);» *Gallery Artists*, Rowan Gallery, London*; *Henry Moore to Gilbert and George – Modern Art from The Tate Gallery*, Palais des Beaux-Arts, Brussels, 28 Sept. – 17 Nov. (exh. cat.).

SELECTED READING

Fenella Crichton, 'London Letter', *Art International*, vol.XVII, no.7, Sept. 1973, p.36

1974

Flanagan visited Ann Stokes several times in her studio in Hampstead to talk about pottery. She recalls how 'Barry wanted to learn about the techniques and experience of the feeling of clay and he made several items using just his hands including some small coiled pots which I then fired.'

Flanagan visited Cortona, Italy, where he made drawings of Etruscan sculptures in the museum, which were included in his exhibition of drawings *1966–1974* at the Museum of Modern Art Oxford. These were also reproduced in the publication *Somethings Etruscan* – which accompanied the Oxford show and his final exhibition at

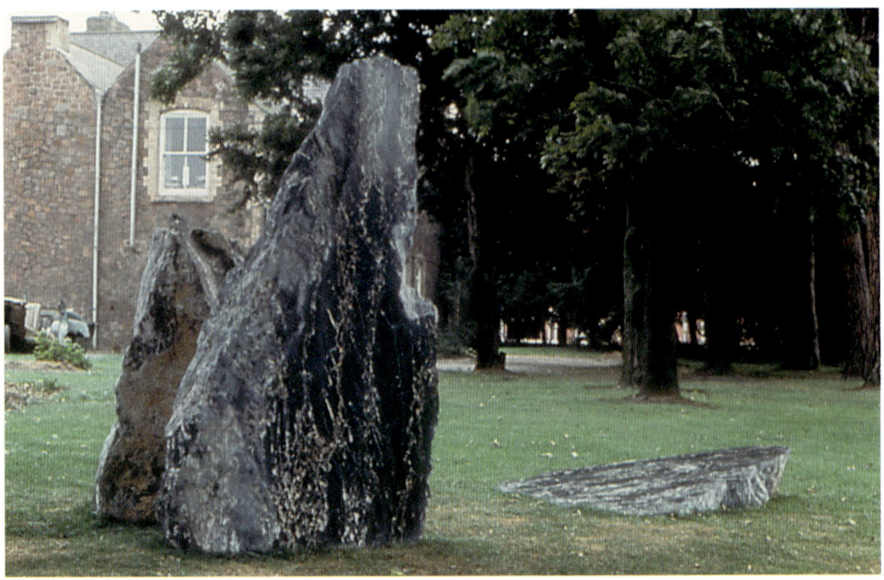

25

24 Private view invitation for *Homework* exhibition, Rowan Gallery 1972
25 *portoro 1* 1973, Rawlins School, Quorn

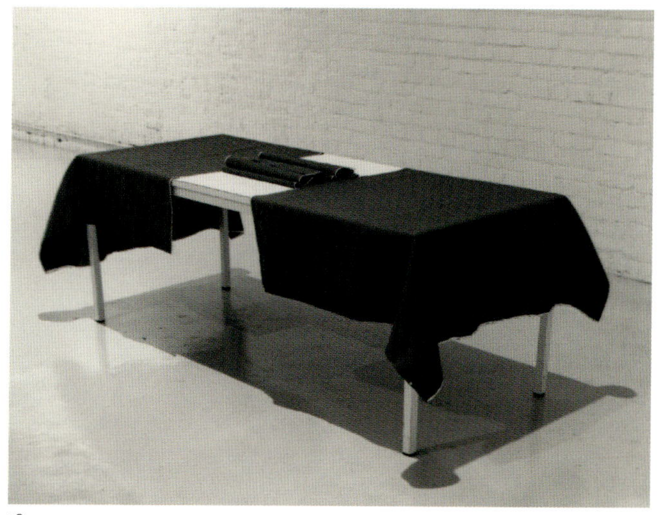

26

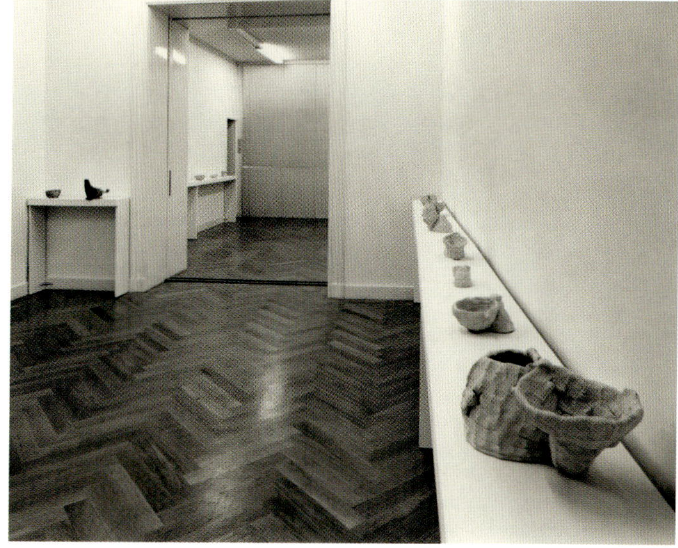

27

the Rowan Gallery later in the year – beside text by David Plante; but although a few advance proof copies were produced, this book was never printed. While in Italy Flanagan also visited Beatrice Monti della Corte at her home Santa Maddalena, Donnini, and her gallery, Galleria dell'Ariete, where he mounted an exhibition of his drawings.

SOLO EXHIBITIONS

Projects: Barry Flanagan, Museum of Modern Art, New York, 18 Jan. – 3 Mar.; *Barry Flanagan: Small works*, Bluecoat Gallery, Liverpool, 27 Feb. – 16 Mar. (exh. cat.); *Barry Flanagan Drawings*, Galleria dell'Ariete, Milan, private view 18 Apr.; *Barry Flanagan Drawing 1966–1974*, Museum of Modern Art, Oxford, 20 Oct. – 24 Nov.; *Somethings Etruscan*, Rowan Gallery, London, 8 Nov. – 5 Dec.

GROUP EXHIBITIONS

Tables, Garage, London, 23 Jan. – 15 Feb.; *Within the Decade*, Solomon R. Guggenheim Museum, New York, 12 Feb. – 24 Mar.; *Graveurs Anglais Contemporains*, Musée d'Art et d'Histoire, Geneva, 5 Apr. – 5 May (exh. cat); *Critic's Choice*, selected by Marina Vaizey, Arthur Tooth & Sons Ltd, London, 23 Apr. – 18 May (exh. cat.); *British Sculptors – Attitudes to Drawing*, Sunderland Arts Centre, Sunderland, 2–26 Oct. (exh. cat.); *Graphics*, Rowan Gallery, London*; *Bob Cobbing and Writers Forum Retrospective Exhibition*, organised by Ceolfrith Arts/Sunderland Arts Centre, 2–30 Nov. (exh. cat.); *Sculpture Now: Dissolution or Redefinition?*, Royal College of Art, London, 11–22 Nov. (exh. cat.); *Christmas Show*, Compass Gallery, Glasgow*.

SELECTED READING

Douglas Crimp, *Art News*, vol.73, no.3, Mar. 1974, p.99

Rosetta Brooks, 'Barry Flanagan and Richard Long', *Flash Art*, no.44–5, Apr. 1974, pp.40–1.

William Feaver, 'Barry Flanagan', *Financial Times*, 20 Nov. 1974, p.3

Caroline Tisdall, 'Barry Flanagan and Richard Long', *Guardian*, 28 Nov. 1974, p.10

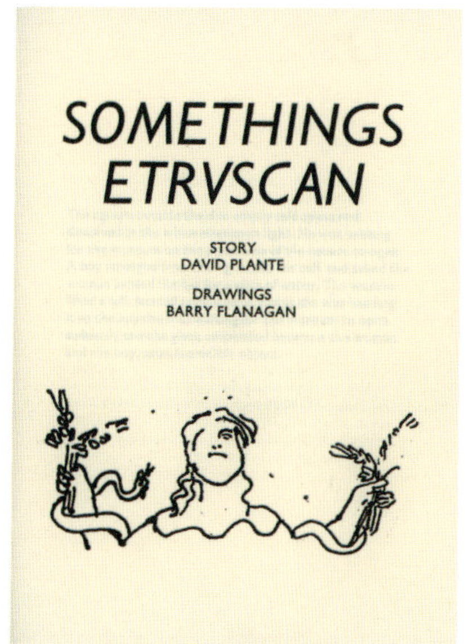

28

26 *tablecloth* 1974, installation at *Tables* exhibition, Garage, London 1974

27 *Coil pinch and squeeze pots*, Art & Project Amsterdam 1975

28 *Somethings Etruscan* title page

1975

Flanagan left London in January for Aston Farm House, Aston-le-Walls, Northamptonshire, where he lived with his family for eighteen months. The house provided land for raising chickens and growing vegetables, and the farm's barns provided studio space, where Flanagan carved local stone. He also installed a printing press and produced a group of wood-fired ceramics. Following a short apprenticeship with Mr Mold in Banbury, he worked as a dental technician.

Flanagan had first met Adriaan van Ravesteijn and Geert van Beijeren in Holland in 1969 during the opening of *Op Losse Schroeven*. The previous year they had founded their gallery Art & Project and after meeting Flanagan in 1969 stayed in contact before offering to show his work. His first (of three) solo exhibitions there presented a group of coil, pinch and squeeze pots that he had made in a Cretan kiln, which Peter Briggs had helped him to build. Flanagan's sister Pat had, much earlier, taken pottery courses at Birmingham School of Art and in the mid 1960s she took a couple of Raku courses given by Bernard Leach in St Ives. At this time both Flanagan and his sister had a shared enthusiasm for the Raku method.

Flanagan resigned from the Rowan Gallery and set up Rowford Process, which became his trading account and under which name a number of projects were conceived. The name derives from Retford, his father's family's stage name; 'Row' was substituted for 'Ret' as he thought it sounded more lyrical in conjunction with the word 'process'. Most publicly it gave its name to the furniture that he designed for, among others, the Hayward Gallery, as well as plinths for his own works. Purchasing materials was much cheaper for him as a trader than as a sculptor.

For a short while Flanagan worked as a stonemason in Jocelyn's Yard, Oxford, blocking out the stone for one of the last of Michael Black's emperors' heads (often called *Philosophers*), which were placed as herms outside the Sheldonian Theatre – the third set of heads to have been produced for the building. The first set lasted for about two hundred years, but by 1868 they were crumbling and replacements were installed; undergraduates, however, daubed these in paint, and the harsh cleaning methods damaged them, leading to their eventual replacement in the 1970s

At the end of the year Flanagan spent five days in Loch Ness. He had intended to attend a conference on the Loch Ness Monster in Edinburgh following recent photographs by Dr Robert Rines, President of the American Academy of Applied Science, but news of the photographs had leaked out to the public and the conference was subsequently cancelled, although Sir Peter Scott announced that the scientific name for the monster would be *Nessiteras rhombopteryx*. This trip informed a group of linocuts published by Bernard Jacobson and the ceramic *Flying Nessies*, first shown by Hester Van Royen the following year in the exhibition *Drawings, Ceramics, Etchings and Linocuts from the 'Loch Ness' Series*.

SOLO EXHIBITIONS

Hogarth Galleries, Sydney*; *Coil, Pinch and Squeeze Pots*, Art & Project, Amsterdam, 18 Nov. – 6 Dec.

GROUP EXHIBITIONS

CAS Art Fair, Mall Galleries, London, 15–23 Jan. (exh. cat.); *British Sculpture and Objects*, Kinsam Morrison Gallery, London, Apr.; «*From Britain '75*, Taidehalli, Helsinki, 22 Mar. – 6 Apr. toured to Alvar Aalto-Museo, Jyvaskyla, 13–27 Apr.; Tampereen Taidemuseo, Tampere, 5–31 May (exh. cat.);» *Recent British Drawings*, Burleighfield House, Loudwater*; *British Exhibition, Art 6 '75 Basel*, Schweizer Muntermesse, Basel, 18–23 June (exh. cat.); *Gallery Artists*, Rowan Gallery, London*; «*Contemporary British Drawings*, XIII Bienal de São Paulo, São Paulo, 17 Oct. – 14 Dec., toured to Fundacão Cultural Brazil, 20–25 Jan. 1976; Museu de Arte Moderna, Rio de Janeiro, 26 Feb. – 28 Mar., 1976; Museo de Bellas Artes, Buenos Aires, May–June, 1976; Museo de Arte Moderno, Bogotá, Aug. – Sept., 1976; Galeria Jose Clemente Orozio, Mexico City, Dec., 1976; Museo de Bellas Artes, Caracas, Feb., 1977;» *Neuvième Biennale de Paris. Manifestation Internationale des Jeunes Artistes*, Paris, 19 Sept. – 2 Nov. (exh. cat.); *Sculpture*, Robert Self Gallery, Newcastle-Upon-Tyne and Billingham Art Gallery*.

SELECTED READING

Fenella Crichton, 'Barry Flanagan', *Art International*, vol.XIX, no.1, Jan. 1975, pp.41–2

Vivian Reed, 'Barry Flanagan', *Art Press*, Sept./Oct. 1975, p.19

1976

Flanagan returned to London in July, moving, by December, to a house at 181 Leighton Road, NW5. The building had a self-contained basement flat that he used as his studio. For a few months he also rented an office in Gloucester Avenue in Primrose Hill.

The month before he returned to London his brother Mike was lost at sea during the Observer Single-Handed Trans-Atlantic Race. The following year Flanagan made a Hessian wall piece called *Eight Storms and Five Days* in memory of his brother, and later the bronze and gold leaf sculpture *Vessel (In Memoriam)* 1980.

Following his departure from the Rowan Gallery he became officially associated with Waddington and Tooth Galleries. Leslie Waddington described his first encounter with Flanagan and how he had seen and admired his work in Ted Powers's flat in Grosvenor Square, where the stone sculpture *Tantric figures* 1973 was positioned on a shelf about twelve feet away from Brancusi's *Fish* 1926 and a Jackson Pollock painting. What struck Waddington was how Flanagan's sculpture stood up well in such company. One day Waddington saw Flanagan by chance in his corner gallery in Cork Street and told him how much he liked the work. Out of that conversation Flanagan joined the gallery and was provided with storage for his work in Clifford Street. His first solo exhibition with the gallery would not be until 1980, however.

In the autumn Flanagan visited, and was captivated by, the *Sacred Circles: 2000 Years of North American Indian Art* at the Hayward Gallery, the first major exhibition of Native American Art to be mounted in Britain.

SOLO EXHIBITIONS

Barry Flanagan. Drawings, Ceramics, Etchings and Linocuts from 'Loch Ness' series, Hester van Royen Gallery, London, 7–31 July; *Barry Flanagan*, CAYC, Buenos Aires, opened 3 Sept. (information sheet with artist's statement)

GROUP EXHIBITIONS

Arte Inglesi Oggi, Palazzo Reale, Milan, Feb. – Mar. (exh. cat. with artist's statement); *Graphics '76 Britain*, University of Kentucky Art Gallery, Lexington, 22 Feb.– 14 Mar. (exh. cat.).

1977

Flanagan produced his first sheet metal pieces in Peter Briggs's studio in Rennes as part of a symposium on sculpture to which he, Jean Clareboudt and Toni Grand were invited. Briggs has recalled how,

'Barry came by himself and made a little trolley that fitted onto the oxy-acetylene cutter I had to guide the cut he made in the steel, the working conditions were rudimentary, we made all the

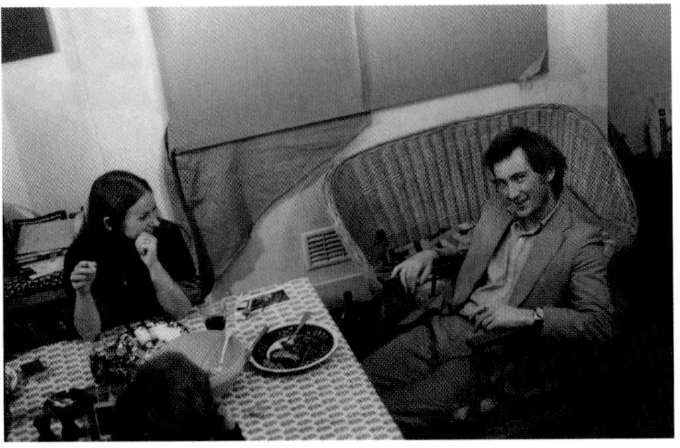

29

29 Sue and Barry Flanagan downstairs at Cliff Road, c.1972

work without any technical assistance, the pieces he cut from steel we tried to pull out using the tow bar on his car – a lot of burnt rubber and little success – so I got a scrap yard that donated the steel to use their crane to lift the centre of the piece having weighed the edge of the pieces down, that worked better. Barry left with one piece completed and one unopened as well as canvas and steel rod works.'

Between 1977 and 1978 Jake Tilson, then a student at Chelsea School of Art, worked as Flanagan's print devil in his basement studio in the house at Leighton Road, experimenting with ink mixes and methods of traditional aquatint. They would often visit the British Museum Print Room together to study works by Goya and Rembrandt.

Flanagan collaborated with the engineer Jonathan Park, who had earlier worked on the house in Cliff Road, to construct the projectors for light pieces at Art & Project in Amsterdam. Earlier in June the Stedelijk VanAbbemuseum in Eindhoven had mounted his first mid-career survey exhibition, which toured in 1978 in a different form to the Arnolfini Gallery, Bristol, and the Serpentine Gallery, London, where he designed a poster using an axolotl motif that mirrored a mason's set square and pair of compasses.

For the first *Hayward Annual* Flanagan produced his third and final installation for the gallery, *Hayward III*. It incorporates a stone sculpture set within an interlaced length of knotted rope running across the gallery floor, a light projection comprising triangular and vertical elements on one wall and, on other walls, a group of banner works, including *Double Eights* 1976. The sculpture and rope was, soon afterwards, given the title *'oh! mind how you cross'*.

SOLO EXHIBITIONS

« *Barry Flanagan Sculpture 1966–1976*, Van Abbemuseum, Eindhoven, 10 June – 10 July, toured to Arnolfini, Bristol, 30 July – 27 Aug. (exh. cat.);» *Barry Flanagan: etsen*, Van Reekum Museum voor Moderne en Hedendaagse kunst , Apeldoorn, 18 June – 24 July; *Light Pieces*, Art & Project, Amsterdam, 2–31 Dec.; *Ceramics*, Hester van Royen Gallery, London, 7 Dec. – 1 Jan., 1978.

GROUP EXHIBITIONS

« *Tolly Cobbold / Eastern Arts National Art Exhibition: an open exhibition of contemporary art*, Fitzwilliam Museum, Cambridge, 1 Apr. – 1 May, toured to Ipswich Museums, Ipswich, 9 May – 4 June; Graves Art Gallery, Sheffield, 11 June – 10 July; Camden Arts Centre, London, 29 July – 28 Aug. (exh. cat.);» *Hayward Annual*, Hayward Gallery, London, 25 May – 4 Juyl and 20 July – 4 Sept. (exh. cat.); *Silver Jubilee Contemporary British Sculpture Exhibition*, Battersea Park, London, 2 June – 4 Sept. (exh. cat.); *Reflected Images*, Kettle's Yard, Cambridge, 22 Oct. – 20 Nov. (exh. cat).

SELECTED READING

Catherine Lampert, 'Notes on Barry Flanagan', *Barry Flanagan: Sculpture 1966-1976*, exh. cat., Van Abbemuseum, Eindhoven 1977

Nigel Gosling, 'Gentle Confections', *Observer*, 21 Aug. 1977, p.24

John McEwen, 'Pinch-pots and skateboards', *Spectator*, 24 Dec. 1977, p.33

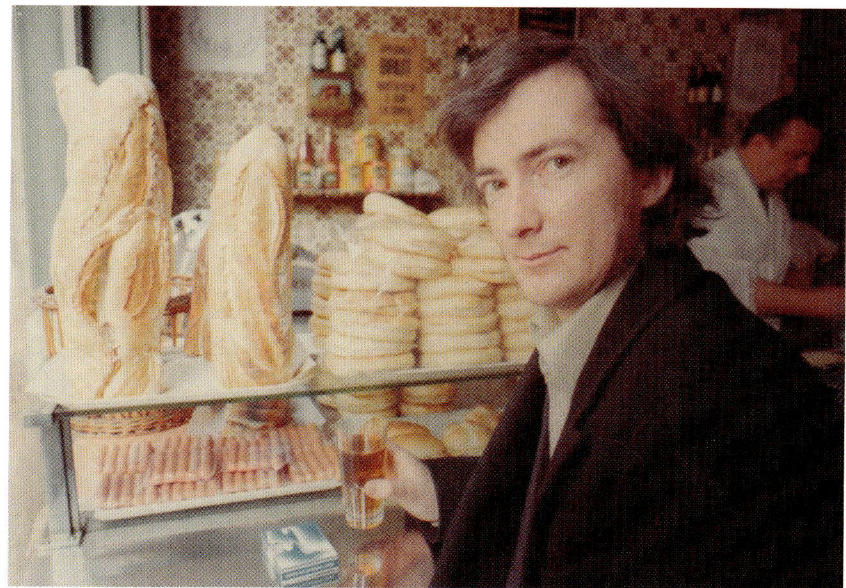

30

1978

Flanagan made a large metal piece at Brown and Tawse in East London, in collaboration with Holborn Metal Works and with Arts Council funding. This was exhibited at the Serpentine and purchased in July by the Ulster Museum, Belfast.

Flanagan was given a copy of the Irish-born sculptor Seamus Murphy's book *Stone Mad* 1966, a story that celebrated the work of the stone carvers and stonecutters with whom Murphy had trained. Flanagan began working with stone selected from Sem Ghelardini's yard in Italy in this year (Ghelardini founded the yard in the 1950s and had worked with sculptors including Henry Moore, César and George Adams). Flanagan imported three tons of stone and produced a number of works, including *'– if marble smell of spring –'*. They were carved in a studio he rented for a year at The Stables, Watlington Park, Oxfordshire, which he maintained on and off for about ten years. Watlington Park itself was the home of the architect Lionel Brett, the 4th Viscount Esher, who was rector of the Royal College of Art 1971–8. John and Myfanwy Piper and Richard Hamilton and Rita Donagh lived nearby. The studio was a flat above the old coach and stable block, and here Flanagan worked with Peter Randall-Page, who first scaled up Flanagan's smaller marble version of *Enlarged Marble Shape* in Ghelardini's marble before working on other sculptures. Flanagan had first met Randall-Page the previous year in Bath, when he had helped him take down his degree show at Bath Academy of Art. Randall-Page was commissioned by Flanagan to examine different methods of scaling up and to work out a technique for him. On his previous visits to Italy Flanagan had observed the triangulation method being used there, but though he was keen to learn how this was done, the Italian stonemasons guarded their secrets well. Randall-Page used a technique he had worked out himself to scale up a number of works in 1978 and 1979. Flanagan then commissioned numerous sculptures in marble from Ghelardini over the next few years, but began to use clay for his maquettes rather than stone.

30 Flanagan in Milanese Bar with *4 casb* made out of bread rolls, 1976

During his time at Watlington Flanagan bought a 40-foot studio: a marquee in a trailer that he could pitch anywhere he wanted, although, as it was not entirely practical, it was never used.

Rowford Process produced a group of table plinths constructed by Caroline Tattersall for Andrew Lord's first solo exhibition *Pottery* at Anthony Stokes Gallery, London; the exhibition was installed by Flanagan.

An interest in the shoebox dioramas his daughter Tara made at school led Flanagan to set up a series of cross-disciplinary lunch meetings with a group of friends at the Museum Tavern near the British Museum, London. Among those attending and giving papers at these monthly meetings were gallerist Barry Barker, artist Michael Craig-Martin, art critic William Feaver, accountant Michael Henshaw, Rembrandt scholar Nigel Konstam, cartoonist Roger Law, writer Paul Levy, poet and novelist David Plante, art historian Brendan Prendeville, Peter Randall-Page and his father, the diorama maker, Charles Randall-Page, actor Graham Seed, artist Jake Tilson and curator Alister Warman. Feaver remembers that the discussion 'was of various forms of connection and reconnection, the role of models (literally in model making) and the various trades and professional specialities that lay outside the conventional parameters of art – specifically sculpture-production'.

SOLO EXHIBITIONS

Barry Flanagan: Sculpture 1965–78, Serpentine Gallery, London, 25 Nov. 1978 – 7 Jan. 1979 (exh. cat. with artist's statement).

GROUP EXHIBITIONS

Critic's Choice, ICA, London, 7 Sept. – 7 Oct. (exh. cat.); *Made by Sculptors*, Stedelijk Museum, Amsterdam, 14 Sept. – 5 Nov. (exh. cat. with artist's statement).

SELECTED READING

Catherine Lampert, 'A further introduction to the work of Barry Flanagan', *Barry Flanagan: Sculpture 1965–78*, exh. cat., Serpentine Gallery, London 1978

Oswell Blakeston, *Arts Review*, vol.XXX, no.25, 22 Dec. 1978, p.698

Tim Hilton, 'Funny and Askew', *Observer*, 10 Dec. 1978, p.17

1979

In November Flanagan began bronze casting in London at A&A Sculpture Casting, which had been founded by Andy Elton and Henry Abercrombie in 1977. This was the first time that Flanagan had worked with bronze since 1969, as he had previously been unable to afford to work with this expensive material. He had acquired a copy of George Ewart Evans and David Thomson's book *Leaping Hare* 1972 from Roger Moss, who had worked on Flanagan's Laundress Green project in Cambridge with Andy Elton. Flanagan had been invited by Elton to work at the foundry but he needed to find a subject. His sighting of hares bounding on the Sussex Downs had inspired him and remained at the forefront of his imagination. Flanagan recalls modelling his first leaping hare having bought one from his butcher. The hare subsequently became a key sculptural motif for Flanagan, and the first *Leaping Hare* was cast on 7 November 1979, in an edition of three. From the same mould he also made the plaster and gesso *leaping hare, embellished, 2/3 jan '80* 1980, which was sized and gilded 'on the first full moon of 1980 (full moon and a lake are conducive to the laying of gold according to the Chinese)'. This was the first hare sculpture to be exhibited, appearing in his solo show at Waddingtons in 1980.

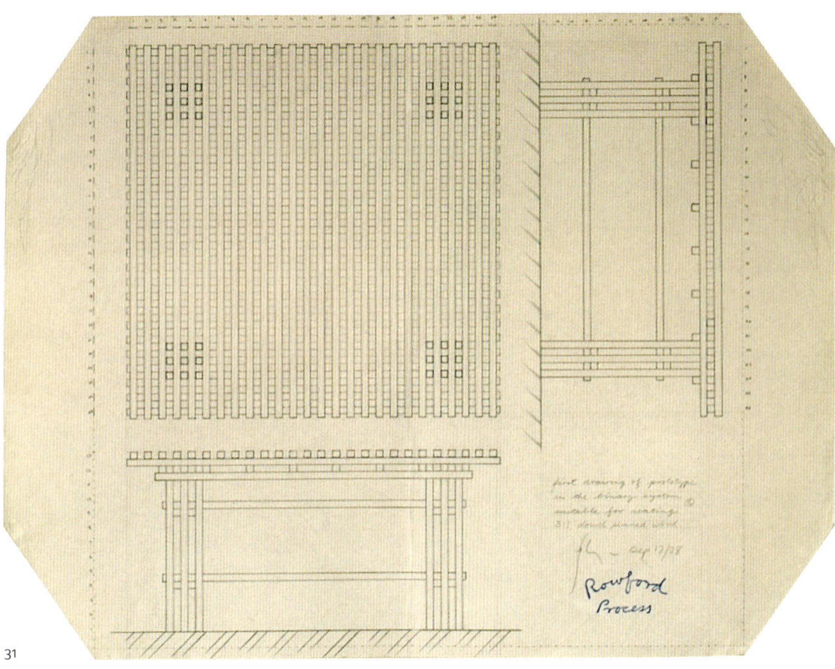

31

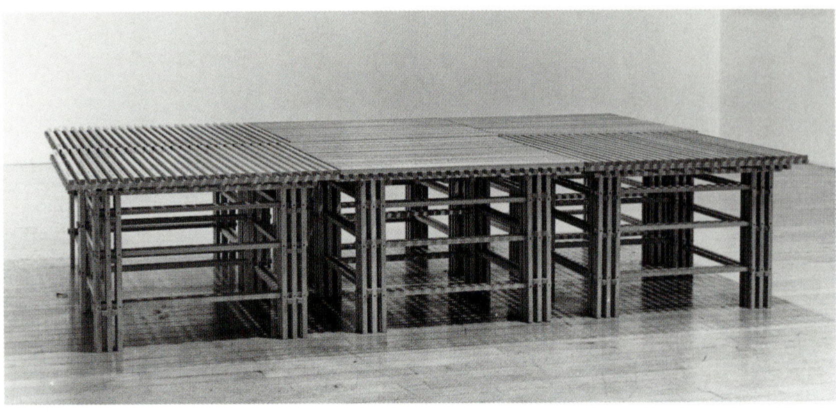
32

31 Drawings of Rowford Process designs, 1978
32 Rowford Process benches, 1980

Flanagan's Rowford Process produced benches for the public areas of the Hayward Gallery, London, commissioned the previous year and fabricated by the Cathedra design group from computer drawings – the first time Flanagan had used such technology to aid the design process.

SOLO EXHIBITIONS
barry flanagan curl snoots, Art & Project, Amsterdam, 27 Sept. – 20 Oct.

GROUP EXHIBITIONS
Said with Feeling. Tactile Sculpture for the Blind and Sighted to Share, Castle Museum, Nottingham, 10 Mar. – 29 Apr. (exh. cat.); *Jp2 Art Actuel en Belgique et en Grand-Bretagne*, Palais des Beaux Arts, Brussels, 31 Mar. – 29 Apr. (exh. cat); *Toasting. "Look all around/yeah"*, Gardner Centre Gallery, University of Sussex Falmer, Brighton, 9 May – 2 June (exh. cat.); *The Native Land*, Mostyn Art Gallery, Llandudno, 11 Aug. – 15 Sept. (exh. cat.); *Sculptors' Drawings*, The Minories Art Gallery, Colchester 15 Sept. – 21 Oct. (exh. cat.); *«gerry schum*, Stedelijk Museum, Amsterdam, 21 Dec. 1979 – 10 Feb. 1980, toured to Museum Boijmans van Beuningen, Rotterdam, 29 Feb. – 13 Apr. 1980; Kölnische Kunstverein, Köln, 30 Apr. – 1 June 1980; Museum voor Hedendaagse Kunst, Ghent, 15 June – 30 Aug. 1980; Vancouver Art Gallery, Vancouver, 1980; A Space, Toronto, 1980 (exh. cat).»

SELECTED READING
Nena Dimetrijevic, 'Barry Flanagan', *Aspects*, 1979, p.8
Catherine Lampert, 'Barry Flanagan', *Artistes*, Dec. 1979 – Jan. 1980, pp.10–17

1980

Although Flanagan had been associated with the gallery for four years, his first solo exhibition at Waddington's was held in April this year. The exhibition was made up of stone works and included *leaping hare, embellished, 2/3jan '80* 1980.

Flanagan received a number of public commissions, making two from cut-out sheet metal: in Ghent he produced an outdoor steel sculpture for the large open space of Sint-Pietersplein; *Camdonian*, made for Lincoln's Inn Fields, London, was the result of a competition funded by Camden Borough Council. Flanagan continued to work on a monumental scale, making studies for a life-size bronze horse in tribute to the Horses of San Marco, after seeing the exhibition *The Horses of San Marco* at the Royal Academy of Art the previous year.

SOLO EXHIBITIONS
Barry Flanagan, Galerie Durand-Dessert, Paris, 22 Mar. – 3 May; *Barry Flanagan: Sculptures in stone 1973–1979*, Waddington Galleries, London, 10 Apr. – 3 May (exh. cat.); *Barry Flanagan*, New 57 Gallery, Edinburgh, 18 Aug. – 6 Sept. (exh. cat.).

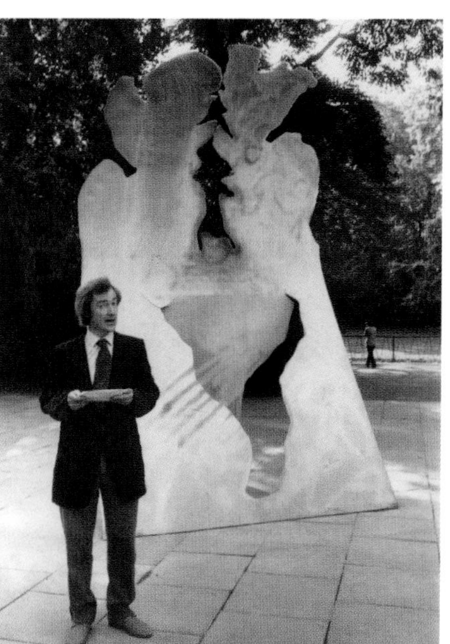

34

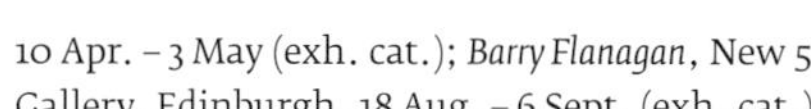

GROUP EXHIBITIONS
Occasional Pieces: Chairs, tables and functional objects, Kettle's Yard, Cambridge, 12 Jan. – 3 Feb. (exh. cat.); *«Pier and Ocean*, Hayward Gallery, London, 8 May – 22 June, toured to Rijksmuseum Kröller-Müller, Otterlo, 13 July – 8 Sept. (exh. cat.);» *"Kunst in Europa na '68"*, Museum voor Hedendaagse Kunst, Ghent, 21 June – 31 Aug. (exh. cat. with artist's statement); *ROSC '80*, University College, Dublin, 6 July – 30 Sept. (exh. cat.); *Introductory Exhibition of Sculpture by Artist-in-Residence Eric Wilson with pieces by Barry Flanagan*, Crawford Centre for the Arts, University of St Andrews, Edinburgh, 4–20 Oct. (exh. cat.); *après le classicisme*, Musée d'Art et d'Industrie, St. Etienne, France, 21 Nov. 1980 – 10 Jan. 1981 (exh. cat); *On Loan*, Coracle Press Gallery, London, 22 Nov. – 19 Dec. 1980 (exh. cat.).

SELECTED READING
Catherine Lampert, 'Stone Sculptures', *Barry Flanagan: Sculptures in Stone 1973–1979*, exh. cat., Waddington Galleries, London 1980
William Feaver, 'Fine Flourish of Flanaganisms', *Observer*, 20 Apr. 1980, p.16
John Glaves-Smith, 'Barry Flanagan', *Art Monthly*, no.36, 1980, pp.17–18

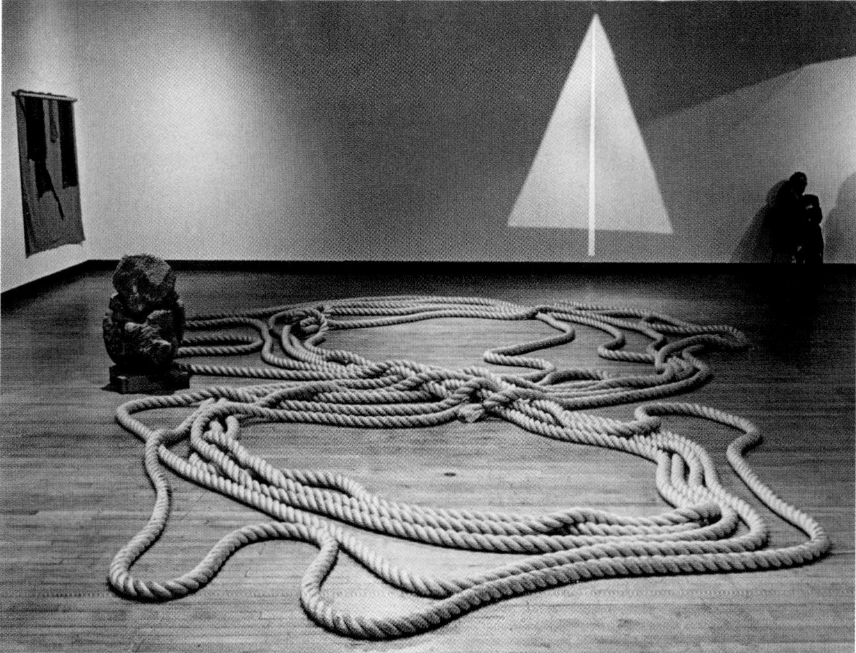

33

33 *'oh! mind how you cross' (Hayward III)* 1977
34 Unveiling of *Camdonian* at Lincoln's Inn Fields, 1980

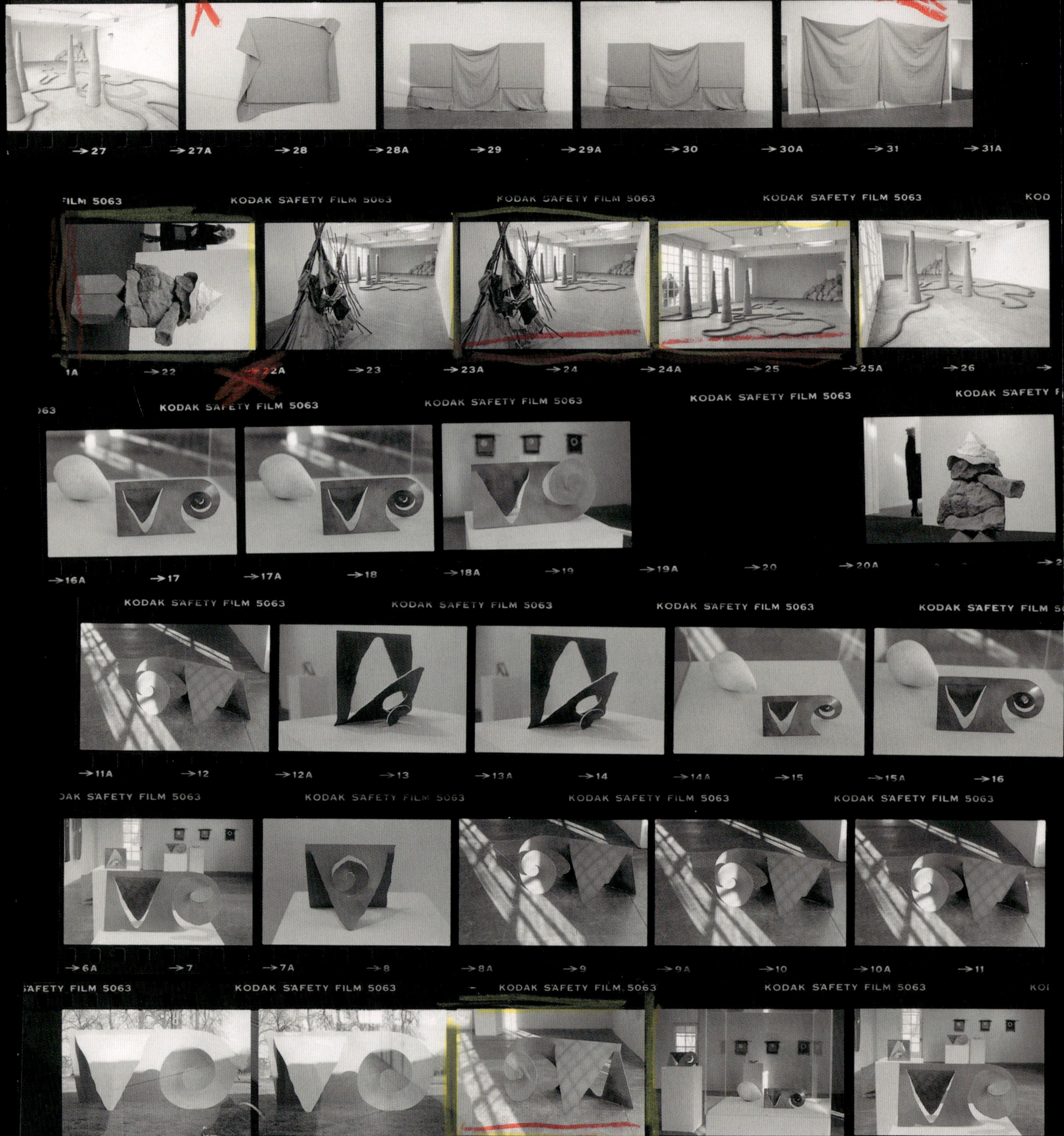

1981

Relatively few of Flanagan's prints of the previous decade had been editioned. Although he had presses in his own studio, he generally just printed a few impressions at will, until the arrival of Colin Dyer in 1981. At Flanagan's request Dyer sorted out the early plates and blocks, and printed archive copies of almost all of them. He printed editions from some early plates as well as editioning Flanagan's new prints from 1981 to 1983 for publication by Waddington Galleries.

Flanagan produced his first carvings in Sem Ghelardini's studio in Pietrasanta, Italy. Encouraged by Catherine Lampert, he went on a study visit to Washington to see the exhibition *Rodin Re-discovered* at the National Gallery of Art. He particularly admired Rodin's ability to model the figure in clay, and went on to make his own versions of *The Thinker* and *Nijinsky*. At the end of the year Waddington Galleries mounted his first exhibition of bronzes.

SOLO EXHIBITIONS

«*Sixties and Seventies, prints and drawings by Barry Flanagan*, Mostyn Art Gallery, Llandudno, 21 Nov. – 12 Dec., toured to John Hansard Gallery, The University of Southampton, Southampton, 31 May – 26 June, 1982; ICA, London, 23 July – 29 Aug., 1982 (exh. cat.);» *Barry Flanagan: Sculptures in bronze 1980–1981*, Waddington Galleries, London, 1–23 Dec. (exh. cat. with artist's statement).

GROUP EXHIBITIONS

Art and the Sea, series of independently organised exhibitions culminating at the ICA, London, 6 Jan. – 7 Feb., (exh. cat.); *Groups IV*, Waddington Galleries, London, 3–28 Feb. (exh. cat.); «*Tolly Cobbold/Eastern Arts 3rd National Exhibition*, Fitzwilliam Museum, Cambridge, 4 Apr. – 10 May (exh. cat.), toured to Christchurch Mansions, Ipswich, 24 May – 21 June; Castle Museum, Norwich, 4 July – 9 Aug.; ICA, London, 14 Aug. – 13 Sept.; Mappin Art Gallery, Sheffield, 19 Sept. – 11 Oct.;» *Summer Exhibition*, Royal Academy, London, 16 May – 16 Aug. (exh. cat.); *Poets' Choice*, 30 May – 28 June, Kettle's Yard, Cambridge (pamphlet); *Sculpture for the Blind*, Tate Gallery, London, 26 Aug. – 1 Nov. (exh. cat.); «*A Mansion of Many Chambers: 'Beauty' and other works*, toured to Cartwright Hall, Bradford, 12 Dec. – 17 Jan., 1982, and subsequently to Oldham Art Gallery; Gardner Centre Gallery, Brighton; The Minories, Colchester; Mappin Art Gallery, Sheffield; City Art Gallery, Worcester (exh. cat.).»

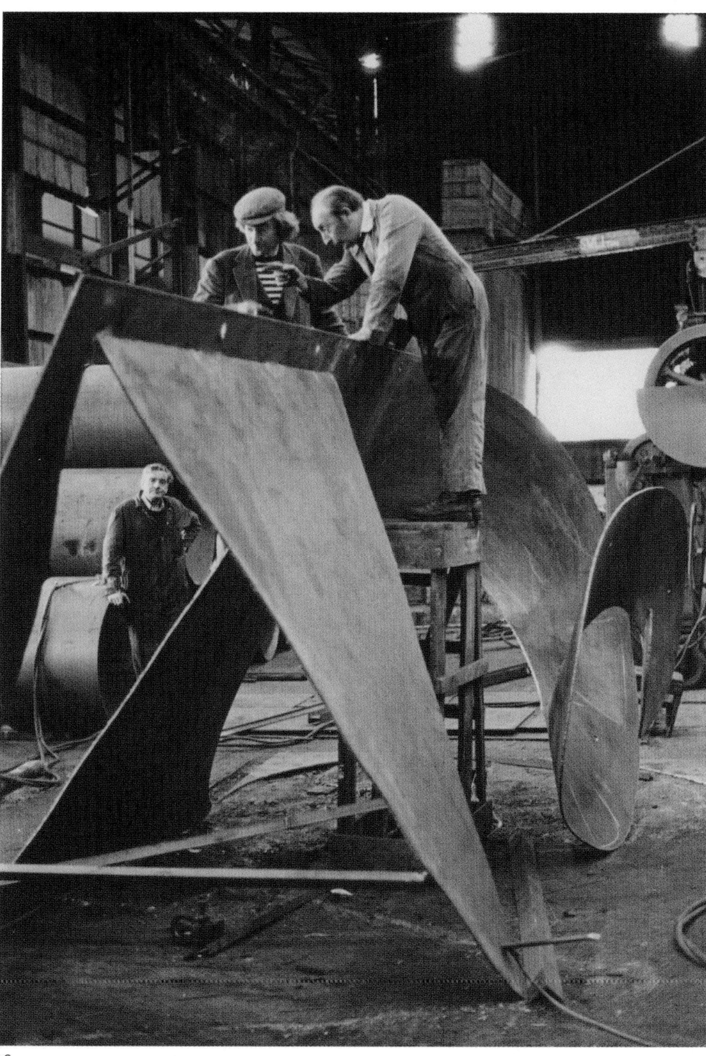

36

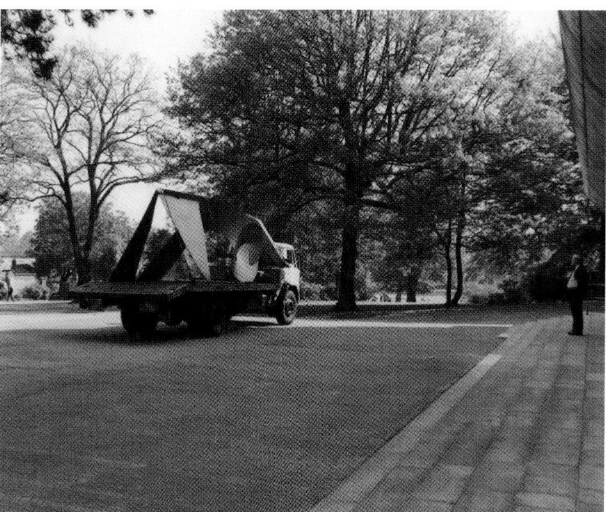

37

SELECTED READING

John McEwen, 'Matters of Imagination', *Spectator*, 19 Dec. 1981

36 At Brown & Tawse, London 1978, making *new metal piece*, first exhibited at the Serpentine Gallery, London

37 *new metal piece* 1978 being transported to the Serpentine Gallery

1982

Flanagan took a studio and living space at A & A Sculpture Casting in Fawe Street, East London. Ted Hickey of the Ulster Museum introduced him to the poet Seamus Heaney and they became friends. Flanagan made a print to illustrate Heaney's translation of the Middle English poem *The Names of the Hare*, which was placed on the page so that three gilded leaping hares formed an arc above the text.

Flanagan was selected to represent Britain at the Venice Biennale, with an exhibition of stone and bronze sculptures dating 1973–81. He presented groups of his recent bronze cast sculptures at *Documenta 7*, Kassel, and *Zeitgeist*, Berlin; in the former show, he exhibited his first large bronze hare sculpture *Large Leaping Hare*.

SOLO EXHIBITIONS

« *Barry Flanagan Stone and Bronze Sculptures*, British Pavilion, XXXX Venice Biennale, 13 June – 12 Sept. 1982, toured to Museum Haus Esters, Krefeld, 10 Oct. – 12 Dec.; Whitechapel Art Gallery, London, 7 Jan. – 20 Feb. 1983 (exh. cat.);» *Barry Flanagan*, Galerie Durand-Dessert, Paris, 16 Oct. – 27 Nov.

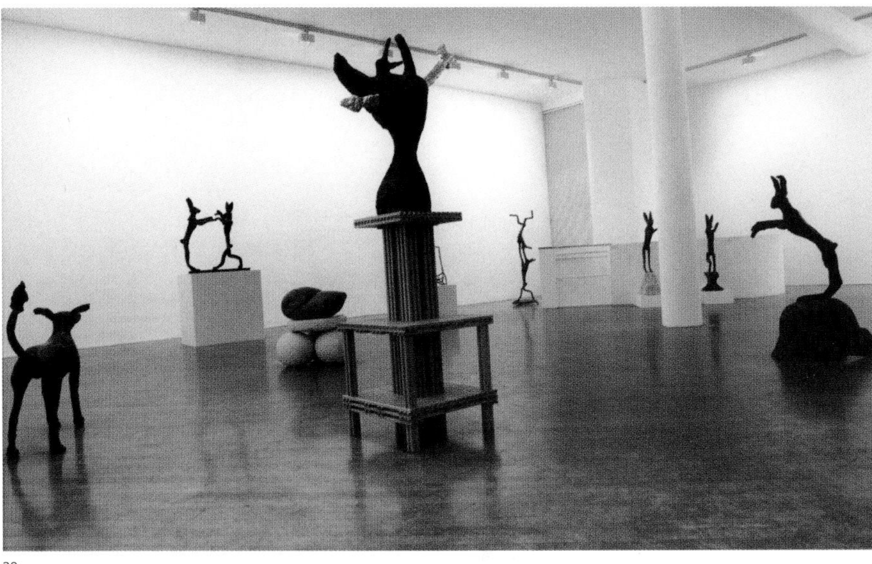

39

GROUP EXHIBITIONS

« *Aspects of British Art Today*, Tokyo Metropolitan Art Museum, Tokyo, 27 Feb. – 11 Apr., toured to Tochigi Prefectural Museum of Fine Arts, Utsunomiya, 24 Apr. – 30 May; National Museum of Art, Osaka, 12 June – 25 July; Fukuoka Art Museum, 7–29 Aug.; Hokkaido Museum of Modern Art, Sapporo, 9 Sept. – 9 Oct. (exh. cat.);» *Arte Povera, Antiform: Sculptures 1966–1969*, Centre d'Arts Plastiques Contemporains de Bordeaux, Bordeaux, 12 Mar. – 30 Apr. (exh. cat.); « *British Drawings and Watercolours*, British Council exhibition toured to China Art Gallery, Peking, 12 Mar. – 9 Apr.; Shenyang 27 Apr. – 19 May; Museum of Art, Hong Kong, 6–30 June (exh. cat.);» *Documenta 7*, Kassel, 19 June – 28 Sept. (exh. cat. with artist's statement); *The Sculpture Walk*, Arts Centre, Great Linford, Buckinghamshire, 3 July – 31 Oct. (exh. cat.); *Hayward Annual 1982: British Drawing*, Hayward Gallery, London, 17 July – 30 Aug. (exh. cat.); *Sculpture*, Waddington Galleries, London, 29 Sept. – 23 Oct. (exh. cat.); *Zeitgeist*, Martin-Gropius-Bau, Berlin, 15 Oct. – 19 Dec. (exh. cat.); *British Sculpture in the Twentieth Century. Part 2: Symbol and Imagination 1951–1980*, Whitechapel Art Gallery, London, 27 Nov. – 24 Jan. 1983 (exh. cat.).

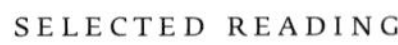

SELECTED READING

Tim Hilton, 'Less a Slave Of Other People's Thinking . . .'; Michael Compton, 'A Developing Practice'; Teresa Gleadowe, 'Stone and Bronze Sculptures', *Barry Flanagan Sculpture*, exh. cat. and pamphlet, British Pavilion, Venice Biennale, 1982

Lynne Cooke, 'Barry Flanagan at Mostyn Art Gallery, Llandudno', *Artscribe*, no.34, 1982, pp.65–6

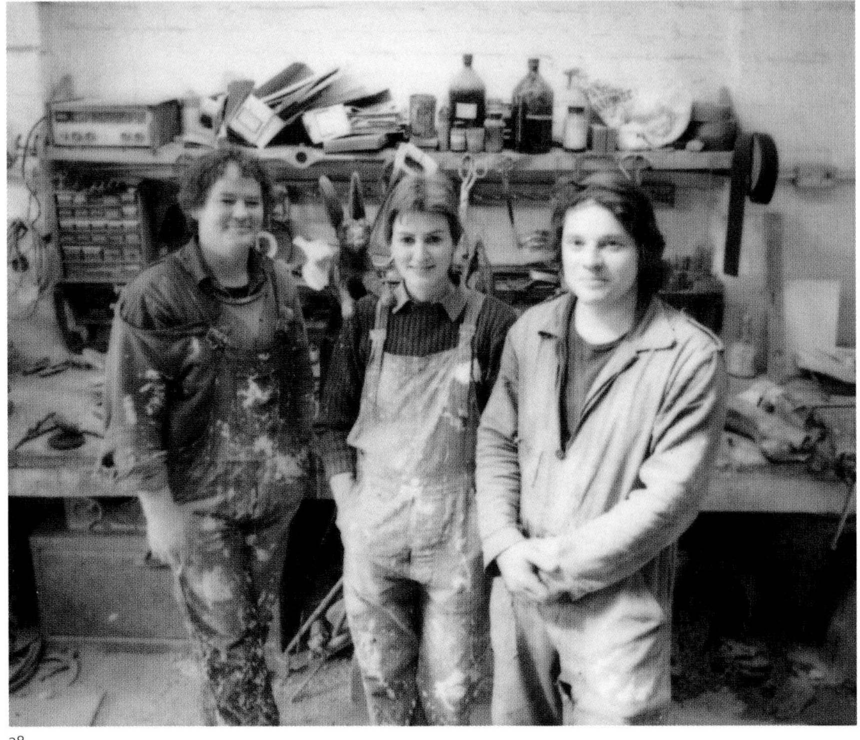

38

38 The foundry at Fawe Steet, London 1980. Left to right: Henry Abercrombie, Jill McManners, Andy Elton

39 Waddington Gallery, London 1981

ADDITIONAL READING

Lucy Lippard, *Six Years: The dematerialization of the art object from 1966 to 1972*, Praeger, New York 1973
Barry Flanagan: Sculptures, exh. cat., Centre Georges Pompidou, Paris 1983
Sixties and Seventies: Prints and Drawings by Barry Flanagan, exh. cat., British Council, London 1983
Barry Flanagan: Etchings and Linocuts, exh. cat., Waddington Graphics, London 1984
Barry Flanagan: Prints 1970–1983, exh. cat., Tate Gallery, London 1986
Barry Flanagan: A Visual Invitation: Sculpture 1967–1987, exh. cat., Laing Art Gallery, Newcastle-upon-Tyne 1987
Barry Flanagan, exh. cat., Fundación 'la Caixa', Madrid 1993
Barry Flanagan, Seeing Round Corners, exh. cat., Waddington Galleries, London 2001
Barry Flanagan Sculpture 1965–2005, exh. cat., Irish Museum of Modern Art, Dublin 2006
Barry Flanagan Works 1966–2008, exh. cat., Waddington Galleries, London 2010

This chronology has been written by Clarrie Wallis, Andrew Wilson, Jo Melvin and Jennifer Powell, with invaluable assistance from Henry Abercrombie, Barry Barker, Ian Barker, Marja Bloem, Peter Briggs, Sue Brown, Michael Craig-Martin, David Curtis, Michael Compton, Jan Dibbets, Andrew Dipper, Colin Dyer, Ger van Elk, Andy Elton, William Feaver, Barry E. Flanagan, Flan Flanagan, Teresa Gleadowe, Alan Gouk, Hilary Gresty, Rupert Harris, Jim Haynes, Jerry Hughes, John James, Phillip King, Catherine Lampert, Paul Levy, Richard Long, Bruce McLean, Jill McManners, Penelope Marcus, Barry Miles, Felix Mottram, Jonathan Park, Judith Patrick, David Plante, Cheryll Potter, Peter Randall-Page, Jasia Reichardt, John Retford, Patrick Reyntiens, Nicholas Serota, John Sharkey, Seth Siegelaub, Ann Stokes, Jake Tilson, Charles Verey, Leslie Waddington, Nicholas Wadley, Brian Wall, Alister Warman, Nick Wayte, Lawrence Weiner and Hester R Westley.

The chronology follows the form set by that compiled, under the artist's direction and with his assistance, by Alexandra Pringle and Teresa Gleadowe (incorporating notebook material 1978–81 and conversations with the artist Jan.–Mar. 1982) in *Barry Flanagan Sculpture* (British Pavilion, Venice Biennale) in 1982. This was updated through conversations with the artist by Clarrie Wallis for *Barry Flanagan* (Fundación 'la Caixa') in 1993.

An asterisk against an exhibition entry indicates that the editors have not been able to verify these details independently.

Exhibition details bracketed by « » indicates a touring exhibition.

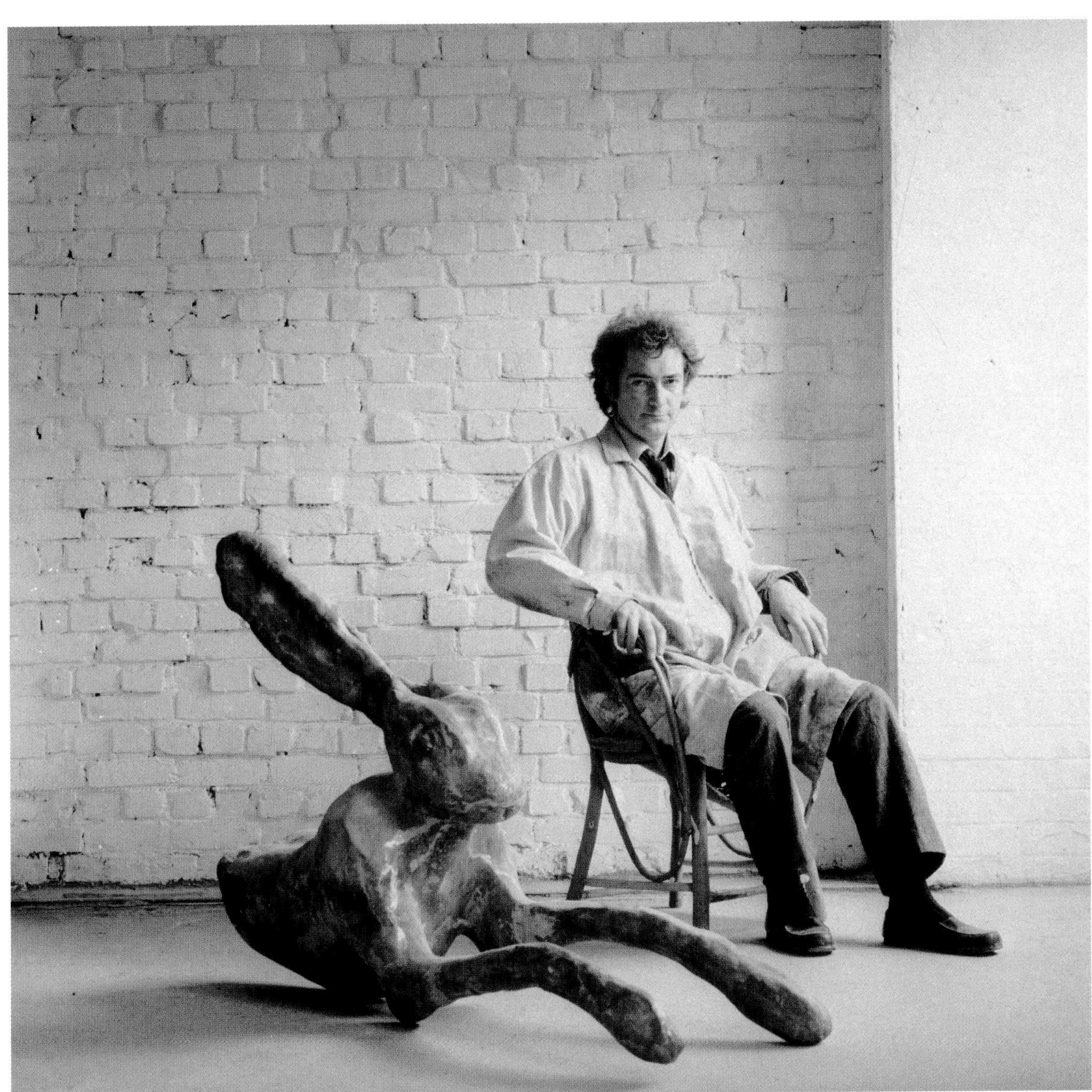

Flanagan in 1982, portrait by Lord Snowdon for *Vogue*

Exhibited Works

Measurements are given in centimeters, height before width and depth.
Where works are illustrated, page numbers are given in bold.

aaing j gni aa 1965
Mixed media
170 × 145 × 145
Tate. Purchased 1969
69

pdreeoo 1965
Cloth, plaster, ink and resin
106.6 × 45.7
Private Collection
70

ringn '66 1966
Sand
50.8 kg
Tate. Purchased 2010
71

sand muslin 2 1966
Mixed media
each 18.1 × 30.2 × 30.2
Tate. Transferred from the Victoria & Albert Museum 1983
71

al casb 4 '67 1967
Canvas, sand and aluminium
80 × 90 × 90
Agnes and Frits Becht Collection, Naarden
72

4 casb 2 '67 1967
Canvas and sand
each 182.9 × 38.1 × 38.1
Tate. Purchased 1976
74–5

ringl 1 '67 1967
Linoleum
183 (maximum circumference) × 0.3 (thickness)
Tate. Purchased 1976
74–5

rope (gr 2sp 60) 6 '67 1967
Rope
6.7 × 6.7 × 3902.6
Tate. Purchased 1976
74–5

bundle 2 '67 1967
Jute, paper and string
36.5 × 62 × 95
Royal Museums of Fine Arts of Belgium, Brussels; Inv. 11533
80

Beutelstuck (bundle) 1967
Burlap and rope
33 × 111.1 × 71.1
Museu Colecção Berardo
81

heap 4 1967
Canvas and sand
60 × 131 × 100
Arts Council Collection, South Bank Centre, London
76

canvas 3 '67 1967
Canvas, rope and wood
155 × 155
Mulier Mulier Gallery, Belgium
84

line 3 '68 1968
Felt and rope
178 × 306 × 3
Collection Liliane and Michel Durand-Dessert, Paris
77

pile 1 '68 1968
Hessian
28 × 48 × 45
Plubronze Limited / courtesy Waddington Custot Galleries, London
78

pile 3 '68 1968/1985
Hessian
31.8 × 52.1 × 48.3
Tate. Purchased 1973
79

june 2 '69 1969
Canvas and wood
292.1 × 508 × 88.9
Tate. Purchased 1973
82–3

light on light on sacks 1969
Hessian sacks and light
200 × 530 × 240
Collection S.M.A.K., Stedelijk Museum voor Actuele Kunst, Gent
86–7

Untitled 1970
Hessian, sticks and string
213 × 213 × 614
Kröller-Müller Museum, Otterlo, The Netherlands
85

no.5 '71 1971
Felt, wood and rope
63.5 × 264.2 × 251.5
Tate. Purchased 1973
85

plant 14 1971
Hessian, mutton cloth, residual sand and resin
117.5 × 45.7 × 42
Private Collection, courtesy Annely Juda Fine Art, London
73

untitled I 1972
Acrylic on canvas
91.3 × 91.3
Private Collection, Amsterdam
95

② feb '73 1973
Hessian, wood and paint
90 × 69 × 5
Karsten Schubert/ Richard Saltoun, London
90

③ feb '73 1973
Hessian, wood and paint
80 × 58 × 5
Private Collection, London
90

Tantric goddess 1973
Carved stone, painted
15.2 × 35.5 × 20.3
Collection Liliane and Michel Durand-Dessert, Paris
106

The Road to Altissimo 1973
White marble
49 × 27.9 × 30.5
Plubronze Limited / courtesy Waddington Custot Galleries, London
105

untitled (3) '73 1973
White marble and granite
121 × 37 × 40
Collection Rijksmuseum Twenthe, Enschede/depot VBVR
111

Untitled once 1973
Painted burlap and wood
114 × 139.5
Collection Van Abbemuseum, Eindhoven
88

flaming red 1973/78
Dyed and painted hessian, string and wood
135 × 58.05
New Art Centre, Roche Court
96

The stone that covered the hole in the road (the skull) 1974
Sandstone
15.5 × 25 × 20
Private Collection, London
108

Coil pot 5 (150 grms) 1975
Ceramic
6 × 10
Collection Rijksmuseum Twenthe, Enschede/depot VBVR
102

Coil pot 7 (1200 grms) 1975
Ceramic
12.6 × 28 × 16.0
Collection Rijksmuseum Twenthe, Enschede/depot VBVR
103

Coil pot 18 (700 grms) 1975
Ceramic
11.5 × 10
Collection Rijksmuseum Twenthe, Enschede/depot VBVR
102

a selection of five pots, VII (250grms) IX (250 grms) XI (210 grms) X (240 grms) VIII (190 grms)
1975–1977
Ceramic
Total area: 7.8 × 37.7 × 27.7
Arts Council Collection, Southbank Centre, London
103

Lamb/Fish 1975
Hornton stone
19.6 × 25.4 × 62.8
Collection Professor Pieter Sanders
109

Nauts and crosses '76 1976
Hornton stone, painted
96 × 57 × 60
Kunsthaus Zürich, Vereinigung Zücher Kunstfreunde
110

Ubu of Arabia 1976
Hornton stone, acrylic and canvas
109 × 76 × 25.5
Agnes and Frits Becht Collection, Naarden
39

Double Eights 1976
Hessian, plastic, wood and paint
172 × 198 × 5.6
Plubronze Limited
89

stand '76 1976
Canvas, wood, cord and paint
160 × 160
Private Collection
91

Hello cello 1976
Clipsham stone on constructed wooden base
41 × 25 × 22.5
stand: 96 × 41 × 41
Edinburgh, Scottish National Gallery of Modern Art. Bequeathed by Gabrielle Keiller 1995
104

and then among Celts N. '77 1977
Hessian and wood
49 × 63
Plubronze Limited
97

and then among Celts N.W. '77 1977
Hessian and wood
49.5 × 63
Private Collection
97

Light Piece 1977
Light, etched copper plate projector
Dimensions variable
Agnes and Frits Becht Collection, Naarden
49

'oh! mind how you cross' 1977–8
Hornton stone, wood and rope
Stone 90 × 38 × 35; rope 2000
Museum Boijmans Van Beuningen, Rotterdam
100–1

a nose in repose 1977–9
Hornton stone and elm wood
89.5 × 75.1 × 30.5
Tate. Purchased 1980
99

shadow catchers '77/79 1977–9
Wood, rope and jute
192 × 120 × 42
Agnes and Frits Becht Collection, Naarden
94

'–if marble smell of spring–' 1978
Marble
20.3 × 51 × 24
Arts Council Collection, Southbank Centre, London
112

VII 78 moon thatch 1978
Painted mild steel
44 × 96 × 43
British Council Collection
93

VII 78 the corn's up 1978
Painted metal
22.8 × 25.4 × 17.8
Lewis Biggs
92

VII 78 as night 1978
Painted metal
24 × 26 × 20
Private Collection, Paris
92

Cornish BuB 1979
Oil paint on granite
55.8 × 32 × 36.5
Tate. Presented by the Trustees of the Chantrey Bequest 2010
107

untitled light blue 2 '79 1979
Dyed hessian and paint
163 × 63 × 9.5
Private Collection, London. Courtesy Richard Saltoun / Austin Desmond Fine Art
96

Bye Bye the Elephant 1980
Hornton stone on wood base
45 × 57
Southampton City Art Gallery
98

Double Bell 1980
Bronze with striker
91.4 × 60.6 × 60.6
Collection Liliane and Michel Durand-Dessert, Paris
31

leaping hare, embellished, 2/3 jan '80 1980
Gilded gesso and paint on wood
75 × 100 × 24
Tate. Purchased 2010
116

Opera Dog 1981
Bronze
82.6 × 83.8 × 22.9
Plubronze Limited / courtesy Waddington Custot Galleries, London
115

Soprano 1981
Bronze with gilding on constructed wooden base
90 × 80 × 50
stand: 95 × 50 × 50
Private Collection Switzerland, courtesy Galerie Karsten Greve AG, St. Moritz
32

The Long Man of Wilmington 1981
Bronze
104.1 × 52.7 × 45.7
Private Collection
114

untitled (carving no. 13/81) 1981
Limestone
35.5 × 141 × 58.5
Tate. Purchased 1983
112

untitled (2b × 4) 1982
Romano-Chiaro marble
29.2 × 60 × 30.5
British Council Collection
113

Large Leaping Hare 1982
Bronze and steel
282 × 282 × 112
Plubronze Limited / courtesy Waddington Custot Galleries, London
116–17

Works on paper

(O for orange U for you: poem for the lips) juno965 1965
Pen on paper
23.4 × 20
Plubronze Limited
38

feb '66 1966
Blue and black pen and ink on paper
35.8 × 25.4
Plubronze Limited / courtesy Galerie Lelong, Paris

feb '66 1966
Blue pen and ink on paper
35.6 × 25.3
Plubronze Limited / courtesy Galerie Lelong, Paris

feb '66 1966
Blue and black pen and ink on paper
35.6 × 25.3
Plubronze Limited / courtesy Galerie Lelong, Paris
68

feb '66 1966
Blue and black pen and ink on paper
35.6 × 25.3
Plubronze Limited / courtesy Galerie Lelong, Paris

feb '66 1966
Blue and black pen and ink on paper
35.6 × 25.4
Plubronze Limited / courtesy Galerie Lelong, Paris

feb '66 1966
Blue and black pen and ink on paper
35.8 × 25.4
Plubronze Limited / courtesy Galerie Lelong, Paris

feb 10 '66 ② 1966
35.6 × 25.4
Blue pen and ink on paper
Plubronze Limited / courtesy Galerie Lelong, Paris

feb 10 '66 ② 1966
Blue pen and ink on paper
35.6 × 25.3
Plubronze Limited / courtesy Galerie Lelong, Paris

sep '66 ① 5/22 1966
Blue and red pen and black ink on paper
15.5 × 27.5
Plubronze Limited / courtesy Galerie Lelong, Paris

sep '66 ① 6/22 1966
Red, blue and black pen and black ink on paper
15.5 × 27.6
Plubronze Limited / courtesy Galerie Lelong, Paris
68

sep '66 ① 7/22 1966
Red, blue pen and black ink on paper
15.5 × 27.6
Plubronze Limited / courtesy Galerie Lelong, Paris

sep '66 ① 12/22 1966
Red and black pen and ink on paper
27.8 × 15.3
Plubronze Limited

sep 4 '66 ① 13/22 1966
Red, blue and black pen on paper
15.5 × 27.6
Plubronze Limited / courtesy Galerie Lelong, Paris

sep '66 ② 19/19 1966
Blue, red and black pen on paper
15.6 × 27.5
Plubronze Limited / courtesy Galerie Lelong, Paris

sep '66 ③ 4/12 1966
Pen on paper
15.6 × 27.5
Plubronze Limited / courtesy Galerie Lelong, Paris

sep '66 ③ 7/12 1966
Pen on paper
15.6 × 27.5
Plubronze Limited / courtesy Galerie Lelong, Paris

nov '66 1966
Pen on paper
25 × 19.8
Plubronze Limited / courtesy Galerie Lelong, Paris

nov 24 '66 1966
Pen on paper
20.2 × 29.9
Plubronze Limited

nov29 '66 1966
Pen on paper
25 × 20.2
Plubronze Limited / courtesy Galerie Lelong, Paris

nov269 '66 1966
Pen on paper
25.2 × 20.2
Plubronze Limited / courtesy Galerie Lelong, Paris

nov29 '66 1966
Pen on paper
25 × 20.2
Plubronze Limited / courtesy Galerie Lelong, Paris

jan 19 '67 2 ⑮ 1967
Ink on paper
15.5 × 27.6
Private Collection
128

jan 19 '67 15 ⑮ 1967
Ink on paper
27.6 × 15.5
Boulanger Collection, Suisée Belgique
128

may 18 '67 1967
Red, blue and black pen on paper
26.1 × 20.2
Plubronze Limited

may 18 '67 1967
Red, blue and black pen on paper
26.1 × 20.2
Plubronze Limited
47

diagram aug '67 1967
Pen on paper
26 × 20.5
Plubronze Limited

diagram aug '67 1967
Red and blue pen on paper
26 × 20
Plubronze Limited

diagram aug '67 1967
Red and blue pen on paper
26 × 19.8
Plubronze Limited / courtesy Galerie Lelong, Paris

diagram aug '67 1967
Pen on paper
26 × 19.8
Private Collection

c.1967
Blue and black pen on paper
26 × 20
Plubronze Limited / courtesy Galerie Lelong, Paris

collage '68 1968
Purple and yellow paper on paper
26 × 19.8
Plubronze Limited / courtesy Galerie Lelong, Paris

collage '68 1968
Blue, purple and green paper on paper
20 × 26
Plubronze Limited / courtesy Galerie Lelong, Paris

collage '68 1968
Purple paper on paper
19.8 × 26
Plubronze Limited / courtesy Galerie Lelong, Paris

june '68 1968
Blue and orange paper on paper
20 × 26.1
Plubronze Limited

june '68 1968
Blue and orange paper on paper
20 × 26.1
Plubronze Limited

june '68 1968
Blue, green and orange paper on paper
26 × 19.8
Plubronze Limited / courtesy Galerie Lelong, Paris

june '68 1968
Blue, green and orange paper on paper
26 × 19.8
Plubronze Limited / courtesy Galerie Lelong, Paris

Appointment Book – a struggle with disapointment, to keep the house from falling down 1972
Intaglio print on paper
19.9 × 24.5
Tate. Presented by Sue Flanagan, the artist's former wife 1985
25

Tom Raworth 1972
Intaglio print on paper
20.1 × 25.2
Tate. Presented by Sue Flanagan, the artist's former wife 1985

Michael Craig-Martin 1972
Intaglio print on paper
24.8 × 19.6
Tate. Presented by Sue Flanagan, the artist's former wife 1985

Larry Weiner 1973, reprinted circa 1983
Intaglio print on paper
24.8 × 19.7
Tate. Presented by Sue Flanagan, the artist's former wife 1985

Jack Wendler 1973
Ink on paper
36.9 × 30.8
Tate. Purchased with funds provided by Tate Fund 2010

Rome 1974
Pen on paper
25.5 × 35.5
Plubronze Limited / courtesy Galerie Lelong, Paris
128

Landscape 1974
Pen on paper
22.6 × 29
Plubronze Limited / courtesy Galerie Lelong, Paris
129

drawing for day and night 1974
Pen on paper
13.4 × 8.9
Plubronze Limited / courtesy Galerie Lelong, Paris
102

drawing for day and night 1974
Pen on paper
13.4 × 8.9
Plubronze Limited / courtesy Galerie Lelong, Paris

Cup drawing I 1974
Pen on paper
13.4 × 8.8
Plubronze Limited / courtesy Galerie Lelong, Paris

Cup drawing II 1974
Pen on paper
13.4 × 8.7
Plubronze Limited / courtesy Galerie Lelong, Paris

Cup drawing III 1974
Pen on paper
13.4 × 8.8
Plubronze Limited / courtesy Galerie Lelong, Paris

Cup drawing IV 1974
Pen on paper
13.4 × 9
Plubronze Limited / courtesy Galerie Lelong, Paris

Cup drawing V 1974
Pen on paper
13.4 × 9
Plubronze Limited / courtesy Galerie Lelong, Paris

Cup drawing VI 1974
Pen on paper
13.5 × 8.8
Plubronze Limited / courtesy Galerie Lelong, Paris

Ubu Sketch 1: Punch and Judy 1974
Pen on paper
13.4 × 9
Plubronze Limited / courtesy Galerie Lelong, Paris

Ubu Sketch 2: Pere Ubu 1974
Pen on paper
13.4 × 9
Plubronze Limited / courtesy Galerie Lelong, Paris

Ubu Sketch 3: Pere Ubu 1974
Pen on paper
14.7 × 9.2
Plubronze Limited / courtesy Galerie Lelong, Paris
24

Alfred Jarry loves Rrose Sélavy 1974
Pen on paper
25.8 × 20.2
Plubronze Limited / courtesy Galerie Lelong, Paris

Trumpeter Swans 1976
Pen on paper
35.4 × 25.4
Plubronze Limited / courtesy Galerie Lelong, Paris
129

Swans Nestling 1976
Pen on paper
35.4 × 25.4
Plubronze Limited / courtesy Galerie Lelong, Paris

Abstract Adam and Eve Theme Feb 3/78 1978
Pen on paper
22.8 × 18
Plubronze Limited / courtesy Galerie Lelong, Paris
48

West Country Point to Point 1978
Pen on paper
22.5 × 29.1
Plubronze Limited / courtesy Galerie Lelong, Paris

Bashful 1980
Pen on paper
13.4 × 8.85
Plubronze Limited / courtesy Galerie Lelong, Paris

Drawing for Running Sea Jul80 1980
Pen on paper
24.1 × 19.9
Plubronze Limited / courtesy Galerie Lelong, Paris

Hare in coil design for day march 12/80 1980
Pen on paper
13.25 × 8.9
Plubronze Limited / courtesy Galerie Lelong, Paris

Notes May 80 1980
Pen on paper
24 × 19.7
Plubronze Limited / courtesy Galerie Lelong, Paris
51

Remembered Image of Cricketer 1980
Pen on paper
14.7 × 9.2
Plubronze Limited / courtesy Galerie Lelong, Paris

Three legged 1980
Pen on paper
13.5 × 8.8
Plubronze Limited / courtesy Galerie Lelong, Paris

Long man of Alfreston Nov 18/80 1980
Pen on paper
24 × 19.5
Private Collection
114

Long Man of Wilmington Jan 1/81 1981
Blue pen on paper
24.5 × 19.8
Plubronze Limited / courtesy Galerie Lelong, Paris

a cunning stunt oct 30/81 1981
Pen on paper
13.4 × 8.8
Plubronze Limited / courtesy Galerie Lelong, Paris

Brick bat, Cricket bat oct 30/81 1981
Pen on paper
13.4 × 8.8
Plubronze Limited / courtesy Galerie Lelong, Paris

Hare on Sand Nov 1/81 1981
Pen on paper
13.4 × 8.9
Plubronze Limited / courtesy Galerie Lelong, Paris

Try Three Cultures Oct 5/81 Nov 3/81 1981
Pen on paper
13.5 × 8.9
Plubronze Limited / courtesy Galerie Lelong, Paris

Inverted pyramid Dec 13/81 1981
Blue pen on paper
24.5 × 19.5
Plubronze Limited / courtesy Galerie Lelong, Paris

Group Feb 10/82 1982
Pen on paper
13.5 × 8.7
Plubronze Limited / courtesy Galerie Lelong, Paris

Game Plan Feb 10/82 1982
Pen on paper
13.4 × 8.8
Plubronze Limited / courtesy Galerie Lelong, Paris

Cart Feb 4/82 1982
Pen on paper
13.4 × 8.8
Plubronze Limited / courtesy Galerie Lelong, Paris

Artistic Hare Feb 10/82 1982
Pen on paper
13.4 × 9
Plubronze Limited / courtesy Galerie Lelong, Paris

Index

Page numbers in bold type refer to illustrations.

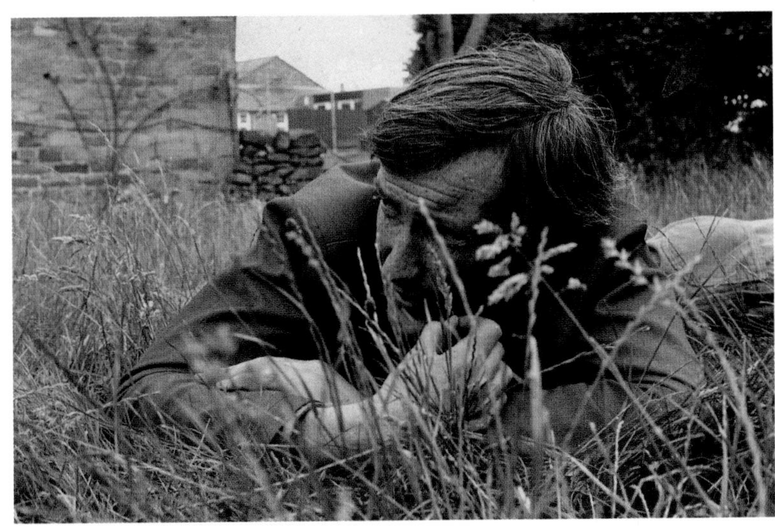

Barry Flanagan at Aston Le Walls, c.1975

Lenders and credits

Lenders

PUBLIC COLLECTIONS

Arts Council Collection, South Bank Centre, London
British Council Collection
Collection Rijksmuseum Twenthe, Enschede/ depot VBVR
Collection S.M.A.K., Stedelijk Museum voor Actuele Kunst, Ghent
Collection Van Abbemuseum, Eindhoven
Edinburgh, Scottish National Gallery of Modern Art
Kröller-Müller Museum, Otterlo, The Netherlands
Kunsthaus Zürich, Vereinigung Zücher Kunstfreunde
Museu Colecção Berardo
Royal Museums of Fine Arts of Belgium, Brussels
Southampton City Art Gallery

PRIVATE COLLECTIONS

Agnes and Frits Becht Collection, Naarden
Boulanger Collection, Suisée Belgique
Collection Liliane and Michel Durand-Dessert, Paris
Collection Professor Pieter Sanders
Karsten Schubert/ Richard Saltoun, London
Lewis Biggs
Mulier Mulier Gallery, Belgium; Museum Boijmans Van Beuningen, Rotterdam
New Art Centre, Roche Court
Plubronze Limited / courtesy Galerie Lelong, Paris
Plubronze Limited / courtesy Waddington Custot Galleries, London
Plubronze Limited
Private Collection, Amsterdam
Private Collection, London, courtesy Richard Saltoun / Austin Desmond Fine Art
Private Collection, courtesy Annely Juda Fine Art, London
Private Collection, London
Private Collection, Paris
Private Collection Switzerland, courtesy Galerie Karsten Greve AG St Moritz

Copyright

Photo credits

Cross-references are to page numbers
© ANZAÏ 55, 146
Courtesy Arts Council, Southbank Centre, London 76, 77 left
Courtesy Arts Council, Southbank Centre, London. Photo: Jonty Wilde 2011 103 bottom
Courtesy Arts Council, Southbank Centre, London. Photo: Mike Fear, 2003 112 top
Corry Bevington 143 top
Southampton City Art Gallery, Hampshire, UK / The Bridgeman Art Library 98
Courtesy British Council 93, 113
Guy Braeckman 91
Peter Cox, Eindhoven, Netherlands 88
Chris Davies 10, 148 bottom, 149 bottom, 150, 151 left
Documenta Archive, Kassel 29
Courtesy Liliane and Michel Durand-Dessert 31, 77, 106
© Evergreen Review 133 bottom right
Courtesy the estate of Barry Flanagan 2, 4, 8, 22, 23, 27, 44, 57, 62, 65, 99, 103, 132, 133 top, 134, 135, 138, 139, 141, 142 bottom, 143 bottom, 144 bottom, 145 top right and bottom, 148 top, 151 right, 152 top, 157
Courtesy Flan and Tara Flanagan 131 top, 136 top, 147
Courtesy University of Glasgow Library, Special Collections 33 top far right
John Goldblatt cover back flap, 136 bottom
Hugh Gordon 142 top right
R. Klein Gotink 102 top right, 102 bottom, 103 top, 111
© Estate of Charles Harrison 58, 141 bottom
Tom Haartsen front cover, 39
© Errol Jackson 130
Courtesy Annely Juda Fine Art 73
Courtesy Galerie Karsten Greve, St. Moritz, Switzerland 32
Courtesy Kröller-Müller Museum 66–7, 85 bottom
© 2011 Kunsthaus Zürich 110
Courtesy Galerie Lelong, Paris/ Photo by Fabrice Gibert 24, 48, 51, 68, 102 top left, 128 top left and bottom, 129
The Lewinski Archive at Chatsworth 43, 142 top left, 144 top
Jochen Littkemann 30
Courtesy Jill McManners 152 bottom
Courtesy Mulier Mulier Gallery 84
Courtesy Museum Boijmans Van Beuningen 100–1
Estate of Barry Flanagan courtesy Plubronze Limited / New Art Centre, Roche Court 96 left, 97 left
NI Syndication / Photograph by Bill Warhurst 149 top
Courtesy The 'Pataphysical Museum, London 133 bottom left
Dirk Pauwels 86–7
Prudence Cuming Associates 114 right
Paulo Raimundo 81
Courtesy Richard Saltoun 140
Scottish National Gallery of Modern Art 104
Snowdon / Vogue / Camera Press 153
Speltdoorn 80
Anthony Stokes 159
Tate Photography, London 2011 19, 25, 38 top right, 69, 74–75, 85 top, 107, 116; Lucy Dawkins 90 right, 92 top; Samuel Drake 82–3, 95, 113 bottom; Samuel Drake and Lucy Dawkins 78, 105, 108, 114 left, 115, 117; Mark Heathcote 71, 72, 79, 90 left, 92 bottom, 94, 96 right, 99, 109; Rod Tidnam 40, 118; Rod Tidnam and David Lambert 21, 38, 47, 50, 89, 97 right
Eileen Tweedy 145 top left
Cor van Weele 49
Peter White, FXP 70